Dr. R. Henry Migliore

STRATEGIC PLANNING AND MANAGEMENT

FOR THE

NEW MILLENNIUM

STRATEGIC PLANNING AND MANAGEMENT
FOR THE NEW MILLENNIUM

by

R. Henry Migliore

Professor Emeritus Northeastern State University

President Managing For Success

ISBN 978-0-578-21020-9

Copyright © 2018 by

R. Henry Migliore

Managing for Success

10839 South Houston

Jenks, Oklahoma 74037

www.hmigliore.com

January 2011

Illustrations by Mike Kelly

Table of Contents

Cases

Readings

Forward for
Strategic Planning and Management

Among the leading figures in the field who have made management by objectives (MBO) a practical system of management, Henry Migliore is distinguished by his innovative approach. Not only does he understand the fundamentals, which he stresses in his writing and consulting, but his agile mind and energetic approach press him into areas of application and practice that others could have discovered but did not. His work in blue-collar applications of MBO is still so far ahead of the field that he stands practically alone in that huge area of application. This grows out of his actual experience in the factory at Continental Can, a bias I share with him, having held a similar post with the competitor in that industry many years ago.

In the present work he has shown his breadth of view by seizing on the top-level applications of MBO in long-range and strategic planning. Considerable pressure exists on firms to sharpen strategic planning and the contribution of this book to that important area of concern is considerable. It enlarges the old applications of MBO to encompass multiyear plans and strategies, which are the major concerns of top management in today world of rapid change. The content is terse and fact-based, and it comprises a model for management that top management can expand upon to widen their MBO efforts to encompass a new and highly valuable area.

GEORGE S. ODIORNE
Amherst, Massachusetts

Dr. Odiorne wrote this forward for an earlier version of this book. He passed away a few years ago and was and remains an inspiration. He encouraged and helped me write my first published article at The University of Michigan. Odiorne was open and accessible to everyone all his life. I first met him in 1968 when I attended one of his seminars. For 25 years he was a friend and constant helper. As a role model, I am inspired to help others with the same spirit and vigor that he helped me. George, thanks.

Henry Migliore is once again a step ahead of his time. His work at Continental Can in the mid sixties pioneered Blue Collar MBO. In the seventies, he simplified strategic planning. In the eighties he made innovative applications in a variety of not-for-profit settings. In the nineties he has pioneered a simplified approach to planning into books for churches, hospitals, non-profit higher education and athletes.

This book brings his very practical ideas and practices on strategic planning on line for application in the next century and beyond. It is unique because it covers in detail the development of planning in the four vital areas of production, marketing, finance, and human resources. The emphasis on teamwork among functional areas ties them all together in a way that is both creative and workable.

Finally, Migliore uses this book to introduce his Culture Index. His understanding of corporate cultures and its importance in organizational planning, management, and control systems provides, indeed, a twenty-first century perspective.

DR. ROGER FRITZ

Preface

An ever-present problem with organizations is determining strategic direction, developing a plan, and then managing the plan. Small organizations, particularly those under one owner/manager/organizer, usually cope fairly easily in the early years. But growth, addiction of personnel, and expansion soon turn a one-time simple problem into one much more complex. Unless management keeps fully abreast, an organization can become sluggish and victimized by a loss of direction.

Large organizations can be drifting and have no real direction. They are often plagued by a lack of innovation and an inability to respond to problems and opportunities.

This book discusses a philosophy of management that has convincingly demonstrated its value in bringing order out of chaos. It compels the management team to agree to direction. It is simple to understand. Once in motion it acquires a natural rhythm. It offers the opportunity to satisfy higher-level needs. Finally, and highly important, it provides a foundation to manage the organization. It gets everyone involved in the planning process.

I have assisted in applying this management philosophy in large and small enterprises, including a railroad, a coal mine, a pipeline company, manufacturing companies, churches, athletic department hospitals, government units, medical practices, educational units, and personal lives. Results have invariably been gratifying. I sincerely hope that the book will help the reader to plan and manage effectively.

In the 21st century there is a dual concern for survival and growth. The planning and management system outlined here can assist the organization in achieving both.

Organization of Book

Chapters 1 and 2 set the base for the introduction of my strategic planning and management system in chapter 3. They bring together for the reader a condensed version of what has been said by others.

Chapter 1 contains the purpose and importance of justification for the book. The objective for Chapter 1 has been to set the stage of the book and give the reader an unbiased look at Strategic Long-Range Planning.

The state of the art of strategic planning, management by objectives, and strategic management are summarized in chapter 2. Various sources of secondary data are used to validate and trace MBO from its origin to the present. The objective for chapter 2 has been to show that Long-Range Planning/MBO comes from our early industrial development and is not a fad. The chapter shows the emphasis to strategically manage the organization. Chapters 3, 4, and 5 develop the actual long-range planning process. Here is where I introduce my own thinking. If the reader works his way through these chapters and fills in the appropriate, required information, he will have a rough draft of a strategic long-range plan. Chapter 6, 7, 8, 9, and 10 cover how to develop functional plans. Chapter 11 covers how to stragically manage the plans. Chapter 12 covers the appraisal and reward process. Chapter 13 describes how to evaluate organizational effectiveness. Chapter 14 describes actual Long-Range Planning/MBO experiences. Chapter 15 covers corporate culture and how culture affects the organization. Chapter 16 summarizes the Long-Range Planning/MBO and strategic management process. The readings and cases at the end of the book cover articles I have written on a wide range of subjects. There is a common thread of accountability that runs through the theme of each article.

Acknowledgements

I would like to acknowledge the following persons for contributions and insights that helped me to develop this planning system: my professor at the University of Arkansas, Dr. Richard Johanson, and Dr. George Odiorne. Both provided me hours of review and discussion in arriving at the final product.

Persons who presented ideas and thoughts for me on the basis of a study of their work were Peter Drucker and Dale McConkey.

I would also like to acknowledge the many companies and organizations that I have worked with over the past 30 years. This interaction provided the learning opportunity through actual practice to develop the theories and concepts presented.

A special note of thanks goes to Elaine Drain in the Word Processing Center at Oral Roberts University.

These women have been special friends and helpers over a long period of time. Marilyn N. Argabright, Sandra E. Stephenson, Janel L. Cook and Elizabeth Burgett.

The joy and balance provided by my wonderful family were a blessing. Finally, I thank God for the experience, skills, and insights given to me in order to write this book to serve others.

R. Henry Migliore

Definitions

A. *Strategic Planning* – This is the process of developing direction for an organization. It is both a product and a process. The product is the plan itself. The plan is in writing and clearly defines where the organization intends to be in the long term, usually three to five years. The plan includes objectives, strategy, and the short-term steps to ensure overall success. The process is the interaction that takes place in developing the plan. Everyone involved in executing the plan should be involved in its development.

B. *Functional Plans* – These are developed to support the overall organizational strategic plan. Functional plans include the following areas: finance, manufacturing, personnel, research, and marketing. They use the same philosophy and process in the strategic planning definition.

C. *Systems Approach* – This concept views the organization as a whole with interacting subsets. The financial plan is an element of the whole organizational plan. Systems thinking considers the action of each element, and that each action or reaction affects other organizational functions. The systems approach recognizes that a firm is a dynamic organism with all parts, or subsystems, operating toward the common purpose of the firm as stated in its strategic plan. The firms financial system provides the implementation of its strategic plan and is a segment of the total system.

D. *Strategic Management* – This is the philosophy of managing with a planning process. It is a flow of decisions and actions, which effectively execute the strategic plan. The strategic management process includes the way the management team directs the organization within the framework and promotion of the strategic plan.

E. *Management by Objectives* – This is a process whereby the superior and subordinate managers of an organization jointly identify its common goals, define each individuals major area of responsibility in terms of the results expected of him/her, and use these measures as guides for operating the unit and assessing the contribution of each of its members.

F. *Zero-Base Budgeting* – This basic concept of attempting to reevaluate all programs and expenditures every year?hence the term zero-base?is not new. The process requires each manager to justify his entire budget request in detail and puts the burden of proof on him to justify why he should spend any money.

G. *Purpose* – This term designates the broad reason for being for the enterprise.

H. *Environmental Analysis* – This focuses on items external to the firm. A Corporation operates within an extremely dynamic situation, which is affected by economic, technological, social, and political influences.

I. *Strengths and Weaknesses* – These include an organizations people, buildings, money, machines, and internal situation.

J. *Assumptions* – These are a temporary hypotheses regarding a very important probability development that cannot be predicted with accuracy and over which you have no significant control.

K. *Objectives* – These are used in dynamic planning to designate the intermediate targets en route to achieving purpose. They entail specific measurable results that outline exactly what is to be accomplished in a time frame.

L. *Strategy* – This is a broad course of action selected from among alternatives as the optimum way to use resources. One must decide how, where, and when to commit resources to achieve objectives.

M. *Long-Range Operational Plan* – This generally includes the determination, for at least five years ahead, of long-term corporate objectives, goals, strategies, and planned commitment of resources. Action is the key: Who is responsible for what?

N. *Short-Range Operational Plan* – This is a plan which relates to the annual corporate budget for guiding current business actions.

O. *Time-Out Period* – Before any plan goes into action, it is important for the whole organization to look it over. It supports the old adage that those who execute the plan need to be in on the plan. This time-out period helps eliminate mistakes. Top management of any organization cannot possibly know all details, opportunities, and problems. There is talent in all organizations, and the time-out period gives the organization a chance to use that talent and listen. Too often plans are made and announced with little or no input. The time-out period helps assure the people will support the plan. You can guarantee apathy and little support if the strategic direction is set with no input.

P. *Total Quality Management* – The philosophy, plans, objectives and strategy to achieve the quality objectives of the organization. This definition views TQM as a subject of the SLRP.

Q. *Rudge Approach to Productivity and Action Teams* – Success is clear and carefully outlined: (1) Determine the facts. What are the problems of the organization? The key to answering this question is the characterization of problems as seen by workers as well as management. (2) Feed back the results of the fact-finding to all members of the organization. Make it clear that the organization has listened to all with interest and an open mind. (3) Design indices to measure improvement and clearly define the factors to be tracked and measures to show improvement. (4) Structure the organization for action by involving everyone in task forces to make recommendations for improvement. (5) Implement those recommendations.

Rudges theory rests on the premise that the way to gain the support needed to accomplish smooth change is to give everyone concerned a piece of action. He also believes that increased involvement is the key to increased productivity and involvement is the wave of the future. I wholeheartedly agree with these principles.

R. *Types of Benchmarking* – Benchmarking seeks out best in-class performers inside or outside your organization, studying them to determine why they are the best at what they do, and applying what you have learned to your own organizations.

S. *Quarterly Review Process* – Each manager reports performance against objectives in their functional plan. The presentation is done with transparencies and handouts. Each presentation lasts 15 to 20 minutes. After the formal part of the presentation the group has an opportunity to respond and interact with the presenter. Each manager points out red flags that are problems in their area.

The last presentation is the CEO. He responds to what he has heard. He gives an evaluation of the preceding quarter.

The entire group then looks at a 5-year plan. What needs changing or adjusting? Is the ship on course? What "red flags" have popped up? The group discusses and fine-tunes the plan.

T. *Problem Definition* – identification of the root cause of the problem. Problem identification comes after considering all symptoms.

U. *Alternatives to Problem Solution* – clear well stated approaches to solve root problems. May be different courses of action.

V. *Recommendation Solution* – is the best of the three alternatives after weighing cost/benefit of each alternative.

Chapter 1
Introduction: Planning Perspectives

You can never plan the future by the past.

EDMUND BURKE
English Statesman

A well-defined mission serves as a constant reminder of the need to look outside the organization not only for "customers" but also for measures of success.

PETER DRUCKER
Management Expert

We can no longer assume we know what our various constituencies need and want.

SUNSHINE JANDA OVERKAMP
Senior Vice President, United Way of America

If you think what exists today is permanent and forever true, you inevitably get your head handed to you.

JOHN REED
Chairman, Citicorp

If you don't know where you are going, you won't know if you got there.

YOGI BERRA
New York Yankee Baseball Hall of Fame

You cannot achieve goals if you don't have any - - - if not you look at the past and wonder where it went.

EVELYN ROBERTS
American writer, spiritual leader, and respected personal friend of the author

Management's job is not to see the company as it is . . . but as it can become.

JOHN W. TEETS
CEO, Greyhound Corp.

Change is the law of life . . . those who look only to the past or the present are sure to miss the future.

JOHN F. KENNEDY
35th President of the United States

People are afraid of the future, of the unknown . . . a person can have control of their destiny. That's exciting to me. Better than waiting with everybody else to see what's going to happen.

JOHN H. GLENN, JR.
American Astronaut, U.S. Senate

WHAT IS STRATEGIC PLANNING?

The word "strategic" means, "pertaining to strategy." Strategy is derived from the Greek word *strategos,* which means generalship, art of the general, or more broadly, leadership. The word "strategic" when used in the context of planning provides a perspective to planning, which is long-run in nature and deals with achieving specified end results. Just as military strategy has the objective of the winning of the war, so too, strategic planning has as its goal the achievement of the organization.

Strategic decisions must be differentiated from tactical decisions. Strategic decisions outline the overall game plan or approach, while tactical decisions involve implementing various activities, which are needed to carry out the larger strategy. For example, a company which decides to change locations because of shifting population trends and industrial development around the present location is making strategic decisions. Then many other decisions must be made about the exact location, size of building, parking facilities, and other major details. These all have long-term implications and are therefore strategic in nature.

Then other decisions such as wall colors, decor, communications and air conditioning must be made. These are tactical decisions needed to carry out or implement the strategic decision previously made. Thus, strategic decisions provide the overall framework within which the tactical decisions are made. It is critically important that leaders of all organizations be able

2

to differentiate between these types of decisions to identify whether the choice has short-term or long-term implications.

THE STRATEGIC PLANNING PROCESS

The strategic planning process is basically a matching process involving internal resources and its external opportunities. The objective of this process is to peer through the "strategic window" and identify opportunities the individual organization is equipped to take advantage of or respond to. Thus the strategic management process can be defined as *a managerial process which involves matching the organization capabilities with its opportunities.* These opportunities are identified over time, and decisions revolve around investing or divesting resources to address these opportunities. The context in which these strategic decisions are made is (1) the firm's operating environment; (2) the firm's purpose or mission; and (3) the firm's organization-wide objectives. Strategic planning is the process, which ties all these elements together to facilitate strategic choices that are consistent with all three areas and then implements and evaluates these choices.

The successful results of planning described earlier can be achieved through implementing an effective strategic planning process. The following breakdown of this process is a complete outline of a system capable of creating true changes in a firm's attitudes as well as its productivity.

It is important to recognize at this point what we call "the two P's." The first "P" means Product: get the plan in writing. The plan must be something you can hold in your hand, a written product of your efforts. If the plan is not in writing, it is called daydreaming. When it is in writing, you are telling yourself and others you are serious about it. The second "P" represents Process; every plan must have maximum input from everyone. Those who execute the plan must be involved in construction of the plan in order to gain their commitment. The best way to ensure a plan's failure is to overlook both the product and the process. They are equally important.

While there are many different ways in which a firm can approach the strategic planning process, a systematic approach that carries the organization through a series of integral steps helps focus attention on answering a basic set of questions each organization must answer:

1. *What will we do?* This question focuses attention on the specific needs the firm will try to meet in the marketplace.

2. *Who will we do it for?* This question addresses the need for the firm to identify the various market segments whose needs will be met.

3. *Why do our customers want to do business with our firm?*

4. *Why do our employees work for our company?*

5. *Who is our <u>real</u> competition?*

6. *How will we do what we want to do?* Answering this question forces thinking about the many avenues through which the firm's efforts may be channeled.

7. *How big should the firm be in the future? What is the optimum size?*

8. *What changes are taking place?*

Strategic Planning: A Definition

Strategic Planning and Management is a philosophy of managing based on identifying purpose, objectives, and desired results, and establishing a realistic program for obtaining these results and evaluating performance in achieving them.

The following nine-point breakdown of this process is productivity. This definition establishes a true strategic long-range planning and management system.

Such a philosophy involves:

1. Defining an organization's purpose and reason for being.

2. Monitoring the environment in which it operates.

3. Realistically assessing its strengths and weaknesses.

4. Making assumptions about unpredictable future events.

5. Prescribing written, specific, and measurable objectives in principal result areas contributing to the organization's purpose.

   a. Negotiating and bargaining at every level from top line and staff positions down to the blue-collar level.

   b. Recognizing a performance contract embracing the agreed-upon objectives.

6. Developing strategies on how to use available resources to meet objectives.

7. Making long-and short-range plans to meet objectives.

8. Constantly appraising performance to determine whether it is keeping pace with attainment of objectives and is consistent with its defined purpose.

   a. Being willing to change or modify objectives, strategies, and plans when conditions change.

    b. Evaluating progress at every stage so that needed changes can be made smoothly.

    c. Making sure that rewards are thoughtfully considered and are appropriate for the accomplishment; recognizing the strengths and weaknesses of the extrinsic and intrinsic rewards.

9. Reevaluating purpose, environment, strengths, weaknesses, and assumptions before setting objectives for the next performance year.

This definition has been sent to dozens of academic, consulting, and business people for review and suggestions. Many shared in the final wording of the definition. Nearly all the respondents agreed that this definition advances the state of the art and better demonstrates that a planning and management system can be the center of managing the organization for survival, growth, and a more efficient organization.

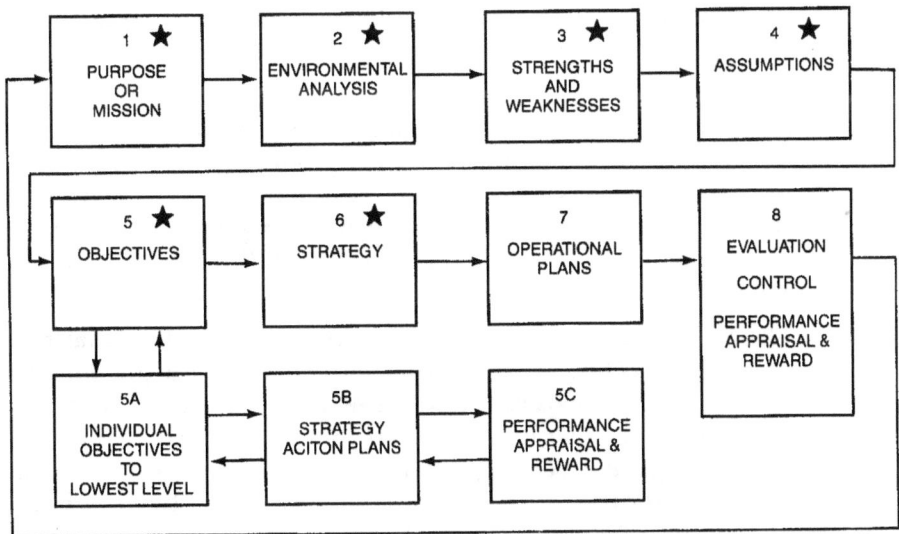

1 ★ PURPOSE OR MISSION	2 ★ ENVIRONMENTAL ANALYSIS	3 ★ STRENGTHS AND WEAKNESSES	4 ★ ASSUMPTIONS
5 ★ OBJECTIVES	6 ★ STRATEGY	7 OPERATIONAL PLANS	8 EVALUATION CONTROL PERFORMANCE APPRAISAL & REWARD
5A INDIVIDUAL OBJECTIVES TO LOWEST LEVEL	5B STRATEGY ACITON PLANS	5C PERFORMANCE APPRAISAL & REWARD	

It is important to remember that the strategic planning process is as important as the product. The nine steps are important because of the questions the organization is forced to consider. Each step requires organization levels to discuss, study, and negotiate. This process develops a planning mentality. When the nine steps are complete, you do have a product: a strategic plan. Managing the strategic plan is a learned art. The longer you use the tool, the better you are able to manage it.

If an organization uses the nine-step Strategic Long-Range Planning process outline, it can count on the following benefits: (1) the organization will determine where it is going; (2) opportunities and risks will be identified; (3) all organization members will be forced into a consensus as the direction for the organization is identified; (4) a surge of excitement will be experienced as managers have the opportunity to have input into the planning process; (5) communication in all directions will be instantly improved; (6) nonproductive persons will fall by the wayside; (7) increases should be expected in all measurable areas-profitability, productivity, turnover, etc.; (8) within a year, a personal training and development plan will evolve for all persons in the organization.

Importance and Justification

The United States economy, and the capitalistic concept, must continue to be a system for the world to follow. A properly functioning planning system organizes men, money, and machines to be more effective and productive.

As we move into the new millennium, the economy is strong with low inflation and a low unemployment rate; productivity is on the rise. The majority of employees are satisfied with their jobs yet experience more job insecurity due to the trend in downsizing, rightsizing, and reengineering as companies struggle to be more competitive in an increasingly global business environment.

The Council of Economic Advisors reported in early 1999 that the country's longest peacetime expansion had occurred over the previous 93 months due to the economy's continued growth (2). The nation's unemployment rate is at a 29-year low at 4.2 percent (3). Productivity the last two quarters of 1998, at 4 percent and 4.3 percent respectively, was the best six-month performance since 1983. These productivity gains have been attributed to continued cost reduction strategies and extensive use of technology such as computers for increased efficiency.[1]

The "Working Trends" survey conducted by the John J. Heldrich Center for Workforce Development at Rutgers University and the Center for Survey Research and Analysis at the University of Connecticut revealed that 88 percent of employees surveyed were satisfied with their jobs and 54 percent considered themselves to be "very satisfied." However, 71 percent had concerns about job security.[2] A two-year study by a New York nonprofit research group, the Families and Work Institute, revealed that due to downsizing trends over the last five years, one third of employees felt "somewhat likely or very likely" they would be laid off within the next few years.[3]

Downsizing has occurred in both the private and public sectors. According to the U.S. Bureau of Labor Statistics, over 3.3 million employees were laid off between 1996 and 1998. Between 1989 and 1998, there was a 33 percent reduction in the armed forces, impacting over 700,000 people.[4] According to the Office of Personnel Management, over 200,000 civil service jobs were eliminated between 1993 and 1998.[5]

Companies are trying to learn to "rightsize" and respond quickly to continual changes in the marketplace. As employees in one part of a company are selectively being laid off, another area of the company may be hiring. Other factors impacting this "rightsizing" trend are mergers and acquisitions as well as rapid growth in technology. According to a 1998 American Management Association survey on downsizing, 41 percent eliminated jobs yet two thirds of those were at the same time creating new jobs.[6]

Need for Strategic Planning

Not to be overlooked is the importance of planning to ensure the survival of the firm. With competition, new products and services, and an ever-changing complex world, a firm must have a system of managing that forces it to think through its alternative. A more detailed planning gap discussion is covered in Chapter 5.

What is needed is a management mentality to help organizations and managers survive as we enter the 21st century. We can no longer count on doing business the way we have in the past. I believe that of the existing American business organizations, one-third will fall by the wayside by the year 2010. The complexities in the marketplace, political arenas, and new product improvement will require organizations to adapt to changing situations. The Strategic Planning Process is the key tool in helping managers manage through the turbulent times ahead.

Any entity unable to adapt to changing times, whether it is dinosaurs, buggy whips, or whale oil, will not make it in the future. Organizations that did not adapt include the Penn Central Railroad, W.T. Grant, Pan American and Eastern Airlines to mention a few.

I am sure that years ago their management teams would have scoffed at the idea they would no longer be in existence today. IBM, General Motors and Sears adapted only after losing market share.

Peter F. Drucker makes an all-important point: "All institutions live and perform in two time periods: today and tomorrow. Tomorrow is being made today irrevocably in most cases."[7] The key point Drucker is emphasizing is that today we are making decisions that will affect the organization in the future. The planning process outlined in this book will help to make those important, far-reaching decisions in a scientific and logical manner.

We are in an era that must emphasize long-range thinking. Dale O. Cloninger, in the article, "American Myopia," believes that our very way of life has contributed toward a concern with only short-term results. He states, "As a whole Americans tend to be impatient, insisting on 'instantness'- instant success, instant gratification, instant service, and instant satisfaction." [8]

I believe this mentality has permeated our management system. Cloninger also says, "What is reasonable is to expect a greater emphasis on long-term planning and a recognition of the importance of patience through the realization that care, planning, hard work, and progress towards longer term goals carry their own rewards." I believe we are in an era in which management systems must seek out and reward those managers who can skillfully guide organizations toward longer term purpose and objectives and with less emphasis on the short-term profitability and reward. This Strategic Planning Process, by its very nature, forces a forward-looking view.

A portion of this book addresses the planning problem. When I assumed the responsibility of long-range planning at Continental Can Company's Elwood plant, I realized that I was not to run a one-man show. For the program to work, I acknowledged that everyone had to be involved. I was fully aware of my limited knowledge about manufacturing, engineering, and traffic, all of which would have to be meshed into the planning program. For any plan to succeed it had to have the support of every phase of the operation, otherwise what would evolve would be my plan and not that of the whole organization. By having this kind of involvement in the planning process, all of the persons needed to assure successful decisions would have been involved in the process.

Richard P. Nielsen observes in a recent article, "When an institution decides to develop a strategic plan often it is important that key individuals and groups reach consensus on the decision." What is being emphasized here is the need for this consensus and discussion, so that once the plan is agreed upon the implementation will go quickly.[9]

Our American management system generally makes fast decisions with only a few persons involved and then struggles for years and sometimes unsuccessfully getting the decisions implemented. The Japanese are one up on us in this area. They spend seemingly endless time analyzing the situation, studying the problem, looking at all avenues of the decision-making process before making a decision. Everyone has his/her say before the decision is made. Typically, they then move much faster in getting the decision implemented than we do in our American system. I believe the planning system discussed here brings out the best in our decision-making process, the need to react quickly, and it also brings people together so that the consensus is made and decisions can be implemented quickly. How important is strategic planning? Robert Albanese of Texas A&M notes:

> One study of 58 business organizations with identifiable formal planning functions (not necessarily planning departments) found that the individuals responsible for formal planning spend half their time working alone, reading and writing reports. The study suggests that the formal planner's relative isolation from meetings with managers and other organization members may be one factor contributing to a lack of planning effectiveness. The danger of such isolation can be reduced if planning is not separated from the implementation of plans.[10]

A study done in 1998 of 177 firms in the six-million-dollar revenue range in the Midwest confirmed the hypothesis for firm is the higher the level of strategic planning in small business, the greater the level of firm performance. This suggests that the higher the level of perception environmental uncertainty, the greater the level of strategic planning.

The results presented provide support for Hypothesis 4 ($p < 0.05$). The regression results show that strategic planning has a positive association with performance when using Return of Assets (ROA) as dependent variable. This suggests that the higher the level strategic planning committed by the small business, the higher the level of business performance. The higher the level of strategic planning in small business, the greater the level of firm performance.11

The planning system described here guards against the problems Albanese mentions. All management levels are involved and are responsible for executing the plan.

Sidney Schoeffler and co-authors found in a study of 57 corporations with 620 diverse businesses that there is a relationship between strategic planning and nonprofit performance. In his summary, he says that it has been demonstrated that strategic planning can have a positive impact on profits.[12]

Planning systems can cover a varied set of time frames. My wife, Mari, in her tenure as president of the Oral Roberts University Women's Club, had a planning horizon of one year. Once the plan was set, it became a process of execution, re-planning, and evaluation to finish the term of office. Planning for Colowyo Coal Company to mine its federal lease covers more than five years. Weyerhaeuser's corporation plans its tree crops for 20 to 40 years. The planning system described in this book can cover any time frame. It can be used by any individual, organization, business (profit or nonprofit) group.

Ronald J. Kudia reports in a study of the effect of strategic planning on the returns of stockholders that he found no significant differences between the shareholders of planning and non-planning firms. Other companies, including 3M and Bendix, attribute planning to superior performance. Kudia discusses a number of studies that indicates strategic planning resulted in positive effects. [13]

In a 1996 *Business Week* article, John A. Byrne observed that after 10 years of slashing and downsizing to remain competitive in the global marketplace, strategic planning is on the rise as organizations seek to improve the bottom line with their reengineered and right-sized organizations. Strategic planning sessions include staff from all levels of the organization, not just those at the top; even customers and suppliers participate with each offering unique perspective. Byrne added that a study by the Association of Management Consulting Firms revealed that "executives, consultants and [business] school professors all agree that business strategy is now the single most important management issue and will remain so for the next five years." Byrne notes that with sound strategy "companies are pursuing novel ways to hatch new products, expand existing businesses and create the markets of tomorrow."[14]

Peter Drucker asserts that there are seven management principles that are no longer valid in today's environment.[15] He notes the following as fallacies: "(1) there is only one right way to organize a business (2) the principles of management apply only to business organizations (3) there is a single right way to manage people." Early management thinking theorized that the only way to organize operations was with functional departments managed separately with all reporting to the CEO at the top.

This centralization was followed by decentralization, and now the team concept in various forms is popular. Drucker emphasizes "in any enterprise . . . there is a need for a number of different organizational structures coexisting side by side" and says "the executive of the future will need to be able to use each one properly and to think in terms of mixed structures rather than pure structures." The management guru also makes the case that every organization, whether a business corporation, religious or charity organization, healthcare group, or university or government agency, needs to follow similar sound management principles in order to achieve success. He adds that the difference between these types of organizations "applies to only 10 percent of the work which is determined by the organization's specific mission, its culture, its history, and its vocabulary. The rest is pretty much interchangeable."

Drucker insists that just as there is no one right way to organize a business there is also not one single way to manage employees. He states his philosophy in the past had been consistent with Theory Y in that that people want to work, and managers just need to motivate them. His thesis changed after reading *Eupsychian Management* by Abraham H. Maslow in 1962 in which Maslow demonstrated "conclusively that different people need to be motivated differently." Drucker notes most of today's employees are not true subordinates who are there just to do what they are told but are "knowledge workers"-they can do their job better than the boss-and thus should be managed as associates. He adds that the same things that motivate volunteers motivate knowledge workers: "above all, challenge, the need to know the organization's mission and to believe in it, a need for continuous training, and a need to see results." Managers need to lead rather than "manage" and can help the organization by "aligning the employee's goals with those of the organization and vice versa."

The other management theories that were valid in the past and are now considered outdated by Drucker are:

That technologies, markets and end users are fixed and rarely overlap.

That management's scope is legally defined as applying only to an organization's assets and employees.

That management's job is to "run the business" rather than to concentrate on what is happening outside the business. That is, management is internally, not externally, focused.

That national boundaries define the ecology of enterprise and management.

Drucker insists that one new assumption is that "the technologies likely to have the greatest impact on a company and its industry are technologies outside of its own field." One example highlighting this point was the development of the transistor by Bell Labs, part of AT&T. Thinking that the applications for this new invention were mainly outside the telephone industry, they sold it for a mere $25,000 to any company that was interested. These companies included Intel, Sony, and Compaq.

End users are not fixed. Markets change and companies need to adapt. Few businesses achieve greater than 30 percent market share, leaving 70 percent as potential customers if an organization can determine how to meet their needs.

Drucker notes that:

"The rapid decline of the American department store in the 1970's and 1980's was not caused by their customers deserting them. The 30 percent of American housewives who were their customers remained loyal, but a new breed of educated working women did not adopt the department store habit. She didn't have the time. Since she was not a customer, the department stores paid little attention to her. By the time she became the biggest part of the affluent middle class, it was too late for the department store to win her loyalty. Instead, by catering to its regular customers, these retailers ended up catering to a dying breed.

Drucker also states that the scope of management needs to be refined to include the entire economic process where main suppliers are involved in joint planning, development, and design and both work as partners to create value. We are operating in an increasingly global environment. Drucker notes that companies have been operating internationally for some time. The difference is that in the past whole companies did business in a foreign country; now, different pieces of the business process are being produced in different countries, resulting in multinational products and a broader scope internationally.

A manager's principal job is not to run the organization but to innovate, Drucker insists. He asserts that "an enterprise, whether a business or any other institution, that does not innovate or does not engage in entrepreneurship will not long survive." He considers four entrepreneurial practices to be essential: "(1) the organized abandonment of products, services, processes, markets, distribution channels and so on that are no longer an optimal allocation of resources, (2) to organize for systematic, continuing improvement, (3) to organize for systematic and continuous exploitation, especially of . . . successes, (4) to organize systematic innovation, that is, to create the different tomorrow that makes yesterday obsolete and, to a large extent, replaces even the most successful products of today in any organization."

Strategic Management

Strategic Management is a philosophy of managing with a planning process. It is a stream of decisions and actions, which effectively execute the strategic plan. The strategic management process is the way the management team directs the organization within the framework and promotion of the strategic plan.

Strategic decisions are a means to achieve ends. These decisions encompass the definition of the business, products and markets to be served, functions to be performed, and major policies needed for the organization to execute these decisions to achieve objectives.

Strategic management provides a strong incentive for employees and management to achieve company objectives. It serves as the basis for management control and evaluation. It allows a firm to innovate in time to take advantage of new opportunities in the environment and reduce its risk because it anticipated the future. Strategic management is a continuous process.

The importance of strategic management became apparent when many organizations developed plans and then put them on the shelf. The yearly planning process would be completed, and the organization went back to its old way of doing things. Strategic management evolved because of the need to manage the plan.

Long-range planning helps remove some of the risks and ambiguity associated with organizational memberships. Strategic management allows an enterprise to base its decisions on long-range forecasts, not spur-of-the-moment reactions. It allows the firm to take action at an early stage of a new trend and consider the lead-time for effective management. This helps ensure full exploitation of opportunities.

Strategic management allows a firm's top executives to anticipate change and provides direction and control for the enterprise, while it allows them to have unified opinion on strategic issues and actions. It also helps educate managers to become better decision-makers; it helps them examine basic problems of a company. It improves corporate communication, the coordination of individual projects, the allocation of resources, and short-range planning such as budgeting. Strategic management focuses on business problems, not just functional problems such as those of a marketing or financial nature.

Strategic management focuses on "second-generation planning," analysis of the business, and the preparation of several scenarios for the future.

This is not to say that strategic management is all you need to make a success of your business, but it should prove to be informative. A good example of both strategic planning and strategic management is at Ford Motor Company. The management style of retired Ford Motor Company's Donald Petersen will be a model for chief executives for years to come. Ford's U.S. market share climbed in the 1980's to about 22 percent from 16 percent. Some of Petersen's handiwork was unique to Ford: He broke the habit of following GM's lead. Here are Petersen's lessons-and how they are applied.

1. Be obsessed with quality. Petersen hired the late W. Edwards Deming, a quality master who taught the Japanese the secrets of statistical process control.

2. Empower your workers. Petersen tapped into the creative power of every Ford worker.

13

3. Tap the power of teams. Petersen forced the people who design cars to work in close-knit teams with Ford's engineers and marketers.

4. Compete globally. Petersen turned Ford into the USA's first truly global automotive company.[16]

Included in the area of strategic management is management responsibility to create a positive productive work environment. A 1998 Fortune survey of most admired companies conducted by the Hay Group revealed that "the single best predictor of overall excellence was a company's ability to attract, motivate, and retain talented people."[17] The corporate culture of those companies was crucial in the achievement of this goal according to their company's leaders. Bruce Pfau, a VP of the Hay Group and an expert in cultural assessment, notes that "the corporate cultures of high performing companies are dramatically different from those of average companies." Average company goals were "minimizing risk, respecting the chain of command, supporting the boss, and making budget" while high-performing companies valued "teamwork, customer focus, fair treatment of employees, initiative and motivation." The survey emphasizes that companies in the lead for their industry such as Southwest Airlines, Squibb, Toyota, JP Morgan, UPS, Intel, Dow Chemical, have top leadership that places high priority on cultural issues and knows how they measure up in comparison to those goals.

WHAT IS PLANNING?

Planning may be defined as a managerial activity that involves determining your fundamental purpose as an organization, analyzing the environment, setting objectives, deciding on specific actions needed to reach the objectives, and then adapting the original plan as feedback on results is received. This process should be distinguished from the plan itself, which is a written document containing the results of the planning process. The plan is a written statement of what is to be done and how it is to be done. Planning is a continuous process that both precedes and follows other functions. Plans are made and executed, and results are used to make new plans as the process continues.

TYPES OF PLANS

There are many types of plans, but most can be categorized as either *strategic* or *tactical*. Strategic plans cover a long period of time and may be referred to as *long-term*. They are broad in scope and basically answer the question of how an organization is to commit its resources over the next three to five, possibly even 10 years. Strategic plans are altered on an infrequent basis to reflect changes in the environment or overall direction of the organization.

Tactical plans cover a short time period, usually a year or less. They are often referred to as *short-term or operational plans.* They specify what is to be done in a given year to move the organization toward its long-term objectives. In other words, what we do this year (short-term) needs to be tied to where we want to be five to 10 years in the future (long-term).

Traditionally, managers who have been involved in planning have focused on short-term rather than long-term planning. This is better than no planning at all; but it also means each year's plan is not related to anything long-term in nature and usually falls short of moving the organization to where it wants to be in the future.

Programs and events also require planning. A *program* is a large set of activities involving a specific area of capabilities, such as planning for a new outpatient surgery service or a new managed care system. Planning for programs involves:

1. Dividing the total set of activities into meaningful parts.
2. Assigning planning responsibility for each part to appropriate people.
3. Assigning target dates for completion of plans.
4. Determining and allocating the resources needed for each part.

Each major program or division within an organization should have a strategic plan in place to provide a blueprint for the program over time.

An *event* is generally a project of less scope and complexity. It is also not likely to be repeated on a regular basis. An event may be a part of a broader program, such as the grand opening of a new service, or it may be self-contained, such as an annual recruiting fair at the local mall. Even for a onetime event, planning is an essential element to accomplish the objectives of the project and coordinate the activities that make up the event.

THE GREATEST NEEDS OF TODAY'S ORGANIZATIONS WORLDWIDE

In informal surveys I have made over the years, leaders of organizations appear strong in their beliefs that strategic planning is important. Yet simple acknowledgment of its importance is not enough for success. To put matters into perspective, let us try to translate success and better understand what makes the organization successful.

$$X = f (A, B, C, D, E, F, G, H, I \dots)$$

In this case X represents success, a dependent variable, and is on the left side of the equation. The = sign means a balance, or equal to what is on the other side; the "f" means "a function of," indicating on what that success depends. On the right side are all the independent variables that affect success:

A. Chief Executive as Leader/Manager/Planner

B. Management Team Working Together

C. Planning System

D. Organizational Structure

E. Control System

F. Reward System

G. Integrity/Ethics of Organization

H. Empowered Employer

I. Etc.

Only a few independent variables are listed, but the possibilities are endless. Notice that success is not necessarily equated with size. We are defining success in broader terms than number of employees, budget, and so forth. There seems to be a widespread notion that size is the only barometer of success, but we do not subscribe to that belief.

Untapped leadership exists in many organizations. I believe the greatest problems holding back these leaders and the organizations they serve involve some combination of independent variables C, D, and E. Management, planning, organization, and control are some of the greatest needs of all organizations.

Most people assume that all administrators are leaders to some degree, or they could not remain in their executive positions. However, their leadership efforts and the success of their organizations are in direct proportion to variables C, D, and E. If you assume all other variables remain unchanged and full effort goes into C, D, and E, then the X factor (success), the dependent variable, has to increase. Without training and knowledge in the area of planning and management, your chief executive places a ceiling on success. No organization can get any bigger than the capacity of its managers to manage. The hindrance is not the needs of the constituents, because the needs are always there.

If every executive could improve each of these areas just a little each year, they would be much more successful. They could reduce drastically all the obvious errors in direction, false starts, dissipated efforts, staff frustration, and waste. They could also successfully challenge a world rife with criticism about waste and inefficiency in organizations.

Organizations cannot afford to wait until someone comes along and stirs up a big scandal. We need to put our shoulders to the wheel and pay attention to management, planning, organization, control, and people. If we do not, on the whole, many of our organizations will not accomplish nearly as much as they might.

My observation is that many people in leadership positions are reluctant to plan, do not want a plan in writing, and do not ask for advice. The tendency is to be led by intuition, which is sometimes based on a whim or emotional impulse. This reflects our general American inclination to "hang loose." Probably 75 percent of the organizations the author has observed or worked with have the same problem. Yet the 25 percent who have the discipline to plan and manage properly, far outperform those that do not. Higher revenue surpluses, better service and lower turnovers are but a few of the rewards of thoughtful, well-executed planning. Good fortune comes to those organizations that have the discipline to plan and manage effectively.

Many times there is the tendency to say that forces outside our control caused a plan or project to go sour. And sometimes that is the case. But too often we are our own worst enemies, holding ourselves back. Many business failures can be traced to poor planning, failure to get people involved in the planning and generally poor management.

Even where planning is done, we often sense a spirit of extreme urgency. Here the atmosphere is permeated with a "let's go for it-if it is a worthwhile service, it will prosper" mentality. What is the rush? Many HCO's need to slow down and plan. Often they have rushed around in circles for several years. If the organization provides a worthwhile service, it deserves our best efforts at careful planning. Included in doing our best is using the best planning and management philosophies and techniques available.

Fundamental to these efforts is effective goal setting. Its importance is to provide direction and unity of purpose. Where planning in organization occurs without quantitative goals clearly understood and widely supported, vigorous progress is unlikely and probably impossible. Planning is not easy, but the alternative is to be tossed to and fro, buffeted by every unforeseen circumstance, and blown off course.

And on a personal level, every leader needs a vision or a dream. Mission statements and dreams are the vessels through which personal desires can be fulfilled. Yet without specific goals, a vision is no vision.

In a society where many institutions are becoming stagnant, it is imperative that firms have an expanding vision. Thus, we see creative planning as the organization's best hope for a successful future. Solid purpose, long-range dreaming, and visionary thinking should be basic to a firm's operation. Too often planning in an organization has been met with little enthusiasm. Even in larger organizations, the enthusiasm for a plan seldom extends beyond a year unless it involves something tangible, such as a new building. Yet no matter how misunderstood and poorly appreciated planning is, it is a major factor in effective organization performance. The time for strategic planning in all organizations is *now*.

PLANNING PERSPECTIVE

All organizations do at least some planning even if it is largely informal and even largely unintentional. One writer states, "planning has to be defined by the *process* it represents" (18). The process is largely informal in many institutions which means it is also incremental (each decision builds upon prior planning decisions). Informal planning, however, leads to misunderstandings because there are few records of planning decisions which have been made, planning efforts are sporadic, and it is likely that the effort will not result in a completed plan. There is also no system of follow-through. Informal planning is not likely to be comprehensively implemented. Effective planning is a disciplined process.

If we have authority and responsibility in an organization, we find ourselves observing how the present is evolving into the future and how things we would like to see happen are sometimes (and sometimes not) becoming a part of that future. The extent to which we think about such things is the extent to which we are beginning the planning process. Planning begins with (1) the assumption that there is a future, and that (2) maybe it should be different than the present, along with (3) realizing that we can do something about that future, and then (4) resolving that we will take action. Let us look at these four concepts.

All of us know that there is a future. Not all of us care about the future. Most of us know that it will be at least a little different from the present even if we do nothing to bring about the difference. Many of us are content to have the fascinating future be created by others and are willing to sit back and take in the benefits of what that future might bring. Part of this is due to the expectation that the future will be better than the present. We point to the progress of this century. If we are from the United States or Canada, we look at how inventions, the standard of living, health care, and other improvements have come about without much effort on our part. Why mess up a good thing? If we continue as we have for the past 40 years and continue to avoid a major war, we expect prosperity, stability, convenience, better health, more wealth, and most other things that we value. In short, why plan when the world is getting better every day without planning effort on our part?

The second concept is determining whether we want the future to be different from the present and the past. Some of us say why bother? Some of us, on the other hand, find the future possibilities exciting. We consider ways in which the future will be different due to major forces such as the increased role of technology and technological break-throughs, or the opportunities we face due to a strong economy and political freedom that encourage entrepreneurial and creative activities on our part and which work toward fulfilling our urges and interests.

The third concept is realizing that we can do something about that future. This requires vision, the ability to dream, to visualize what could happen if the right efforts take place. It begins with an understanding that the future can be different from the present, that you and others around you can help shape that future. It must include the understanding that the present is going to change anyway. The rapid rate of change in society today affects every aspect of organization's life.

And then we have the fourth concept, resolving that we will take action to mold that future. This is the tough one. This means taking action based upon our vision of what we would like the future to be. The number of people who are serious in this category on a consistent basis is relatively small. The need for positive people in this category is very high. They are the ones who shape the world. These are the people who lead the world and create the interesting setting in which the rest of us live. The greatest opportunity is that each of us can decide whether we want to be in this category. There are no elections, no dues to pay, just leadership to exert and the satisfaction that comes from seeing something happen that has come about because of our leadership and the leadership of others.

STRATEGIC THINKING

Strategic thinking is akin to critical thinking, a familiar concept in management theory. Traditionally, critical thinking has been identified with the field of logic and the mental ability to reason in the abstract. Today, critical thinking is an essential element of most disciplines including management, leadership, and strategic planning. Strategic thinking might be explained as focusing on higher-level learning and more complex thinking abilities. Thus, categories in the cognitive domain such as analysis, synthesis, and evaluation are rich fields for critical thinking. However, the focus is that of strategic planning in a practical and applied context. Therefore, we must direct critical thinking beyond knowledge within a discipline to application:

- Between disciplines.
- To real-world predictable problems.

19

- To real-world unpredictable problems.

Strategic thinking also emphasizes:

- Asking and seeking answers to penetrating questions, which affect survival of the organization.

- Scanning the environment, both external and internal, for unique ways of "doing more with less at higher quality."

A leader who thinks strategically will focus on the following:

- Conceptualize direction-setting actions for the organization.

- Identify areas of change that will impact the vision, mission, and overall objective of the firm.

- Look at the big picture across traditional boundaries and beyond the next two to three years.

- Emphasize the why and the how (instead of what) of strategy design and implementation.

- Search for the best competitive advantage, or best competitive position relative to other key institutions, which may target similar markets and donors.

Strategic thinking emphasizes development and implementation of organization-wide or overall strategies with accountability toward effectiveness, efficiency, and quality in mind. Perspectives of strategic thinking can be illustrated with the question, "Who are the two most important persons responsible for the success of an airplane's flight?" Typical responses would be:

- the pilot and the navigator.
- the pilot and the maintenance supervisor.
- the pilot and the air traffic controller.
- the pilot and the flight engineer.

All of these responses recognize the day-to-day hands-on importance of the pilot. They all introduce one of several other important support or auxiliary functionaries to the answer. However, each of these responses ignores the one person who is perhaps the single most important individual to the ultimate success of the airplane-the designer. Perhaps the pilot and the designer are the two individuals most important to the success of an airplane's flight-because of the pilot's day-to-day responsibilities in commanding the craft and the designer's ability to create a concept that can be economically constructed, easily operated by any normally competent flight crew, and safely maintained by the ground crew.

Most contemporary administrators of organizations perceive themselves as the "pilots" of their institutions taking off, landing, conferring with the navigator, and communicating with the air traffic controller. They generally view themselves as the chief hands-on operational managers. However, what has been most lacking in these institutions in the past few years has been an appreciation for the strategic planning viewpoint. There is a need for more emphasis on an integrated "designer-pilot" approach to operating an education venture. A well-conceived, continuously updated strategic planning system can facilitate this emphasis.

An organization without a strategic planning perspective faces a tough situation. Instead of moving steadily toward its goals, the institution will continually swerve off course due to the endless supply of distractions that can prevent an institution from pursuing its vision and mission. Thus, strategic planning is one of the keys to success of any undertaking, and nowhere is it more important than in all organizations.

Ethics, Integrity, and Religious Principles in Business

Drucker's[18] quote "the ultimate test of management is integrity" caught my attention in 1974 with the publication of his book, *Management: Tasks and Practices.* (19) At the time I thought no way. What about profits, market share and customer service? By the early 80's, I began to understand what he was saying. Now as we enter the 21st century I agree 100 percent. Oral Roberts, then president of Oral Roberts University, spoke at a business seminar on the ORU campus. In his opening remarks he said, "Your product better be better than your sales pitch." In a brilliant, spirit-led speech before bankers from 38 states Roberts went on to relate the similarity between his product, ORU and students raised to hear His voice, and products and services sold by the banks. As we look at promotions and deals by a wide range of organizations, it appears to me we are full circle back to "buyer beware." More and more there is "fine print," a hidden agenda.

How do we define integrity, ethics and character? The dictionary gives us "firm attachment to moral or artistic principle: honesty and sincerity."

How are our society and business organizations measuring up to this definition? Some would say the trend is disturbing. The nation's CEO is still in office. His behavior would have resulted here in Tulsa with immediate removal from office. Our society does not seem to care. Many people went to prison over the savings and loan scandal. An international insurance company with questionable sales practices is refunding premiums. Instead of immediate refunds, they set up a cumbersome bureaucracy for the refund. The administration of the claim process problem amounts to more than the claim. Right after, we see ads on TV to "trust" this company. Another corporate giant admits to breaking the law collecting from customers. "That is big business!!"

Some would say, "Not here in Tulsa!" How about a 50 percent off coupon that a local company used recently. Upon investigation, the company almost doubled the original price and honored the 50 percent offer. This resulted in a real saving to the customer of only 10 percent instead of the advertised 50 percent. Good business practice? Short term, maybe. But what about the long term? These customers might not be back.

Peter Drucker said, "The ultimate test of management is integrity" in his 1974 look at management. I thought, "Come on profits and market share, return on investment." Any principled person could not argue against integrity, but management's "ultimate test"?

Twenty-five years later, I submit Drucker hit it on the head. Lawyers, laws, and court systems are not going to help you get a fair deal. My suggestion is deal only with organizations and people you can trust. Trust is gained over time. The issue is not what you say, as much as what you do.

My father, the late Roscoe Channing Migliore taught me an early lesson in life. He was a merchant in Collinsville. Briefly, a freezer was delivered to a farmer on the verge of losing a freezer full of meat. Mr. Migliore, a union electrician, noticed the problem was in the electric cord. He fixed it in minutes. In the short run, he lost a sale. But, in the long run, his action confirmed what everyone in the Collinsville area already knew. You could trust Roscoe. Many, Many years later he and the farmer by chance were in a nursing home together. Forty years later they still were discussing the incident.

I submit that integrity, ethics and character are traits that are not only morally correct, but gain a trust that makes people want to do business with your organization.

Seven privately held companies that I have had close dealings with operate in an ethical way with a high degree of integrity. All seven companies are founded on Christian principles. They are The Oklahoman Eagle, Parker Drilling, and T.D. Williamson, Inc., Tulsa, OK; Cross Manufacturing, Overland Park, KS; Michael Cardone Industries, Philadelphia, PA; and Brasfield Construction, Jackson, TN and Aftermarket, Phoenix, Arizona. Except for Parker Drilling, I have been a consultant to the other six for many years. I am familiar with Parker Drilling because they are here in Tulsa, OK.

Many of my students work for Parker Drilling as do many of our friends. I am privileged to count Bobby Parker, Chairman of the Board, as as a friend. I have been in countless strategy, operational meetings with the six companies mentioned. Each CEO has conferred with me on numerous decisions. Not once has any decision or action not met the highest standard of conduct. I count it as a privilege to have worked with and count these people as close friends.

Competitive Advantage

Competitive Advantage in the rapidly changing, fiercely competitive marketplace can be gained when the firm uses good planning and management principles. Michael E. Porter has made a significant contribution to the understanding of competitive advantage. His books *Competitive Strategy* [19] and *Competitive Advantage* [20] go into great detail on how to gain and maintain the competitive edge. He states that "Competition is at the core of the success or failure of firms. Competition determines the appropriateness of a firm's activities that can contribute to its performance, such as innovations, a cohesive culture, or good implementation. Competitive strategy is the search for a favorable competitive position in an industry, the fundamental arena in which competition occurs. Competitive strategy aims to establish a profitable and sustainable position against the forces that determine industry competition."[21]

I submit that the firm that understands is committed and has the discipline to use the concepts in this book will gain a competitive edge.

SUMMARY

I have attempted to establish in this chapter the belief that: (1) the demands of a volatile environment create an urgency for the planning concept; (2) many of the identifiable organization failures cannot be blamed solely on unforeseen and uncontrollable factors; yet (3) many leaders do not believe that there is a need for planning; but (4) there is a crucial place for better planning and management; (5) new planning creates opportunities and helps eliminate failures and last (6) the firm gains a competitive advantage using the principles in the book.

The philosophy of this book is that in order for everyone in an organization-the board, the executive staff, the employees-to be successful, a strategic plan is desperately needed. If you look at the mistakes of the past, it is obvious that many organizations have floundered because they lack strategic direction. Over years of consulting with these types of organizations, the authors have observed this exact pattern in a large number of them. However, if you take the time and effort to study this book, apply the format prescribed here, and follow up with your people, this is what I believe you can expect:

1. A sense of enthusiasm in your organization.
2. A five-year plan in writing to which everyone is committed.
3. A sense of commitment by the entire organization to its overall direction.
4. Clear job duties and responsibilities.
5. Time for the leaders to do what they need to do.
6. Clear and evident improvement in the health and vitality of every member of the organization's staff.
7. Accountability, responsibility, and delegation moving down and lower organization ratios.
8. Rewarding results and behavior that are important to the firm and to the benefit of organization members.
9. Measurable improvement in the personal lives of all those in management positions with time for vacations, family, and personal pursuits.

IMPORTANT POINTS TO REMEMBER

1. A workable Strategic Long-Range Planning/MBO program should include a specific pre-objective-setting procedure
2. We have a productivity problem in this country.
3. Long-range planning is essential to survival.
4. A general state of apathy and dissatisfaction exists at lower levels of the work force.
5. Problems have arisen with MBO when it is not used properly.
6. Many companies worldwide have had successful experiences with MBO.
7. There is scientific evidence of the merit of Long-Range Planning/ MBO.
8. It is management's responsibility to provide the leadership to solve the productivity and planning problem.
9. There is a need for a simple, easy-to-understand long-range planning tool.
10. The strategic plan must be strategically and systematically managed.

If you are struggling with any of the following problems or questions, this book may be very important to you:

- Why is there so much confusion among our vice presidents and department heads about what we are trying to accomplish?
- Why is there so much dissension and disagreement in this organization?
- Why is there such a high turnover of people in our organization, especially in leadership positions?
- Why did we spend money on new services when they are not being used?
- As CEO (Chief Executive Officer) why am I working 12 hours a day, and can never keep up?
- Why have we been less than successful on a number of projects and programs?
- Why have our revenues dropped off?
- Why does this organization lack enthusiasm?
- Why has the board asked me to resign after everything I have put into this organization?

If you are wrestling with any of these questions, the answer might be that your organization lacks effective long-term strategic planning and management.

References
Chapter 1

[1] Laabs, Jennifer, "Has Downsizing Missed Its Mark?" Workforce, Costa Mesa, April 1999.

[2] Hinden, Stan, "Forced to Retire Before You're Ready; The Merge and Downsize IRA's layoffs Hit Older Workers Especially Hard," *The Washington Post,* Washington, June 6, 1999.

[3] Miller, Rich, "Worker Output up 4%; Productivity bodes well for economy," *USA Today,* Arlington, May 12, 1999.

[4] U.S. Dept. of Labor Statistics. Shepard, Scott, "Workers say job steals family time," *The Atlanta Constitution,* Atlanta, GA. March 18, 1999.

[5] Joyner, Tammy, "Massive Study Finds Workers Tired, Insecure," *The Atlanta Constitution,* Atlanta, GA, April 15, 1998.

[6] Cavsey, Mike, "Downsizing Hits Home," *The Washington Post,* Washington, March 1, 1999.

[7] Peter Drucker, "Managing for Tomorrow," *Industry Week,* April 14, 1980, p. 55.

[8] Dale O. Cloninger, *The Collegiate Forum,* Fall 1981, p. 6.

[9] Richard Nielsen, "Toward a Method for Building Consensus During Strategic Planning," *Sloan Management Review,* Summer 1981, p. 29.

[10] Robert Albanese, Managing: Toward Accountability for Performance, p. 108-109, and Larry E. Greiner, "Integrating Formal Planning into Organizations," in F.J. Aguilar, R.A. Howell, and R.F. Vancil, eds., *Formal Planning Systems,* 1970 (Cambridge, Mass.: Harvard University, Graduate School of Business Administration, 1970), p. 88.

[11] Charles H. Matthews, Choy Hoon Lee. Antecedents and Consequence of Strategic Planning in Small Business: An Empirical Study. Competitive paper presented during the 44th World Conference of the International Council for Small Business (ICSB), June 20-23, 1999, Naples, Italy. Please contact second author.

[12] Sidney Schoffler, Robert D. Buzzell, and Donald F. Heaney, "Impact of Strategic Planning on Profit Performance," *Harvard Business Review,* March-April 1974, p. 137.

[13] Ronald J. Kudl, "The Effects of Strategic Planning on Common Stock Returns," Academy of Management Journal, Vol. 23, No. 1, p 5

[14] Byrne, John, *Business Week,* August 26, 1996. p. 26-51.

[15] Peter Drucker, *Managements New Paradigms* Forbes, Oct. 6, 1998. p. 152.

[16] John Hillkink "Peterson's Style Is a Model for the 1990's," *USA Today,* March 1, 1999. p. 813.

[17] "What Makes a Company Grow?" *Fortune.* October 26, 1998. p. 210

[18] Drucker, Peter F. *Management: Tasks and Practices.(New York: Harper & Row, 1974, p79)*

[19] Porter, Michael E. *Competitive Strategy.(The Free Press1980)*

[20] Porter, Michael E. *Competitive Advantage. (The Free Press 1980)*

[21] Porter, Michael E. *Competitive Strategy.(The Free Press1980)*

Chapter 2
State of the Art

The purpose of this chapter is to develop a historical overview of management by objectives and how it is developing into a planning system. The evolution from strategic planning into strategic management is covered. The acronym MBO was first used in 1954 by Peter Drucker.[1] George Odiorne told me he remembers the graduate class at New York University in which Drucker first discussed the concept in the early fifty's. Odiorne and Dale McConkey, both students under Drucker, were certainly influenced by his work as we all have been. Ronald G. Greenwood credits Harold Smiddy, a long-time vice president of General Electric, with a great contribution to Drucker as he developed the concept. He credits Smiddy with being the first to actually practice MBO as we know it today.[2] However, many of the elements used in MBO were actually developed before Drucker's time; the early development of these elements is traced chronologically. Various authors, managers, and consultants contributed to the growth of MBO from Drucker in 1954 to the present day; their contributions are also traced. Odiorne, McConkey, George Morrisey, and others are credited with giving MBO a substantial boost about 1965. The relative merits of installing and encouraging the use of MBO by a staff entity (the so-called personnel view), or by top management (the "organization view"), are examined. The importance of planning and its part in MBO are covered. My feeling that strategic planning is the trend of the future for MBO is examined. The fact that MBO is applicable at lower levels is introduced. My recent experiences with MBO in the nonprofit sector are discussed. Finally, the controversy surrounding MBO is discussed in greater detail, and a brief discussion of MBO's relevance to academia is given.

MBO Definition and Origins

Management by objectives has been described as "a process whereby the superior and subordinate managers of an organization jointly identify its (the organization's) common goals, define each individual's major area of responsibility in terms of the results expected of him, and use these measures as guides for operating the unit and assessing the contribution of each of its members."[3] The even broader definition in chapter 1 considers the firm's purpose, the environment in which the firm operates, the firm's strengths and weaknesses, and makes assumptions before setting objectives.

The sequence of steps used by Alcoa of America a number of years ago in its MBO system provides an instructive example of a pre-1980 system in actual use:

1. A person lists his major performance objectives for the coming year and his specific plans including target dates for achieving these objectives.
2. He submits them to his boss for review. Out of the discussion comes an agreed-upon set of objectives.
3. On a quarterly basis, he verbally reviews progress toward these objectives with his boss. Objectives and plans are revised and updated as needed.
4. At the end of the year, the person prepares a brief "accomplishment report" which lists all major accomplishments, with comments on the variances between results actually achieved and results expected.
5. This self-appraisal is discussed with the boss. Reasons for goals not being met are explored.
6. A new set of objectives is established for the next year.[4]

In my view this definition, like most companies' systems, is incomplete in that it begins with goal setting and leaves out the preliminary considerations I detailed in steps 1-4 (in chapter 1). My firm belief, thoroughly tested over the years since I was responsible for long-range planning at Continental Can's Elwood plant, has always been that it is necessary to consider a firm's purpose, the environment in which it operates, and its strengths and weaknesses, as well as to make assumptions about future events, before setting objectives. Otherwise, the MBO process runs the risk of being ill-grounded and in the end irrelevant. A workable system can then be devised, building on the remaining points in my definition.

Based on this representative description and company practice, the following specific elements in MBO can be identified:

- Planning
- Setting of objectives and goals
- Negotiation
- Performance review
- Feedback, communication, and involvement
- Evaluation

McConkey emphasizes that the key word in MBO is management, not objectives. The historical development of these elements is discussed in the following paragraphs. Drucker and the Odiorne-McConkey group in 1965 represent focal points in the analysis.

Profit-center accountability was first introduced by Donaldson Brown, DuPont's treasurer from 1918 to 1921. Brown created the idea of controlling through accounting responsibility by linking the various organizational sub-units to a planned rate of return on controllable expenses.[5] He left DuPont and joined Alfred P. Sloan, Jr., at General Motors. At General Motors, Brown installed the accounting responsibility system into Sloan's organization plan in 1923.

Sloan's organizational plan—centralized control of policy and decentralized operations—had many of the elements of management by objectives.[6] In the early 1920s, division managers submitted yearly estimates of their expected operating results for the ensuing year. Later, these forecasts became commitments, and the division managers were held accountable for their attainment. In 1924 and 1925 General Motors used a system of statistical reports that supplied feedback as to progress in attaining commitments.

In 1918, a management bonus plan had been worked out. Each manager was eligible for a bonus; however, he had to earn the bonus based on his performance. Sloan defended this financial incentive plan, emphasizing that each manager was encouraged to think he was "the boss" of his particular entity.

Edward N. Hay recognized the value of this "accountability management" concept in the 1930s and defined its basis as the concept that an organization's goals are most effectively attained by establishing and distributing specific accountabilities and objectives relating to those goals among the organization's management group.

Around this concept Hay built a consulting business that has helped install accountability management in organizations around the world. Albanese stresses the accountability in his new book, *Managing: Toward Accountability for Performance.*

A number of consulting firms affirm the value of this managerial style, including the well-known Booz, Allen & Hamilton and McKinsey & Co. J. O. McKinsey wrote a book in 1922 called *Budgetary Control.*[8] Many elements of MBO are included in the book. In many of these firms' varied consultations they have used management-by-objectives concepts, making major contributions from the 1940s to the present.

As described by Henry Fayol, the setting of objectves and goals became increasingly important in 1916.[9] Ralph C. Davis emphasized planning, objectives, and goal setting in 1934[10] and may also have been influenced by Frederick Taylor's scientific management. Luther Gulick, in his notes on the theory written in 1936, and Urwick, in *The Making of Scientific Management: Thirteen Pioneers in 1948,* emphasized planning and objectives.

McConkey has credited Drucker with bringing the importance of objectives to the forefront: "Objectives of one variety or another have been known and used by managers since Biblical times. It remained for Drucker, writing in 1954, to utilize them as the basis for a management system."[11] Drucker was understandably influenced by the work of Taylor, Fayol, Davis, Gulock, Urwick, and others before 1954.

Contributions by the Behavioral Scientists

Elton Mayo, from the Hawthorne Studies, started the behavioral scientists' contribution to MBO.[12] The behavioral scientists emphasized the importance of participative management and the role of the individual.

Lester Coch and John French contributed the idea that a greater commitment to organizational goals could be obtained and satisfactions enhanced by participation in decision making.[13]

Abraham Maslow introduced his theory of human needs in 1943.[14] The existence of higher order needs for such things as recognition and achievement, and the attempt to fulfill them in an organizational system are basic to MBO. A manager needs to recognize the motivational power of satisfying these higher-level needs.

The concepts of the decentralized profit center originating with Sloan and the objectives and planning contributed by Fayol, as well as the importance of commitment and participation advanced by the behavioral scientists beginning with Mayo, were all specific contributions to the development of MBO prior to Drucker's synthesis. Drucker, however, crystallized the MBO concept by synthesizing the various influences and advancements in thinking which had already been conceived. He wrote the following as an explanation of the purpose of MBO:

> What the business enterprise needs is a principle of management that will give full scope to individual strength and responsibility, and at the same time give common direction of vision and effort, establish teamwork and harmonize the goals of the individual with the common will. The only principle that can do this is management by objectives and self-control.[15]

The behavioral scientists contributed again to MBO in the late 1950s and early 1960s. Frederick Herzberg advanced the two-factor theory in an effort to explain what motivates managers.[16] Herzberg contends that the things that tend to motivate people more today are primarily related to people themselves and their images of themselves. Opportunities for advancement, greater responsibility, promotion, growth, achievement, and interesting work are identified as the kinds of factors that make work experiences enjoyable, challenging, meaningful, and interesting. By its very nature MBO can be people oriented, gives the opportunity to satisfy needs, and therefore has a positive effect.

Rensis Likert argued for participative management.[17] Likert's "linking pin" concept recognizes the organization's structure and clearly defines who reports to whom. The concept gets its name from the fact that the manager of each unit is linked to a higher unit in the organization. The value to MBO in this type of organization design is in its clarity of defined responsibilities. All subunits in the organization are linked together to make up the whole, and each is answerable for its accomplishment to the next higher level. MBO has a better chance for positive results in an organization in which duties and functions are clearly defined. The defining of responsibility areas helps in the derivation of the goals and objectives for that specific area.

Robert L. Kahn and Daniel Katz felt that particular leadership styles were important for maximum effectiveness.[18] They discovered that effective foremen did not supervise their workers closely, apparently giving them more freedom to set their pace and approach to their performance of assignments. Katz and Kahn encouraged more participation by the worker in the management of his own work. Their major contribution to management by objectives and successful supervision is that they emphasize the elements of self-control and participation.

Douglas McGregor contributed his Theory X and Theory Y.[19] The Theory Y type of management recognizes the value of the individual, assuming that people will exercise self-direction and self-control in the achievement of organizational objectives to the degree that they are committed to these objectives. Theory-X-oriented managers, on the other hand, have a basically limited view of people and their capabilities, and believe they must be strictly controlled in order to make them produce. McGregor's contribution to management by objectives is his emphasis on the value of human resources and their potential and, along with Maslow, on satisfying certain "higher-level needs," such as self-esteem, recognition, self-actualization, and so forth. The MBO philosophy enables the individual to satisfy his higher level needs. MBO provides the opportunity for recognition and independent thought.

Robert M. Blake and Jane Mouton have emphasized leadership styles in their concept of the "managerial grid."[20] A leader's behavior can be understood in terms of his concern for both production and people, and the emphasis he places on each of these concerns. An ideal management is generally regarded as one that seeks mission accomplishment with primary emphasis on people and production. Blake and Mouton's important contri-

31

bution to management by objectives is their identifying of different leadership styles, and realizing that the opportunity for positive results is greater with a balanced managerial style.

All of these contributions are directly or indirectly related to the problem of management by objectives and tend to advance the state of the art.

1965 Books

The next major focal point in the history of management by objectives came in 1965 with Odiorne's *Management by Objectives: A System of Managerial Leadership,* and McConkey's *How to Manage by Results.* A number of other authors made contributions during this period, including J. D. Batten, Marvin Bower, Chuck L. Hughes, Alfred J. Marrow, Phillip Marvin, George Morrisey, David E. Olsen, and Edward C. Schleh. They had the benefit of Drucker's thinking, had been active as consultants, and saw the motivational effects of the various behavioral scientists from 1954 until the early 1960s. Most of these authors saw MBO in a broader context than merely performance appraisal. They reinforced Drucker's view that it was a total system of management.

The Personnel View

The so-called personnel view is defined as MBO conceived, implemented, and encouraged by a staff entity such as personnel. In this view the personnel department reviews goal attainment with the managers, and the organization thinks of it strictly as a personnel program.

J. W. Enell and G. H. Hass reported successful early MBO programs at Standard Oil Company (Ohio); Intercity Papers, Ltd.; and Smith, Kline, and French Laboratories.[21] These programs emphasized performance appraisal, not goal attainment.

Howell[22] and McConkey[23] noted that performance appraisal through the personnel function was the dominant theme of MBO in the late 1950s. The evaluation techniques measured the degree to which managers were thought to possess, or fail to possess, highly subjective traits.

At General Electric in the 1950s it was found that performance appraisal alone did not work.[24] Odiorne has stated, "The system of management by objectives is viewed in a larger context than that of a mere appraisal procedure. It regards appraisal as only one of the several subsystems operating within the larger system of goal-oriented management."[25]

Wilkstrom[26] and Reddin[27] have also pointed out the problems associated with MBO as a personnel scheme or an appraisal system. These problems created conditions that changed the emphasis on MBO.

The Organization View

Howell indicated that during the mid-1960s the emphasis was on integrating the objectives of the organization with the objectives of the managers.[28] The impetus for MBO came from top management, not from personnel, during this period. Other organizations such as General Motors and Edward N. Hay & Associates, where MBO principles became a way of life, did not go through the personnel phase. For these organizations the emphasis was from the top as MBO was started and continued as a management philosophy.

The importance of the negotiation of goals between superior and subordinate became more evident during this period. Howell has compared the negotiation process to that of working out a budget, stating, "Just as the approved budget is the result of revisions and trade-offs, so the objective-setting process is the result of compromise."[29] The involvement of each manager in setting his own goals provided the opportunity to feel a sense of belonging and recognition, and a favorable climate for employee motivation.[30]

The Bureau of Industrial Relations at the University of Michigan started conducting seminars in the 1960s on the MBO system of managing. Honeywell, Northwest Bancorporation, Ford Motor Company, and Continental Can are but a few of the companies that sent representatives to these seminars throughout the late 1960s. These seminars and the publication of the books previously mentioned encouraged organizations to use the MBO concept.

Marvin Bower, in his book, *The Will to Manage*, emphasized a theme germane to MBO when he stated, "The key to corporate success is a leader with a strong will to manage, who inspires and requires able people to work purposefully and effectively through simple and traditional managing processes that are integrated into a management program or system tailored to the nature and environment of the business."[31] This important principle, that management must have the courage of its convictions, runs through the entire history of MBO. The backbone of any management philosophy must be firm, with a management that has the courage and stamina to attain predetermined objectives. This will to manage with MBO is stronger where the organization as a whole supports MBO.

Planning

One of the most significant contributions of MBO was the emphasis on planning as a part of the MBO process. Wilkstrom stated:

Targets set by individual managers are relevant to the company's goals because the entire management group is involved in the total planning process. Mechanisms have been involved to ensure that individual plans contribute to larger goals. In setting targets, managers develop detailed plans, perhaps with several alternative contingency plans, for achieving their targets. If totally unforeseen events require a change in direction, all concerned are aware of this long before the annual appraisal period, and the required adjustments are made.[32]

Similar concepts were advanced by Odiorne concerning long-range planning and the five-year plan, as follows:

Hence, long-range plans are most valuable when they are revised and adjusted and set anew at shorter periods. The five-year plan is reconstructed each year in turn for the following five years. The soundest basis for this change is accurate measurement of the results of the first year's experience with the plan against the target of the plan.[33]

Edward C. Schleh has stated, "Whenever a man has a responsibility for a result, he should also have the responsibility for planning ahead to prevent crises that may prevent the accomplishment of that result."[34]

Further evidence of the evolution of long-range planning and management by objectives is found in Richard Johanson's dissertation, *A Systematic Approach to Corporation Planning.*[35] The MBO process has become a subset in a greater management system that requires a total organization view. It is an ongoing, cybernetic system, a "way of life." The features of MBO are built into the dynamic planning process. The five-year plan in the dynamic planning process is based on consideration for environmental factors, strengths and weaknesses of the company, assumptions, criteria. The broad objectives are determined, and measurable goals are set to meet those objectives. The five-year plan then charts a course to meet those goals.

The principles of MBO are used in setting the five-year plan. The yearly operating plan is then just the first year of the five-year plan. Each year the five-year plan is updated, with the first year of the new five-year plan the operational plan for the next year. The dynamic planning process is described as "cybernetic" because it allows for changes in the environment, relative strengths in the company, assumptions, criteria, objectives, goals, or anything that affects the company during the planning period. Dr. Johanson developed this process while with Continental Emsco in the 1950s, and he has since perfected it further and assisted in installing it in a wide variety of firms, government units, and nonprofit organizations.

I was greatly influenced by Dr. Johanson as I developed the management system discussed in chapter 1. I had the opportunity to study under him in 1971 at the University of Arkansas in the Management Ph.D. program.

"Planagement," developed by Bob Randolph, is another system that has evolved from successful elements of MBO.[36] Like Johanson's work, it emphasizes taking a long, detailed look at many things before objectives are set. International Harvester is but one of many organizations achieving very successful results with Planagement. Ed Green recognized this total look at MBO. He developed a unique planning book. T. D. Williamson, Inc., is one of many organizations using many elements of his planning system.

I found, in a survey of 297 managers in manufacturing and banking, that a direct relationship exists between the extent of MBO and the amount of planning being done.[37] This book is an extention of the planning evolution. The discussion in chapter 3 describes my long-range planning system.

Blue-Collar MBO

I documented the application of MBO at the blue-collar level as early as 1964-65 at Continental Can.[38] Performance, measured by engineered standards, increased dramatically from 83 percent to 97 percent as the basic elements of MBO were introduced. Similar programs were in effect by 1967 in other Continental Can plants. Frank Habic, when he was at the Duluth, Missabe & Iron Range Railway, has had a successful experience with MBO at the blue-collar level as well.[39] Chris Kenna assisted Hugh McKnight in setting up the entire planning system in the Tulsa Parks and Recreation Department. Kenna was responsible for implementing the system right down to the lowest organization level.

In an article for the *Management By Objectives Journal*, "Blue-Collar MBO," I discussed the theory, application, and recommendations surrounding lower-level application of MBO.[40] Odiorne has stated, "If you listen carefully to the experiences of Texas Instruments and Ohio Bell, and to those of Henry Migliore of Northeastern State University/University Center at Tulsa and Fred Schwarz of the University of Wisconsin, it is apparent that MBO can be applied in the blue-collar ranks if we are sufficiently committed."[41] It appears that MBO could make a significant contribution toward solving the job-satisfaction, blue-collar-blues problem.

Management by objectives can make a contribution to job satisfaction and increased productivity, according to some researchers and practitioners. To this end, scientific research should be directed toward determining the validity of the MBO concept. Based on the findings of these efforts, a valid appraisal of the strengths and weaknesses of MBO can be made.

Coupled with and a first cousin to the productivity problem is the lack of fulfillment at the lower levels of most organizations. As discussed in chapter 1, the Opinion Research Corporation, of Princeton, New Jersey, indicated that 38 percent of the lower-level organization workers are dissatisfied with their work.[42] This is up from 24 percent in 1952. Karl Marx predicted that capitalism would fall because the worker would become an appendage to the machine. With due respect to the production line and simplification of work, we have created a monster. Our standard of living is high because of capital, technology, and automation. A cost/benefit ratio is associated with any alternative. It appears that our higher standard of living has been achieved at the cost of dehumanizing the workplace. Pride, loyalty, and commitment on the part of craftsmen seem to be eroding. Replacing these characteristics is the general mood of apathy, gripes, and sometimes total "antiorganization" view. Studs Terkel found this in the research for his book, *Working.*[43] We seem to have convinced ourselves that high pay for lower-level jobs should be enough.

I have had the opportunity to do manual labor on the farm and in the oil fields, clerk in a retail store, serve as lifeguard, and teach at a swimming pool before completing a college degree. Much of my first three months on Continental Can's management-training program was spent learning and performing almost all of the lowest-level jobs in the plant. These jobs ranged from checking the specifications on the cans to loading a punch press. I am convinced, based on these experiences and in-depth study, that the people at the lower levels have the same needs for achievement, autonomy, recognition, and self-worth as do persons at the higher levels.

The basic attitude of management has traditionally been rather paternal. I'll make the decisions, you do the work. Capitalism cannot survive another 100 years without the enthusiasm and commitment of approximately 30 million members of the work force at the lower levels.

MBO by its very nature brings management and labor together. It demands mutual respect. It creates the opportunity for better positive communication. Recognition and feedback are almost automatic. Setting goals creates unity, a team spirit, and harmony. It is not the final answer to the problem, but I have not seen one shred of evidence that it won't help, usually dramatically. I reported my experience with blue-collar MBO in my book, *MBO: Blue Collar to Top Executive.*[43]

Nonprofit MBO

Morrisey and McConkey have led MBO practitioners into a new era. Both Morrisey's *Management by Objectives Results in the Public Sector* and McConkey's *MBO for Nonprofit Organizations* describe theories in the application of MBO to nonprofit and governmental units.[45]

There is an early indication that MBO is applicable in these areas. The entire country has been appalled by the lack of efficiency and effectiveness in charities, churches, and in local, state, and federal governments. The zero-based budgeting for governmental units has most of the elements of MBO. My brand of long-range planning/MBO has been successfully installed in the Tulsa Parks and Recreation Department, at the upper level of Tulsa Christian Fellowship, World Evangelism, Tulsa's First Methodist Church, Brush Creek Boys' Ranch, and the Schools of Business and other schools at Oral Roberts University. The results of my work were presented in a special nonprofit/MBO workshop at the International MBO Conference in 1979. Dr. Richard P. Rettig, working as a special consultant for the State of Oklahoma, used a modification of the Planning/MBO system in an earlier printing of this book to help develop a reform program for juvenile offenders. He presented the paper, "Confronting Deviance in a Juvenile Institution through the Implementation of a MBO Program," at the March 1979 meeting of the Criminal Justice Association. He helped implement a comprehensive long-range plan there.

Bob Bullock, an industrial engineer when he was with St. John Medical Center in Tulsa, has done a good job developing MBO for lower-level application. It is incorporated into such jobs as the insurance claim processors.

I have assisted American Red Cross, National Head Start Program, YMCA, Salvation Army, and other nonprofit organizations in the development of strategic plans.

Staff Use of MBO

I have discussed staff use of MBO with many authorities in the field including Morrisey, McConkey, Varney, and Odiorne. They agree and have discussed many times the applicability of staff use of MBO. We are in an age of accountability. To exclude one group from the long-range planning/MBO process would be a mistake.

As a department head in charge of industrial engineering at Continental Can's Elwood plant, I successfully implemented many elements of MBO. Persons at all levels of the organization became involved in cost-reduction terms. Our objective in 1967 was to develop $27,000 in cost reduction. The teams worked hard and came up with $493,000 in savings. This is just one of many examples I have seen where concrete measurable results can be obtained.

Strategic Planning in Churches and Ministries

In the last five years, I have trained about 10,000 pastors in the strategic planning/management processes. The book, *Strategic Planning for Ministry and Church Growth*, covers what I have learned and experienced working with this sector. Briefly, all the same principles apply.

Pastors, elders, theology faculty, and graduate students analyzed this material and concluded along with me that there is biblical back-up to the planning process. Note what we found:

PURPOSE, MISSION, VISION

Proverbs 11:14: "For lack of guidance a nation (or in our case 'a person') falls, but many advisers make victory sure." (NIV)

Proverbs 15:22: "Plans fail for lack of counsel, but with many advisers they succeed." (NIV)

Proverbs 20:18: "Every purpose is established by counsel ..."

Proverbs 16:20: "He that handleth a matter wisely shall find good ".

Proverbs 29:18: "Where there is no vision, the people perish ..."

Proverbs 23:7: "As a man thinketh in his heart, so is he" (paraphrased).

Joel 2:28: "...Your old men shall dream dreams, your young men shall see visions."

Acts 2:17: (Essentially the same as Joel 2:28.).

Romans 12:3: "For by the grace given me I say to every one of you: Do not think of yourself more highly than you ought, but rather think of yourself with sober judgment, in accordance with the measure of faith God has given you." (NIV)

OBJECTIVES

Nehemiah 2:4: "For what dost thou make request? . . ." (What do you want?)

STRATEGY

Matthew 5:15: "Neither do people light a lamp and put it under a bowl. Instead they put it on its stand, and it gives light to everyone in the house" (paraphrased).

OPERATIONAL PLAN

2 Timothy 2:15: "Study to shew thyself approved unto God, a workman that needeth not to be ashamed . . ."

2 Timothy 3:17: ". . .Complete and proficient, well-fitted and thoroughly equipped for every good work." (AMP)

Luke 14:28: "For which one of you when he wants to build a tower does not sit down and calculate the cost?" (paraphrased).

James 1:23: "For if any be a hearer of the word, and not a doer, he is like unto a man beholding his natural face in a glass."

I Corinthians 14:40: "Let all things be done decently and in order."

Galatians 6:34: "If anyone thinks he is something when he is nothing, he deceives himself. Each one should test his own actions. Then he can take pride in himself, without comparing himself to somebody else . . ." (NIV)

Ephesians 4:1: ". . .I urge you to live a life worthy of the calling you have received." (NIV)

Psalm 37:4: "Delight yourself in the Lord and he will give you the desires of your heart." (NIV)

Matthew 6:33: "But seek first his kingdom and his righteousness, and all these things will be given to you as well." (NIV)

ENVIRONMENTAL ANALYSIS

Proverbs 25:2: "It is the glory of God to conceal a thing: but the honour of kings is to search out a matter."

STRENGTHS AND WEAKNESSES

Luke 12:48: "To whom much is given, much is required" (paraphrased).

2 Timothy 3:17: ". . .Complete and proficient, well-fitted and thoroughly equipped for every good work." (AMP)

Proverbs 20:5: "A plan in the heart of a man is like deep water." (paraphrased).

Proverbs 24:3: "Through wisdom is an house builded; and by understanding it is established."

I Corinthians 14:33: "For God is not the author of confusion, but of peace . . ."

REWARD

I Corinthians 3:8: "Now he who plants and he who waters are one; but each will receive his own reward according to his own labor." (paraphrased).

Proverbs 13:21: " . . .The righteous will be rewarded with prosperity." (paraphrased).

Philippians 3:14: "I press toward the mark for the prize of the high calling of God in Christ Jesus."

I Corinthians 16:9: "For a great door and effectual is opened unto me, and there are many adversaries."

Philippians 4:13: "I can do all things through Christ which strengtheneth me."

Colossians 3:17: "And whatsoever ye do in word or deed, do all in the name of the Lord Jesus . . ."

Proverbs 16:9: "We should make plans—counting on God to direct us." (TLB)

Proverbs 16:3: "Commit thy works unto the Lord . . ."

Colossians 3:23: "Whatever you do, work at it with all your heart, as working for the Lord, not for men" (NIV).

Nehemiah 2:4: " . . .For what dost thou make request? So I prayed to the God of heaven."

PLAN IN GENERAL

Proverbs 15:22: "Plans fail for lack of counsel, but with many advisers they succeed." (NIV)

Proverbs 16:10: "A divine sentence is in the lips of the king: his mouth transgresseth not in judgment."

Proverbs 19:20: "Hear counsel and receive instruction, that thou mayest be wise . . ."

Strategic Planning in Athletics

We just completed a study of the use of strategic planning in Intercollegiate Athletics: "The Effect and Usage of Strategic Planning in Intercollegiate Athletic Departments in American Colleges and Universities."[50] The purpose was to determine the level of usage of strategic planning in Intercollegiate Athletics and the effect that planning has on the results of competition.

It was conducted by a random sampling of athletic directors who are members of the National Association of Collegiate Directors of Athletics. A questionnaire was mailed to 300 potential participants. One hundred thirty-eight were returned. The departments completely involved in strategic planning reported better results. These results held true for all classifications of study including review by division and by geographic region. In addition, all the strategic planning variables showed a positive relationship with results.

The most important predictor of results was the purpose statement. Ninety-three percent of all the schools that reported excellent results had a written statement of purpose. Other predictors of success included the depth of environmental analysis, the depth of assessing strengths and weaknesses, the method of selecting a competitive strategy, and the management system used by the athletic department.

Better results are achieved when a formal system of strategic planning is implemented to guide the expended energies of the athletic department staff toward desired objectives. Departments that see themself as winners utilize more thorough and formal channels of planning in preparing for competition. Start the planning process by defining the purpose or mission of your department as it relates to the school. Eighty percent of the institutions that had results that were classified as good or excellent had a formal written statement of purpose.

Next, conduct a competitive analysis of all sports on an annual basis. Two-thirds of the high achievers conducted both internal assessments of strengths and weaknesses as well as an assessment of the competitive environment and their rivals.

Include the staff in the development of realistic goals and the subsequent strategies utilized to achieve them. Goals are more readily accomplished when they are internalized and personal. Keep an open mind in this phase. Almost twice as many high achievers reviewed a complete list of alternative strategies as does the average department.

Tie the performance appraisal and compensation of the coaching staff to their performance on the desired objectives. The group that accomplished the highest results stated that their performance appraisal was tied to the negotiated objectives at a rate that was 63 percent higher than the general respondent.

	ALL	RESULTS 4&5	RESULTS 5
Number in Sample	138	109	14
Budget under 1MM	78%	76%	71
Purpose Written	72.5	80	93
EA Year	52	52	67
EA Scope (Conference)	30.7	34	55
EA Depth (All)	64	70	83
SW (Year)	67	67	71
SW (All sports)	83	88	100
Assume (All)	49	52	62
Strategy Analysis			
of Alternatives	34	40	57
Objectives Negotiated	80	85	79
Coach Performance Appraisal			
(Considerable)	36	38.5	57

X Mean	ALL	RESULTS 4&5	RESULTS 5
Number	138	109	14
Purpose	3.51	3.66	3.93
EA Time	2.26	2.31	2.42
Scope	3.07	3.20	3.36
Depth	3.22	3.38	3.67
SW Time	2.34	2.42	2.43
Depth	3.61	3.73	4.00
Assume	2.67	2.76	2.92
Strategy	3.69	3.85	4.21
Objectives	2.75	2.79	2.79
Appraise	2.57	2.70	2.85
Coach Performance Appraisal	3.03	3.19	3.43
Result	3.83	4.13	5.00

I have had the opportunity to work with a Division I top 20 athletic program the past 18 months. The same philosophy and format used in this book was used to develop an overall strategic plan. Over the years I had worked with a few athletic departments. The results have been positive. All involved feel progress is being made. The biggest problem from a planning and organization stand point has been the need to change culture and mind-set on how to do business. After years of success, regular sell outs, there was really no reason for serious change. The new environment for athletics has changed dramatically. Those athletic departments that adapt will be successful in the year 2000. Those that don't won't succeed or perhaps survive.

Declining student interest in football attendance, funding for women and minor sports are examples of problems that need strategy funding and action.

The entire staff went through the planning process. Long and short term objectives and strategy were discussed. Problems were addressed and analyzed. Athletic Departments need strategic planning to succeed.

Government

All governments worldwide are challenged with the changing needs of society. Citizens expect more from government. There is a noticeable decrease in revenue everywhere. City managers are called upon to increase service with fewer resources.

The format used in this book has been used successfully in city government. I have had the opportunity to work with cities of Plano and Denton Texas. In Tulsa, Oklahoma, I have worked with the Department of Parks and Recreation and the Department of Public Works. Again the results have been positive.

The city of Calgary Alberta, Canada has an extensive well thought out strategic plan. It is well thought out and professionally bound and printed. The plan reflects strategic direction. It represents input from all segments of the community.

The Controversy

As successes and failures occurred in organizations, as experiences were documented, and as theory was developed, the conditions for controversy became apparent. The *Management by Objectives Newsletter* recently stated that 83 percent of business firms in the United States are using management by objectives.[46] However, John M. Ivancevich presented a paper at an International Conference on MBO at Salt Lake City, Utah, in August 1974, that raised some questions about the applicability of MBO. Fred E. Schuster and Alva F. Kindall have completed a study of the Fortune 500 and found that only 10 companies in the United States are properly using MBO and getting good results.[47] There is obvious disagreement as to whether it is indeed the solution it is hailed as being.

As a result of MBO's growth and the controversy surrounding it, many scholars and practitioners have devoted time to its study and implementation. Main contributors to the general MBO philosophy have been Walter Wilkstrom, Anthony Raia, John Humble, Henry Tosi, Stephen Carroll, W. J. Reddin, J. M. Ivancevich, J. F. Donnelly, Glen Varney, J. D. Battan, Douglas McGregor, Dale McConkey, George Morrisey, and Richard Johanson, all of whose work has been mentioned briefly here. Important contributions have been made in various forms, with MBO being called management by objectives, management by results, improving business performance, goals management, work planning and review, objectives, strategy, tactics, 3-D MBO, and other terms. Daniel Glasner attempted to show the differences among some of them in an article, "Patterns of Management By Results."[48]

Rob Albert found in a master's study and paper on the MBO implementation method that the support of top management is critical for overall organization success.[49] He studied my implementation methods and methods used by other consultants. He assisted and did much of the work on the ORU Dental School Long-Range Plan as a model. The results of his findings agree with others on the same subject.

Strategic Management

Strategic management is the alert, philosophical, foreward thinking managing of the strategic plan. For too many years organizations went through the planning process, created a document, applauded its completion, and then put it on the shelf. Yes, the planning process helped, but no, it didn't attain its full potential, because very little attention was given the plan through the year. A perennially wasteful exercise is the academic self-study. As dean of a business school, I watched this waste of time each year—self-study—on the shelf—self-study—on the shelf. Can you imagine the contribution higher education could make if they had a plan and managed it?

Summary

This chapter described the growth of MBO from the early part of this century to the present. Drucker was the first focal point in the development of MBO in 1954. Odiorne, McConkey, and several other authors are considered the second focal point in 1965. Wilkstrom, Randolph, and Johanson have made contributions on planning along with other authors. The development of the two views of MBO, the personnel view and the organization view, has been traced. The notion that MBO is applicable at the blue-collar level, nonprofit sector, and staff use was discussed as well as the present controversy on the value of MBO to the firms that have actually initiated it in their operations. Ivancevich and Donnelly presented a paper at the Academy of Management meeting in Dallas, Texas, in March 1974. They stated that the years 1954-1974 were a growth era and that MBO has stood the test of the first 20 years. They noted that the future appears bright and encouraging in spite of the present controversy.

In the mid-seventy's as strategic planning became "in," and it seemed "MBO" was out. Then in the late eighty's, strategic management is "in." The buzz words change, but the fundamentals don't. Whatever you want to call it, it makes sense to operate with a few key fundamentals addressed in the following questions. Where are we now and where are we going? What are we trying to accomplish? What is target market? How do we best position ourselves to get there? What are key long-term measures of success? How are plans coordinated? How do we operate in an ethical, proper way and make a contribution to society?

I would like to suggest the new phase for the ninety's be common sense management. Common sense in terms of returning to the fundamentals. There will be increased emphasis on the importance of the human resources. The dramatic change in all aspects of the labor force will bring attention to the human resources area. Finally, are we providing a safe, healthy work place and a rewarding long term career opportunity for our people?

IMPORTANT POINTS TO REMEMBER

Any philosophy of management must have:

1. Planning
2. Objectives
3. Feedback
4. Communication
5. Review and accountability
6. Rewards
7. Delegation
8. Responsibilities
9. Needs of participants met
10. Esprit de corps

References
Chapter 2

[1]Peter Drucker, *The Practice of Management* (New York: Harper & Row, 1954), pp. 121, 126, 128, 129, 131.

[2]Ronald G. Greenwood, "Management by Objectives: As Developed by Peter Drucker, Assisted by Harold Smiddy," *Academy of Management Review*, Vol. 6, No. 2, 1981, p.225.

[3]George Odiorne, *Management by Objectives: A System of Managerial Leadership* (New York: Pitman Publishing Co., 1965), p. 55.

[4]Walter S. Wilkstrom, *Managing by-and-with Objectives, Studies in Personnel Policy, No. 212* (New York: National Industrial Conference Board, 1968), p. 3.

[5]Ernest Dale, *The Great Organizers* (New York: McGraw-Hill Co., 1960), p. 260.

[6]Alfred P. Sloan, Jr., *My Years With General Motors* (Garden City: Doubleday, 1964).

[7]Edward N. Hay Associates, *Accountability Management, Men and Management Series: 174* (Philadelphia: Edward N. Hay Associates, May 1966), p. 2.

[8]James O. McKinsey, *Budgetary Control,* (New York: Roland Press, 1922).

[9]Henry Fayol, *Industrial Administration* (London: Sir Isaac Pitman, 1949).

[10]Ralph C. Davis, *The Principles of Business Organization and Operation* (Columbus: H. L. Hedrick, 1935).

[11]Dale D. McConkey, "MBO—Twenty Years Later, Where Do We Stand?" *Business Horizons*, Aug. 1973, p. 25.

[12]Elton Mayo, *The Human Problems of an Industrial Organization* (New York: Macmillan Co., 1933).

[13]Lester Coch and John French, Jr., "Overcoming Resistance to Change," *Human Relations*, Vol. 1, 1948, pp. 512-513.

[14]Abraham Maslow, "A Theory of Human Motivation," *Psychological*

Review, Vol. 50, 1943.

[15]Peter Drucker, *Managing for Results* (New York: Harper & Row, 1964), p. 25.

[16]Frederick Herzberg, *Work and the Nature of Man*, (Cleveland: World Publishing, 1960).

[17]Rensis Likert, *Developing Patterns of Management, General Management Series No. 182* (New York: American Management Association, 1956), p. 8.

[18]Robert L. Kahn and Daniel Katz, "Leadership Practices in Relation to Productivity and Morale," *Group Dynamics* (Evanston: Row, Peterson, & Co., 1960).

[19]Douglas McGregor, *The Human Side of Enterprise* (New York: McGraw-Hill, Inc., 1960), p. 47.

[20]Robert M. Blake and Jane Mouton, *Managerial Grid* (Houston: Gulf Publishing Co., 1964).

[21]J. W. Enell and G. H. Hass, *Setting Standards for Executive Performance* (New York: American Management Association, 1966).

[22]Robert Howell, "Managing by Objectives—A Three-Stage System," *Business Horizons*, Feb. 1970, p. 42.

[23]McConkey, op. cit., p. 26.

[24]Alfred J. Morrow ed., *The Failure of Success* (New York: American Management Association, 1972), p. 231.

[25]George Odiorne, *Management By Objectives* (New York: Pitman Publishing Co., 1965), p. v.

[26]Wilkstrom, op. cit., p. 27.

[27]W. J. Reddin, *Effective Management By Objectives* (New York: McGraw-Hill, 1971), p. 16.

[28]Howell, op. cit., p. 43.

[29]Howell, op. cit., p. 54.

[30]Wilkstrom, op. cit., p. 27.

[31]Marvin Bower, *Will to Manage* (New York: McGraw-Hill, 1966), p. vi.

[32]Wilkstrom, op. cit., p. 29.

[33]Odiorne, op. cit., p. 19.

[34]Edward C. Schleh, *Management by Results* (New York: McGraw-Hill, 1961), p. 12.

[35]Richard Johanson, *Systematic Approach to Corporation Planning* (Denton: North Texas State University, unpublished Ph.D. dissertation, 1969).

[36]Bob Randolph, *Planagement* (New York: AMACOM, 1975).

[37]R. Henry Migliore, "Planning and MBO," *Long Range Planning*, August 1976, pp. 58-65.

[38]R. Henry Migliore, "The Effects of Knowledge of Results on Worker Productivity," *Management of Personnel Quarterly*, Summer 1970, pp. 26-30.

[39]Frank Habic and R. Henry Migliore, "An Application of MBO at the Blue- Collar Level at the DM&IR Ore Docks." Fourth Annual International MBO Conference, Bowling Green, Ohio.

[40]R. Henry Migliore, "Blue-Collar MBO," *Management By Objectives*, 4 (1974), pp. 27-33.

[41]George Odiorne, "Where Job Enrichment and MBO Meet," MBO, Inc., (1975).

[42]Supra, p. 6.

[43]Studs Terkel, *Working*, (New York: Pantheon, 1972).

[44]R. Henry Migliore, *MBO: Blue Collar to Top Executive* (Washington Bureau of National Affairs, 1976).

[45]George Morrisey, *Management by Objectives and Results in the Public Sector*, 1976; and Dale D. McConkey, *MBO For Nonprofit Organizations* (New York: Amacom, 1975).

[46]*Management By Objectives Newsletter*, (Westfield: MBO Incorporated, February 1974), p. 1.

[47]Fred E. Schuster and Alva F. Kindall, "Management By Objectives Where We Stand—A Survey of the Fortune 500," *Human Resources Management*, Spring 1974, pp. 8-11.

[48]Daniel M. Glasner, "Patterns of Management By Results," *Business Horizons*, February 1969, pp. 37-40.

[49]Rob Albert, *The Development of a Systematic Method for Implementing MBO* (Unpublished master's thesis, Oral Roberts University, May 1980).

[50]David Dyson, Mark Manning, William A. Sutton, and R. Henry Migliore, "The Effect and Usage of Strategic Planning in Intercollegiate Athletic Departments in American Colleges and Universities," paper presented at North American Society for Sport Management, University of Calgary, June 1-3, 1989. Also refer to Strategic Planning For Collegiate Athletics, Miliore with co-authors Haworth Press, July 2000.

Chapter 3
Purpose, Environmental Analysis, Strengths, and Weaknesses

This chapter will present discussions of the first three steps in the strategic planning process: on the mission and purpose of an organization, the environmental analysis, and how to assess strengths and weaknesses of the organization. The reader should be able to explain why these three steps must be completed before anything else is undertaken.

Further, the reader will be expected to be able to give an example of a purpose, an example of environmental analysis, and an example of strengths and weaknesses.

Purpose

The first and likely most important consideration when developing a long-range plan with this new definition of SLRP/MBO is to define the purpose of or the "reason for being" for the organization or any specific part of it. This is usually a difficult process. Peter Drucker was the key influence in my logic to put this step first. I believe I never fully realized the importance of this until 1974, when Drucker's book came out. Oral Roberts is another that emphasized the purpose and mission of ORU. Drucker, in his book, *Management—Tasks, Responsibility and Practices*, defines the purpose of organization. Here he starts with the marketing concept, which says to organize a business to satisfy a need in the market place. Drucker says, "It is defined by the want the customer satisfies when he buys a product or a service. To satisfy the customer is the mission and purpose of every business."[1] He continues, "Business enterprise, however, requires that the theory of the business be thought through and spelled out. It demands a clear definition of business purpose and business mission. It demands asking, 'What is our business and what should it be?'"[2]

The purpose statement defined here encompasses the mission, dream and vision for the organization. It defines the reason for being, identifies needs in the market place. The scope of the operation, declares ethical and moral responsibility. It makes clear what business the organization is in.

The organization members must be continually reminded of the "reason for being."

Drucker stoutly declares, "Only a clear definition of the mission and purpose of the business makes possible clear and realistic business objectives. It is the foundation for priorities, strategies, plans, and working assignments. It is the starting point for the design of managerial jobs and, above all, for the design of managerial structures."[3] He continues, "Clearly, if purpose is defined casually or introspectively, or the list of key result areas neglects some of the less obvious threats and opportunities, the fabric of organization objectives and resources rests on shaky foundations. As Calvin Coolidge puts it: 'No enterprise can exist for itself alone. It ministers to some great need, it performs some great service not for itself but for others; or failing therein it ceases to be profitable and ceases to exist.'"[4]

When I was dean of a College of Business, at the beginning of our planning sessions the administration and faculty of the School of Business defined, reviewed, and discussed our purpose statement. This practice kept us aware of and in tune with the world about us. Every business, organization, family, or person must have a clearly defined purpose. Note the purpose statement for M. Cardone Industries and Trammell Crow.

Statement of Purpose

M. CARDONE INDUSTRIES is a business enterprise. As a business, we realize a profit by meeting the needs of people. Profit permits expansion and strengthening of the business for the benefit of its owners, employees, customers and community. To this end, we pledge ourselves to:

1. HONOR GOD IN ALL WE DO
2. HELP PEOPLE DEVELOP
3. PURSUE EXCELLENCE
4. GROW PROFITABLY

Our business is the Remanufacturing of Automotive Products. Our market is the Automotive Aftermarket.

Our purpose is to:

1. Provide the automotive after market with products of the highest quality, a 100% order fill and the most responsive efficient service available in the industry.

2. Contribute to the conservation of America's natural energy and mineral resources through our recycling of automotive parts.

3. Continually seek ways to offer our customers the greatest potential for profit.

We are an equal opportunity employer seeking to provide for our employees a safe, healthy, comfortable working environment. We encourage a holistic family atmosphere in our working relationships and seek to foster the belief that everyone at M. Cardone Industries is a vital part of a unified, precision team.

M. Cardone Industries is committed to conducting its business relationships in such a manner as to be a credit to God, its owners, our employees, their families, our customers, and the community. Each, though a separate entity, is part of a unified family and the mutual benefit of the whole is achieved as the needs of one another are considered.

Our position is that of a pioneer and proud leader in the automotive remanu-facturing industry. We constantly pursue excellence and believe that . . .
"If you want a long and satisfying life . . . never forget to be truthful and kind. If you want favor with both God and man, and a reputation for good judgment and common sense, then trust the Lord completely . . . In everything you do, put God first, and He will direct you and crown your efforts with success."
Selections from the Bible:
Proverbs 3:
The Living Bible

Trammell Crow Company Philosophy

Serving Our Customer
As a marketing company, we have a preeminent commitment to serving the needs of our present and prospective tenants by developing buildings of the highest quality and providing superior building management and other services.

Our Valuable Relationships
We strive to nurture and expand mutually successful relationships with the financing, construction, brokerage, design and other firms with whom we have the privilege of doing business. We are committed to creating and managing real estate properties for our lenders and investors that meet or exceed their investment objectives and to providing prompt, thorough and accurate reporting on the performance of the investments.

Our Business Family
We are a company owned by our people. Because we believe our people are our greatest asset, we choose not to conduct ourselves as a large, imper-sonal company, but rather to operate as a business family with stewardship responsibilities to one another. Our company has been built around the dig-nity and worth of the individual and the recognition of personal achievement. We encourage full development of the talents of all our people, and are committed to reward and promote on the basis of merit. We manifest our pride in our people by providing each individual a personal stake in the

profitability of our business. We want our people to enjoy their work and we encourage a balance between work responsibilities, family life and community involvement.

Profitability

By providing excellent service to our customers, by enhancing our outside relationships and by fostering the well-being of our people, we will generate cash flow, profits and equity appreciation to capitalize our growth and achieve our other objectvies.

Our Business

We believe in:

- Individual entrepreneurship with local office autonomy
- Informal, consensus style of management
- Growth through shared experiences and mutual support
- Long-term ownership of assets
- Opportunities for management and ownership to those who distinguish themselves
- High quality, cost effective central services provided by a lean staff
- Honesty, integrity, excellence, hard work and fun

We are an evergreen company; we believe our prosperity in the future depends on our doing the right things today.

With confidence in the future and in each other, yet with humility born of experiencing the cyclical nature and the risks inherent in our business, we strive for excellence, hoping to do the best job we can do and become the best people we can be.

Defining purpose is not always easy. Drucker describes how American Telephone & Telegraph Company defined its business purpose as:

> Our business is service. This sounds obvious once it has been said. But first there had to be the realization that a telephone system, being a natural monopoly, was susceptible to nationalization and that a privately owned telephone service in a developed and industrialized country was exceptional and needed community support for its survival. Second, there had to be the realization that community support could not be obtained by propaganda campaigns or by attacking critics as "un-American" or "socialistic." It could be obtained only by creating customer satisfaction.[5]

Another way to help understand purpose in organizational subunits comes out in the Bacone College story. When Charles Holleyman, former president of Bacone, took over, he recalled, "We took every position, including mine, and theoretically fired everyone. Then we started placing them back and justifying their positions."[6]

What they did in effect was to determine the purpose each function had to offer in terms of its overall contribution. If it couldn't be justified, it was combined with others that were only partially justified.

Statement of Purpose of
Tulsa Christian Fellowship

Tulsa Christian Fellowship purposes to be an expression of the body of Christ (the Church), submitted to the Lord Jesus Christ in all things, patterned after the elements of New Testament church order that are reproducible in our context, and dedicated, through the power of the Holy Spirit:.

To evangelize the unconverted to a saving faith in Jesus Christ; to apply the healing gospel of Jesus Christ to all kinds of social and personal sins, diseases, and disorders;	Matt. 28:19 Prov. 11:30 John 10:10
To reproduce the life and character of the risen Christ in a growing congregational expression of the Body of Christ; to disciple participants producing in them wholeness and maturity; to develop spiritual leaders who can multiply themselves and meet the needs of others;	Phil. 2:5-11 Matt. 28:19 II Tim. 2:2
To adore and glorify God in the liberty of the Holy Spirit through public and private worship; and to administer the sacraments or ordinances.	Rev. 19:10b I Cor. 6:20 Psa. 150 Matt. 28:19 I Cor. 11:23-34
To experience and express love as the intended relationship of God and man, and man and man;	John 13:34-35 Matt. 22:37-40
To encourage and strengthen other expressions of the Body of Christ, especially in Tulsa; and to promote unity and harmony in the Body; and	I Cor. 14:12 Rom. 14:29
To discover, nurture, and commission people whom the Holy Spirit has called to minister beyond Tulsa.	Matt. 28:19 Matt. 9:37

Another example is proposed purpose statement for Sambo's in early 1980s.

The mission of Sambo's Restaurants, a national profit-making company and a leading provider of family style dining, is to utilize capital resources to maximize owner and employee wealth. Demonstrating a sense of responsibility to public interest and earning the respect and loyalty of its customers, Sambo's maintains the highest standards of ethics, quality, and service while protecting both the environment and society. Sambo's Restaurants will become the standard by which family style dining is measured.

The late Dr. L. D. Thomas, senior pastor of Tulsa's First United Methodist Church, used a regular Wednesday evening bible study to get the church congregation involved in bible study, prayer, and development of a formal statement of purpose for the church. That purpose statement set the foundation and continued under the direction of Dr. James Buskirk, the current senior pastor. Buskirk does a good job of translating the dream and the plan into his sermons. It is important for all members of an organization to understand the directions being taken.

The purpose statement must include:

1. What is the business you are in? Example: Colowyo is in coal mining.
2. What is the scope of the organization? Example: T.D. Williamson is an international corporation.
3. What need is satisfied in market place? Example: First Methodist Church satisfies the spiritual growth of its members.
4. Who are your customers? Example: Colowyo serves utilities, steel mills, etc.
5. Is it profit or nonprofit? Example: Brush Creek Ranch is nonprofit.
6. What are your ethics? Example: Phillips Petroleum Company is committed to protect the environment.

Gauging the Environment

It is vital for the organization to gauge the environment within which it operates. This stage is that in which you check the pulse of conditions at the current time frame. You look back for trends. You do studies to forecast the future. Care must be taken not to confuse this stage with the assumption base discussed later. Environmental analysis should be standard practice for all organizations, including universities, churches, and nonprofit units. Southwestern Bell Telephone Company asked me to do a study and present to its managers my thoughts on what the business environment would be like in the mid-1980s. This is the type of futuristic inquiry needed to plan for the future. I had the opportunity to talk to Ean Wilson, a futurist for General Electric. His job is to look ahead and tell G.E. what the world will be like.

My own experience and study have convinced me of the importance of realizing that anything that can happen ultimately will happen.

Just five years ago who would have predicted the dramatic fall of the teleevangelists? I remember conducting a planning seminar for dentists years ago. At that time tooth decay/treatment was a major revenue generator for dentists. Look how floride has transformed their business.

As late as 1970 few would have believed there would be an oil embargo, one energy crisis after another, and the shift in economic power. What this is telling us is that we are in effect managing change. The only way we can manage change is to constantly monitor the environment within which we operate. This gives us clues to changes. Examples for a college of business might be the trends we see in education, the nationwide increase in MBA enrollment, the coming decline in college-age young people, faculty salaries, ethical and social responsibility, and increased growth of adult education, to mention a few. The environmental analysis for Colowyo Coal Company resulted in the following data:

1. While initial projections calling for coal output of 1.2 billion tons by 1985 have been scaled back somewhat, planned production increases remain impressive but seemingly within reach.
2. According to estimates obtained from the Bureau of Mines in mid-1977, U.S. coal production is expected to reach 830 million tons by 1980 and 1.05 billion tons in 1985, up from 671 million tons in 1976.
3. U.S. has coal reserves containing more than 10,000,000 trillion Btu's.
4. Of the 10 largest steam coal companies, which accounted for roughly 45 percent of 1976's domestic steam coal output, three were associated with oil companies (Continental Oil, Occidental Petroleum, and Gulf Oil); three with utilities (American Electric Power, Pacific Power & Light, and Montana Power); one with a mining company (AMAX INC.); and one with a railroad (Burlington Northern).
5. According to a mid-1977 report by the Federal Power Commission (FPC), captive coal's share of utility coal usage is projected to rise to nearly 19 percent in 1985, or about 145 million tons, from about 11 percent in 1976, or around 48.7 million tons. Production at underground mines per man per day fell to 8.50 tons in 1976, from 9.54 tons in 1975.
6. At surface mines, output per man per day dropped to 25.50 tons in 1976, from 26.69 tons in 1975, 33.16 tons in 1974, and 35.71 tons in 1969.

Cross Manufacturing Company, a manufacturer of parts for farm equipment centered in Overland Park, Kansas, provides an example of how environmental analysis is used in the strategic plan. After having used this strategic planning process for approximately a year, major changes started taking place in the marketplace. Higher interest rates and lower commodity prices started having a negative impact on farm income and farm spending.

Some of Cross's major customers, such as International Harvester, started cutting back. Economic conditions got so bad that International Harvester almost went out of business.

It is the job of strategic planning processes to systematically provide management the means to make decisions for tomorrow. How the management system uses the information is another subject. The Cross Manufacturing team recognized that a turndown in business was on them, but assumed that this environmental information was so drastic that a turn-around would be just around the corner. In analyzing the organization's strengths and weaknesses, the management team felt it could hold off a fur-ther cutback and be in a position to go into the marketplace much stronger if production and activity were not curtailed. As it worked out, the assump-tion was erroneous and business activity did not turn around. Some of Cross's major customers like International Harvester found themselves going into an ever deeper hole. The whole chain reaction of high interest rates, depressed farm income, Russian grain embargoes, and other factors caused a slack demand for farm equipment. This caused problems for the International Harvesters and their suppliers such as Cross Manufacturing. The latter used the Strategic Planning System improperly and got caught in making an incorrect assumption.

All companies and organizations must study the present business cli-mate so that they can make good decisions for future activity.

Prophet Management Information Systems (PMIS) sells computer-based accounting and information systems to oil jobbers. Their success is dependent on a number of factors that include the profitability of its cus-tomers, the oil jobbers. There were other environmental factors that during the early eightys would be considered by petroleum-related companies: (1) Crude oil supplies have become plentiful—it is now a buyers' market (*Standard & Poor's*, May 7, 1981, p. 47). (2) Saudis are flooding the market and new production from non-OPEC areas such as Mexico, the North Sea, and Egypt is adding to the glut (*Standard & Poor's*, May 7, 1981, p. 47). (3) Net earnings fell 17%, reflecting current industry trends with losses in mar-keting production caused by high crude oil prices and falling consumption (*Moody's Handbook*, Summer 1981). (4) On January 28, 1981, President Reagan decontrolled the price of crude oil, gasoline, and propane (*Wall Street Journal*, January 29, 1981, p. 1). (5) An increase in oil production next year was projected by the Independent Petroleum Association of America (*Tulsa Tribune*, October 20, 1981, p. 1b). (6) Increased foreign and domestic taxes, among other things, reduced 1980 profits in the oil industry (*Moody's Hand-book*, Summer 1981).

Like Cross Manufacturing, PMIS was faced with planning in a market with unfavorable environmental factors. These factors must be considered along with the present strengths and weaknesses of the company before good, measurable objectives and strategies can be developed.

An example of environment analysis for the food and restaurant industry is the trend of America toward eating more and more meals outside the home. Since 1970, restaurant sales have risen from 42.8 billion dollars to the present 227.3 billion dollars in 1989. In 1985, restaurant sales were 178.4 billion dollars. That's a 50 billion dollar increase in four years. This is information that needs to be considered if you are looking at that business.

Obviously there are many more factors to consider. Companies like Sambo's in 1981 could see the obvious trend. By 1985 overall restaurant sales went from 119.6 billion to 178.4 billion. We know what happened to Sambo's during that period—they went out of business. A positive trend doesn't guarantee success as Sambo's (Source *USA Today*, Sept. 26, 1989 on National Restaurant Association).

Environmental factors that Sambo's considered in 1981:

1. Nation's 100 largest food service companies double market share to 44% in 1980 compared to 24% in 1970.(1)
2. Food service industry sales will grow 82% from $115 billion in 1979 to $400 billion in 1995.(2)
3. Food service industry will rise from third to first place in domestic retail sales by 1987.(3)
4. Full service restaurants increasingly use early bird special dinners at low prices to fill tables.(4)
5. Denny's fast food chain installed distributed processing networks.(5)
6. Restaurant chains boosted advertising outlays in 1981 to exceed $456 million in 1979.(6)
7. Congress passed a bill that allows restauranteurs to offer cash-paying patrons unlimited discounts.(7)
8. Single person households are shifting toward fast-food restaurants for eating out.(8)

   (1) *Food S Market*, 8/81, p. 8.
   (2) *Food Stuffs*, 4/27/81, p. 10.
   (3) *Foods Products*, 1/81, p. 18.
   (4) *Nations Restaurants*, 3/02/81, p. 3.
   (5) *Laser Focus*, 8/81, p. 99.
   (6) *Nations Restaurants*, 5/25/81, p. 1.
   (7) *Nations Restaurants*, 8/03/81, p. 6.
   (8) *Nations Restaurants*, 4/13/81, p. 2.

The purpose of the environmental analysis stage in the Strategic Planning Process gives the organization managers a complete understanding of what they are facing in the marketplace to be successful.

The following is from Newman and Logan, *Strategy, Policy, and Central Management*, summary for chapter 2:

An essential part of company strategy is a plan for adapting company action to its environment. This is no simple matter because the environment is continously changing. New technology, social shifts, political realignments and pressures, as well as the more commonly recognized economic changes, all create problems and opportunities. The many examples of exciting new developments noted indicate how dynamic the setting of business is. To adjust most effectively, central management should try to predict important changes before they occur. And these predictions should not only identify the new factors, they also should anticipate how such shifts in the dynamic environment will affect the company.

Industry surveys, marketing research, Dow Jones stock averages, and recent commodity prices are all environmental factors. When we get up in the morning we look to check the weather. This affects our plans for the day, what we wear, etc. It is in this same vein that a company wants to check external conditions before proceeding with a plan.

In practice, no company can systematically monitor every part of its environment that might change. The task is too big. So the process involves (1) identifying crucial aspects of the dynamic environment, (2) selecting a forecasting method and making frequent forecasts for each of these aspects, and (3) taking steps to ensure that company executives actually use the forecast in formulating plans. Since the ability to make good long-range forecasts is limited, especially in the technical-social-political areas, management needs arrangements for frequent measurement. Built-in flexibility in the planning mechanisms is also needed. In other words, the total managing process that this paper examines is no one-time affair; it is a recycling, never-ending—and challenging—undertaking.

A helpful way to relate shifts in the dynamic environment to current operations of a company is to move first from the general environment to an industry analysis, and then to assess how the particular company stands in that industry.

In this environmental-analysis stage we look at the past, identify trends, and in effect take the pulse of the environment in which the organization operates. Environmental analysis should not be confused with our assumption base discussed later.

Industry studies done by the associations, universities, and the Standard & Poor's Industry Surveys[7] are other examples of information generated for environmental analysis. They represent valuable starting points for the environmental analysis. Another step in a thorough analysis is a complete audit of the organization. There are a number of audits, but the best I have seen is the "General Survey Outline" done by McKinsey in his 1922 book, *Budgeting Control*.[8]

One of the latest pieces of work in terms of a planning audit has been done by Thomas H. Naylor of Duke University. He has developed a questionnaire called "The Planning Audit." He presents a method for auditing the planning system. It reviews the planning environment, organization structure, management philosophy and style, planning process, and other organization factors. The result is a thorough understanding of the strengths and weaknesses of the planning system. It differs from McKenzie's work in that McKenzie's is a complete audit of the organization whereas Naylor's work is an audit of the planning system.[9]

Also in environmental analysis is the classification of products in the product life cycle. The product life cycle classifies the firm's existing products on a continuum from R&D through introduction, growth, maturity, and the decline stage. For example, Liberty Industries classified wood pallets in the mature stage of the product life cycle. Recognizing this "cash cow" in mature stage helped them see the long term importance of developing their machinery packaging products.

Another client, who asked to remain anonymous, discovered as we went through this exercise that all of their products were in mature and growth stages. There was an obvious gap coming in three to four years. They immediately made the decision to put more resources into R&D. The vice president of R&D told me privately that after 39 years with the company, it was the first time he and his division felt like they were part of the team. The continuing emphasis in this book is team work. All segments of the organization must be in on developing the overall plan.

Here are examples of two environmental factors in 1990. William K. MacReynolds, forecasting director for the U.S. Chamber of Commerce, said the report "shows that the economy has no clear direction," and that "Florida led all states in the nation last year and Orlando ranked fourth among metropolitan areas in landing new corporate facilities and expansions of existing businesses." The rankings were published in *Site Selection Handbook*, a publication produced by Conway Data, Inc., a publisher of economic development news. The survey considered only new corporate facilities and expansions meeting at least one of three criteria: an investment of at least $1 million, creation of at least 50 jobs, or at least 20,000 square feet of new space. This report stated the top 10 states in 1989 in new plants/explansions are Florida, California, Alabama, North Carolina, Texas, Ohio, Pennsylvania, New York, Virginia, and George. The top five metro areas in 1989 in new plants/explansions are Dallas/Fort Worth, Portland, Oregon, Atlanta, Orlando, and Los Angeles/Long Beach.[10] Forecasts for the future are included in environmental analysis. Here are some that were made this year in *The Futurist*, the magazine of the World Future Society: By the year 2100, the number of U.S. banks will be fewer than 100, compared with about 15,000 in the 1980s. The number of Americans over age 75 will grow by almost 35 percent by the year 2000. Managers study this data and base their plans on what they think will happen and include assumptions.

Long-Range Planning/MBO Audit

Sections:
I. Purpose
   A. Is it written?
   B. Show purpose as written, or develop one.
   C. How is the purpose statement being used?
II. Environmental Analysis
   A. National trend
   B. Industry trend
   C. Go to library and get facts
III. Strengths and Weaknesses
   A. Human
   B. Financial
   C. Market position
   D. Facilities
   E. Equipment
IV. Assumptions — List at least four
V. Functional Analysis: list each as strength and/or weakness.
   A. Financial analysis.
      1. Analyze current financial situation — Financial statements
      2. What tools would be beneficial in analysis?
         a. Pro forma statements
         b. Cash budget
         c. Capital budget
         d. Ratio analysis
         e. Operating and/or financial leverage
         f. Time value of money
         g. Break even (C.V.P.)
         h. Rate of returns
         i. Project tock and/or bond prices
      3. Analysis of current financial policies
         a. Cash policies

        b. Accounts receivable
          (1) Factoring
          (2) Discounts
          (3) Aging schedule
          (4) Collections
        c. Accounts payable
          (1) Discounts
        d. Inventory levels
        e. Debt retirement
        f. Dividends/retained earnings
    4. Synopsis of current financial situation
B. Accounting analysis
    1. Analysis of current accounting policies
        a. Depreciation
        b. Tax considerations
        c. Decentralized/centralized operations
        d. Responsibility accounting
    2. Tools beneficial in analysis
        a. Budgeting (short- and long-range)
        b. Variance analysis
        c. Breakeven/C.V.P.
        d. Costing methods
        e. Contribution margin analysis
    3. Synopsis of current accounting situation
C. Market analysis
    1. Analysis of current marketing policies
        a. Consumer
        b. Competition
        c. Product (type of product, type of demand, market position)
        d. Distribution channels (place, middleman, etc.)
        e. Pricing (markups, discounts, commissions, contribution, etc.)
        f. Promotion (advertising, selling, budget policies)
        g. Profit analysis (variable production and/or promotion levels).
    2. Synopsis of current market situation
D. Management analysis
    1. Planning—Do they have planning system? How does it work?
    2. Organize—Is organization of resources correct? (Show present organizational chart)
    3. Direct—Centralized or decentralized?
    4. Staff—What needs do they have for people?
    5. Control—Are controls in evidence? What are they?
    6. Is there a motivation problem?

7. Is strategy defined? What is strategy now?
8. Synopsis of management situation?
9. How efficient is production function?
10. Analyze —
    a. Quality control
    b. Production control
    c. Engineering
    d. Maintenance
    e. All major departments
11. Synopsis of Current Management Situation

As I discussed earlier, McKinsey wrote the "General Survey Outline" in 1936 to accomplish many of the same things.[11] His outline is more comprehensive and detailed. If an organization has the time and resources to go through the General Survey Outline, it has advantages over this shorter analysis. It is at this stage that the organization is set for making assumptions.

A complete study of the organization industry, products, management, policies, and procedures is needed. Also included in this environmental analysis is a study of the management system outlined in chapter 13. The management questionnaire gives management information on the effectiveness of the management system and brings major problems to the surface. Also discussed is concept of organization culture and how culture affects performance.

Strengths and Weaknesses

After we have identified our purpose and considered the environment in which we operate, we must assess the strengths and weaknesses of our organization. Howard H. Stevenson states, "Business organizations have certain characteristics—strengths—which make them uniquely adapted to carry out their tasks. Conversely, they have other features—weaknesses—which inhibit their abilities to fulfill their purposes. Managers who hope to accomplish their tasks are forced to evaluate the strengths and weaknesses of the organization . . ."[12] Some of the things normally looked at would be your key resources: human, financial, facilities/equipment, natural resources/patents, product line, and others. The controller must analyze the financial statements and break out the strengths and weaknesses. It is relatively easy to identify the strengths in each. When you attempt to define weaknesses, it becomes a little more painful. Often organizations must call in outside consultants to be able to candidly pinpoint their limitations. But weaknesses and limitations must be recognized before you move on. You can't develop an achievable plan without knowing your strengths and weaknesses.

One good method to ascertain and bring out strengths and weaknesses is to have the management team break into five discussion groups. Each group is charged with the responsibility of determining strengths and weaknesses in the seven areas listed.

STRENGTHS	WEAKNESSES
1. Human	1. Human
2. Financial	2. Financial
3. Facilities/Equipment	3. Facilities/Equipment
4. Natural Resources/Patents	4. Natural Resources/Patents
5. Product lines	5. Product Lines
6. Other	6. Other

Strengths and weaknesses can be determined with the use of the worksheets on the following pages. Whatever you wish to measure is classified into one of four categories: dog, problem child, star, or cash cow. For example, a product line with high potential and high performance is a "star." A product line with high potential and low performance is a "problem child."

Blake and Mouton have developed a six-volume series on how to assess the strengths and weaknesses of a business enterprise. It allows the manager to go even deeper into assessing this important area. The series fits logically at this point in the planning process. It helps the manager assess strengths and weaknesses in operations, marketing and sales, research and development, personnel management, financial management, and corporate leadership.[13]

Before considering the development of a Strategic Planning MBO System, the organization must consider the following factors: (1) Is the organization's management style compatible with the strategic planning MBO process? (2) Is there sufficient backing by the chief executive officer to implement the planning process? (3) Is the organization willing to stay with getting the planning system started long enough to give it a fair trial?

Important Points to Remember

1. The first and most important consideration of a long-range plan is to define the purpose of the organization or any specific part of it.
2. The organization must gauge the environment within which it operates.
3. Strengths and weaknesses of the organization must be realistically assessed.

```
        10
     P
                         Cash
     E

     R

     F

     O           Cows                    Stars

     R
        5    ─────────────────────────────────────────
     M

     A

     N           Dogs                    Problems

     C

     E

          1              5                      10
                     POTENTIAL
```

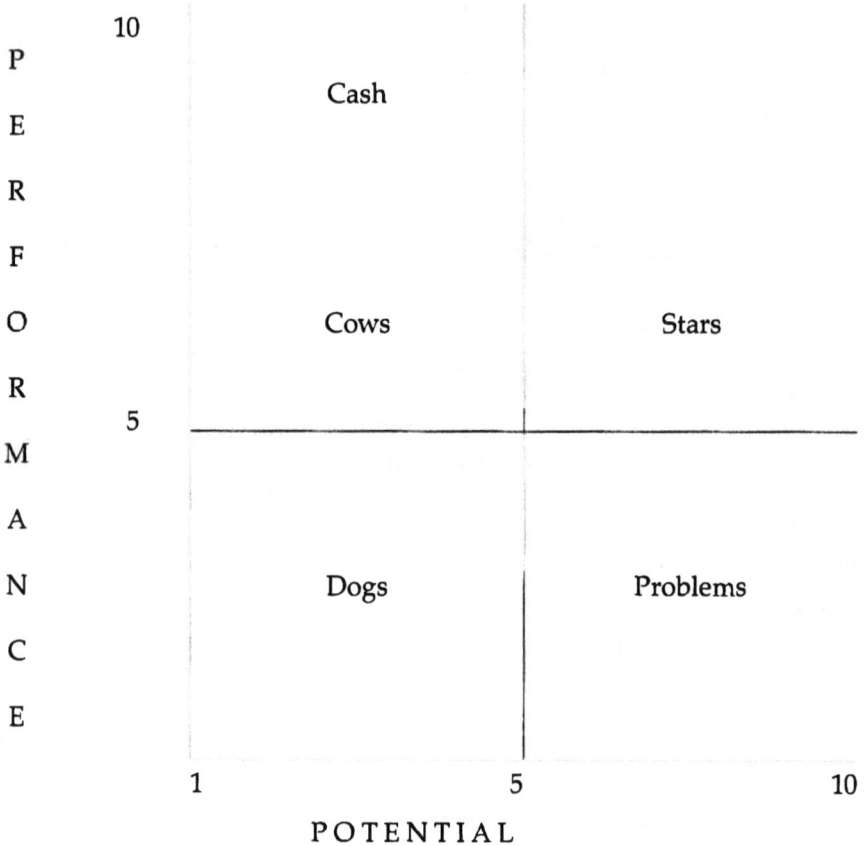

This basic evaluation tool can help an organization evaluate a wide range fo things. The organization can evaluate production lines, people, facilities, buildings, etc.

PRODUCT LINES

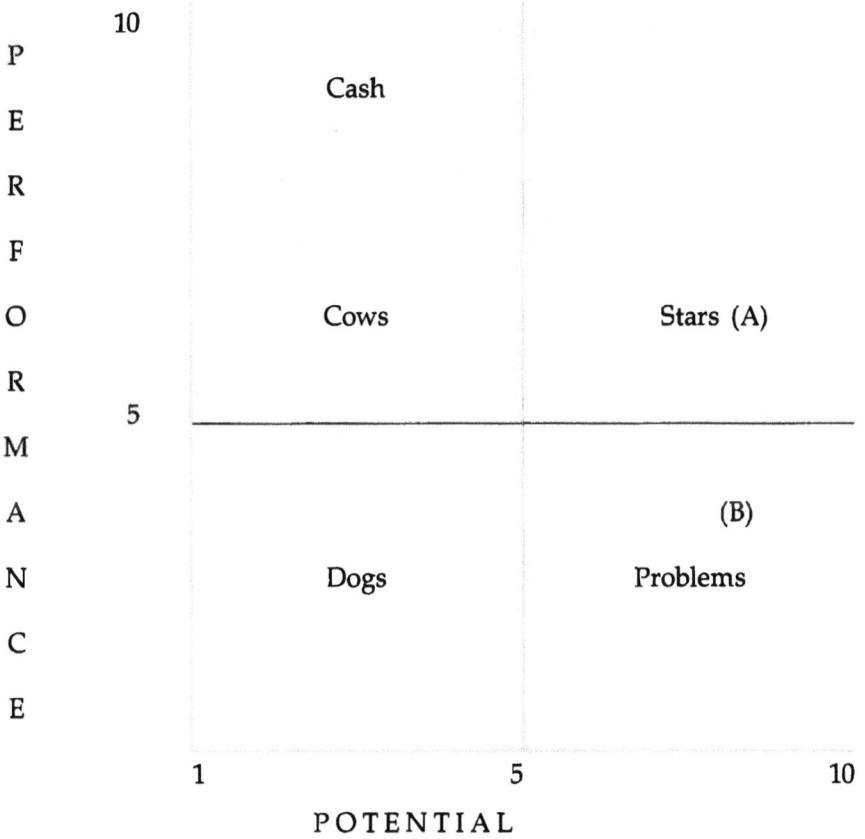

```
        10 │
 P         │
           │         Cash
 E         │
           │
 R         │
           │
 F         │
           │
 O         │         Cows          Stars (A)
           │
 R         │
         5 ├─────────────────────────────────────
 M         │
           │                          (B)
 A         │
           │         Dogs          Problems
 N         │
           │
 C         │
           │
 E         │
           └─────────────┬──────────────┬──────────
           1             5             10
                    POTENTIAL
```

For example, Product Line A might be a "star" with (8.7) rating. B might be a "problem" with a (8.4) rating.

PRODUCTION LINES

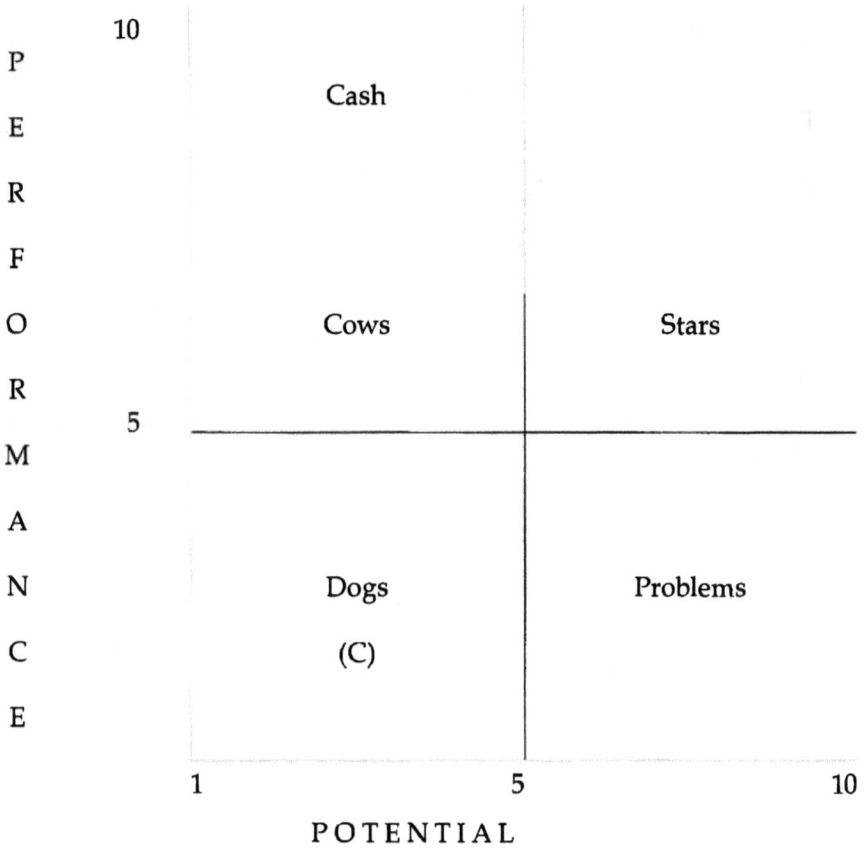

```
        10
    P
               |                          |
    E           |         Cash            |
               |                          |
    R           |                          |
               |                          |
    F           |                          |
               |                          |
    O           |         Cows             |        Stars
               |                          |
    R           |                          |
         5  ────┼──────────────────────────┼──────────────────────
    M           |                          |
               |                          |
    A           |                          |
               |                          |
    N           |         Dogs             |       Problems
               |                          |
    C           |         (C)              |
               |                          |
    E           |                          |
               |                          |
            1           5                         10
                    POTENTIAL
```

For example, Production Line C would be a "dog" if it had a (3.3) rating.

HUMAN RESOURCES

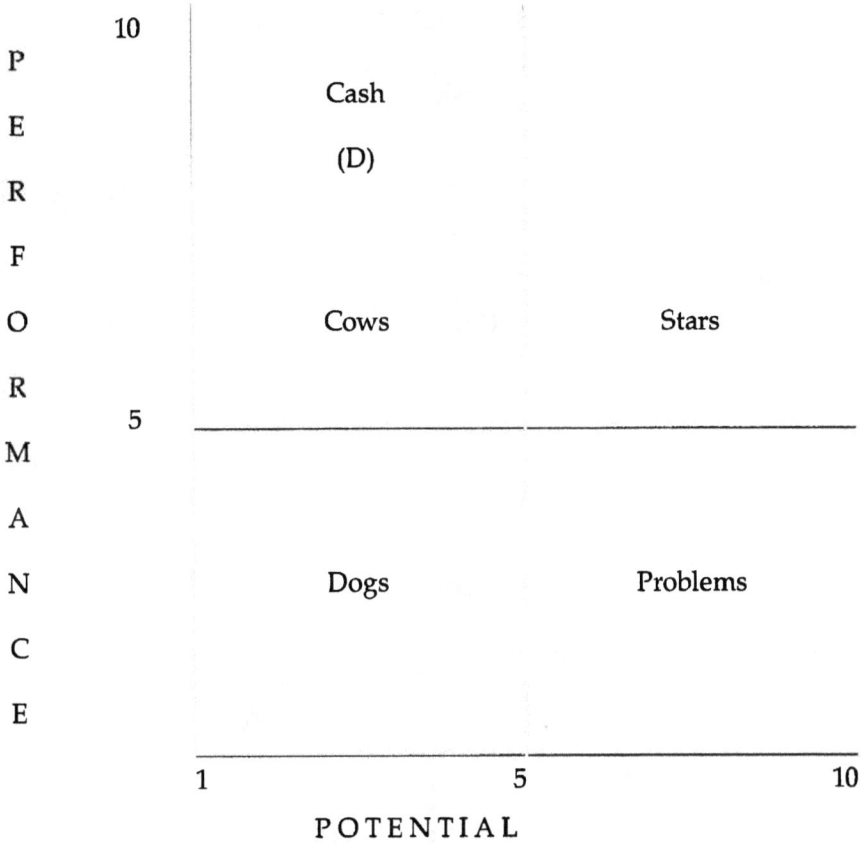

```
  10 |
P      |
       |              Cash
E      |
       |              (D)
R      |
       |
F      |
       |
O      |              Cows              Stars
       |
R      |
   5   |_____
M      |
       |
A      |
       |
N      |              Dogs              Problems
       |
C      |
       |
E      |_____
        1                 5                      10
```

POTENTIAL

For example, Person D might be a (3.8) — a cash cow.

BUILDINGS

```
        10 |                          '
    P       |                              (E)
            |         Cash
    E       |
            |
    R       |
            |
    F       |
            |
    O       |         Cows         Stars
            |
    R       |
         5 _|_____
    M       |
            |
    A       |
            |
    N       |         Dogs         Problems
            |
    C       |
            |
    E       |
            |
         1              5              10
              P O T E N T I A L
```

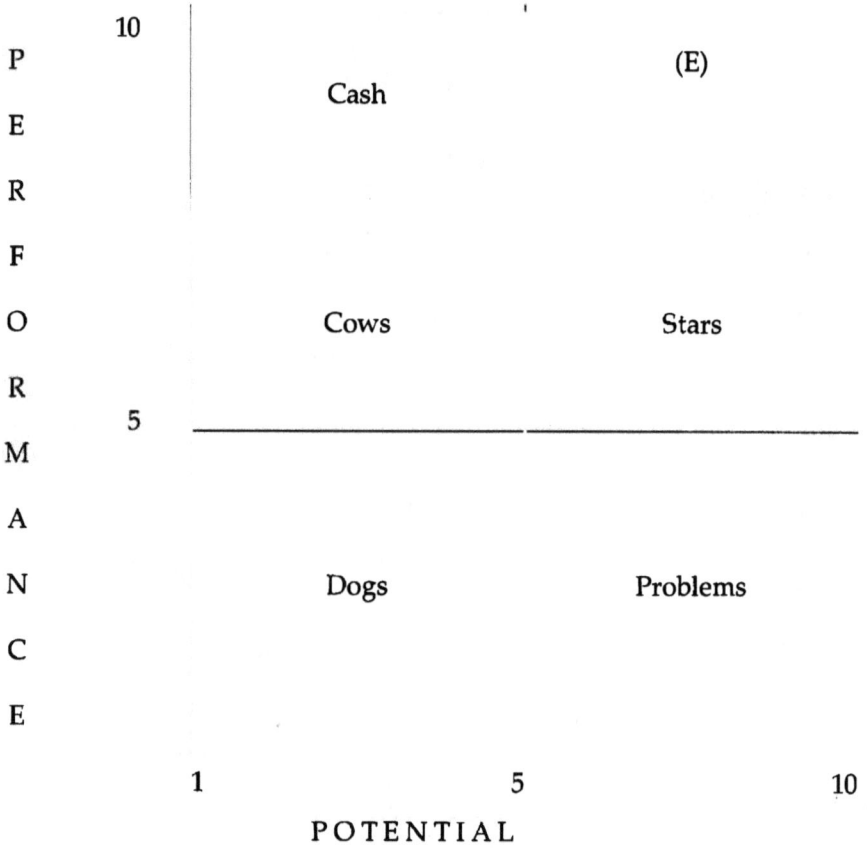

For example, a new plant, well laid out, might be E, a (9.9) — a star.

MACHINES/EQUIPMENT

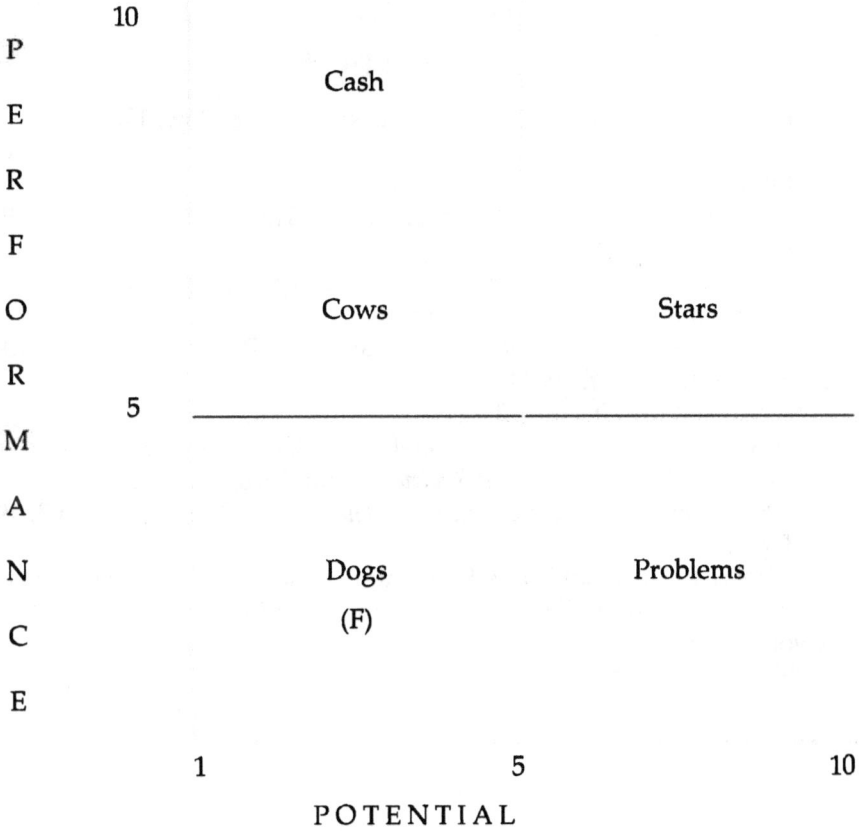

```
        10
P
                        Cash
E

R

F

O                       Cows                    Stars

R
        5       _____
M

A

N                       Dogs                   Problems

C                       (F)

E

        1                 5                      10
              P O T E N T I A L
```

For example, a piece of machine (F) might have a (3.3) rating and be classified as a "dog."

References
Chapter 3

[1]Peter Drucker, *Management* (New York: Harper & Row, 1974), p. 79.

[2]Ibid, p. 75.

[3]Ibid.

[4]John Humble, "Social Responsibility — The Contribution of MBO," *MBO Journal*, Vol. 5, No. 3, p. 19.

[5]Peter Drucker, *Management* (New York: Harper & Row, 1974), p. 77.

[6]Business Success Story, *Tulsa World*.

[7]*Standard & Poor's Industry Surveys*, Standard & Poor's Corp., 345 Hudson Street, New York, N.Y. 10014.

[8]McKinsey, op. cit., pp. 52-94.

[9]Howard H. Stevenson, "Defining Corporate Strengths and Weaknesses," *Sloan Management Review*, Spring 1976, pp. 52-67.

[10]"Economic Barometer Levels Off," *The Orlando Sentinel*, March 3, 1990, See B, p. 1.

[11]Robert R. Blake and Jane S. Mouton, *How to Assess the Strengths and Weaknesses of a Business Enterprise*, (Austin: Scientific Methods, Inc. 1972) A six-volume series.

[12]Ibid.

[13]Ibid.

Chapter 4
Assumptions, Objectives, Performance Contracts, and Ways to Measure Success

This chapter deals with making assumptions, writing objectives, negotiating objectives, and agreeing on objectives to form a performance contract. You should be able to explain the reasoning behind making assumptions before writing your objectives. Furthermore, you should be able to write objectives and be able to discuss the concept of the performance contract. This chapter covers these topics in detail.

Assumptions

You should make your major assumptions about spheres over which you have little or absolutely no control—for example, the external environment. A good way to start is to extend some of the items studied in the environmental analysis.

Should the assumption stage appear to be relatively unimportant in developing a long-range plan, consider the following:

1. If by studying the environment of a college of business it could be assumed there would be a dropoff in demand for the MBA, the school would not have had an objective of hiring one more faculty member.
2. More than likely all the automotive companies have assumed that no oil embargo will be imposed next year. Consider how their plans and objectives would change if they assumed an embargo was in the offing.
3. A few years ago I was leading a planning session for a major oil company. At that time they assumed $35/barrel of oil.

Some PMIS assumptions from their 1984 plan:

1. The oil glut will continue until mid-1984.
2. Interest rates will stay above 15 percent for another year.
3. Profit margins for oil jobbers will stay tight.
4. The predictions of some economists is correct and the turnaround in activity will not come until 1984.

Assumptions for most organizations for 1990 could likely be:

1. There will be a continued lowering of prime rate to about 10 percent.
2. There will be no major labor strikes.
3. West Texas Intermarket crude will be in the $18-20 range.

These assumptions could be included in the strategic plan for GISI. Because PMIS is a supplier of computer and accounting systems to oil jobbers, their assumptions extended from the environmental analysis greatly affect the objectives and strategies to be set later in their strategic plan. All of these assumptions seem to indicate tight markets and margins for the customers of PMIS. These environmental factors and assumptions then become the basis for developing sound, measurable, and obtainable objectives. Because of this situation, PMIS is developing strategies to provide more services to current customers rather than to emphasize the gaining of new customers. In order for GISI to meet its long-term sales and production objectives, this strategy of concentration on its current customers makes sense because of the environmental conditions and the assumption that these conditions are going to stay the same.

This is a key example of how the management team must use different steps in the strategic planning process as a base on which to make decisions in other steps of the process. If, for example, the environmental analysis showed a period of prosperity, high gross national product, tight oil supplies, and high profit margins such as those evidenced in the embargo era of the mid-1970s, then an assumption could be made that these conditions would remain the same over the next operating period. If that were the case, then the GISI management would probably develop a strategy to go after more new customers with positive cash positions.

It should also be noted that the top management team must indicate the assumptions in the strategic plan that have the most opportunity and risk for the organization. If any of those key assumptions are incorrect, then a contingency plan must be developed to handle the unexpected assumption change.

An example of a contingency plan is that made by a group of students on a class project for the City of Tulsa. The city government assumed after the oil embargo that there would not be another embargo. However, at the time the threat of another embargo seemed to me to be great enough to require a contingency plan that could be implemented immediately if tight petroleum supplies should again prevail. A detailed contingency plan was developed and agreed on. Every department knew specifically how to react if supplies were cut drastically. For example, the routes and frequency rates for the city trash pickup, police traffic patterns, and other areas of fuel consumption were provided with a plan that could be immediately implemented if needed.

William L. Schubert, an economist from California, has done extensive study on business cycles. An organization uses specialists like Schubert in the environmental analysis state. The organization then makes its own assumptions, perhaps agreeing and building elements of its plan around these assumptions.

Rate of change trend analysis suggests that 1990 will be a good but unexciting year for the economy. Interest rates will cycle mildly within their present range, the stock market will continue to rise despite intermittent declines, and business activity will begin to reaccelerate in the first quarter. Consumer price inflation will oscillate between 4.5 and 5 percent with no sign of blow-off. Very long term analysis shows that inflation is now on the down side of the long 54-year cycle. There is no reason why the current growth rates cannot be maintained provided the government doesn't do anything foolish. The entire decade can be one of continuous, vigorous growth as we now come out of the low point of the long Kondratieff economic wave.

Some years ago the Public Service Company of Oklahoma wanted to develop a procedure for monitoring and identiyfing significant internal data series which might signal need for management attention. The task force assigned to the project decided that ROC Trend Analysis would be the best means of identifying and focusing attention on critical areas. Starting with the monthly Operating Statement, all important categories of revenue, product sales, expenses, and other various operating ratios were converted to rates of change with an analytic report prepared once every quarter. More than 80 series were monitored, compared, and analyzed. The first report was compiled in 1983, and rate of change charts showed graphically that expenses were growing at a much more rapid rate than revenues and that the rate of growth was accelerating. While the data came from accounting statements, the import was not obvious, but the problem was made immediately apparent by the extreme divergence in growth rates made dramatically evident by the ROC curves. Martin Fate, president of PSO, observed that the rate of change analyses gave him insights he had not had before. Fate emphasized the value of the methodology, saying, "We instituted significant cost control measures and a new resource allocation process which enables us to continually improve our planning, primarily as a result of ROC Trend Analysis. The result has been a one-time reduction of total expenses by 11 percent with even greater improvement of profits."[6]

The assumption may seem elementary, but it must be done. It helps you to identify all the important factors that you feel will remain constant. If any one of them changes drastically, major revisions in plans might be needed. As an exercise, list the assumptions for your organization on a separate piece of paper.

Objectives and Goals

Management by objectives (MBO) has caused a stir in all areas of organizational life over the past 40 years. It is well to remember that the word *management* is the key. Management by objectives is the use of objectives to help manage for results. Before any discussion of writing objectives can begin, we must again refer to the new definition of MBO presented in chapter 1. The purpose of the organization must be defined, environmental analysis made, strengths and weaknesses assessed, and assumptions made. Then and only then can objectives be considered. The examples that follow are from a wide range of industries.

Objectives must be clear, concise, written statements outlining what is to be accomplished in a key priority area, in a certain time period, in measurable terms that are consistent with the overall objectives of the organization.[1] Objectives can be classified as routine, problem-solving, innovative, team, personal, and budgetary.[2] Drucker feels that "objectives are not fate; they are direction. They are not commands; they are commitments. They do not determine the future; they are means to mobilize the resources and energies of the business for the making of the future."[3] Without objectives we tend to fall into managing by habit, staying busy in an "activity trap," as Odiorne often refers to it. We have a tendency to work hard, not smart. Objectives help you to see where you are going. Evelyn Roberts has said:[4]

> You can't achieve goals if you don't have any. Sometimes this idea is so simple that many people pass it by. In order to accomplish anything, we've got to first purpose in our hearts to do it. We've got to make up our minds. If we don't, we just waste our time and energy and find ourselves going around in circles, looking back at the past and wondering where it went.

Objectives are those clear, measurable targets. You don't just get in your car and drive somewhere. Family members agree to go somewhere, perhaps to dinner and have a destination in mind at a certain time. Plans can be organized when you know where you are going; dress and distance are all considered. How many organizations in America are "just going for a drive"? No one knows where he is going but works very hard and sometimes is efficient at going nowhere. We need specific measurable objectives to make organizations work. After objectives are set, you develop a strategy to get there, and then you work hard at getting there.

Objectives can be set at upper organizational levels in profitability and growth, market position and penetration, productivity, product leadership, employee morale, development, and attitudes, physical and financial resources, and public responsibility.[5] You should set an objective in each of these areas in the long-range plan of your organization or company.

The top management team must set organization objectives in the following areas:

1. Profitability and sales
   (a) profit to sales
   (b) sales in volume and dollars
2. Production and productivity
   (a) units
   (b) cost per unit
   (c) efficiency
3. Product characteristics
   (a) quality
   (b) research and development
   (c) engineering
4. People
   (a) safety
   (b) training
   (c) management system balance sheet/culture index
5. Financial resources and performance
   (a) return on assets
   (b) earnings per share
   (c) The five to 10 key financial ratios depending on the organization must be set here. An example is the current ratio or inventory turnover.
6. Public responsibility
7. Overall budget.

The discussion here centers on objectives in a range of settings. Objectives in these seven areas can be further broken down into routine problem-solving, innovative, personal, team, and budgetary objectives. The study of objectives in these categories is purely academic. I usually emphasize that the organization or unit identify its five to ten most important results. It is a good idea, however, to understand each of the objective types.

Routine Objectives

Routine objectives have to do with those activities, jobs, or work assignments that occur regularly and predictably. An example of a routine objective for the foreman of a machine shop might be: "Complete a preventative maintenance check on all equipment each calendar quarter in 1990." Notice that the objective states what is to be accomplished: "complete a preventative maintenance check" on all equipment in a certain, measurable time period, "each calendar quarter."

Other routine objectives might be:
1. I will spend an average of 15 minutes per week in 1990 discussing safety with my group.
2. I will review each machinist's objectives and accomplishments quarterly.
3. I will attend every department meeting.

Problem-Solving Objectives

Problem-solving objectives identify existing, recognized problem areas and state a time period for solution.

An example of a problem-solving objective for a dental dean might be: "Develop a syllabus and a teaching plan for dental hygiene by August 1990." Other problem-solving objectives might be:

1. Develop a plan for faculty internship with local dentists by January 1990.
2. Develop a set of criteria for admitting dental students by October 1990.
3. Hold a one-day symposium on the spiritual and mental health of dentists and prepare summary minutes and recommendations by November 1990.

Innovative Objectives

Innovative objectives look to the future, suggest a completion date, and usually improve an existing situation. For example, an innovative objective for a personnel manager might be: "Devise a better system of screening new hires by July 1, 1990." Another innovative objective might be: "Develop a method or methods to give supervisors feedback on their performance. At least one method will be implemented by May 1, with another method implemented by June 1."

Personal Objectives

Personal objectives relate directly to the person, and they are those he or she wishes to achieve during the year. Examples for a shipping foreman are:

1. To improve my understanding of management, I will read Dr. Migliore's *MBO: Blue Collar to Top Executive* and attend at least one

Executive Action Seminar at Northeastern State University during the fall semester.

2. I will develop a career development plan by October 1990.

Team Objectives

Team objectives are those that need to be accomplished with another member of the organization team. An example for a librarian might be: "I will work with the library consultant to revise our new library classification procedure for law books. We will discuss it in May and introduce the new procedure in July 1990."

Another example might be: "I will work with the library consultant to develop a faster way to handle outside inquiries. We will develop a system by October 1, 1990."

Budgetary Objectives

Budgetary objectives are quantitative, measurable, and usually set on a yearly time frame consistent with the organization's financial year. An example might be: "The Press Department will operate within its $100,000 yearly budget during 1990-91." Budgetary objectives are usually felt to be the most important because of their financial nature, but all other objectives are just as important to support the total MBO program.

How to Measure Performance

One practical, easy way to record, communicate, measure, and update objectives is through a "Performance Plan Book" or "Management Plan Book." All steps in the planning process, including objectives for the organization, are in this book. The objectives are reviewed periodically, usually each quarter, and updated. Table 1 shows how objectives can be listed, kept track of, and presented for review. Each manager reviews his progress on goal attainment each quarter. Sample college of business objectives and samples from a number of areas are included. This is a method I developed at Continental Can Company in 1967. It greatly reduces paper work and provides a convenient method for review. The planning book is kept up to date by that person in the organization who coordinates the long-range plan.

Now that you have made the asumptions, take time to write objectives in these seven areas. Use the seven areas as guides.

1. Profitability and Sales

	Sales	Percentage Profit/Sales	R.O.I.
1st year			
2nd year			
3rd year			
4th year			
5th year			

2. Production and Productivity

	Units	Cost/Unit	Efficiency
1st year			
2nd year			
3rd year			
4th year			
5th year			

3. Product Characteristics
   Quality
   R & D
   Engineering

4. People
   Safety
   Training
   Management System Balance Sheet

5. Financial Resources

6. Public Responsibilities

7. Overall budget

Note the general worksheets on the following pages that suggest areas for objectives. The key is to use these suggested worksheets to find those few that best represent what needs to be measured.

	Last Year Actual	Next Year	Five Years
SALES			
Total sales/revenue			
Net sales per dollar of net worth			
Net sales per dollar of total assets			
Net sales per dollar of net working capital			
Cost of sales per dollar of inventory			
Net sales per dollar of depreciated fixed assets			
MARKET POTENTIAL			
Percent regional market share			
Percent national market share			
Percent world market share			
Percent products in introductory stage			
Percent products in maturity stage			
Percent products in declining stage			
MANUFACTURING/PRODUCTIVITY			
Total output = labor + materials + energy + capital + miscellaneous input			
Number projects completed			
Number projects scheduled			
Units produced			
Hours worked			
Sales			
Employee			
Quality			
Customer Service			

	Last Year Actual	Next Year	Five Years

Labor Productivity

1. Items produced per employee
2. Quantities produced per employee-hour
3. Labor Index = $\dfrac{\text{equivalent employee-hours of output} \times 100}{\text{actual total employee-hours}}$

4. Labor Productivity Index = $\dfrac{\dfrac{\text{price weighted output (period 2)}}{\text{total labor costs (period 2)}}}{\dfrac{\text{price weighed output (period 1)}}{\text{total labor costs (period 1)}}} \times 100$

Materials Productivity
1. Output per constant dollar of total material cost

Energy Productivity
1. Output per energy consumer (BTU's)
2. Energy Productivity Index = $\dfrac{\dfrac{\text{output}}{\text{BTU (constant period)}}}{\dfrac{\text{output}}{\text{BTU (base period)}}} \times 100$

OR

Energy Productivity Index = $\dfrac{\dfrac{\text{output in current period}}{\text{output in base period}}}{\dfrac{\text{BTU in current period}}{\text{BTU in base period}}} \times 100$

Capital Productivity
1. Quantity of output per quantity of capital input

2. Capital productivity = $\dfrac{\text{quantity of output}}{\text{quant. of capital of input}}$ = $\dfrac{\text{units prod./day}}{\text{units inventory}}$ = $\dfrac{\text{units produced/day}}{\text{machine (process unit)}}$

People
1. Man-hours worked without lost time from accidents.
2. Various other safety objectives.

Quality
1. Zero defects.
2. Acceptance rates vs. various sampling plans.

FINANCIAL

SALES

Return on Investment
1. Net profit after taxes/net worth
2. Net profit after taxes/total assets
3. Net profit after taxes + depreciation +
   noncash expense/total assets

Return on Sales
1. Net sales per dollar of net worth
2. Net sales per dollar of total assets
3. Net sales per dollar of net working capital
4. Net profit after taxes/net sales
5. Cost of sales per dollar of inventory
6. New sales per dollar of depreciated fixed assets

Financial Leverage
1. Debt/equity ratio
2. Total debt/total assets
3. Times interest earned

Current Ratio
1. Current assets to current liabilities
2. Cash and receivables to current liabilities
3. Cash and equivalent to current liabilities
4. Current liabilities to net worth
5. Acid-test ratio (current assets-inventory)/
    (current liabilities)

Activity
1. Inventory turnover
2. Accounts receivable turnover
3. Average collection period
4. Total asset turnover
5. Fixed asset turnover

Market Ratios
1. Earnings per share
2. Dividends per share
3. Dividend payout ratio
4. Book value per share
5. Price/earnings ratio
6. Dividend yield

OBJECTIVES

	Last Year Actual	Next Year	Five Years
FACILITIES			
Yearly safety check			
Annual energy audit			
PEOPLE/TRAINING/MORALE			
Management system balance sheet			
Yearly people development audit			
25 hours training per employee/year			
Quality circles (participation teams) implemented			
Turnover			
Performance/reward system			
Benefits			
Compensation levels			
Wellness			
Manpower forecast			
Recruiting objectives and costs			
Succession planning			
PUBLIC RESPONSIBILITY			
100% United Way			
Sponsor Junior Achievement Co.			
200 working days per year volunteers			
Pay all taxes, wages, and bills			
Contribute $300,000 to civic projects			
Meet OSHA safety requirements			

After the president or chief operating officer has gathered the staff to think through the major objectives, the subunit managers must develop their plans and objectives to support the overall objectives. The key subunit persons should be involved in the supporting subunit objectives.

After the top management team has worked through the top organization objectives based on all the previous steps and discussion in the strategic planning process, each subunit manager is beginning to perceive what his organizational unit must do to support the overall plan. After the various strategies are developed for each of the major objectives, the subunit manager must gather his team and go through the same process. At this point, one of two steps can be taken. Each organizational subunit, such as the vice president heading marketing, the vice president of production, and perhaps the controller, can start with step one, the purpose, and develop the purpose, say, for the controller's area, work on salient environmental factors in the controller's area, study its unit strengths and weaknesses, make assumptions specifically important to the controller's area, and then develop specific overall objectives that contribute to the overall strategic plan for the organization. Other organizations I have worked with prefer to let the analysis that has taken place in the organization plan be the stage setting and to go directly into setting objectives for their particular units. For example, A. B. Steen, president of T.D. Williamson, Inc., brings his managers from around the world to Tulsa for a yearly planning meeting. They chart the direction of the company over the long term. Each individual functional manager then develops a game plan to support the overall plan. For example, to achieve the sales volume objective for T.D. Williamson, Inc., the unit managers of the marketing and service divisions set objectives as follows:

- Marketing—increase penetration of the gas-distribution market in 1990, to achieve the following share of market by 1994: Product A, 45%; Product B, 30%; Product C, 45%.
- Manufacturing—develop an integrated manufacturing control system by July 1, 1991.
- T.D.W. Services Division—complete the development of a quality control program for all services performed by October 1991.

The concept of an effective objective is not measurable, but it is important. An example from ORU is appropriate. To the degree that the university achieves these purposes and the student responds to these opportunities the student will:

1. Develop a concept of personal honor based on the principles of integrity, common sense, reverence for God, esteem for man, and respect for social and spiritual laws.
2. Develop a sense of responsibility and citizenship, which enhances his or her moral and spiritual growth.
3. Apply himself or herself to the development of the full powers of the mind.
4. Practice good health habits and regularly participate in wholesome physical activities.
5. Employ his or her professional expertise in the world.
6. Endeavor to seek the will of God for his or her life and to exemplify Christlike character.

Notice the effective objectives for ORU attained will tend to support the ORU purpose.

IMPORTANT POINTS TO REMEMBER

1. Without proper objectives, managing is a day-to-day crisis.
2. Direction is difficult if you don't know where you are going.
3. With proper objectives there is a sense of direction.
4. George Morrisey calls objectives the results you wish to achieve.
5. How can you guide and measure a person's performance if you first

don't agree on what is to be accomplished?
6. The objectives must be clear, concise, written statements outlining what is to be accomplished in a key priority area, within a time frame, and in measurable terms.

Conclusion

The objectives become a performance contract after they have been:
1. Properly written and submitted to the supervisor.
2. Discussed and negotiated with the supervisor.
3. Resubmitted to the supervisor.
4. Approved by both parties.
5. Signed by both parties.

The objectives once negotiated are the just measurable results confirmed in the strategic long-range plan. Every previous step was to set the stage for proper long- and short-range measurable targets and results expected.

In my 1986 news column in the *Tulsa Tribune*, I specifically forecast three events by the year 2000. One was an event beyond anyone's imagination in Europe. No, I didn't know the Berlin Wall would come down. My forecast was not that spectacular. More specific, the column called for U.S. involvement in major military action in the mid-east. The Gulf War came along as predicted. The Third was a major world wide economic downturn year 2000.

Each of these predictions came from a report I developed for a major U.S. corporation. I was asked to report to top management and the board on world conditions and economic situations in the year 2000.

After looking at all the forecasts from 1950 - 1985, the pattern was obvious. Almost all the ecomonic models crunch their numbers and predict changes in a fairly narrow range. No legitimate service, to my knowledge, predicted the economic highs and lows from 1950 to 1985. Right now you will notice, no one is predicting a high or low. Common sense says there are highs or lows in the future.

Now look at the Kondratieff curve. Very interesting!!! Guess where we are on the cycle? Don't guess here are the facts. We are on the downward slop of the curve. The 50- 55 year cycle of the Kondratieff curve has been on accurate predictions of business cycles.

So what do we do??? Ignore the obvious warnings??!! Full speed ahead? Or is it time for a wake-up call!

The question is how we manage our organizations and personal lives. Who will be in the drivers seat in the year 2010? Trust to luck or try to weave your way through the icebergs.

References
Chapter 4

[1] For an excellent view of how company and organizational objectives are set, refer to Dr. Richard Johnson's dissertation, *A Systematic Approach to Long-Range Planning* (1969), North Texas State University. Before objectives can be set, the organization must monitor its environment, make assumptions, set criteria, and assess its strengths and weaknesses. Only then is it in a position to set objectives and goals. Also refer to my book, *MBO: Blue Collar to Top Executive* (Washington: Bureau of National Affairs, 1977), pp. 2 and 3. I suggest defining purpose and then the other stages before objectives are set. Also refer to George Morrisey's book, *Management by Objectives and Results*, pp. 62 and 63, for guidelines and sample objectives. Roger Fritz has excellent educational examples in a manuscript he developed for a conference at ORU entitled, "Colleges Can Be Managed."

[2] The Penton Publishing Company Education Division has an excellent MBO cassette/text programmed learning course. It recommends and gives examples for these types of objectives: routine, problem-solving, and innovative.

[3] Peter Drucker, *Management*, Harper & Row, 1974, p. 102.

[4] Evelyn Roberts, *Daily Blessing*, Tulsa: ORU Press, Jan. - Mar., 1977, pp. 10 and 11.

[5] Paul Mali, *Managing Objectives*, New York: Wilby, 1972, p. 117.

[6] For more information, contact Mr. William L. Schubert, Business Strategy and Planning, Business Cycle Analysis and Forecasting, 8298 Sugarman Drive, La Jolla, California 92037.

Chapter 5
Strategy and Long- and Short-Range Planning

In this chapter, ideas of strategy and long- and short-range planning are discussed. By the end of this chapter you should be able to distinguish between objectives and strategies and should be able to write strategies in order to meet the objectives stated in chapter 4. Also, you should be able to write a long-range plan (five years) to accomplish the objectives stated, using the strategies set forth.

Finally, you should be able to distinguish between long-range and short-range plans and be able to develop the short-range plan of your five-year plan.

Strategy

After the objectives and goals have been set, a strategy must be developed to achieve the goals and objectives. A good way to outline a strategy is to ask yourself: "How and where am I going to commit my resources?" Your answer will be your strategy. Or you might describe strategy as your "game plan." A basketball coach could use a strategy of shifting from a man-to-man defense to a zone press. A university could consider the strategy of allowing "accountable time" to one professor each semester to do proper research. Some examples of marketing strategy are:

1. Demarketing
2. Changes in product mix
3. Changes in price policy
4. Changes in promotional strategy.

It is during the strategy phase that we consider organizational structure. Drucker says, "The best structure will not guarantee results and performances. But the wrong structure is a guarantee of nonperformance."[1]

Strategy also concerns timing. The timing of the introduction of a new product can be very important. An example of strategy in a real estate setting would be the decision whether or not to expand into a new area of a city. Another strategy would be determination of the amount and type of advertising. Remember that strategy is not "doing." It is the thinking process. The "doing" comes in the five-year and one-year operation plans. For more information on strategy, refer to Hanna,[2] Richard and Nielander,[3] and Hutchinson.[4]

The strategy phase begins to receive more and more attention after the organization has been on the strategic planning process the second and third year. Until this time, most of the attention has gone into the previous steps. This is not to say that strategic decisions haven't been made, and in many cases, made properly. We all use strategy daily. We are looking into the environment when we arise in the morning, look outside, and make an assumption on how the weather might change as we make the strategic decision of what to wear that day and whether or not to take an umbrella. Organizations used strategy long before they recognized the need for overall planning. What the strategic planning/MBO process is doing is creating the framework so that when strategy decisions are made, they are made within the context of the overall business situation. As we have seen, specific strategies must be developed for the overall key corporate objectives. Another example of strategy is Sears, Roebuck, & Company's going into the field of financial services. Sears obviously has had objectives to attain sales in the $18-billion range. Using a planning system, Sears appears to have recognized the environmental factors already discussed here, to have recognized that their profits have tumbled since 1977, and to have been faced with a tougher job in meeting the overall sales and profits objectives needed for the company to survive. Within this framework, it appears that they have decided to commit resources and that they believe the timing was correct to introduce financial services into their product mix. They are taking advantage of one of their great strengths—that being the confidence of the American consumer and the millions of people who regularly patronize the Sears stores. I believe this has been a well-considered strategic move. Using its customer base for carefully targeted loans and other financial services should bolster the company's profitability.[5]

Colowyo general strategies include buildup of production capacity, and buying equipment needed for future operations at attractive prices caused by the downturn in the copper and uranium industries.

Bendix Corporation at one time kept about one-sixth of its assets in the bank and in liquid securities. Bendix earned attractive interest while looking for the right opportunities to use the cash to help the company.

Another example of strategy is the difficult question of pricing. In spite of all the sophisticated pricing models, it appears that the pricing decision cannot be scientifically determined. In some cases, the higher the price of certain products, such as a luxury car or some other status product, the more desirable the product becomes. When J.C. Penney Company went into its "plain pockets" jeans and its shirts with the fox emblems, it was an example of price-cutting strategy against the Levi Strauss & Company's jeans and Alligator shirts. The strategy was that the lower price would result in a more profitable product line.[6]

An example of strategy in the food business is Wendy's strategy on their hamburger. In order to combat McDonalds' frozen, pre-cooked, and warmed hamburger, Wendy's wanted to have a hamburger cooked on the spot. There is risk in continually cooking hamburgers. If they are not consumed fresh and on the spot, they become tomorrow's Wendy's chili.

Another example of strategy in the food/restaurant business has been the drive-through window. Coupons, sales, price reductions such as Arby's five hamburgers for $5 after 5:00 p.m. are strategies. Some characteristics of a successful strategy are (1) It is understood by all in the organization; (2) It is flexible; and (3) It reacts to changes in the environment and assumptions.

In the strategic phase, the organization must recognize its driving force. Benjamin B. Tregoe, chairman and CEO of Kepner-Tregoe, Inc., defines driving force:

> The notion of driving force is crucial to the strategy formulation and implementation process.
>
> Briefly, driving force is the primary determiner of the scope of future products and markets of an organization. Determining driving force will help the top team answer such questions as "Why are we in our current businesses and not others? Why are we making the products we are making and not others?"
>
> Research suggests that there are nine possible driving forces. Here are the nine: (1) products offered, (2) market needs, (3) technology, (4) production capability, (5) method of sale, (6) method of distribution, (7) natural resources, (8) size-growth, and (9) return profit."

A major important area of planning is in the area of the planning gap. The planning gap is represented by Figure 5-1.

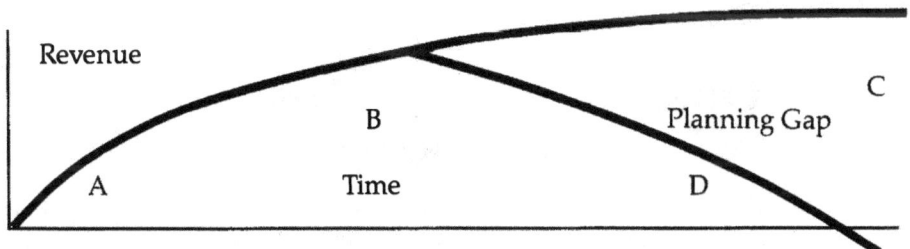

With the firm's total revenue on the vertical axis and time being represented by the horizontal axis, we can see the planning gap concept. The total revenue curve, ABD, is what a company can expect in returns from its present products and services. At the present rate of innovations, inventories, and improvements, all these things begin to become obsolete. Notice the BD portion of the curve. What the firm must have is continuing revenues represented by the curve of ABC, expressed in terms of an objective. The gap between BC and BD can be overcome only by good planning, which is done at the strategy stage of long-range planning/MBO. After the objectives are set on sales or total revenue following the ABC objective, management must then develop the specific strategy or game plan to achieve this result.

T. D. Williamson, Inc., has a good planning system started by the late Ed Green in the middle 1970s. Green was a recognized leader in the planning field. The company was founded by the late T. D. Williamson, Sr., passed on to his son, T. D. Williamson, Jr., and now is headed by the very capable A. B. Steen. Steen is the type of chief executive officer who can get the most out of the planning process. He practices what he preaches, sets objectives, measures people by their results, and rewards accordingly.

He asked me to lead his company's 1979 planning conference. The main theme after setting the stage was to develop specific strategies to overcome the planning gap. Good solid objectives were set through 1985. Steen then turned the conference over to me to bring out the opinions and creativity of the management team. Not many chief executive officers have the courage and confidence to show this type of participation. We arrived at four specific strategies. I am sure you can perceive the commitment the T. D. Williamson management team will have in implementing their strategies. How would the management team feel if outside consultants came in and worked with Steen to develop the strategy for the company? They would not have liked it!

One strategy developed at T. D. Williamson was to move company operations to where the customers are located. The strategy to move company operations to the Mideast and Southeast Asia was developed.

As an exercise, the reader can develop a set of strategies to meet each of the objectives.

Operational Plans: Long- and Short-Range

After all the steps have been taken and a strategy has been developed to meet our objectives and goals, it is time to develop both long- and short-range plans. Examples of long-range plans are found in building, equipping, hiring people, developing curriculum, and so on. It is important not to confuse the long- and short-range plan with strategy. This is the *action* or *doing* stage. Strategy was the thinking stage. Here you hire, fire, build, advertise, and so on. In every long-range plan I have ever been involved with, we have developed pro forma income and balance sheets for five years. We also have developed contribution analysis by product line for five years. The sales forecast for five years should also be included in this section. In manufacturing, the master production control schedule fits this area. For maintenance, the overhaul and preventive maintenance schedule fits here also.

Personnel managers can line up training activities and plans for all their people over the next five years in this section. Ideally, each person has assessed his strengths and weaknesses and then set his own training and self-improvement objectives.

In short, a five-year operating plan must be developed for every function of the business. Marketing, finance, personnel, accounting, manufacturing, etc. must develop a plan that insures the success of the overall company plan. When the objectives in chapter 4 are set for the organization and strategies are developed, each organizational unit must do its part to insure that it makes the proper contribution to the success of the plan.

Zero-Base Budgeting in a Short-Range Plan

There has been a big movement toward zero-base budgeting (ZBB) in recent years. Allen Austin found in a survey of 481 enterprises that there are definite benefits to zero-base budgeting.[7] Zero-base budgeting has a natural fit in the planning process. It probably is more applicable in business than in government, where the results have been mixed. Zero-base budgeting can be defined as follows:[8]

> The basic concept of attempting to reevaluate all programs and expenditures every year—hence the term zero-base—is not new. The process requires each manager to justify his entire budget request in detail and puts the burden of proof on him to justify why he should spend any money.

Former President Carter defined zero-base budgeting this way:[9]

> In contrast to the traditional budgeting approach of incrementing the new on the old, zero-base budgeting demands a total rejustification of everything from zero. It means chopping up the organization into individual functions and analyzing each annually, regardless of whether it is 50 years old or a brand-new proposal for a future program.

The budget is broken into units called decision packages, prepared by managers at each level. These packages cover every existing or proposed activity of each department. They include analyses of purpose, costs, measures of performance and benefits, alternative courses of action, and consequence of disapproval.

Zero-base budgeting can be summarized as a further sophistication of the regular budgeting process. Every expenditure and activity is rejustified at the budget proposal stage. Those activities and functions that have been part of the organization's regular activities are thought through again.

As Peter Drucker in 1954 was given credit for putting all the elements of management by objectives together, it appears that Peter A. Pyhrr has been the one key person to put all the elements of zero-base budgeting together in his book, *Zero-Base Budgeting,* published in 1973.[10]

It is in this stage that ZBB and MBO most logically fit together. The yearly budget and activities that go along with the budget under MBO are the first year of the five-year plan. I see that ZBB, with its yearly "let's start from point zero" requirement would make units and subunits reanalyze their purpose or reason for being.

Because the yearly budget is entrenched in our organized society (families, government, industry, and nonprofit groups), ZBB could be the catalyst to force more and better long-range planning. Every manager in every organization is sensitive to his budget, and ZBB then becomes the mechanism to force him to learn to manage with his budget. Too many units see the budget as only "What do we have to spend?" and then find ways to spend it. We need to move to "What needs to be done?" and then "How much does it cost?"

It seems more logical to me for the organizational unit to define its purpose, analyze its environment, its strengths, its weaknesses, and make to a few key assumptions. Then it sets its objectives and makes up a strategy and plan to meet these objectives. Top management then submits a five-year budget that represents the cost to implement that plan. Then and only then can the first year's budget be judged on its merit. Top management needs to see what the subunit can produce and what its cost will be. Accountability needs to be forced into the budget process. Once the budget is agreed on, the unit manager freely manages his part of it. If he can't manage it properly, you get a new manager who can. There is no need for elaborate controls in the budget process. Too many organizations overcontrol, which is more costly in the long run.

In using long-range planning/MBO, we should not confine the handling of the everyday, regular problems to the short term. We will use this decision model for problem analysis. This decision model should not be confused with the overall planning process. With the strategic plan in mind, a manager uses this outline to systematically solve problems and make short-term decisions. You might want to use this model as you manage your real estate company, for example, to analyze the problem of high turnover of real estate salespeople. You could also use it for other problems such as an overdrawn bank account or a poor cash flow. It is important to use this problem-solving model within the context of the overall strategic planning process. Problems are easier to determine if an organization knows where it is going. I always make sure the group considers purpose, what is going on at the time, strengths and weaknesses, assumptions, objectives, and strategy to set the stage for problem identification.

1. Defining the problem
2. Analyzing the problem
3. Developing alternative solutions
4. Considering the effect each alternative solution will have on:
   a. Finance
   b. Accounting
   c. Marketing
   d. Management.
5. Deciding on the best solution
6. Converting decisions into effective actions, what you are going to do and when.

An example of the outlining format using the decision model follows:

I. Defining the problem
    A. Labor turnover too high.

II. Analyzing the problem
    A. High anxiety
       1. Poor indoctrination
       2. Lack of training
    B. Low pay

III. Developing alternative solutions
    A. Indoctrination program
       1. Welcome speech
       2. Written booklets
       3. Films
       4. Training
    B. Raise commission of sales to community average
    C. Keep hiring to cover turnover
       1. Little loyalty
       2. Bad reputation in community

IV. Deciding on the best solution(s)
    A. Note choice "A" and "B"

V. Converting decisions into effective actions
    A. Convert storeroom to lounge by October 1, 1991
    B. Buy training film by November 1, 1991
    C. Develop booklets covering benefits, insurance, etc. by October 1, 1991; review rough draft by September 1, 1991
    D. Train the trainers on each job; training session September 5 - October 8, 1991
    E. Budget 1-week break in period on job.

Note further discussion of this problem-solving approach in chapter 10— Strategic Management.

Think of one highly important problem facing you. Follow the outline suggested to determine a tentative solution, and as an exercise, develop a tentative decision using the model.

The use of PERT is another tool that is used in the five-year, or operational, plan. A PERT schedule is an excellent way to implement a strategy to achieve some overall objective. PERT is used in project-oriented or building-related projects.[11]

Operational planning is what you are going to do in each year; no results, no strategy, no thinking, just doing! Remember that the short-range plan is the first year of the five-year plan. This is what you are doing to implement the strategy to achieve the objectives set previously. Look at one of your objectives and the strategy determined to meet that objective. Now determine exactly what must be done to implement the plan. For example, the objective of the Northeastern State University College of Business might be to have 125 MBAs in the 1990-91 class. The strategy to attain that objective might be to concentrate on the recruiting of NSU seniors, both business and nonbusiness graduates. To implement this strategy, NSU might (1) *develop* a special brochure, (2) *meet* with Admissions, (3) *announce* in class, and 4) *award* scholarships to 3.5 students. Note the action words in italics.

Note that in the five-year plan lower organizational units pick up these operational tasks and reword them as objectives.

Brasfield Construction Company of Jackson, Tennessee, developed a comprehensive strategic plan. They followed the exact outline in the book. All of the managers of Brasfield Construction took part in the planning. After the total plan was agreed upon each manager developed a support plan. Note the format they agreed upon for each construction job. Also note on the bottom of the form where those involved "sign off" on the agreement.

JOB GOALS

JOB DESCRIPTION: _____ JOB # _____

Estimated Job Costs		Actual Job Costs	
Labor			
Material			
Subcontractors			
Other			
TOTAL COST			
Contract Amount			

	GOAL	ACTUAL
1. Increased Profit Goal		
2. Labor Saving Goal		
3. Bonus Goal		
4. Job Schedule Improvement Goal		

OTHER OBJECTIVES

1. Complete buy out of job and computer estimate input within two weeks of contract.
2. Develop job schedule with superintendent and subcontractors participation.
3. Monitor schedule and adjust with superintendent.
4. Preconstruction conference with men and subcontractors.
5. Annual sales goal of ($_____). Sales goal for personally identified job ($_____).
6. Develop new contacts (_____) per month.

It is important to have any work group or individual have a voice in determining how their work is to be measured. The Brasfield Construction Job Goals is a good example. It is equally important that goals and performance be revised periodically. Ken Brasfield, president of Brasfield Construction, has developed a very generous reward system if the goals are met.

Examples of Strategy

All organizations are faced with strategic choices. They include: hiring full time vs. temporary workers, length of time to pay bills, whether or not to use alliances, partnerships, merges or acquisitions, centralize or decentralize, pricing of goods and services. Other examples of strategy include:

Restaurants
1. Expand or cut back menu
2. Provide a drive in or pick up service
3. Start catering division

Airlines
1. Raise or lower airfare
2. Senior citizen and/or children discounts
3. Free ticket if flight late

Sports Teams
1. Special attractions, give away promotions
2. Season ticket packages
3. Starting time of games

University
1. Programs offered
2. Decision to go into adult non-credit courses
3. Research or teaching enrollment

Hotel
1. Free local phone calls
2. Breakfast and/or happy hour included in room rate

Procter and Gamble
1. Cuting back choices and sizes of detergents, disposable diapers, bathroom tissues and other household items

Ruffin Properties
1. Converted Galleria Shopping Mall to office complex

NCAA Athletics
1. University of Oklahoma replacing turf with grass

Soft Drinks
1. Pepsi relying on Ray Charles and Michael Jackson promotions
2. Coke strategy was signing up fast food chains

University/Colleges
1. Oklahoma City University started a lock-step one year MBA program in Tulsa.
2. Northeastern State University added a master in technology at UCT in Tulsa.

References
Chapter 5

[1] Peter Drucker, *Management* New York: Harper & Row, 1974.
[2] Hanna, "Marketing Strategy Under Conditions of Economic Scarcity", *Journal of Marketing*, (39-1), 1975, pp. 63-67.
[3] Richard and Nielander, *Readings in Management*, Reading No. 23, pp. 234-235.
[4] Hutchinson, *Readings in Management Strategy and Tactics*, No. 6, 7.
[5] "The New Sears," *Business Week*, Nov. 16, 1981, pp. 140-46.
[6] "Pricing of Products is Still an Art," *Wall Street Journal*, November 21, 1981, p. 25.
[7] Allen Austin, *Research Report*, New York: American Management Association.
[8] Peter Pyhrr, *Zero-Base Budgeting*, New York: John Wiley & Sons, 1973, p. xi.
[9] President Jimmy Carter, "Jimmy Carter Tells Why He Will Use Zero-Base Budgeting," *Nation's Business*, January 1977, p. 24.
[10] Op. cit.
[11] Jerome D. Wiest and Ferdinand K. Levy, *A Management Guide to PERT/CPM*, Englewood Cliffs: Prentice-Hall, 1969.

Chapter 6
Integrating the Functional Marketing Plan with the Corporate Strategic Plan

A problem that appears to persist in planning environments is the failure to integrate the functional plans with the strategic plan. Such a failure reduces the effectiveness of the planning effort and is counterproductive to the whole planning process.

At the root of this failure is a lack of understanding of the planning hierarchy that integrates the functional plans with the strategic plan. This chapter addresses this issue by providing a clear explanation of the marketing planning process and presents a hierarchical model which focuses on the integration of functional/strategic plans.

Functional Plans

After all members of the top management team have worked on and contributed to the overall plan, it is time to work on functional plans and to get input from marketing, finance, production, research and development, human resources, etc. After the general draft of overall strategic direction is developed, it is time for each functional area to study and give advice on the overall plan. This is called *time-out period.*

Time-Out Period

Before any plan goes into action, it is important for the whole organization to look it over. It supports the old adage that those who execute the plan need to be in on the plan. This time-out period helps eliminate mistakes. Top management of any organization cannot possibly know all details, opportunities, and problems. There is talent in all organizations, and the time-out period gives the organization a chance to use that talent and to listen. Too often plans are made and announced with little or no input. The time-out period helps assure that people will support the plan. You can guarantee apathy and little support if the strategic direction is set with no input.

Personnel in each functional area, production, marketing, etc., discuss the overall plan and submit a written critique in a four- to six-week period.

Then top management get together and rethink each step in the overall plan. Adjustments are made and an overall plan is set.

Strategic Plans

In review, strategic planning is the philosophy of managing with a planning process. It is both a product and a process. The product is the plan itself. It is in writing and clearly defines where the organization intends to be in the long term, usually three or more years in the future. The plan includes strategy and the short-term steps to ensure overall success. The process is the interaction that takes place in developing the plan. Everyone involved in executing the plan should be involved in its development.

Functional plans are the strategic plans developed to support the overall corporate strategic plan. Functional plans include manufacturing, personnel, research and development, marketing, and finance. They are basically the same philosophy and process described in chapter 1.

In review, the firm must establish its overall long-term strategic plan first. The essence of this plan is determining where the organization wants to be five to ten years in the future and mobilizing its resources to get there. Recall that the top management team must meet and work together through the following steps:

1. Defining the organization's purpose and reason for being.
2. Monitoring the environment in which it operates.
3. Realistically assessing strengths and weaknesses.
4. Making assumptions about unpredictable future events.
5. Prescribing written, specific, and measurable objectives in principal result areas contributing to the purpose.
6. Developing strategies on how to use available resources to meet objectives.
7. Constantly appraising performance to determine whether it is keeping pace with attainment of objectives and is consistent with defined purpose.
8. Reevaluating purpose, environment, strengths, weaknesses, assumptions objectives, and strategies before setting objectives for the next performance year.

The strategic planning and management process should be viewed as a continuing, ongoing, orderly process. It is cybernetic in nature as developed in chapter 1 and presented again in Figure 1. The top management team works together developing Steps 1 through 7. The overall direction of the organization is determined, usually focusing on five years, but with a view toward the future. Note Figure 1 demonstrates the overall planning process.

Figure 1
The Strategic Planning Process

FIGURE 1-1. Strategic long-range planning process

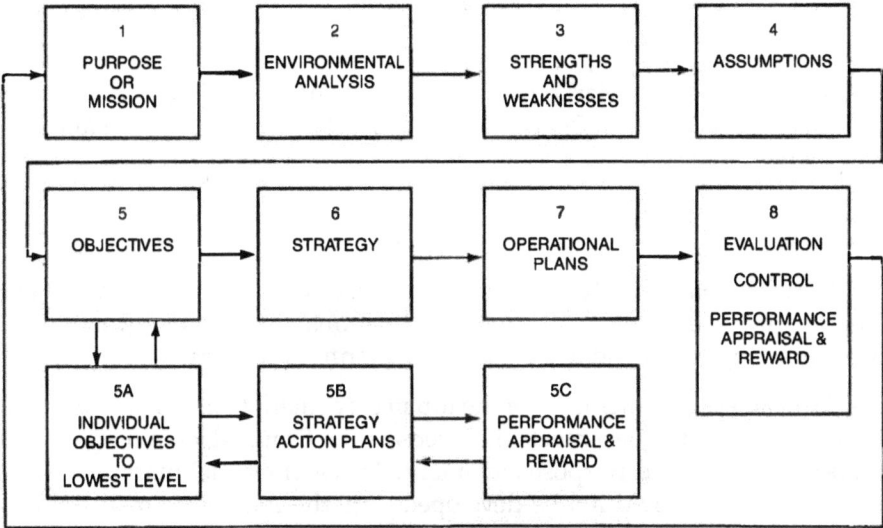

The strategic planning process should be viewed as a flexible, dynamic, and continuous process that assumes a democratic or participative style of management. It integrates various plans by providing appropriate linkage between short- and long-term plans. Its purpose is to allocate scarce resources in order to ensure continuous achievement.

Once the overall direction of the firm has been determined, then each functional area must develop a functional plan to support the overall strategic plan. These support plans include, for example, the marketing plan, human resources plan, financial plan, R&D plan, and production plan. Note Figure 2 demonstrates the relationship between the overall plan and the functional plan.

Figure 2

```
                    ┌──────────────┐
                    │  Corporate   │
                    │    Plan      │
                    └──────────────┘
                           │
     ┌──────────┬──────────┼──────────┬──────────┐
┌──────────┐ ┌──────────┐ ┌──────────┐ ┌──────────┐
│Production│ │Marketing │ │Financial │ │ People   │
│  Plan    │ │  Plan    │ │  Plan    │ │  Plan    │
└──────────┘ └──────────┘ └──────────┘ └──────────┘
```

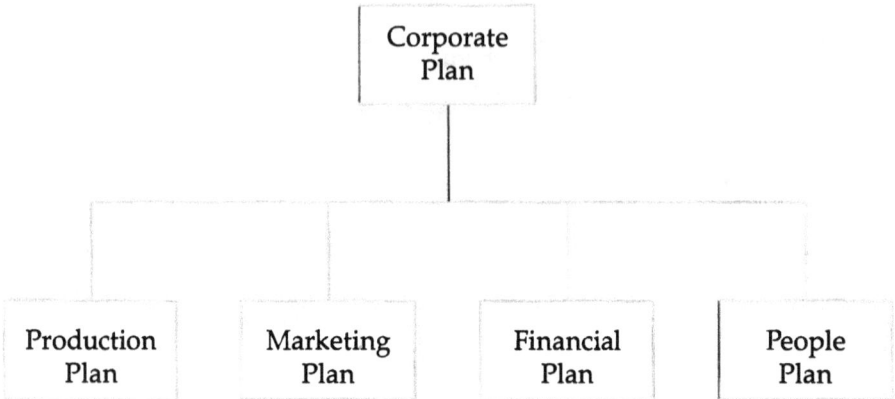

Too often, each functional entity works to develop its own plan without coordinating with other areas. In those situations, one functional area plan, like marketing, may tend to dominate the planning process.

To avoid this, all members of the top management team need to develop the overall plan that best meets the needs of the firm and keep it striving to serve its mission and purpose statement. This is the benchmark plan. The marketing plan should not be developed until the marketing management team can see the overall direction of the firm and how the marketing plan fits with other functional area plans. The marketing manager should participate in the overall planning of the firm to ensure the integration of the marketing plan with the strategic plan.

For example, the company might decide to be an international supplier of widgets. It wants to grow to a certain sales-and-profit position and be a leader in the international marketplace. With this in mind, the optimum production plan might call for production facilities near the customer. Service and fast delivery might be considered as keys to the marketing plan. This results in higher manufacturing costs, but lower transportation costs. The optimum-size plan must be developed to serve each of the individual markets. In some market areas it might be cheaper to supply the market from a central plant, pay higher transportation costs, and let the market develop. Capital budgeting decisions must be made to ensure the right plant and equipment are at the right spot to maximize profitability. None of these functional area decisions should be made without a full view of the strategic direction of the business.

An example of how complex and forward-thinking marketing/production strategy must be comes from the motorcycle industry. The normal view is to look at a least-cost manufacturing alternative. Standardize everything, make few changes, build to plant capacity, and try to optimize the plant capacity at the bottom of the long-run average cost curve. This produces a least-cost manufacturing product—in this case, motorcycles, motorcycle engines, and parts. However, standardization contributes to replacement by competition. It allows entry by other firms into the lucrative replacement parts and repair business. The Japanese constantly redesign, remodel, and change after shorter production runs to discourage this kind of competition. Even though the engineering research and short-term production costs are higher, the long-term overall profits to the firm are maximized[2].

The Japanese change their oil filter design every year on their engines to keep the big oil filter makers out of the replacement-parts business. The money to be made in motorcycles, as in so many other products, is with the replacement-parts market. This is not necessarily the best strategy in all types of business. The main point here is to emphasize the fact that top management must look at the long-term potential of the firm, recognizing the characteristics in the marketplace and the overall long-term best return on assets for the organization. The emphasis should be to look at the total picture and make the functional plans fit neatly into the overall plan of the firm. The emphasis must be on the firm and maximizing the achievement of all the firm's specific measurable objectives.

Marketing Planning

Nowhere in the organization is planning more needed than in marketing. The complexity of today's environment in terms of social, legal, environmental, economic, competitive, and resource constraints requires a high degree of skill to provide structure to a course of action an organization can follow to achieve desired results.

For the marketing managers, the marketing planning process becomes paramount. The marketing concept or philosophy has its major impact on an organization's operating procedures when it is reflected in the performance of the administrative function of planning. The customers needs are the focus of an organization's operations under the marketing philosophy, and this can be paramount in the planning process. Which customer segments will the organization try to serve? How will the marketing functions be performed? Who will perform them? What sales volume will be generated? These are all questions which are answered by a well-thought-out and carefully written marketing plan. In essence, the plan becomes a tool through which the marketing concept is implemented into the decision-making procedures.

The marketing plan does not necessarily differ in format from the strategic plan. In fact, it must cover some of the same basic topics—objectives, strategies, and so forth. The difference is in scope and time frame. The corporate plan is broad in scope and may lay out a strategy which is never departed from if successful. The strategic marketing plan focuses on the marketing decisions needed to support the overall plan. This is then used to develop the operating plan. This plan is a short-run plan and normally coincides with the organization's fiscal year. The operating plan deals only with the current operating environment and specifically addresses only important events that influence changes in the detailed tactical decisions in such areas as advertising themes, product changes, etc.

The marketing plan, whether strategic or operational, is a written document which contains seven basic elements: (1) purpose of talent; (2) a summary of the environmental analysis, including general developments, consumer analysis, competitive analysis, and opportunity analysis; (3) strengths and weaknesses; (4) a set of objectives; (5) a detailed strategy statement of how the marketing variables will be combined to achieve those objectives as well as the financial impact of the strategy; (6) sales management plan; (7) performance appraisal; (8) a set of procedures for monitoring and controlling the plan through feedback of results. An outline of the format for a marketing plan is shown in Table 1.

Table 1
Outline of a Marketing Plan

I. Purpose of marketing
II. Environmental analysis
   A. Market analysis
   B. Customer analysis
   C. Competitive analysis
   D. Opportunity analysis
III. Strengths and weaknesses
IV. Objectives
   A. Sales objectives
   B. Profitability objectives
   C. Customer objectives
V. Strategy
   A. Overall strategy
   B. Marketing mix variables
   C. Financial impact statement
VI. Marketing operating/sales management plan
VII. Performance appraisal
VIII. Keeping the marketing plan on target.

The logic of this approach to planning is clear: We must (1) determine where we are now, (environmental analysis), (2) decide where we want to go (objectives), (3) decide how we are going to get there (strategy), and (4) decide what feedback we need to let us know if we are keeping on course (performance appraisal). A well-designed marketing plan provides the answers to these questions.

The feasibility of combining products together for planning purposes depends on the similarities of the needs of customers and the similarities of the marketing variables required to meet their needs. For example, a firm may develop a plan for a whole line of products aimed at the same customers. Frigidaire has used this approach with its line of appliances and the theme "I should have bought a Frigidaire."

Integrating Corporate and Functional Plans

For planning to produce optimum results, there must be an interrelationship established in the plans developed at the corporate, business, functional, and operational levels. The logical flow of such plans is depicted in Figure 3. The corporate mission determines the appropriate corporate objectives. The corporate strategy is then developed to accomplish these objectives. If there are several strategic business units, each should develop a strategic plan including a mission statement, objectives, and strategy. These are referred to as business level because they relate to a specific SBU.

With most companies, a single set of overall objectives does not provide sufficient detail for operating management. Rather there is a hierarchy of objectives which reflects the specificity of the contribution of the part to the whole. In other words, overall corporate objectives would be expected to be more general in nature than business level ones. Business level objectives, in turn, would be more general than functional area objectives. The greater the degree to which the contribution of a department, product group, or product can be specified, the more specific the objectives.

Figure 3
The Organizational Hierarchy of Objectives and Strategies

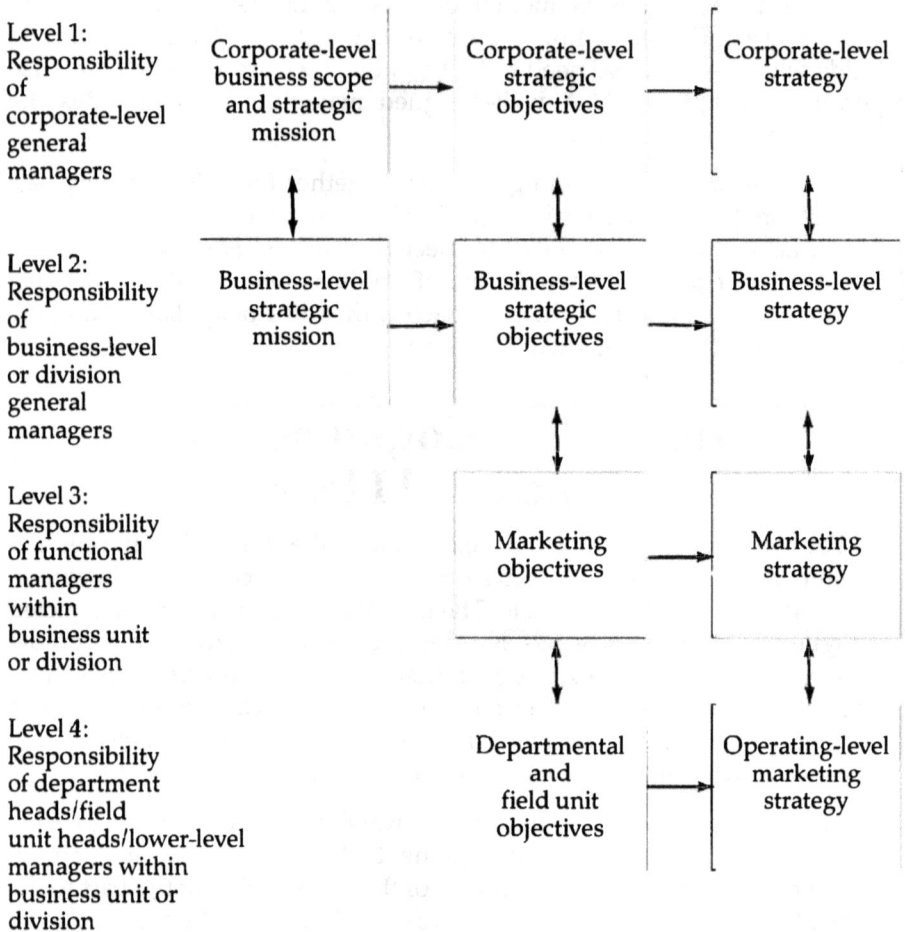

Level 1: Responsibility of corporate-level general managers	Corporate-level business scope and strategic mission →	Corporate-level strategic objectives →	Corporate-level strategy
Level 2: Responsibility of business-level or division general managers	Business-level strategic mission →	Business-level strategic objectives →	Business-level strategy
Level 3: Responsibility of functional managers within business unit or division		Marketing objectives →	Marketing strategy
Level 4: Responsibility of department heads/field unit heads/lower-level managers within business unit or division		Departmental and field unit objectives →	Operating-level marketing strategy

Source: Adapted from Arthur A. Thompson, Jr. and A.J. Strickland III, *Strategy Formulation and Implementation*, Third Edition, Business Publications, Inc., Plano, Texas, 1986, p. 58.

Although objectives may originate anywhere in the organization, the most logical sequence is to start at the top and flow down to lower levels in the structure. Knowledge of and alignment with this hierarchy is mandatory to integrate the total organization by fostering commonality of purpose and unity in decision making.

In most planning scenarios, strategy follows objectives. Thus the development of the corporate strategy follows the identification of corporate objectives. Just as there is a hierarchy of objectives which flows from corporate to functional to operational, there is also a hierarchy of strategies. Strategies in the functional areas (marketing, production, and finance) must support the overall corporate strategy.

The functional marketing plan, along with plans for other functional areas, must be developed to support the business level strategy. It is the strategic plan for the functional area. The operating marketing plan is then developed as the short-run plan which details the tactical decisions in the marketing area for the operational planning period, usually a year.

The interrelationship that should exist in this planning hierarchy is demonstrated in Figure 4. This figure shows the corporate, business, functional, and operating strategies for a movie theater chain. Note the flow from corporate to operating strategy. Each strategy is developed to support the strategy at the next highest level. However, the strategy development flows from top to bottom, i.e. the corporate strategy must be established first so that the business level strategy can be developed to support the corporate strategy. This flow continues down to the lowest level of planning in the firm, the operating level.

Figure 4
Integration of Strategies for
a Movie Chain

Corporate Strategy: Movie Theatres

Maintain and selectively expand lending nationwide position in the movie exhibition industry to provide positive cash flow for corporate diversification opportunities.

Functional Marketing Strategy

Seek only first-run films by outbidding competition in each local market, locate in popular regional shopping centers, provide family-oriented movies, and maintain an admission price only slightly above local competition.

Operating Marketing Strategy

Offer concurrent movies of varying classifications (G, PG, R) at multiscreen locations to simultaneously attract different audiences at the same location.

Price: Adults $4.00
        Children $2.00

Promotion: Weekly Newspaper
            Ads, Spot Radio

The corporate strategy is to grow through diversification from cash provided from the movie division of the company. The marketing strategy focuses on generating cash flow through showing first-run movies at multiscreen locations to generate the volume needed for profitable levels of operations.

The operating strategy is more specific and even specifies current prices and promotional plans. These short-term aspects of the operational plan may change several times during the year based on competitive moves, special matinees, or promotions. The lower price for children reflects the strategic orientation toward families.

There must be alignment of the functional and operational strategy with the corporate strategy. This assures consistency in the functional areas to support the overall corporate strategy in achieving organizational objectives.

Sales Management Plan

Everyone involved in executing the plan needs to be in on the plan. Cross Manufacturing brought all their sales and marketing representatives into Kansas City recently in order to get firsthand input on helping develop the marketing plan. That set the stage to develop the sales plan. The sales plan includes sales force organization, selection, training, motivation, compensation, and evaluation.

If you are involved in business on an international level, are you spending enough time drinking mint tea, playing polo, or sailing in the Riviera? According to expert business managers, time spent in developing a strong understanding of cultural norms and in cultivating relationships built on mutual trust and acceptance is of the essence in the international business scene.

T. D. Williamson, Inc. (TDW), a Tulsa-based international firm serving the pipeline and petrochemical processing plant segment of the energy industry, conducts 55 percent of its business outside the United States and is a proven example of how corporate strategies successfully deal with vast cultural differences. Employing a sophisticated strategic long-range planning process, each level of TDW's management works conjunctively with the levels immediately above and below to synchronize the agreed-upon objectives and strategies. When the top functional managers from all over the world convene annually to discuss the strategies and new objectives based on strengths, weaknesses, and environmental factors, they discover profitable opportunities and dedicate a long-term effort to capitalize on those opportunities. For example, during the past year, TDW has emphasized the strategy of maximizing its worldwide production capabilities by selectively placing orders in the factory having available capacity but not necessarily the regular source of supply. The customer will accept an alternate source of supply, provided he has confidence and trust in the individual with whom primary contact is maintained, preferably a national.

This is good planning and simply good management, true, but unless the corporate plans are carefully adapted to the individual foreign segments based on local custom, the company's options are reduced. In this particular case, an order to a foreign customer was moved from a United States manufacturing plant to a TDW plant in Belgium. The TDW Belgium plant is not running at capacity, and it is against the social fabric to lay off workers in Belgium as it is in the United States. Recognizing this, the order was placed in Belgium.

TDW managers have found that the key difference in strategic planning for foreign operations is the perspective time. In most countries it is essential to spend enormous amounts of time establishing personal relationships, building trust. This is where TDW does its homework. "You can't go into a foreign country with preconceived ideas. You have to play by their rules, use their methods to accomplish the ultimate objectives. If you don't, you'll get heavy resistance and probably failure," a TDW executive commented. He cited one instance in which he learned this lesson the hard way when he was setting up the company's operation in France. The home office wanted increased sales from particular key accounts, and the strategy was to take a typically American, aggressive approach to convince these clients of their need for TDW's equipment through seminars. After numerous frustrating attempts to build up these accounts, the French sales manager suggested a more relaxed approach, one in which personal relationships could be established through long lunches and participation in local social activities. Convinced there was a better way, top management moved the operation closer to the location of the key account companies. For a year the sales manager demonstrated to his clients his willingness to listen to their complaints and to participate in their pastimes—with satisfactory results. Trust was soon established between the two companies and sales for TDW began to soar.

TDW's manager of customer service commented that the same principles apply to the Middle East countries, which he says will continue to be the "hot spot" for American international business for many years to come. It is, therefore, vital that American business people understand the Arab culture and how the differences affect business management in those countries. "They need us and we need them. They need our engineering ability and we need their energy resources."

In Saudi Arabia, where the pace is much slower than in the United States, business executives must learn to like drinking hot mint tea. This is not an option. It is customary, and to refuse this form of Arab hospitality is a grave insult.

Also, to understand Islam, the religion of the Middle East, is to understand the law. Their religion is tied to everything. There is also a strong emphasis on family relationships. Because of Western dominance, the only stability they really know stems from family connections. This means that in order to be successful in these countries, a management team must first recognize the power structure, learn who calls the shots, and establish a local contact base—usually a family enterprise and often tied to a government power. These are the threads of commonality weaving throughout the Muslim countries.

Generally speaking, most Arabs are very capable businessmen. Females do not participate in social or business activities; therefore, to send a woman in a management capacity to one of these areas would be unthinkable. They love to bargain, and in negotiations they will never accept the first offer. Arabs just don't consider a transaction a bargain unless they have spent long, grueling hours haggling over it.

These extremely proud, emotional, and expressive people may have little concern for time, but they do place a high premium on integrity, trust, and service after the sale. A TDW executive remarks of the Arab businessman, "If you stick to the same facts without wavering, you'll keep his business, but he will always be checking you out, scrutinizing everything."

There is usually a good reason why a local custom differs from yours, if you only take the time to find out the background.

It has become apparent to the authors that for American businesses to successfully enter foreign regions, they must take time, *lots of it*, to understand the many cultural differences, and adjust their strategies to the difference in the perspective of time itself. This puts a new twist to the American adage, "Time is money."

This same advice holds true for North American businesses. Relationships must be established with the people you do business with. More emphasis in serving and helping, and less "selling" is important.

Keys to Successful Selling

The key to the sales management plan is *service*. The old "hype-up-the-sales-force" and "the martini lunch" days are over. Customers are becoming increasingly knowledgeable and sophisticated in their dealings with suppliers. Sales people should do their homework in their area before ever making a call. The first meeting with a client should be to get acquainted.

What are the needs of the customer? What problems is he having? What can the selling company do to improve product and/or service? Then *follow-up* like a bulldog. Increased sales start taking care of themselves.

Summary

This chapter has emphasized the importance of integrating the marketing plan with the overall strategic plan for an organization. Failure to integrate the functional plans with the business level and corporate plan will result in lower optimization in planning and reduce the likelihood of successfully achieving corporate objectives. In turn, such a failure can result in constant conflicts among functional managers as each strives to position his own plan as the driving force in the company.

References
For Chapter 6

Migliore, R. Henry and Walt Thrun, *Production and Operations Management: A Productivity Approach* New Jersey: G P Publishing.

This chapter is adapted from article coauthored with my longtime friend and associate, Dr. Robert E. Stevens.

As a reminder, objectives can be set in the following areas:

SALES

Total sales
Net sales per dollar of net worth
Net sales per dollar of total assets
Net sales per dollar of net working capital
Cost of sales per dollar of inventory
Net sales per dollar of depreciated fixed assets

MARKET POTENTIAL

Percent regional market share
Percent national market share
Percent world market share
Percent products in introductory stage
Percent products in maturity stage
Percent products in declining stage

MARKETING RESEARCH

Usually on a project basis
Objectives set on every project

SALES MANAGEMENT

Revenue per territory
Quotas/objectives for sales teams
Quotas/objectives per person

THE MARKETING PLAN MUST ADDRESS THESE QUESTIONS:

Where do products fit product life cycle?

How do products fit performance/potential matrix?

What is optimum product mix?

What is present contribution to profit per product line?

What is expected contribution to profit per product in 1995?

What products should be added to present product mix?

What products should be dropped from present product mix?

How do you react to a rapidly changing market place?

What opportunities are available due to changes in Soviet Union, Europe 1992, Pacific Rim, etc.?

OBJECTIVES:_____Marketing_____

OVERALL
RESPONSIBILITY:_____ _____ _____

STRATEGIES: ____ Product, Market Position, Distribution Channel and ____

Pricing

START DATE:	ACTION STEPS:	DUE DATE:	RESPON-SIBILITY:	STATUS:

OBJECTIVES: Research and Development

OVERALL RESPONSIBILITY:

STRATEGIES: Percentag eof p rod ucts in what stage of research

START DATE:	ACTION STEPS:	DUE DATE:	RESPON- SIBILITY:	STATUS:

Contemporary Marketing

What goes around comes around.

James O. McKinsey in the early 1920's used a creative strategy to get to know his customers. McKinsey throughout his career used the business lunch as an effective marketing tool. He scheduled lunches with a wide range of community leaders. The lunches were not restricted to just business leaders and customers. He got to know education, clergy, government and community leaders. There was no sales pitch. He didn't try to sell anything. He wanted to know how they felt about different issues. He was interested in their plans and problems.

Today McKinsey is one of the worlds most respected international consulting companies.

Marketing and sales for years seemed to center around developing a product and "selling" it to a customer. My roommate back in my single days was an IBM salesman. I recall in the evenings he would practice his "sales pitch." His presentation was polished, the handouts and support material were as expected, BIG BLUE quality.

The science and art of closing the sale remains today an intriguing process. From my perspective organizations worldwide used this process for selling their products. Guess what . . . the "new" trend in marketing is called by IBM COS, customer oriented selling and Xerox Canada called it solution selling. The "new" concept calls for going to the customer, find out about future plans, problems and products. The marketing manager in this last decade of the century has learned to be customer focused.

The key is to find out how your organization can help the customer solve problems, gain market share and be more profitable. With the information gathered, you go back and put together a multi-level, multi-discipline task force to see what specific products, services and solutions your company can come up with. This is not a "let's adapt what we have and see if it will fit approach". It is a creative, innovative look at the customer and perceived needs.

The "solution" might mean a capital investment. It could require a complete change in what you considered time honored policy and procedure.

Your customer is eager to have the follow up meeting. There is a keen interest in finding out what you have to offer.

This customer focus, whether you call it customer oriented selling or solution selling becomes one of the ways you differentiate your company from your competitor. You don't want selling price to be the only criteria your customers can judge you by.

The trend I see over the past few years is for customers and suppliers working together strategically for a common good. When I grew up working for my father in a Western Auto Store in Collinsville, Oklahoma, I recall one of his favorite themes "a good business deal is one that benefits both parties." Every organization that adds value to the product and/or service must receive a fair reward for their labor. There is a Biblical principle that states "A man is worthy of his hire."

The Three Reasons We Are Here

To keep existing customers

To create new customers

To make ourselves and our organization the kind that people want to do business with

---

Chapter 7
The Importance of Production/Operations Management in the Development of the Organization's Strategic Long-Range Plan

This chapter establishes the importance of the production- management plan and key operations officers in the development of the overall strategic long-range plan for an organization. Over the past 20 years, most strategic plans have been either inspired by marketing or financing. Little attention has been paid to the production process as the strategic plan has been developed. In many cases, representatives of production and operations management are not even involved in the planning and decision-making process.

Also stressed is the importance of the systems approach in coordinating the production plan with other functional plans as they support the overall strategic plan.

The objectives for the chapter are to (1) understand the concept of strategic planning for the firm; (2) see how the production manager fits into the overall planning process; (3) show how the production plan contributes to the overall strategic plan; (4) explain why the production plan is important and necessary; and (5) introduce the systems approach to the production process.

The production plan cannot be made unless the production management team can see the overall direction of the firm and how the production plan must fit the financial and marketing plans. The production manager must participate in the overall planning of the firm.

In my first planning responsibility as chief industrial engineer of a Continental Can Company, Inc. manufacturing plant in the mid-1960s, we went through the typical process. Everything started with a marketing forecast and then all other parts of the organization adapted their planning process to the marketing plan. This is absolutely the wrong approach. The marketing plan often can't recognize the financial implications, and most certainly has little insight into the production implications of some of its decisions. I learned that lesson as manager of press manufacturing at another Continental plant two years later.

As I drove down the Dan Ryan Expressway one morning, I heard an unusual "easy open" can being advertised for an automobile product. I remember thinking ... "I'm glad I'm not in his production manager's shoes." Later that week my boss informed me that R&D was coming in to start adapting equipment and running experiments for developing the new "easy open" can for an automobile product. Clearly production and research were not involved in any of the planning. The product was advertised to be on the shelf in a big Memorial Day campaign. Independence Day found the top research and engineering people in the company assembled in Chicago trying to figure out why the manufacturing process wasn't working properly. Poor planning, marketing dominance, and lack of input had created a monstrous situation.

A company might decide to be an international supplier of widgets. It wants to grow to a certain sales and profit position and be a leader in the international marketplace. With this in mind, the optimum production plan might call for production facilities near the customer. Service and fast delivery could have been determined as a key to the marketing plan. This results in higher manufacturing costs but lower transportation costs. The optimum size plant must be developed to serve each of the individual markets. In some market areas it might be cheaper to supply the market from a central plant, pay higher transportation costs, and let the market develop. Capital budgeting decisions must be made to ensure the right plant and that equipment is at the right spot to maximize profitability. None of these decisions can be made without a full view of the business.

Recall the example in the previous chapter from the motorcycle industry. A least-cost manufacturing alternative can have an adverse affect on the company. Standardize everything, make few changes, build to plant capacity, and try to optimize the plant capacity at the bottom of the long-run average cost curve. This produces a least-cost manufacturing product—in this case motorcycles, motorcycle engines, and parts. However, standardization contributes to replacement by competition. It allows entry by other firms into the lucrative replacement cost and repair business. The Japanese constantly redesign, remodel, and change after shorter production runs to discourage this kind of competition. Even though the engineering, research, and short-term production costs are higher, the long-term, overall profits to the firm are maximized. Many manufacturing executives have trouble with their strategies. I know I did early in my career with Continental Can. In that era, I don't believe any of us in manufacturing felt like we were part of the team. We fought for long runs and few changeovers.

Recall that the Japanese change their oil filter design every year on their engines to keep the big oil filter makers out of the replacement-part business. The money to be made in motorcyles, as in so many other products, is with the replacement-parts market. This is not necessarily the best strategy in all types of business. The main point here is to emphasize that top management must look at the long-term potential of the firm, recognizing the characteristics in the marketplace and the overall long-term best return on assets for the organization. Too often in our experience we rush into production and operations design, manufacturing, and quality problems using traditional approaches. The emphasis is to look at the total picture and to make the production operations plan fit neatly into the overall plan of the firm. The emphasis must be on the firm and maximizing the achievement of all of the firm's specific measurable objectives.

The eighth and ninth steps in the strategic planning process implicitly state that a firm operates as a system. Consider that a system basically is an array of components designed to accomplish a particular objective according to plan.

As the strategic plan is the expression of the firm's reason for being, so the goods and services are the expression of the strategic plan. How many types of firms or business entities exist without producing goods or providing services? Strategic plans are expressed in terms of goods and services. Examples: (1) capture a 25 percent share of the world market for widgets in three years; (2) develop substitute composite materials to replace aluminum in commercial aircraft within five years; (3) operate a motel chain at 85 percent occupancy level for next three years; (4) enter the hydraulic-valve market within two years; (5) employ wide-body jets in transpacific flights before Braniff is revived.

A very obvious void exists between the firm's strategic plan and the "goods and services" segment. The implementation of the strategic plan is missing. The missing segment is the firm's production plan! A firm need not be a manufacturer to have a production plan. Let's reconsider the aforementioned five examples of strategic planning items.

1. The firm desiring a 25 percent share of the widget market may not be a manufacturer at all; it may be a distributor for several brands of widgets. If in fact the firm is in the distribution end of the business, the production plan might well involve transportation and storage facilities.
2. Strategy to develop substitute composite materials for aluminum might be an aircraft manufacturer, an engineering firm, the D.O.D., or a university research department. Once again, the gathering of resources to meet the strategic plan is the production plan.
3. The objective to operate a motel chain at a given occupancy rate requires a production plan to provide for energy, maintenance help,

cleaning service, and many other related services.

4. The strategy to enter the hydraulic-valve market could be for a manufacturer of completed products, say pumps, or a supplier of component parts such as a foundry which would cast the valve body itself. In either case, the production plan would involve manufacturing processes, equipment and tooling acquisition, training of the labor force, provisions for raw material, etc.

5. The strategy to employ wide-body jets in its service would most likely be for a commercial airline. The production plan would involve providing for larger staging areas at the airports to be served, additional sanitation disposal service, and additional cabin service among other things.

The above five items all have one very basic thing in common. They all represent portions of a firm's strategic plan which are accomplished by means of the production plan. Without proper input from operations executives, it would be difficult for the organization to achieve its purpose.

It can be confidently stated that all strategic plans are implemented and/or achieved via the production of goods and/or services.

The production plan, therefore, is perhaps the most important segment of the total system representing a firm or business entity. A production plan exists whenever a strategic plan exists.

The absence of a formal production planning process results in an informal system in which companies inefficiently react to situations rather than taking well-coordinated and thought-out steps in anticipation of events.

In manufacturing environments, the production control function should play a vital role in the process of developing strategies and goals that will support the implementation of the production plan. However, a great majority of companies today still fail to use a formal system that could generate information to develop plans that other people could be held accountable for executing. This results in production planning and control becoming just an order launching and expediting function. This area generates orders, puts due dates on them, and then the expediting system tries to determine what material is really needed and when. This reacting mode creates an atmosphere of distrust, and many persons become dissatisfied because of their inability to work effectively.

A case in point is a small manufacturing plant in the southwest that produces a variety of highly engineered products for the process-control industry. No formal planning process existed. Marketing, engineering, and manufacturing all recognized that costs were excessive, inventories inflated, and that the customer was not receiving the kind of service that would keep this company competitive in the marketplace. This cycle was never ending, beginning at the first of each month and culminating with the month end rush that ineffectively tried to meet demand.

In an effort to resolve this problem, general management instigated a "production meeting." Representatives from marketing, engineering, accounting, production planning and control, and manufacturing were required to sit down four times a week for approximately two hours. These were middle-management personnel whose sole objective was to generate daily action steps that would end their inability to meet marketplace requirements.

Upper management ultimately recognized that this daily production meeting was not a substitute for a formal planning process. Management addressed the problem and developed a planning process that would provide the necessary information and decision-making capabilities to effectively operate the business.

This process became so effective that the daily production meeting became almost obsolete. The meeting is now held on a once-a-month basis in which each area is responsible for reviewing performances and contributing to the modification of future plans.

Objectives, strategies, and action plans must be set for equipment overhaul, preventative maintenance, check maintenance, and running maintenance.

An army travels on its stomach. A manufacturing company travels on its machinery. Good sound maintenance programs pay off in the long run. A manufacturing company either acts or reacts. It acts with sound maintenance, cleanup, and lubrication. It reacts if it just runs equipment until there is a breakdown.

Conclusion

For the firm to develop and execute an overall strategic plan, it must include top executives from the production/operations function. The production plan must contribute to the overall organization strategic plan. The firm can be more profitable if all functional plans are coordinated.

As a reminder, objectives can be set in the following areas:

MANUFACTURING/PRODUCTIVITY

Total output = labor + materials + energy + capital + miscellaneous input.

Number projects completed
Number projects scheduled

Units produced
Hours worked

Sales
Employee

Labor productivity

1. Items produced per employee
2. Quantities produced per employee-hour
3. Labor Index = $\dfrac{\text{equivalent employee-hours of output} \times 100}{\text{actual total employee-hours}}$

4. Labor productivity index = $\dfrac{\dfrac{\text{price weighted output (period 2)}}{\text{total labor costs (period 2)}}}{\dfrac{\text{price weighed output (period 1)}}{\text{total labor costs (period 1)}}} \times 100$

Materials productivity

1. Output per constant dollar of total material cost

Energy productivity

1. Output per energy consumer (BTU's)

2. Energy productivity index = $\dfrac{\dfrac{\text{output}}{\text{BTU (constant period)}}}{\dfrac{\text{output}}{\text{BTU (base period)}}} \times 100$

OR

Energy productivity index = $\dfrac{\dfrac{\text{output in current period}}{\text{output in base period}}}{\dfrac{\text{BTU in current period}}{\text{BTU in base period}}} \times 100$

Capital productivity

    1. Quantity of output per quantity of capital input

    2. Capital productivity = $\dfrac{\text{quantity of output}}{\text{quantity of capital of input}} = \dfrac{\text{units produced/day}}{\text{units inventory}} =$

$$\dfrac{\dfrac{\text{units produced/day}}{\text{machine}}}{\text{(process unit)}}$$

    3. Inventory within certain percentage vs. standard

People

    1. Man-hours worked without lost time from accidents
    2. Various other safety objectives

Quality

    1. Zero defects
    2. Acceptance rates vs. various sampling plans

Maintenance

    1. Overhauls

    2. Preventative

    3. Check

    4. Running

    5. Lubrication and Clean-Up

Cost Reduction
Continental Can Plant 50
Elwood, Indiana

OBJECTIVE:

Develop $25,000 in implemented cost reduction in 1967.

STRATEGY:

Develop cost reduction teams.

Set objectives/goals for each team.

Meet periodically as teams with coordination from I.E. staff.

Reward is dinner and night out for winning team at Elwood Country Club.

ACTION PLAN:

Task	Who is Responsible	Date Completed
1) Set meeting agenda	Adams	9/15/67
2) Tape agenda and notes	Bentley	In 24 hours
3) Plan Program	Daniels	10/15/67

(Note: In 1967 we installed $471,000 in implemented cost reductions against the objective $25,000. The next year I took the same approach to the Chicago Stockyards with similar results. I have used the same approach year after year, client after client. It works! (The keys are participation, recognition, objectives, reward, environment, and follow-up.)

Objectives: _____Purc h a ing_____ Overall Responsibility:_____Hamlin_____

1. Purchase price variance at 0.
2. Timely delivery.
3. Inventory at certain level.

Strategies: _____Neg otate ne w c otracts, interacti onwit h otbr deputu te_____
on requirements

START DATE:	ACTION STEPS:	DUE DATE:	RESPON-SIBILITY:	STATUS:
11/20	Inflation Forces, T all materials	12/30	Stewart	
11/29	Set purse standards	1/15	Camp	
11/29	Set up negotiation	2/1	Jones	

Chapter 8
Financial Planning and the Organization's Strategic Plan

Financial planning practices vary from very sophisticated, fine-tuned financial planning with a long-range focus, to developing a strategic plan and allowing the financial plan to take care of itself.

In some cases, organizations have financially driven, budget-oriented planning, but mistakenly call this strategic planning. This particular effort does not take into account the overall direction of the firm and its particular strategies in such areas as product mix, pricing, and diversification.

Granted, all organizations plan differently for the future, and, because of many factors such as financial officers, personalities, strengths, and weaknesses, the organization may use those persons differently in plan development.

These observations and experiences, along with a search of the literature, provide the basis for this chapter and a study of financial planning practice of corporation. Also discussed is how the capital budget ties into the financial plan.

Background

The financial implications of either strategy formulation or implementation are often given only a cursory glance or are completely ignored; however, recent environmental changes have forced many CEOs to question the viability, and even feasibility, of their originally developed strategic plans (Malernee and Jaffe, 1985). Malernee and Jaffe offer an integrative approach to strategic and financial planning. The authors give an example of how a company developed a strategic plan with a growth strategy that was impossible because of financial implications. If a financial plan had not been developed, the company would have followed the wrong path and realized its mistake too late after resources had been allocated.

Applications of financial analysis and planning models to strategic management have been discussed by Duhaime and Thomas. They define the concept of strategy and the nature of strategic problems, and then present a useful organizing paradigm of the strategic management field. Against that backdrop, the discussed financial analysis applications various financial analysis and planning models are reviewed, focusing on their usefulness to strategic management.

The relationship between formality of planning procedures and financial performance was examined for a sample of small U. S. banks by Robinson and Pearce. They describe how small banks without formal planning systems performed equally with small banks with formal plans. Regardless of formality, each set of banks placed equal emphasis on all aspects of strategic decision making except formalized goals and objectives. Results suggest that managers responsible for strategic planning activities in smaller organizations do not appear to benefit from a highly formalized planning process, extensive written documentation, or the use of mission and goal identification as the beginning of a strategic planning process.

Strategic planning tasks should emphasize the two dimensions of thought (Grawoig and Hubbard 1982: 9-10). Decision makers should develop the firm's overall picture. Usually one prepares detailed budgets based on chain reasoning models, such as financial accounting. Such an apparent paradox has led to some half-truths such as "Models are not much help in solving policy problems." Unless a problem solver conceptualizes the overall system, and unless he employs intuition and creativity, plans will certainly be inadequate if not outright failures.

During the first quarter, the corporate financial planning group should request each profit center to provide its five-year financial plan (Allio and Pennington). The annual objective should become the first year of the five-year plan. During the second quarter, profit-center financial plans should be reviewed, analyzed, and consolidated by the corporate financial planning group, and then presented to top management for review and comments. After necessary revisions are made in line with the overall corporate strategy and management judgment, the long-range financial plan is submitted to the board of directors for approval. The plans are updated for known changes and reviewed by top management and the board of directors each quarter.

The strengths and weaknesses of corporate-strategic planning systems have been reviewed by Allen, (1985). In 1979, fewer than 25 percent of respondents indicated that their companies had corporate strategic plans. When the study was repeated again in 1984, more than 75 percent said they had strategic plans. Five years ago, business planning was centered heavily on financial plans and objectives, and was relatively weak in the area of strategic analysis.

A recent study indicates that 48 percent of companies surveyed with over 251 employees had a written strategic plan with defined long-term objectives (*Wall Street Journal,* 1986). The study stated: "(1) a large percentage of the respondents did not use a specific financial leverage measure as a constraint on the mix of debt and equity; (2) a majority of the firms did not have a target financial structure that they maintained; and (3) many did not see a relationship between the use of debt financing and the cost of capital. Consistent with earlier cited research, a larger percentage of the large firms utilized the above mentioned concepts" (Lamberson, 1988).

We recently conducted a study to determine actual financial planning practices and opinions of practitioners in the field. The study investigated and then suggested how financial planning can support an organization's overall strategic plan. This chapter suggests how a financial plan should be developed.

Research Methodology

The data gathered and conclusions for the chapter came from three sources: (1) mailed questionnaires, (2) personal interviews with 10 financial officers of major companies, and (3) the authors' experience. The responses to the mailed questionnaires were entered into a machine readable form and computer analyzed using SAS. One-way and two-way frequency tables were generated as well as appropriate statistical tests such as chi-square and t-test. The following subgroups were compared:

A. Firms with annual planning meetings versus those with more frequent meetings
B. Firms that have five-year financial objectives versus those not setting five-year financial objectives
C. Smaller firms ($100 million in sales or less) versus larger firms.

Study I

A total of 78 questionnaires were mailed to members of the Northeastern Oklahoma Financial Executives Institute (Appendix B). The purpose of the study was to determine actual financial planning practices and opinions of practitioners in the field. A total of 38 responded by the cutoff date and their responses were analyzed. Overall results of the study are in Appendix B and are presented on the questionnaire.

The following 15 conclusions were drawn from the survey responses:
1. Few organizations (18.4%) do not have regular strategic planning meetings that focus on three to five years.
2. Of those with long-range strategic planning which focused on three

to five years, almost all (96.9%) responded that someone from the finance function is usually at these meetings.

3. Of those with the finance function being represented at the strategic planning meetings, more than half (54.8%) reported that the finance participant is very active at these meetings.

4. Those firms that had annual planning meetings generally did not set measurable objectives for the break-even point (16.7%), while firms with more frequent meetings did set measurable objectives for the break-even point (60.0%).

5. Those firms with five-year financial objectives almost always set a measurable objective for NPAT on net worth (93.3%), while those not setting five-year financial objectives were much lower (64.3%).

6. Those firms with no five-year financial objectives more frequently set financial objectives for NPAT on net sales (76.9%) than those firms with five-year objectives (42.9%).

7. Smaller firms ($100 million in sales or less) almost always (90.9%) mention current assets/current liabilities as a measurable objective, while larger firms reported more infrequently (61.9%).

8. Larger firms seldom mentioned break-even point (19.1%) as a measurable objective, while smaller firms generally did (70.0%).

9. Capital Structure was the most frequently mentioned function within the finance discipline for which measurable objectives were set for five years. Financing cash requirements was second and asset management was third. The most infrequently mentioned objective was foreign exchange exposure.

10. NPAT on net worth was the most frequently mentioned category for which a measurable objective was set. Current assets/current liabilities was second, current and long-term liabilities/Net worth was third, and average collection period was fourth. Net sales/dollar of depreciated fixed assets was the most infrequently mentioned objective.

11. Firms which set five-year measurable objectives for the finance function rated NPAT on net worth (profitability) the most frequently mentioned objective. Those firms without five-year measurable objectives for the finance function mentioned current assets to current liabilities (liquidity) most frequently and NPAT on net worth tied for fourth.

12. Larger firms mentioned NPAT on net worth most frequently, while smaller firms mentioned current assets to current liabilities most frequently.

13. Larger firms generally had annual planning meetings (62.5%), while smaller firms generally met more frequently than one time per year (62.5%).

14. Larger firms generally had five-year measurable objectives for the

finance function (57.9%), while smaller companies generally had no five-year measurable objectives (33.3%).

15. In the smaller firms, the finance participant was much more active (75.0%) as compared with larger firms (47.6%).

Study II

A total of 50 questionnaires were mailed out to the 50 largest public corporations in Oklahoma with a total of 24 responding. The purpose of Study II was to follow up and expand on Study I which had been sent only to members of the Oklahoma Financial Executives Institute. The questionnaire was expanded and improved as a result of the information gained from completing Study I. Overall results are in Appendix C.

The following seven major conclusions were drawn from Study II:

1. Most companies set objectives and have these objectives written down (86.4%).
2. Someone from the finance function is at the long-range strategic meeting (88.2%).
3. The finance function generally has measurable objective for one year (85.7%); only approximately half have for three years (50.0%) and five years (45.5%).
4. Examining functions within the finance discipline:
   A. Measurable objectives were always set for capital structure, cash management, and financing cash requirements. Measurable objectives are generally not set for foreign exchange exposure (71.2%).
   B. Internal auditing (47.1%) generally had objectives set for only one year.
   C. Capital structure (63.2%), tax compliance (56.3%), asset management (85.6%), and financing cash requirements (55.6%) generally had objectives set for five years.
5. Examining measurable objectives:
   A. The current ratio (current assets to current liabilities) was most frequently mentioned (66.7% - definitely).
   B. Net profit after tax on net worth and average collection period were second and third percentages.
   C. Net sales per dollar of depreciated fixed assets was least frequently mentioned (11.8% - definitely).
   D. Net sales per dollars of net working capital and cost sales per dollar of inventory were second and third from last percentages.
6. Liquidity was the most frequently mentioned objective (current ratio), with profitability second (NPAT/NW and NPAT/net sales) and activity third (average collection period).

7. The firms surveyed rated the effectiveness of their management team and their organization's communications very high. Planning in the organization and the performance appraisal system appear to need improvement.

QUOTES/OBSERVATIONS FROM INTERVIEWS OF FINANCE EXECUTIVES

1. Accountant/finance person is often not involved in the master plan—after the fact, or mostly used as a catch-up. He is generally brought in to confirm someone else's thoughts rather than at the beginning.

2. The financial person has a better chance of respect if he has worked himself up from the bottom. How the CEO views the financial person has a great influence upon whether or not he/she is considered as being a major contributor to the strategic planning process.

3. Financial persons are not involved in the strategic planning of most organizations.

4. The financial person is viewed as the weakest link in the planning process.

5. The financial plan is one leg of a three-legged plan; it should be part of strategic plan. There is no strategic plan that overrides the financial plan.

6. The financial plan is more a facilitator of the strategic plan.

7. Financial people are making a more significant contribution to the strategic plan, because now CEO's are less dictatorial and more people are becoming involved.

8. Some objectives will conflict, for example, in the case of cash flow and profitability. The decision will rest upon whether the firm is after cash flow at a particular time or profitability. Strategies drive numbers, numbers don't drive strategies. Measurable objectives should be benchmarked:

   A. Net profit after taxes on net worth

   B. Net profit after taxes on net sales

   C. Cost of sales per dollar of inventory

   D. Current assets to current liabilities

   E. Current and long-term liabilities to net worth

   F. Break-even point (% of capacity)

    G. Average collection period

9. ROI would rather use invested capital, equity, and long-term debt as investment base.

10. Our company uses net profit after taxes on net worth, net profit after taxes on net sales, and current and long-term liabilities to net worth.

Conclusion

The senior executive of the finance function should play a major role in the development of the organization's strategic plan. In this role he wears first the hat of a team manager, but uses his functional expertise to interpret financial implications into the strategic plan. The strategic planning group, which incorporates major functional areas, works as a team to define purpose, analyzes the operating environment, assesses the organization's strengths and weaknesses, makes assumptions, and determines long-range objectives (Migliore, 1984, 1987). After the organization's total plan is developed, each functional manager must develop a support plan to assist the organization in achieving its purpose and stated long-term objectives.

Proforma balance sheet and income statements should be developed by the finance function to support the expected results of the strategic plan. Cash should be managed strategically over the long term to enhance profitability and allocate scarce resources.

The survey indicated that the finance function was present in those companies that had three- to five-year long-range strategic planning. However, no conclusion could be reached as to the extent of their participation in integrating the financial implications with the long-term strategic plan.

Every organization should determine for itself the three to five key long-term financial objectives. These objectives should be reflected in the firm's overall strategic plan. Some measures of either return on capital or return on equity must be included. They join the firm's other overall objectives which might include total revenue, market share, productivity, human resources, and ethics.

The financial plan then should monitor all other financial benchmarks and ratios. If any of these indicators or ratios exceed a predefined range, they should be "red flagged" and reported to management. The overall strategic plan and financial plan should address the issues of which assets and divisions within the firm businesses should funds be invested, what is the best source of funds, and what is the best mix of funds. Also to be considered is the dividend or capital appreciation strategy to the investors/owners of the firm.

Recommendations for expanding and improving the study would include expanding the study to a nationwide base with a much larger and diversified number of responses. The expanded study could include questions to probe the extent of the finance function participation in integrating the financial implications with the long-term strategic plan. Also, the analysis of smaller versus larger firms could be expanded to examine firms in each of the sales/revenue categories. Different industries could be examined separately as well as possibly public versus private firms and profit versus nonprofit firms. Also, the number of finance functions and measurable objectives could be expanded. Examples of financial objectives from actual plans:

1. Bring accounts payable from 35 days in 1988 to 31 days in 1989.
2. Increase ROA from 5.3% to 6% by the end of 1989.
3. Increase profit margin from 0.5% to 1% by end of 1989.
4. Increase current ratio from 1.31 X to 2 X by the end of fiscal year 1993.
5. Increase debt/asset ratio from .73 to .55 by the end of fiscal year 1993.
6. Keep times interest earned ratio at no lower than 10 X.
7. Increase corporate PM to 3% by the end of fiscal year 1993.
8. Increase return on assets to 10% by the end of fiscal year 1993.
9. Increase return on equity to 25% by the end of fiscal year 1993.
10. Increase PS/DD GM to 25% by the end of fiscal year 1993.

As a reminder, objectives can be set in the following areas:

FINANCIAL

Return on Investment.

1. Net profit after taxes/net worth
2. Net profit after taxes/total assets
3. Net profit after taxes + depreciation + noncash expense/total assets.

Return on Sales.

1. Net sales per dollar of net worth
2. Net sales per dollar of total assets
3. Net sales per dollar of net working capital
4. Net profit after taxes/net sales
5. Cost of sales per dollar of inventory
6. New sales per dollar of depreciated fixed assets.

Financial Leverage.

1. Debt/equity ratio
2. Total debt/total assets
3. Times interest earned.

Current Ratio.

1. Current assets to current liabilities
2. Cash and receivables to current liabilities
3. Cash and equivalent to current liabilities
4. Current liabilities to net worth
5. Acid-test ratio (current assets-inventory)/(current liabilities).

Activity.

1. Inventory turnover
2. Accounts receivable turnover
3. Average collection period
4. Total asset turnover
5. Fixed asset turnover.

Market Ratios.

1. Earnings per share
2. Dividend per share
3. Dividend payout ratio
4. Book value per share
5. Price/earnings ratio
6. Dividend yield.

Appendix A

A study of the strategic planning practices of 62 major companies was conducted. A preliminary study of 38 (Study I) was conducted with a structured questionnaire and then expanded to 24 more (Study II) organizations. The results were discussed and more ideas gathered from ten financial officers of major organizations. The purpose was to determine specifically how both long- and short-range financial planning was being conducted. Companies with defined long-range plans have more financial input than those that focused on short-term planning. There is a different concept of financial planning in larger and smaller firms.

Information on financial tools used and other comparisons was presented. The authors concluded that a long-term financial plan must be developed to support a firm's overall strategic plan and that the chief financial officer should play a vital role in developing the firm's strategic plan. Finally, each firm should pick a minimum of three to five key long-term financial targets. All other financial ratios should be monitored and be part of the formal financial plan.

Appendix B
Results of Study I
Firms in Northeastern Oklahoma

The respondents had these definitions in responding to the questionnaire:

A. **Strategic Planning** is the philosophy of managing with a planning process. It is both a product and a process. The *product* is the plan itself. It is in writing and clearly defines where the organization intends to be in the long term, usually three to five years. The plan includes objectives, strategy, and the short-term steps to ensure overall success. The *process* is the interaction that takes place in developing the plan. Everyone involved in executing the plan should be involved in its development.

B. **Functional Plans** are developed to support the overall organization strategic plan. Functional plans include the following areas: finance, manufacturing, personnel, research, marketing, etc. They use the same philosophy and process in the strategic planning definition.

C. **Systems Approach** is a view of the organization as a whole with interacting subsets. The financial plan is an element of the whole organizational plan. Systems thinking considers the action of each element and that each action or reaction affects other organizational functions. The systems approach considers that a firm operates as a dynamic organism with all parts, or subsystems, operating toward the common purpose of the firm as stated in its strategic plan. The firm's financial system provides the implementation of its strategic plan and is a segment of the total system.

D. **Objective** is a specific measurable result that outlines exactly what is to be accomplished within a time frame.

E. **Strategy** involves how, where and when to commit resources to achieve objectives.

Study I
Questions and Responses

1. Does the organization you work for (or local division) have regular strategic planning meetings that focus on three to five years?

    Yes **81.6%**   No **18.4%**   Don't Know **0.0%**

1A. If the answer to question 1 is yes, how frequent are the planning meetings?

Weekly	0.0%	Semiannually	28.6%
Monthly	3.6%	Annually	50.0%
Quarterly	10.7%	Other (explain)	7.1%
		Don't Know	0.0%

1B. What are titles of others in the meeting?

2. Is someone from the finance function usually at these long-range strategic planning meetings?

    Yes **96.9%**   No **3.1%**   Don't Know **0.0%**

If the answer to question 2 was No, or Don't Know, go on to question 3.

2B. If the answer to question 2 is Yes, how active is the finance participant—on a scale of 1 to 5, with 1 being inactive and 5 being very active?

inactive	1	2	3	4	5	very active
	0.0%	9.7%	16.1%	19.4%	54.8%	

3. Are measurable overall organization objectives outlined in a few key areas for years 3 through 5? (Example revenue, sales, ROI, production, etc.)

    Yes **78.4%**   No **21.6%**   Don't Know **0.0%**

3A. Are strategies developed to meet these objectives?

    Yes **87.1%**   No **12.9%**

4. Does the finance function have measurable objectives for:

One year	Yes 94.1%	No 2.9%	Don't Know 2.9%
Three years	Yes 71.0%	No 22.6%	Don't Know 6.5%
Five years	Yes 48.4%	No 45.2%	Don't Know 6.5%

4A. Does the finance function have specific strategies to meet the finance objectives?

Yes **85.7%**   No **5.7%**   Don't Know **8.6%**

5. If the answer to any part of question 4 is Yes, are measurable objectives set for the following functions within the finance discipline?

	Yes			
	One Year	**Three Years**	**Five Years**	**No**
Capital structure	42.1%	39.5%	31.6%	5.3%
Tax compliance	42.1%	18.4%	7.9%	26.3%
Tax planning	52.6%	28.9%	18.4%	21.1%
Accounting policies	47.4%	10.5%	13.2%	15.8%
Financial reporting	52.6%	15.8%	15.8%	15.8%
Financing cash	68.4%	44.7%	26.3%	2.6%
Requirements cash management	63.2%	26.3%	21.1%	5.3%
Pension plan investment	18.4%	13.2%	7.9%	50.0%
Performance internal auditing	28.9%	0.0%	7.9%	36.8%
Foreign exchange	23.7%	7.9%	5.3%	52.6%
Exposure risk management	42.1%	21.1%	13.2%	34.2%
Payout ratios	23.7%	5.3%	15.8%	34.2%
Asset management	55.3%	31.6%	23.7%	13.2%

6. Are measurable objectives set for the following?

	Yes	**No**
Net profit after taxes on net worth	77.1%	22.9%
Net profit after taxes on net sales	58.8%	41.2%
Net sales per dollar of net worth	16.7%	83.3%
Net sales per dollar of total assets	31.3%	68.7%
Net sales per dollar of net working capital	40.0%	60.0%
Cost of sales per dollar of inventory	46.7%	53.3%
Net sales per dollar of depreciated fixed assets	6.7%	93.3%
Current assets to current liabilities	73.5%	26.5%
Cash and receivables to current liabilities	36.7%	63.3%
Cash and equivalent to current liabilities	33.3%	66.7%
Funded debt to net working capital	30.3%	69.7%
Inventories to net working capital	13.3%	86.7%
Net fixed assets to net worth	22.6%	77.4%
Current liabilities to net worth	25.8%	74.2%
Current and long-term liabilities to net worth	66.7%	33.3%
Accumulated depreciation to original cost of fixed assets	19.4%	80.6%
Break-even point (% of capacity)	33.3%	66.7%
Average collection period	60.0%	40.0%

BREAKDOWN OF COMPARISON IN STUDY I

Million

5.6%	$5 or less
0.0	6 to 10
13.9	10 to 50
13.9	51 to 100
66.7	over $100
0.0	Don't Know

Appendix C
Results of Study II
Firms in State of Oklahoma

Questions and Responses Study II

[4]   1.   Does your organization set objectives that are specific and quantifiable, and outline exactly what is to be accomplished in the future?

(86.4%)[1] Yes (13.6%)[2] No.

[5]   1A.   Are these objectives written down?

(86.4%)[1] Yes (9.1%)[2] No (4.5%)[3] Don't Know.

       1B.   How long are these written objectives for? (Check all which apply.)

[6]   5 years (45.5% said yes)
[7]   2-4 years (45.5% said yes)
[8]   1 year (63.6% said yes)

[9]   2.   Does the organization (or local division) you work for have regular strategic planning meetings that focus on three to five years?

(63.6%)[1] Yes (31.8%)[2] No (4.5%)[3] Don't Know

[10]   2A.   If the answer to question 2 is yes, how frequent are the planning meetings? (Check the most appropriate one.)

(0.0%)[1] Weekly	(33.3%)[4] Semiannually
(6.7%)[2] Monthly	(26.7%)[5] Annually
(20.0%)[3] Quarterly	(13.3%)[6] Other (explain)
	(0.0%)[7] Don't Know

       2B.   What are the titles of others in the meeting?

[11-12] 2C. How many are involved in the planning meetings?

Mean = 10.1 persons   Median = 10 persons

[13]   3.   Does the organization you work for have a separate strategic planning department?

(22.7%)[1] Yes   (72.7%)[2] No   (4.5%)[3] Don't Know

[14]   3A.   If the answer to question 3 is yes, how frequent are their meet-
                ings? (Check the most appropriate one.)

                        (40.0%)[1] Weekly   (0.0%)[4] Semiannually
                        (20.0%)[2] Monthly   (0.0%)[5] Annually
                        (20.0%)[3] Quarterly   (0.0%)[6] Other (explain)
                                                    (20.0%)[7] Don't Know

[15]   4.   Do each of your major divisions or functional areas in your
               company have regular planning meetings that focus on 3 to 5
               years?

                        (45.5%)[1] Yes   (45.5%)[2] No   (9.1%)[3] Don't Know

[16]   5.   Is someone from the finance function usually at these long-
               range strategic meetings?

                        (88.2%)[1] Yes   (11.8%)[2] No   (0.0%)[3] Don't Know

               If the answer to question was No or Don't Know, go on to
               question 6.

[17]   5A.   If the answer to question is Yes, how active is the finance
               participant—on a scale of 1 to 5, with 1 being inactive and 5
               being very active? (Circle the most appropriate number.)

               inactive   1   2   3   4   5   very active
                          0.0%   0.0%   26.7%   53.3%   20.0%

        6.   For how long does the finance function have measurable objec-
               tives?

[18]   One year
                        (85.7%)[1]   Yes   (9.5%)[2] No   (4.8%)[3] Don't Know
[19]   Three years
                        (50.0%)[1]   Yes   (35.0%)[2] No   (15.0%)[3] Don't Know
[20]   Five years
                        (45.5%)[1]   Yes   (36.4%)[2] No   (18.2%)[3] Don't Know

[21]   6A.   Does the finance function have specific strategies to meet the
               finance objectives?

                        (86.4%)[1]   Yes (9.1%)[2]   No (4.5%)[3] Don't Know

               If the answer to any part of question 6 is Yes, are measurable
               objectives set for the following function within the finance dis-
               cipline?

Maximum Length of Time Mentioned	Yes			
	One Year	Three Years	Five Years	No
[22] Capital structure	21.1%	15.8%	63.2%	0.0%
[23] Tax compliance	25.0%	6.3%	56.3%	12.5%
[24] Tax planning	26.7%	13.3%	46.7%	13.3%
[25] Accounting policies	27.8%	16.7%	50.0%	5.6%
[26] Financial reporting	27.8%	16.7%	50.0%	5.6%
[27] Financing cash requirements	22.2%	22.2%	55.6%	0.0%
[28] Cash management	42.1%	21.1%	36.8%	0.0%
[29] Pension plan investment performance	17.6%	11.8%	41.2%	29.4%
[30] Internal auditing	47.1%	5.9%	35.3%	11.8%
[31] Foreign exchange exposure	7.1%	7.1%	14.3%	71.4%
[32] Risk management	20.0%	6.7%	46.7%	26.7%
[33] Payout ratios	15.4%	7.7%	38.5%	38.5%
[34] Asset management	27.8%	11.1%	55.6%	5.6%

7. Are measurable objectives set for the following? (Circle the most appropriate number.)

			Avg. Score	Defi- nitely	Most of the Time	Some- times	Seldom	Never	Rank
[35]	A.	Net profit after taxes on net worth	2.24	1 (52.9%)	2 (11.8%)	3 (11.8%)	4 (5.9%)	5 (17.6%)	2
[36]	B.	Net profit after taxes on net sales	2.39	1 (50.0%)	2 (11.1%)	3 (11.1%)	4 (5.6%)	5 (22.2%)	4
[37]	C.	Net sales per dollar of net worth	3.53	1 (17.6%)	2 (5.9%)	3 (23.5%)	4 (11.8%)	5 (41.2%)	15
[38]	D.	Net sales per dollar of total assets	3.22	1 (27.8%)	2 (0.0%)	3 (27.8%)	4 (11.1%)	5 (33.3%)	11T
[39]	E.	Net sales per dollar of net working capital	3.71	1 (17.6%)	2 (0.0%)	3 (17.6%)	4 (23.5%)	5 (41.2%)	17
[40]	F.	Cost of sales per dollar of inventory	3.61	1 (27.8%)	2 (0.0%)	3 (5.6%)	4 (16.7%)	5 (50.0%)	16
[41]	G.	Net sales per dollar of depreciated fixed assets	4.06	1 (11.8%)	2 (5.9%)	3 (11.8%)	4 (5.9%)	5 (64.7%)	18
[42]	H.	Current assets to current liabilities	2.00	1 (66.7%)	2 (0.0%)	3 (16.7%)	4 (0.0%)	5 (16.7%)	1
[43]	I.	Cash and receivables to current liabilities	2.44	1 (55.6%)	2 (0.0%)	3 (16.7%)	4 (0.0%)	5 (27.8%)	5

			Avg. Score	Defi-nitely	Most of the Time	Some-times	Seldom	Never	Rank
[44]	J.	Cash and equivalent to current liabilities	2.88	1 (41.2%)	2 (0.0%)	3 (23.5%)	4 (0.0%)	5 (35.3%)	9
[45]	K.	Funded debt to net working capital	2.76	1 (41.2%)	2 (11.8%)	3 (5.9%)	4 (11.8%)	5 (29.4%)	8
[46]	L.	Inventories to net working capital	3.50	1 (27.8%)	2 (0.0%)	3 (11.1%)	4 (16.7%)	5 (44.4%)	14
[47]	M.	Net fixed assets to net worth	3.17	1 (33.3%)	2 (0.0%)	3 (22.2%)	4 (5.6%)	5 (38.9%)	10
[48]	N.	Current liabilities to net worth	2.59	1 (52.9%)	2 (5.9%)	3 (5.9%)	4 (0.0%)	5 (35.3%)	6T
[49]	O.	Current and long-term liabilities to net worth	2.59	1 (41.2%)	2 (17.6%)	3 (11.8%)	4 (0.0%)	5 (29.4%)	6T
[50]	P.	Accumulated depreciation to original cost of fixed assets	3.24	1 (23.5%)	2 (17.6%)	3 (11.8%)	4 (5.9%)	5 (41.2%)	13
[51]	Q.	Break-even point (% of of capacity)	3.22	1 (27.8%)	2 (16.7%)	3 (5.6%)	4 (5.6%)	5 (44.4%)	11T
[52]	R.	Average collection period	2.26	1 (52.6%)	2 (15.8%)	3 (5.3%)	4 (5.3%)	5 (21.1%)	3

Circle the number that most closely describes your feelings on questions 8-13.

[53]   8.   An organization should use the type of management described in the definition for strategic planning.

(9.1%) (4.5%) (9.1%) (36.4%) (40.9%)   Avg. Score = 3.95
1   2   3   4   5

DISAGREE   NOT SURE   AGREE

[54]   9.   I would rate the effectiveness of our entire management team as:

(0.0%) (0.0%) (13.6%) (54.5%) (31.8%)   Avg. Score = 4.18
1   2   3   4   5

POOR   AVERAGE   EXCELLENT

[55]   10.   I would rate the communication in our organization as:

(0.0%) (0.0%) (27.3) (50.0%) (22.7%)   Avg. Score = 3.95
1   2   3   4   5

POOR   AVERAGE   EXCELLENT

[56] 11. I would rate the planning in our organization as:

(0.0%) (9.1%) (31.8%) (50.0%) (9.1%) Avg. Score = 3.59
  1   2   3   4   5

POOR   AVERAGE   EXCELLENT

[57] 12. I would rate the performance appraisal system in this organization as:

(0.0%) (4.5%) (45.5%) (40.9%) (9.1%) Avg. Score = 3.55
  1   2   3   4   5

POOR   AVERAGE   EXCELLENT

[58] 13. Do you feel that financial planning is applicable and beneficial for your firm and the industry you are in?

(0.0%) (4.5%) (4.5%) (18.2%) (72.7%) Avg. Score = 4.59
  1   2   3   4   5

DISAGREE   NOT SURE   AGREE

[59] 14. Sales/revenue of your company or local division

Million

(1)	$5 or less	(4.5%)	(4) 51 to 100	(13.6%)
(2)	6 to 10	(0.0%)	(5) Over $100	(68.2%)
(3)	10 to 50	(4.5%)	(6) Don't Know	(9.1%)

References
Chapter 8

Allen, M. G. "Strategic Management Hits its Stride", *Planning Review*, Sept. 1985.

Allio and Pennington. *Corporate Planning*.

Bergson, L. "The CFO as Corporate Strategist". *Institutional*, 1980

Carleton, W. T. and Davis, J. V. "Financing of Strategic Action." *From Strategic Planning to Strategic Action*, ed. Ansoff. Chichester, England: John Wiley and Sons, 1976.

Donaldson, G. "Financial Goals and Strategic Consequences." *Harvard Business Review*. May/June 1985: p. 37-36.

Donnelly, R. M. "Controller's Role in Corporate Planning." *Managerial Planning* (63), 1981.

Duhainie, I. M. and Thomas, H., (University of Illinois. *Financial Analysis and Strategic Management*, published paper University of Illinois.

Grawoig and Hubbard, *Strategic Financial Planning with Simulation.* New York: Petrocelli Books, 1982.

Higgins, R. C. "How Much Growth Can a Firm Afford?" *Finanacial Management.* Fall, 1977.

Krackou, L. M. and Kaushik, S. K. *The Practical Financial Manager.* New York: New York Institute of Finance. 1988.

Lamberson, M. A survey of financial structure management practices of manufacturers: A comparison of large and small firms. Jan. 27, 1988.

Malermee, J. K. and Jaffe, G. "An Integrative Approach to Strategic and Financial Planning." *Managerial Planning,* Jan./Feb., 1985.

Migliore, R. H., *An MBO Approach to Long-Range Planning.* Englewood Cliffs: Prentice Hall, 1984.

Migliore, R. H., *Strategic Long-Range Planning.* Tulsa: Western Publishing, 1987.

Migliore, R. H. and Haines, S., *Human Resource Planning—a Competitive Advantage; A Redefinition of the Field.* Submitted to Academy of Management Review, August, 1988.

Migliore, R. H. and Stevens, R. E., "A Marketing View of MBO." *Managerial Planning,* March/April, 1980.

Migliore, R. H. and Thrun, W., *Developing a Strategic Plan for Production.* Tulsa: J. Williams Publishing, 1988.

Robinson, R. B., Jr. and Pearce, J. A., III. University of South Carolina. *The Impact of Formalized Strategic Planning on Financial Performance in Small Organizations.*

Stonch, P. J. and Zaragoza, C. E., "Strategic Funds Programming: The Missing Link in Corporate Planning." *Managerial Planning,* Sept./Oct: 3-11, 1980.

Vanderweele, R., "Expanded Role of Controllership in Strategic Planning. *Managerial Planning.* (20) 1980.

Wall Street Journal, Long-range plans. Oct. 31, 1986.

Acknowledgment

Studies I and II presented at Southwest Business Symposium, College of Business, Central State University, April, 1988.

OVERALL
OBJECTIVES:_____Finance_____RESPONSIBILITY:_____

STRATEGIES: ____Dept. Policy, Dividend Policy, Asset Management,____
Capital Structure

START DATE:	ACTION STEPS:	DUE DATE:	RESPON- SIBILITY:	STATUS:

Chapter 9
How Capital Budgeting Fits into the Firm's Financial Plan and Supports the Overall Strategic Plan

After years of experience consulting and working with organizations of all sizes and in a wide variety of industries, I have observed that in many organizations that there is lack of coordination between the capital budget, financial plan, and the organization's overall strategic plan.

Several years ago, the topic of capital budgeting and how it supported the overall plan was raised at a corporate budget meeting. The reaction was that no one seemed to be able to pinpoint the answer. Continued inquiry into corporate practices indicated that there was, in many cases, little connection between the capital budget, financial plan, and the firm's overall strategic plan.

Review of Literature

The following articles suggest relationships among strategic planning, financial planning, and capital budgeting. Each gives a different perspective of the relationship.

The article, "Financial Goals and Strategic Consequences," demonstrates how a company can check whether its strategic and financial goals are consistent with reality. Such an analysis may better prepare the company to make the right trade-offs among conflicting goals and to anticipate what the consequences of its actions may be (Donaldson, 1985:57). Donaldson lists certain characteristics of corporate financial goals systems that have often been overlooked and that contribute to misunderstanding of the goal-setting process. Contrary to popular belief, companies do not put maximum profit before all else . . .

> Mature companies assign priorities to multiple financial goals based on the relative power of the economic constituencies represented by these individual goals . . .

> Companies do not have an inalienable right to "dream the impos-

sible dream" and set any goal . . .

Managing a company's financial goals system is an unending process in which competing and conflicting priorities must be balanced . . .

A company's internal capital market must continuously try to reconcile the demand for and supply of funds . . .

Most managers find it difficult to understand and accept the entire goal system. Although financial goals appear objective and precise, they are in fact relative, changeable, and unstable. Moreover, subordinate managers normally see them from the limited perspective of their immediate responsibilities (Donaldson, 1985:58). By recognizing that all financial goals are interdependent, a company soon learns that a change in one demands a compensating adjustment somewhere else in the funds-flow equation (Donaldson, 1985:62).

In the article, "Financial Planning System and MBO—An Integrated Approach," Garg states a financial planning system (FPS) integrated with MBO can offer great potential for management. Furthermore, he says that an integrated FPS with MBO is a managerial process which does not sacrifice the financial good of the firm but rather instills in the employee a sense of commitment and desire to contribute to commitment and desire to contribute to organizational financial goals (Garg, R. C., 1983:29). Garg affirms:

The relationships between finance and management are intimate ones in principle. Management must have a comprehensive financial plan in order to accomplish organizational goals. At the same time, no financial plan can be effective unless it is integrated with the managerial planning system . . . Combining these two systems of managerial practice can help generate synergistic effects in the functioning of an organization. Both FPS and MBO are to be viewed as mutually reinforcing (Garg, 1983:29).

An integrated version of the FPS with MBO will help in setting financial goals which are mutually acceptable and feasible to the top management and subordinates. Both the conceptualization and the implementation of the financial plan will have the approval of top as well as middle management, as long as the participative management practices are followed (Garg, 1983:31).

Stonich and Zaragoza's article, "Strategic Funds Programming: The Missing Link in Corporate Planning," deals with an approach, strategic funds programming (SFP), that helps companies make strategy happen. SFP is a management system designed to help organizations isolate potential programs having an impact on the future of the business and then to make decisions about which programs to undertake. Thus, concrete actions are taken that affect the future performance of the organization (Stonich and Zaragoza, 1980:3).

Malernee and Jaffe, in "An Integrative Approach to Strategic and Financial Planning," state that the financial implications of either strategy formulation or implementation are often given only a cursory glance or completely ignored, but that recent environmental changes have forced many CEOs to question the viability, and even feasibility, of their originally developed strategic plans. This article offers an integrative approach to strategic and financial planning (Malernee and Jaffe, 1980:35).

In this article, "A Program For Integrating Budgeting and MBO," Babcock and Qureshi develop a methodology for operationalizing the integration of budgeting and MBO. They claim that both budgeting and MBO can be strengthened and mutually supportive by creating a unified MBO-budgeting system, rather than treating MBO and budgeting as separate processes. The result is the development and funding of operational objectives and budgets that effectively allow the enterprise to carry on its ongoing activities, as well as encourage continuing attention to supplemental activities (Babcock and Qureshi, 1980:28).

Dickinson and Herbst, in "Understand Deficiencies of Capital Budgeting Techniques Before Applying Them to Planning," attribute much of the controversy of applying capital budgeting methods to marketing decisions to the fact that the executives who use the methods do so without understanding the implied assumptions. These authors state that the mathematical theorists who developed the capital budgeting methods' assumptions are not based on realistic assumptions such as:

Perfect capital markets exist (that is, the markets appropriately reflect all relevant factors pertaining to the company and all firms have equal access to the capital markets).

Net, after-tax cash flows are appropriately reflected over the total life of the investment alternative, to infinity.

The singular goal is to maximize the current value of cash flow (Dickinson and Herbst, 1984:10).

The article discusses the payback period and the discounted cash flow methods: net present value and the internal rate of return. The payback period method is the time it takes to recover the initial investment. Or, stated another way, it is the return *of* investment. The discounted cash flow methods, internal rate of return, and net present value take into account the time value of money and are directed toward the return *on* investment. From the standpoint of marketers, for the discounted cash flow to be utilized more effectively in making decisions before the planning takes place, six guide-lines to use are:

1. Develop understanding. Being aware of the assumption of the DCF techniques will certainly give a healthy skepticism.

2. Establish different hurdles rates. Qualitatively attractive long-term alternatives should be subjected to lower rates of discount.

3. Set a low discount rate. Insist on justification of requests in terms of their impact on strategy.

4. Use a sequential procedure. Qualitative factors such as mission or image should be constraints on alternative investments.

5. Mix methods. There is no one best method of quantitatively eva-luating investment alternatives. Payback, average return on average investment, net present value, internal rate of return, and computer simulation all can provide useful insights.

6. Seek new methods. Marketers and others faced with uncertainty will have to develop new methods to suit their specific needs (Dickinson and Herbst, March 16:11).

In "The Relationship Between Long-Term Strategy and Capital Budgeting," Steven D. Grossman and Richard Lindhe maintain that capital investment decisions on the program level and specific asset level should be made in conjunction with the objectives, of the organization as a whole. To meet these objectives capital budgeting should be reflected in the short- and long-term strategies. The organization's long-term plan is less imprecise than the short-term plan. However, the organization must understand and monitor the environment in which it will exist and define its resources. Once the organization has done this, it can establish strategies for the short- and long-term plan to meet its objectives.

The authors point out two problems that exist with the present value model in the capital budgeting process. First, the measurement of elements by use of the present value model does not accurately depict the most desir-able alternative in a set of alternatives. They agree with Dickinson and Herbst that a mix of measurement devices is needed. Second, the present value model does not justify how a capital investment decision will interre-late with other elements or parts of the organization. They further argue, "the value of an organization is greater than the sum of its parts, because the special combination of resources and their use derives greater return than the sum of the return of each of those resources used independently" (Grossman and Lindhe, 1984:105).

Connection with Overall Plan

The strategic plan is a flexible, dynamic, and continuous plan that assumes a democratic or participative style of management. It integrates various plans by providing appropriate linkage between short- and long-term plans. Its purpose is to allocate scarce resources in order to ensure continuous achievement of long-term objectives (Vander Weele, 1980:17). The strategic plan's objectives should be specific, measurable, and in a time frame. However, there are objectives that are not directly related to the strategic long-range plan. For example, customer service could lead to increased market share but not be directly aimed at return on investment. The prologue to all functional plans is strategy. The driving force of all strategic planning is the implementation of strategies. After the strategic plan is developed, marketing, production, human resources, finance, and other support plans are developed. Mark Kirk, corporate controller of Purolator Products Company, said, "Strategies drive numbers, numbers don't drive strategies. Good strategies don't produce bad numbers—the unknown element is time."

Note Figure 1-2 which shows the relationship between these plans.

Figure 1-2

The Financial Plan and Capital Budgeting

The financial plan supports the strategic plan. It is that integral part of the strategic plan that permeates all other functional plans of an organization. The financial plan has its own purpose, environmental analysis, strengths and weaknesses, assumptions, objectives, strategy, operational plans, and controls. The plan contains projections of income statement, balance sheet, budgets, cash flow, and sources and uses of funds. It is a forecast of future monetary needs of an organization and the development of ways to generate cash flows to meet the objectives of the strategic plan. Its predictions and forecast illustrate what an organization has to sell or produce to *ultimately* maximize owners' wealth. The theory that a company's main purpose is to maximize shareholders' or owners' wealth is not always the most important issue. Financial objectives and strategic objectives are sometimes at opposing ends. Finance may have a need to decrease production costs while the strategic objective is to increase sales. Companies must assign priorities with conflicting and competing objectives. The monitoring of financial objectives is a continuous ongoing process. The financial performance of an organization depends upon how well the financial plan supports the strategic plan.

The classical concept of capital budgeting decisions is for the firm to accept investment proposals up to that point where marginal costs equal revenues. Firms are restrained from accepting all capital investment proposals. Projects are ranked and based upon some mathematical standard and undertaken until the point reached where either funds are not available or the project's return falls below the firm's hurdle rate (Sherman, 1978:28). Some projects are accepted qualitatively, such as those that are mandatory and/or nonfinancial proposals such as pollution devices, safety programs, or employee benefits. Some proposals are accepted so a company may remain competitive to maintain customer relations, or even to defend its market share.

> Capital budgeting is an integral part of overall corporate objectives, since the objectives provide a framework within which capital budgets must develop. A capital budget is a plan to achieve corporate objectives. Capital budgets may embrace such projects as increasing plant capacity, modernizing equipment, gaining control of a supplier or competitor, expanding a product line, or implementing other cost-saving programs. Capital budgeting concerns include allocating funds among alternate investment proposals so as to optimize long-term profits to the shareholders (Vaughn, Norgarn, and Bennett, 1972:3).

Only strategically defined, thoroughly thought-out qualitative and quantitative capital budgeting proposals will achieve the future expectations of the organization.

Capital budgeting is a subset of the financial plan. It is the process of allocating resources among ideas, projects, and products and then quantitatively and/or qualitatively evaluating alternatives to determine the best investment to be used in the financial plan. It has a synergistic effect; that is, the total effect is greater than the sum of two effects taken independently. It is the most dynamic aspect of the decision-making process. The dynamics of capital budgeting involves many variables. However, the variables are not isolated from each other. They must interact together with an optimal decision (Truitt, 1985:46).

Capital budgeting is at the very heart of virtually all financial planning. In many instances this perspective is not fully appreciated because the term "capital budgeting" has become too associated with the mechanics of DCF economics and yearly, short-term budgeting. In fact, however, key decisions of any planning process—short-term, operational or long-term, strategic — is the determination of which "project" will be funded and pursued to meet the corporation's goals. This is a capital budgeting decision; it is a basic part of planning (Hoyle, 1978:24).

Principal Mathematical Techniques Used in Capital Budgeting

Payback Period is the length of time to pay back the original investment. Advantage: simplicity. Disadvantages: does not recognize the time value of money or revenues generated beyond the pay back period. *Discounted Cash Flow Rate of Return* (internal rate of return) equates present value of the future cash flows with the present value of the original cash outlay. Advantages: Recognizes time value of money, provides for project ranking with the assumption of cost of capital, emphasizes long-term profitability, and recognizes cash flows beyond the payback period. Disadvantages: Trial-and-error procedure and difficult to understand.
Return on Investment (accounting rate of return) measures operations' performance by dividing the average annual income by the assets committed. It is used in planning and evaluation of operations because these functions are enhanced by the ability to examine the components separately. Advantages: Identifies ways to increase returns, is easily understood and offers a basis of comparison against results from existing investments and operations. Disadvantages: Does not recognize time value of money and the real difficulty of ascertaining a "true" income figure and an acceptable measurement of the assets committed.
Net Present Value determines the dollar difference between the present value of the investment outlay and the present value of the yearly cash flows measured against the firm's hurdle rate is the minimum acceptable rate of return. A positive net amount means the project meets the minimum requirements. Advantages: recognizes time value of money.

153

Disadvantages: Hurdle rate is difficult to determine and cash flows are assumed to be reinvested at a constant rate which may not be justifiable. *Benefit-Cost Ratio* (profitability index or present value index) is measured by dividing the present value of the cash flows by the present value of the original investment using the same hurdle rate as used in net present value. Advantages: Recognizes time value of money and establishes a "break-even point" of 1.0. Disadvantages: Requires additional calculations and no positive reference to time frame and cash flows (Sherman:31).

No matter how sophisticated the capital budgeting techniques are, they first must integrate four major analyses into the decision-making process (Sherman:32).

These four interdependent steps are: (1) the defining and the communication of a firm's long-range and strategic plans and goals, (2) the development of a system that permits the orderly gathering and ranking of investment proposal, (3) the determination of the accuracy of the estimates that become utilized in the estimated rate of return calculations, and (4) the determination and assignment of the probabilities of levels of risk to the investment proposals. It is only after due consideration of all these steps as an integrated whole has been taken that a valid "go or no go" decision can be made in regard to capital budgeting decision (Sherman:28).

Conclusion and Recommendation

Capital budgeting fits into the firm's financial plan and supports the overall strategic plan through its future economic benefits to an organization. Its prime decision-making factors are time value of money, cost of capital, and the inherent risk of each project/proposal. Our discussion targets fixed assets. Fixed assets are capable of being used repeatedly over a long period of time and used in the normal course of business. They are long-term present dollar commitments. The capital budgeting decisions to finance these commitments must be made strategically. These decisions are more than far-reaching, they are future reaching.

The consensus of opinion is that the ultimate goal of an organization is to maximize shareholders' or owners' wealth. Maximization is determined by a firm's use of assets, financing of assets, and planning and forecasting. The mechanics of capital budgeting: Payback, Discounted Cash Flow Rate of Return (Internal Rate of Return), Return on Investment, Benefit-Cost Ratio are all paramount to the success of a firm or company in its bid to maximize shareholder wealth.

Firms can identify their target markets in terms of geographical location, consumption habits, levels of income, and levels of education, and then create new products to maintain and increase market share. There is an underlying issue of who are a firm's customers not only today, but tomorrow? Capital budgeting decisions must address this issue *today*. As a starting point, one fact is established. The class of 2000 entered the first grade in 1988. How many are there? Who are they? More importantly, who are their parents? How many parents are customers of a particular industry? Parents influence children's purchasing decisions. Will the birth rate and life expectancy decrease or increase? How sophisticated will their level of education be? How consumer-oriented will they be? How will a firm's mission enhance their quality of life? Another factor that should influence capital budgeting decisions should be how a firm will favor in the coming external environment: short- and long-term interest rates, suppliers, local, state, national, and international governments and competitors, tax laws, and new legislation that will affect financial institutions.

The baby boomers are the largest consumer group in the United States. These people were born between 1946 and 1964. As this population gets progressively older, how will a firm's capital budgeting decisions affect them? How many are presently customers? What is their level of education? How consumer oriented are they? How politically active are they? What services will they demand? The class of 2000 and the baby boomers are two unique and distinct groups with their own inherent needs. These customers when asked the same questions about their needs will give unique and distinct and even opposing answers. Before the allocation of scarce resources become committed, management must take a hard and unbiased look at who are the customers, what they need now, and what they will need in the future. Consumers may need fewer nursing homes and more home health programs, fewer cars and more public transportation, fewer malls and more discount stores, fewer homes and more condominiums. These capital budgeting issues need to be addressed now, and not when the problems arise.

An organization's strategic planning must be receptive and take into account a changing society. The firm must have a willingness to communicate with economists, demographers, urban planners, social scientists, political scientists, health care experts, and others in order to monitor trends. Companies and institutions who investigate the above issues will be able to make a more profitable transition into the twenty-first century. Success in the year 2000 will depend on a well thought out strategic direction. The finance function supports this strategic plan. Capital budgeting decisions support the financial plan, and insure that capital is distributed to assets that are used as a base upon which the execution of the strategy is built.

References
Chapter 9

Babcock, R. and Qureshi, M. A. "A Program for Integrating Budgeting and MBO." *Managerial Planning,* XXIX (6) May/June: 28, 1908.

Dickinson, R. A. and Herbst, A. "Understand Deficiencies of Capital Budgeting Techniques Before Applying Them to Planning." *Marketing News,* March 16:10-11, 1984.

Donaldson, G. "Financial Goals and Strategic Consequences." *Harvard Business Review* May/June: 57-62, 1985.

Garg, R. C. "Financial Planning System and MBO—An Integrated Approach." *Managerial Planning,* XXXI (4) Jan./Feb.: 29-31, 1983.

Grossman, S. D. and Lindhe, R. "The Relationship Between Long-Term Strategy and Capital Budgeting." *Journal of Business Strategy,* Fall: 105, 1984.

Hoyle, R. S. Capital Budgeting Models and Planning: An Evolutionary Process." *Managerial Planning,* XXVII (3) Nov./Dec.:24, 1978.

Malernee, J. K., Jr. and Jaffe, G. "An Integrative Approach to Strategic and Financial Planning." *Managerial Planning,* XXX (4) Jan./Feb.:35, 1980.

Migliore, R. H., Hall, M. J., and Martin, R. T. "Financial Planning and the Organization's Strategic Plan." Paper submitted to the Academy of Management, 1988.

Schall, L. D. and Hatley, C. W. *Introduction to Financial Management.* New York: McGraw-Hill, 1986.

Sherman, J. F. "An Integration Approach to Capital Budgeting Decisions." *Managerial Planning* XXVII (1) July/Aug.:28,31,34, 1978.

Stonich, P. J. and Zaragoza, C. E. "Strategic Funds Programming: The Missing Link to Corporate Planning." *Managerial Planning,* XXIX (2) Sept./ Oct.:3, 1980.

Truitt, J.F. "Synergism: The Forgotten Capital Budgeting Dimension." *Managerial Planning,* XXXIII (5) March/April:46, 1985.

Vander Weele, R. "The Expanded Role of Controllership in Strategic Planning." *Managerial Planning,* XXIX (2) Sept/Oct:17, 1980.

Vaughnm, D. E., Norgarro, R. L., and Bennett, H. *Financial Planning and Management: a Budgetary Approach.* New York: Goodyear Publishing Company, 1972.

Chapter 10
Human Resource Planning—
A Competitive Business Advantage;
A Re-definition of the Field

The Human Resource Planning (HRP) function can lead to a competitive business advantage if an organization chooses to put its emphasis in developing an aggressive, spirited, well-trained and motivated work force.

This chapter traces the evolution of HRP and suggests the next stage of evolution is a redefinition of the field. HRP can become specifically tailored and linked to the four hierarchial levels of a firm's strategic business planning, as adapted from the strategic literature.

Further, this chapter delineates a specific and clear strategic planning philosophy and process that an organization could use to define its strategic direction and tie the human resource plans to it.

Finally, research is discussed that shows firms who strategically plan and manage using their people power have a competitive business advantage.

It has been estimated that the amount of change in the world that occurred in the first 85 years of the 1900s will be matched within the last 15 years of this century. As a result, every company today is facing radical changes in their business. For example, approximately ten million U.S. workers lost their jobs between 1984 and 1988. In 1989, 116 million Americans had jobs. Those jobs are a result of rapid change. Companies with 1-19 employees accounted for 28 percent of the job expansion and concerns with over 5,000 employees lost 13.5 percent. This occurred through a myriad of circumstances including takeovers, mergers, plant closings, deregulation, downsizings, etc., according to the U.S. Department of Labor. These internal business changes may include the downsizings, mergers, global competition, competitive pressures, technology, and government but also may include changes such as a turnaround, a culture change, a high growth situation, a total company transformation, new business start-ups, reorganizations, changing business strategies, cost cutting, repositioning and the like. The ability to successfully manage the complex change, stress, and human aspects associated with this have never been greater.

The need for proactive planning for a firm's attraction, motivation, growth, retention and/or contraction of its human resources has not kept pace with this amount of change in today's world. The proof can be seen in the large number of firms who go from expansion of their workforce to laying off thousands of workers soon afterwards. The planning for a firm's human resources in the broadest sense of those words can, instead, actually be a competitive business advantage.

The organizational area that is responsible for this planning is the Human Resource (HR) function. Within HR, the human resource planning field (HRP) has evolved into its present state over the last half of this century.

This article traces this evolution, and suggests that there needs to be a next level of HRP evolution in order for it to become fully effective, meaningful and relevant to the senior management of organizations. Only then does HR and HRP have the potential to become a bottom-line competitive business advantage for a firm.

This chapter will give an overview of the HRP field and its early developments. It will then explore the differing aspects of the field as it has evolved into a more mature professional discipline. The current state of the art will then be discussed along with some conclusions and a re-definition of the HRP field. Finally issues and barriers to the successful implementation of these new HRP concepts will be discussed. These barriers must be overcome if the promise of HRP as a competitive business advantage is to be fulfilled.

Overview of Human Resource Planning

The notion that a five-year strategic human resources plan is necessary seems to be a novel idea as we begin the last decade of the century. Paul F. Buller reports, "A few studies using more systematic empirical methods have recently appeared in the literature. These studies suggest that high levels of integration between human resources and strategic planning activities do not exist in most large firms" (Paul F. Buller). Stella M. Nkomo did a survey of Fortune 500 firms indicating that 54 percent prepare formal strategic human resources plans with only 15 percent using comprehensive systems. Few firms in the survey reported on integrated linkage between human resources planning and strategic business planning. Nkomo reports "What is clear from this survey is that formal strategic human resources planning is still in its infancy even among Fortune 500 firms. This result suggests that the literature is far ahead of actual organizational practices. The prevailing assumption of most line managers is that appropriate human resources can be found on short notice. Second, strategic planning for human resources has generally lagged behind planning for capital and financial resources. The human resources dimension of planning has been

```
┌─────────────────────────────────────────────────────────────┐
│        Assessment              Recruitment/Selection          │
│                                                               │
│        ■ Map-D                 ■ Sources                       │
│        ■ Psychological         ■ EEO/AAP                       │
│          Evaluations           ■ Interviews                   │
│        ■ Interviews            ■ Reference Checks              │
│        ■ Skills Inventory                                     │
│        ■ Performance                                          │
│          Observation                                          │
│  Managing Personal                                            │
│  Growth                               Compensation            │
│                                                               │
│  ■ Personal Values                    ■ Base Pay              │
│  ■ Career Planning                    ■ Incentive Plans       │
│  ■ Coaching          ┌──────────────┐ ■ Job Evaluations      │
│  ■ Performance       │  TDW HUMAN   │                         │
│    Evaluation        │RESOURCES PLAN│                         │
│                      └──────────────┘                         │
│  Manpower Planning                     Benefits               │
│                                                               │
│  ■ Needs Forecasting                   ■ Retirement           │
│  ■ Succession Planning                 ■ Vacation/Holiday     │
│  ■ Career Counseling                   ■ Insurance            │
│  ■ Career Planning                                            │
│  ■ Job Rotation                                               │
│                                       Training &              │
│                                       Development             │
│          Performance Appraisals       ■ Specific Job Skill    │
│                                         Needs                 │
│          ■ Feedback                   ■ Management            │
│          ■ Coaching/Mentoring         ■ Quality               │
│          ■ Career Counseling          ■ Generic               │
│                                       ■ Personnel            │
│                                         Development           │
│                                       ■ Safety and Health     │
└─────────────────────────────────────────────────────────────┘
```

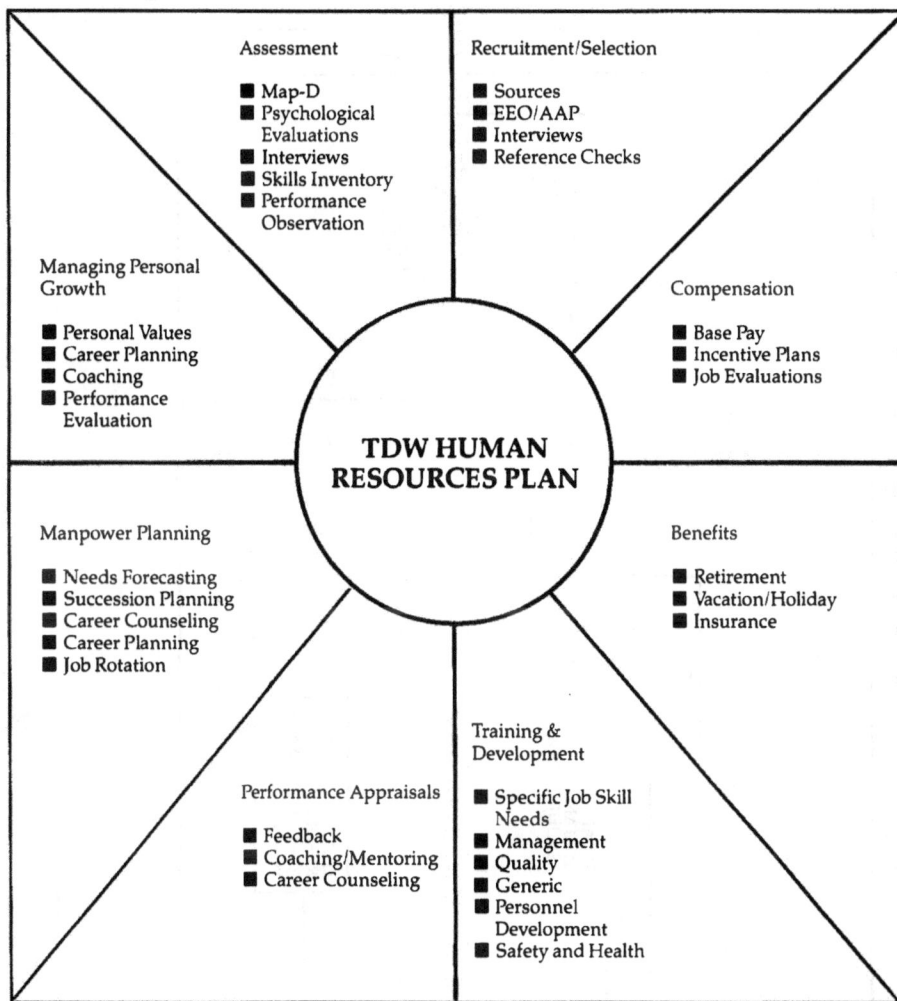

largely treated as a short-term implementation issue rather than a driving force in the formulation of strategic plans (Stella M. Nkomo).

Darrin Harwood, a recent Northeastern State University graduate, worked with me to determine how Muskogee, Oklahoma, area manufacturing firms were using human resources planning. We concluded approximately the same results as Nkomo.

After years of consulting work, I always notice that the human resources plan gets attention only after the corporate plan, marketing, production, and finance plans are in place. At this time I'm working with six firms on the

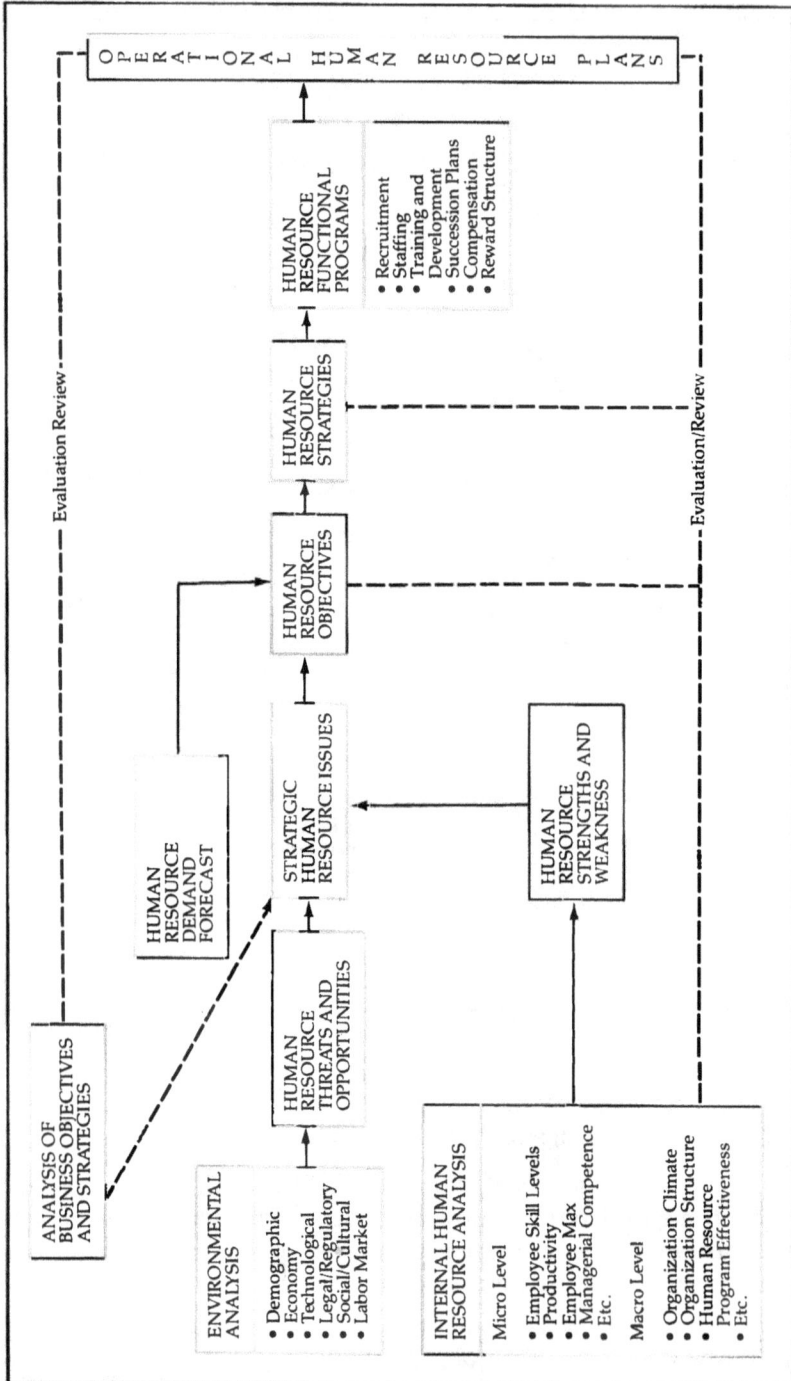

development of human resources plans. In each of these cases the other plans are in place. All are using the model in this chapter. The major theme of the chapter is that the human resources top person must be involved in developing the overall strategic plan. With all my clients, I make sure the human resources function is represented. Unfortunately, in most organizations the human resources function finds out about the overall plan after it is developed. This is a tragic and all too often made mistake. Fellow consultant and friend Steve Haines has been a leader in the importance of human resources as a competitive advantage. I worked with Haines developing a fully integrated human resources plan for Imperial Corporation of California. Another company with a sophisticated five-year human resources plan is T. D. Williamson, Inc. David Miller, Vice President of Human Resources, developed their human resources plan. The human resources plan fits into the overall firm's strategic plan. Note model one on the next page for the TDW plan. Also, note model developed by Stella M. Nkomo.

Anyone not convinced long-term human resources planning is needed might consider a few case histories. One large defense company bid on a big contract. To complete the project they needed specifically trained engineers. They got the contract and had difficulty hiring the engineers. A large multinational aluminum company had to scrap a big sophisticated computerized smelter in Brazil because there was no trained work force to operate the plant.

Any company responding to technological change needs to be planning for the inevitable changes in workforce composition and newly needed skills.

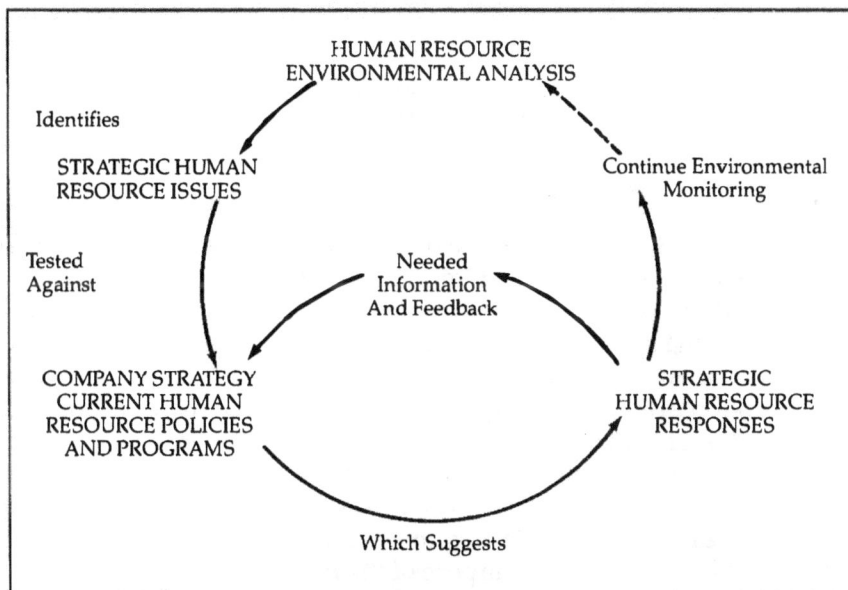

161

LEVEL	RESPONSIBILITY	FOCUS
Corporate	Corporate Human Resource Staff and Corporate Management	Organization Wide Human Resource Strategies and Policies Tailored to Fit the Corporate Mission and Business Portfolio Planning
Business/ Division	Divisional Human Resource Staff and Division Management	Human Resource Strategies and Policies Tailored to Meet Specific Product/Market/Customer Segments
Department	Departmental Human Resource Staff	Human Resource Programs and Policies for Each Functional Area (e.g., Recruitment, Staffing, Compensation, Career Development, etc.)

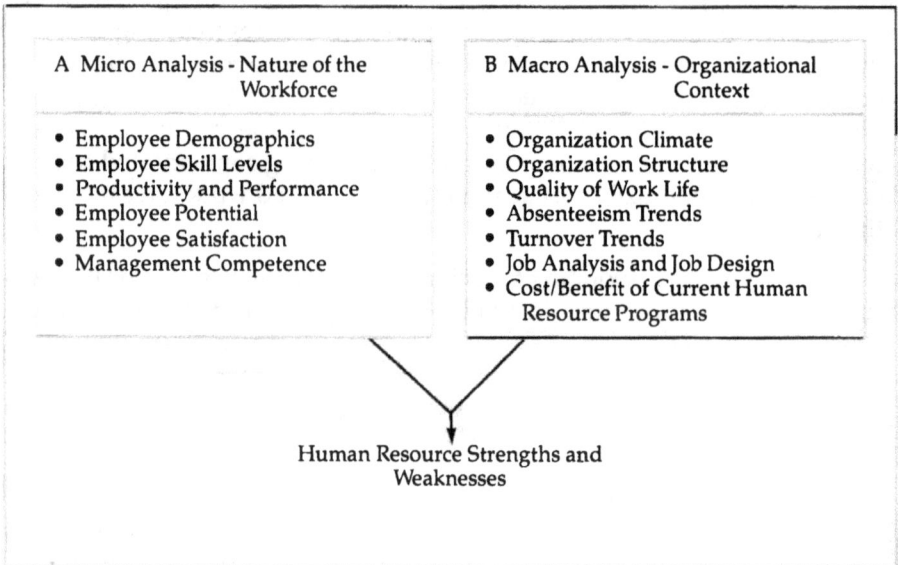

A Micro Analysis - Nature of the Workforce	B Macro Analysis - Organizational Context
• Employee Demographics • Employee Skill Levels • Productivity and Performance • Employee Potential • Employee Satisfaction • Management Competence	• Organization Climate • Organization Structure • Quality of Work Life • Absenteeism Trends • Turnover Trends • Job Analysis and Job Design • Cost/Benefit of Current Human Resource Programs

Human Resource Strengths and Weaknesses

Much of the growth of the field of "human resource planning" parallels the growth of its broader human resources field. The human resource field has gone through various stages in its own evolution that can best be viewed by the changing terminology employed. One of the first terms used was "industrial relations". It dealt with the very rudimentary need to have a small workforce during the early stages of American industrialization. Later, the terms "labor relations" and "employee relations" were used depending on whether or not you were unionized (labor was the union term). As these functions became written into law and a profession began developing around these laws, the term "personnel administration" became popular. It often signified that the main purpose of the field was to administer the necessary paperwork to ensure employees were paid, had benefits coverage, and the firm complied with the increased requirements of the labor and EEO laws.

In the '50's and '60's, as the need to be concerned about employees increased, the term "human relations" came into vogue. It often meant that the firm wanted to be more parental towards its employees. Finally in the '70's and '80's, "human resources" has become the generally accepted term among progressive companies. Ideally, this has meant that the HR function, has become a full strategic partner in the business. In many instances, however, this has been an unfulfilled promise. Changing the terminology alone does not make human resource a strategic partner.

Unfortunately, the same terminology problem has held true for the field of Human Resource Planning. The field is rarely a bottom-line competitive business advantage for most organizations today, despite some claims to the contrary.

While the evolution of HRP may have been over the past half of this century, it was not widely acknowledged as a field until Eric Vetter defined it in 1967 as:

the process by which management determines how the organization should move from its current manpower position to its desired position. Through planning, management strives to have the right number and the right kinds of people, at the right places, at the right time, doing things which result in both the organization and the individual receiving maximum long-run benefits (as quoted in Fiorito 1982).

Early Development and Evolution of HR Planning

The above definition evolved out of the literature on manpower planning, the dominant form of what little personnel planning there was in the 1950's. Manpower planning in the 1950's was usually just the forecasting of numbers of employees needed to run next year's business. This concept wasn't much different from that espoused by economist Alfred Marshall back in 1890. He observed that "the head of a business must assure himself that his managers, clerks, and foremen are the right men for their work and are doing their work well." (quoted in Walker 1979).

Even into the 1970's and '80's this manpower planning concept was the focus of popular articles in the HR literature (Berger 1976, Russ 1982). It was also the dominant focus of James W. Walker (1970, 1971) considered by some to be the father of HRP. During this time frame one of the authors was personally exposed to firms such as TRW, General Electric and Marriott Corporation. They all used a similar process called "manpower reviews" as a key component in their personnel departments' activities.

During the '70s, however, the terms "manpower" and "human resource" planning began to be used interchangeably (Walker 1973, Shaeffer 1976). It was indicative of a broadening focus for the field of HR planning. Allen Janger (1977) observed that the planning for the human resources of an organization was becoming more complex due to changing factors both external to, and within the corporation. These included items such as the changing environment, business strategies, growth and expansion as well as the demographics of the employees themselves. This complexity and the increased need for professionalism to deal with these issues drove the growth of this newer field of human resource planning.

In 1977, a professional society called The Human Resource Planning Society was formed; a sure sign that this fledgling field was growing. Positions for HRP specialists began to be found in the "want ads" and within Human Resource Departments. The authors believe that an accepted definition of HRP at this time might have seen it as a process of analyzing an organization's HR needs under changing conditions and developing the activities necessary to satisfy those needs. Thus, planning *and* developing programs to meet employee needs extended the previous more narrow view of manpower planning.

Edgar Schein (1977) was one of the first to embrace and extend this definition to include not only HR planning but "development" as well. Reid (1977) also reported on HRP at Xerox as "a tool for people development".

Differentiation in the Field of HR Planning

HRP began to have a number of practitioners differentiate their activities from their colleagues. "Work force planning", for example (DeSanto 1983), was seen as an idea whose time had come. He felt it would integrate decisions on the recruitment, development, and utilization of human resources into the overall system of corporate planning.

"Annual HR planning" also began to emerge as something that HR departments should do each year, just as one does annual corporate business planning.

"Executive continuity" and "succession planning" became other key concepts under the HRP umbrella (Mahler and Gaines 1983, Rhodes and Walker 1984).

The term "Management Resource Planning" was coined by Bolt (1982) for use at Xerox. It embodied this succession planning concept and extended the planning for replacements further down into the middle management ranks.

Areas such as "career planning and development" became associated under the HRP umbrella (Hall and Hall 1976), as did "performance appraisal," "performance improvement," and "performance management" (McFillen and Decker 1978).

At various times, other types of planning within the general functions of a human resource department were grouped under this new, almost faddish, concept of HRP. These HR plans included recruitment planning, merit planning, and affirmative action planning (AAP's) among others.

Finally, in order to further confuse the issue, training and development departments and HRP departments are often now called by a single new name, "Human Resource Development" (HRD). It appears this term is becoming a generally accepted one as the umbrella for the entire training and development field (see, for example, University Associates HRD '87 conference).

Current State of the Art in HR Planning

The critical need in the 1980's is for all of these various HRP activities to become more closely linked to the business and more relevant to senior management. While stated in various terms, all the needs expressed by these various types of planning techniques within the broadly defined human resource field have a common theme of becoming more "business oriented".

One school of thought currently looks at HRP from the point of view of the entire human resources function needing to do strategic planning (Goodmeasure 1982, Devanna, Fombrun and Tichy 1980). They included such activities as defining "what should we be doing, and how can we successfully do it"? They also developed a topology of five specific activities that HR personnel should help line executives plan for:

1. matching executives to strategic plans
2. defining long-run managerial characteristics of the firm
3. modifying rewards to encourage strategic objectives
4. changing staffing patterns to help implement strategies
5. appraising key personnel for their future roles in this (Devanna 1980).

Another school of thought about these issues comes from the field of organization design. It is embodied by Jay Galbraith (1973) who works backwards from business plans and strategies towards HRP with what he calls "organization planning". He sees this as more than structure alone. It also includes management processes, rewards, values and people (Galbraith 1986). Even the Planning Executives Institute has now begun to look at planning from a human resource viewpoint much as Galbraith has done (Kaumeyer 1984).

A third view (Miles and Snow 1985) focuses on designing strategic human resource "management systems" as the method for linking HR more to the business and its objectives.

Finally, some of the HRP practitioners themselves, through their HR Planning Society, have focused on the need to link HRP to the strategic plans of corporations. This Society has sponsored research in five major corporations regarding the status of HRP. It found both narrowly focused HRP programs with an emphasis on staffing as well as the more comprehensively focused HRP programs that were tightly linked to the main corporate strategic planning processes (Dyer 1986).

These comprehensive approaches included four key attributes:
(1) a wide range of HR activities,
(2) both a long and short range focus,
(3) covered virtually the entire corporation's employees,
(4) and had a formal planning process that looks at the environment, the business and the employees.

A number of other authors in the '80's have also looked at HRP from the point of view of integrating it with the organization's strategic plans (see Golle and Holmes 1984, Walker 1978, Ulrich 1986, Hennecke 1984, Kelleher and Cotter 1984).

George S. Odiorne sees the major tool of HRP to be the "environmental scan."[1] He sees most HR strategic planning as being environmentally driven as opposed to just market driven. He also sees it organization-wide, multi-year in duration and producing significant changes in the character of the organization.

A Re-definition of HR Planning

While the above may represent the current state of the art in HRP, a further elevating of its importance is only being written about by a few futuristic authors. Gould (1984), Mills (1985), and Ulrich (1987) all discuss organizations gaining a competitive business advantage through their employees and doing strategic planning with their people in mind.

This is a newer school of thought that links employees and the business together with a consequence to both the bottom line of improved business profitability, along with improving the long term organizational health and viability. This is the authors' basic definition of a "competitive advantage"...

A competitive business advantage is that distinct and unique edge an organization has over its competitors and substitutes that:

- the organization is known for, * cannot be readily duplicated,
- can be renewed and viably sustained over a long period of time
- results in a bottom-line organizational success and profitability greater than their average competitors over this time period
- while desired employees grow and thrive.

This competitive advantage notion may have a common sense appeal and face validity. However, it is relatively new ground for HRP and the behavioral sciences in general. They rarely have *explicitly* advocated people as a competitive business advantage. Despite being *implicit* in the value set of the field, it has not been one is which many authors have been comfortable advocating. The lack of valid quantifiable research data has been one key barrier to being more explicit about people as a competitive business advantage.

Instead, competitive business advantages have generally been seen as deriving from traditional business sources such as cost advantages, uniqueness of product, markets, customers or geography (see Porter 1980, 1985).

This article proposes a redefinition of the field of human resource planning to encompass this crucial competitive business advantage concept. Without this notion, the HRP field will continue to be absent from the room when the real strategic decisions of the firm get made. Hence:

Human Resource Planning is that integral portion of the organization's strategic planning process . . .

that deals with identifying, planning, monitoring and reporting on the attraction, motivation, development, reward and retention of desired employees . . .

and results in a sustainable bottom-line competitive business advantage

along with the constant renewal of the organization's health, human spirit, and vitality.

This far-reaching definition of HRP is currently an ideal except for, perhaps, a few of the excellent companies in the recent management literature (see Peters, 1982, 1985, O'Toole 1981, 1985, Waterman 1987). However, to the majority of American companies, this common sense viewpoint that "people are our most important asset" remains an ideal rather than a proven reality. The implications of this gap present an enormous challenge to HR executives and HRP practitioners if they want to make their partnership with senior line management become a reality.

The enormous challenge, discipline and persistence involved in showing senior line management that human resource programs and practices can produce a competitive business advantage in the marketplace is not minimized by any means. This challenge is due to the fact that the ultimate ownership understanding and implementation of this concept (and the outputs of any strategic planning process) are the responsibility of line management.

However, research by Hay Associates, the Institute of Social Research at the University of Michigan, Schuster, and others (see Haines 1987) are now documenting the fact that paying attention to the human side of an organization does result in a competitive business advantage. Interesting enough, Porter (1987) is beginning to agree with this in his strategic planning research, as shown below.

Levels of Strategic Planning

The ability to discuss HRP as a competitive business advantage depends on the level of planning one is discussing. Porter, for example discusses some of these levels in his 1987 Harvard Business Review article. As adapted by the authors, there are actually four levels of business strategies for any organization (see Figure 1).

These include:

LEVEL 1. Corporate Strategy—which is the buying and selling of assets representing businesses in which one desires to compete. Porter lists four (4) main corporate strategy alternatives as a result of his research on 33 large, prestigious U.S. companies from 1950-1986. These strategies include portfolio management, restructuring, transferring skills or sharing activities. He concluded that the track record of corporate strategies is dismal in that they have generally dissipated instead of created shareholder value.

Figure 1.

HUMAN RESOURCES ROLES IN BUSINESS STRATEGIES AND PLANS

– Stephen G. Haines, 1988

BUSINESS STRATEGY LEVELS	HR STRATEGIC ROLE

1. Corporate Strategy
   - Portfolio management (buy/sell assets)
   - Restructuring assets
	1. People/Organization Placement
	   - Industry characteristics (mission formulation)
	   - Transferring employees
	   - Sharing resources
	   - Executive selection
	   - Organization design
	   - Values audit (executive vs. employees)

2. Business Unit Strategy (SBU)
   - Competitive strategies
   - Market
   - Product
   - Financial
   - Employee
   - Manufacturing
   - Miscellaneous
	2a. Employee-Driven Strategies
	   (create a competitive advantage through employees)
	   - Quality
	   - Customer service
	   - Productivity
	   - Selling Channels
	
	  b. HR Involvement in any Potential Strategy
	   - Environmental scanning
	   - Performance/gap audit

3. Functional Strategies
   - All functions
   - Tactical planning
   - Operational planning
	3. Human Resource Strategies
	   - Implementing corporate/SBU strategies
	   - Organization success profile (OSP) of key systems/programs

4. Strategic Management
   - Implementation
   - Leadership
   - Persistence
	4. Change/Transition Management
	   - Transition technology
	   - Organization models/fit
	   - Organizational behavior/assumptions
	   - Organization development
	   - Management training
	   - Human resource development
	   - Action-research
	   - Unfiltered feedback/renewal
	   - Executive advice

Figure 2.

BUSINESS STRATEGIES

I. PRODUCT STRATEGIES
1. Product/service applications
2. Product uniqueness
3. Technology
4. Patents

II. MARKET STRATEGIES
5. Geographic niche
6. Customer segment
7. Marketing effectiveness
8. Large market share

III. FINANCIAL STRATEGIES
9. Low cost price leadership
10. Economies of scale
11. Capital structure
12. Diversification

IV. SPECIAL CIRCUMSTANCES
13. Unique distribution channels
14. Vertical integration
15. Natural resources
16. Production capacity

V. EMPLOYEE DRIVEN
17. Unsurpassed customer service
18. Employee productivity
19. High quality reputation
20. Unique selling channels

LEVEL 2. Business Unit Strategy—or the familiar Strategic Business Unit (SBU) where specific competitive strategies are chosen. A list of competitive strategies in Figure 2 has been distilled from research in this area by one of the authors.

It includes the following strategic categories; (1) markets, (2) products, (3) financial, (4) employee driven, and (5) special circumstances such as manufacturing.

LEVEL 3. Functional Strategies—which include the planning for traditional functions such as finance, marketing, manufacturing, legal, data processing, human resources and the like. While this level of strategies goes by a number of different names such as tactical or operational planning, it is still a strategic set of decisions for the functional executive. It is this area that is most confusing within the HRP literature. Many authors and organizations who focus on HRP or "HR Strategic Planning" are really talking about this level of business planning; strategic from the point of view of the functional executive or department, but far different than the Corporate or SBU strategies of levels 1 and 2.

LEVEL 4. Strategic Management—or implementation of all the strategies set at the higher levels 1, 2, and 3 above. This is the chaotic and difficult task of actually turning strategic plans into reality. It open requires changing an entire organization, a very difficult and time consuming task.

These four levels of strategy have enormous consequences for HR Planning. In order for HR Planning to become a bottomline competitive business advantage, it must, by definition be closely tied in some fashion to an "organization's strategic planning process" (as stated in the authors' redefinition of the field of HRP). The tying of HRP to the organization's strategy

170

depends on what level of strategy one is dealing with; whether it is corporate, SBU, functional, or just strategic management and implementation.

In summary, the concept of strategic planning and the links of HRP to it are not as simple as one would like them to be in today's global world. It is now necessary to articulate the HRP linkages to each level of strategy.

Links to Level One: Corporate Strategy

At this highest level of strategy, the issue for the HR Executive is to understand and be a partner in the organization's complete corporate-wide strategic planning process. One of the more typical strategic planning processes is a model I first presented in 1974. It has since been refined over the years through positive study and work in the field of strategic planning (Migliore 1974, 1984, 1986, 1987, 1988). See Figure 3 for details. This model is being effectively used in a wide range of organizations; not only in the private sector, but also with nonprofit organizations such as hospitals, the public sector and ministries.

Figure 3

Strategic Planning Process

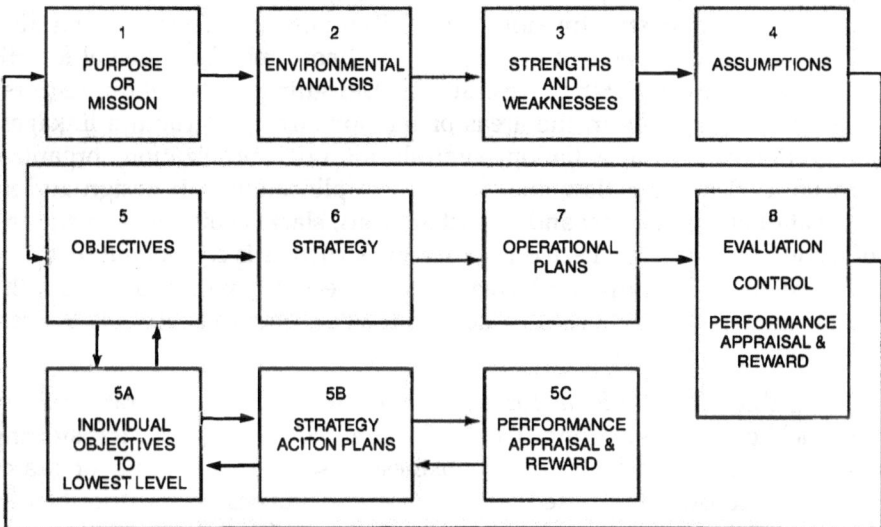

This process covered in earlier chapters and reviewed again here begins with an organization's purpose or mission, next goes through an environmental analysis, the strengths and weaknesses of the firm, and then all the way through the objectives, operational plans, evaluation and rewards. While this process is more fully described in the referenced texts, the role of the HR Executive as a partner in this strategic process depends on the strategy level with which one is involved.

To illustrate, at the Corporate strategy level, there are three main areas of focus for HR Planning. The first is the area of examining the structure and main characteristics of the industry under consideration in order to decide if the mission of the overall corporation should include doing business in this industry. For example, looking at the types and number of employees needed along with their values compared to those of senior management, is crucial to determining whether the corporation's mission includes a particular industry.

Further, the demographics and the values of today's work force have changed dramatically over the past few years. Key issues include the baby boom, baby bust, aging population, employee rights, women in the work force, a greater number of Hispanics, etc. Yankelovich's *New Rules* (1981) has more information on this subject. However, the issue is clear; to determine what is senior management getting themselves in for by entering a particular industry.

The second HRP area of corporate strategy focus is the arena of organization design. It is not just a given that the buying and selling of assets will result in the proper structure for the overall corporation. The understanding of the structural aspects of organizational theory may be unusual for HR Executives to learn, but they are essential. Designing organizations requires knowledge and skills in the areas of mission-strategy-structure linkages, integration and differentiation, centralization-decentralization, organization life cycles, work flow analysis and simplification, job design and its motivational impact, cost and impact analysis, slack resources, and sharing of resources. The issue here is not that one structure is correct but that they all have their strengths and weaknesses. Deciding which problems the senior management chooses to deal with as barriers to success is the real question.

The third areas of focus for an HR Executive during corporate strategy level deliberations is staffing. This includes executive selection, transferring employees into newly acquired business assets, and sharing of scarce employee resources. These activities are also advocated as priorities by Michael Porter (1987) in order to ensure a proper fit of the executives and other employees with the mission-strategy-structural analysis above. Despite much HR preoccupation with developing human resources, initial selection and job-fit is still much more important to overall organizational success, especially at this level.

Links to Level Two: Business Unit Strategy

The HR Executive's issue of being involved in the strategic planning process at this level is similar and yet different from level one. It is similar in that the strategic planning *process* in Figure 3 is the same one at this level. However, while Figure 2 lists the 20 possible strategies an SBU might select, four of them are "employee-driven" strategies. These four are much more fundamentally dependent on employees to achieve success. They include quality, customer service, productivity, and selling channels (see Figure 4 for a graphic illustration).

Figure 4.

ORGANIZATION GOALS AND EMPLOYEE NEEDS
A Unique Competitive Advantage

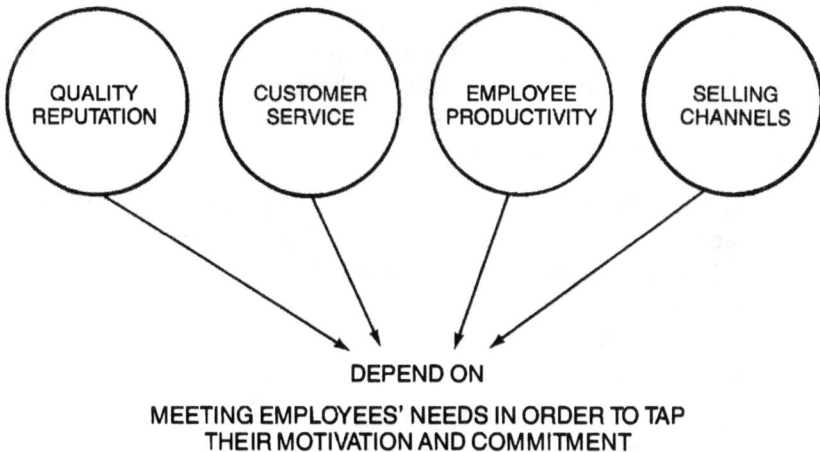

QUALITY REPUTATION   CUSTOMER SERVICE   EMPLOYEE PRODUCTIVITY   SELLING CHANNELS

DEPEND ON
MEETING EMPLOYEES' NEEDS IN ORDER TO TAP
THEIR MOTIVATION AND COMMITMENT

As a example, Ford Motor Company is known for its slogan of "Quality is Job One", and Chrysler for its seven-year, 70,000 mile warranty. Customer service is the hallmark of Marriott Corporation, McDonalds, and Nordstrom's department stores. Productivity as a strategy is key to many Japanese firms. Their car manufacturers can produce a car for half the labor costs of U.S. auto manufacturers. Finally, Tupperware, Avon and encyclopedia companies are known for their unique selling channels.

In all of these employee-driven strategies, the involvement, knowledge and skills of the professional HR Planner and others in HR associated fields is at the core of how to make these strategies succeed.

However, the HR Executive's involvement and role in the selection of the other nonemployee driven strategy choices of Figure 2 is also crucial. HR brings key information and expertise to the table during the phases of Figure 3's strategic planning process concerning (1) environmental analysis (or scanning), (2) strengths and weaknesses (or performance audits and gap analysis), as well as at the (3) mission or purpose formulation (including values audits). This is crucial to determining the final objectives, strategies and operational/tactical/functional plans later in the strategic planning process.

Links to Level Three: Functional Strategy

In actual practice over the years, there is a lack of coordination of the production, marketing and finance plans with overall corporate as well as SBU strategic planning processes. It was apparent that this same fundamental link to the strategies was needed for a firm's people plans *regardless* of the acutal SBU and Corporate strategies chosen. in concept, all of these business functions and departments above should link to the overall corporate and SBU strategic plans in similar fashions.

In regards to HR Planning at this functional strategy level, it needs to occur in exactly the same manner and steps as the strategic planning process in Figure 3. HR Functional Plans must first define their purpose or mission. Next a scan of the external and internal environment must be accomplished, resulting in a diagnosing of the firm's people-related strengths and weaknesses. The rest of the planning steps follow.

Figure 5 shows this overall HR Planning process in detail and how it mirrors the strategic planning process noted in Figure 3.

Of special note, is the need to set clearly defined and measurable objectives just as executives do in finance, operations and the other business functions. Allowing soft and vague phrases such as "improve the productivity, morale, satisfaction, (or whatever) of our human resources" is no more acceptable here than in the other business functions.

There are many areas of the previously cited HR Planning definition where specific objectives can be developed. Each firm's HR Planning process must have its senior executives select their own unique objectives that fit for them. However, in the experience of the authors, areas such as turnover, training, rewards for performance, benefits, compensation levels, wellness levels, survey results, internal advancement, manpower forecasts, recruiting costs, succession candidates, etc. are all examples of areas where firms have successfully set objectives.

Success in HRP must be measurable over both the short and long term. All members of the senior management and human resource staffs must be active participants in this objective-setting process. This is key if an organization is to achieve HR Plannings' maximum potential as a competitive business advantage. This is true regardless of the strategies chosen at the higher strategy levels 1 and 2.

Conclusion

With all the expected, predictable changes coming between now and the year 2000 in the human resource area, organization must be planning now on how to cope with this change. Changing regulations and laws such as the 1993 family leave legislation require proactive, not reactive H.R. planning. Who knows what effects the Clinton Health reform will have on organizations. The only way to manage this changing environment is with a well thought out comprehensive, co-ordinated H.R. plan.

Figure 5
(AS A COMPETITIVE BUSINESS ADVANTAGE)

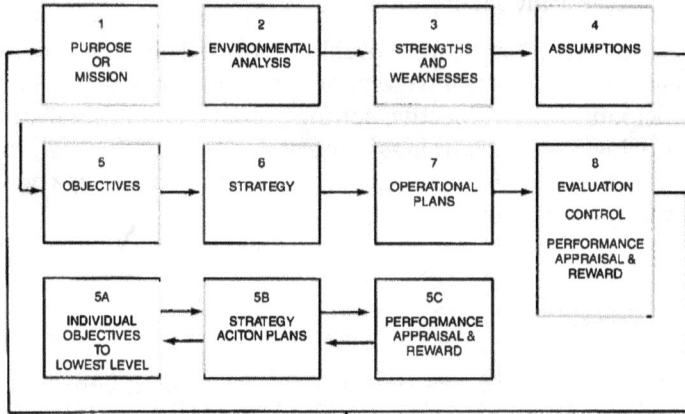

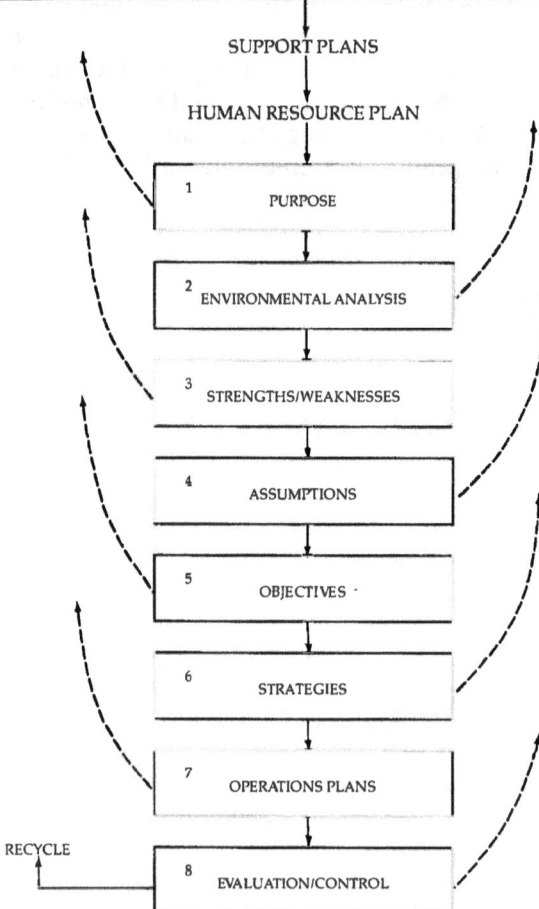

SUPPORT PLANS

HUMAN RESOURCE PLAN

NOTE: DASHES TIE IN EACH STEP IN THE STRATEGIC PLANNING PROCESS TO THE
CORRESPONDING BOX OF THE HUMAN RESOURCES PLAN. THIS IS KEY TO THE
SUCCESS OF THIS PROCESS

Special attention here is necessary regarding two key factors usually missing from HR Planning. First, measures for the objective-setting and tracking of these "soft" areas are usually missing. However, the literature is now beginning to show that this area can be measured (Haines 1987). In addition, one of the authors did in fact set up an effective "Administrative MIS" for all his areas of responsibility (including HR) while an executive vice president at Imperial Corporation of American, an $11 Billion asset-sized financial services company.

Second, the prominent place that the "evaluation and control" step in the strategic planning process plays in its ultimate success is often missing in the HR arena. Reviews of HRP progress by senior management are relatively uncommon in the authors' experiences. Yet, reviews of other traditional business functions (finance, operations, etc.) are usually held by senior management. The stewardship of the employees of the organization is no less important!

Methods to accomplish this review need to be decided early in the process of HRP. One of the most useful methods by firms such as IBM, EXXON, and others is the use of an annual survey-feedback process (see Nadler 1977 for more information). In it, management receives unfiltered and quantifiable feedback on employees' perception of management's results regarding HR and business objectives.

As a result of recent research, it has become clearer that organizational and HR programs help constitute a bottomline competitive business advantage for firms (Haines 1987). Thus, the authors recommend the use of the Organizational Practices Profile (OPP) as an excellent vehicle to measure the status of their effectiveness in creating a competitive advantage through people (Haines 1987).

This OPP survey can be very effectively used to supplement other quantitative data collected on agreed upon HRP objectives. It is important here to note consistency with our redefinition of the HRP field to include its "monitoring and reporting" functions.

Cascio's 1982 book entitled, *Costing Human Resources: The Financial Impact of Behavior in Organizations* makes fascinating reading on the bottomline competitive business advantage of HR functional level Plans. Even Michael Porter (1987) found that the key to successful corporate-level strategies was the sharing of personnel resources or the transferring of executives and managers systematically across different corporate assets or entities. Again, functional HR plans can become competitive advantages regardless of the corporate strategy chosen.

Level Four: Strategic Management

The strategic management and implementation of the HR plan is fraught with numerous barriers to success. Clearly, there are many ways an organization can achieve the same end result. Therefore, any HRP professional who approaches the CEO and senior management with the "one best way" is heading for potential trouble. The authors' HRP redefinition and framework may appear to be quite specific. However, the strategic management of change associated with implementing a strategic plan is dependent on many factors unique to each organization, its senior executives and the situation.

Some of the most important factors are the CEO's preferred leadership style, his or her level of implementation persistence, the firm's culture or norms of behavior, and the existing political realities.

There is obviously a key role that the HR Planner (and the entire HR Department) can play in implementing the plan. First, there are a number of skills and concepts that must be acquired.

These include:
(1) the entire area of "transition and change management technology" (see Beckhard 1977).
(2) a diagnostic model/methodology on how to view an organization as an overall system (see Galbraith 1973, 1977).
(3) the ability to serve as a highly professional adviser and consultant to senior executives.
(4) the facilitator and process skills of the organization's development profession.

As stated, it is beyond the scope of this chapter to delineate the specific change or transition steps needed for each unique situation. Nevertheless, the kinds of issues and barriers to be encountered along the way to strategically managing the implementation process are relatively common. Some of the more recent articles that highlight these barriers include Rowland (1981), Mackey (1981), Leskin (1984), and Burack (1985). For ease of presentation, they are grouped into two categories; strategy formulation (i.e. Business Strategy Levels 1-2-3) and strategy management and implementation (Level 4).

Strategy Formulation Barriers:

1. Lack of a champion
2. The skills, business acumen and credibility of the vice-presidents of both human resources and the planning function
3. No clear sense of the vision and strategic direction of the overall firm

4. Inability of the HR head to be involved
5. Lack of a close tie-in between HR and corporate planning
6. Not having senior management committed at every level of the strategic plan
7. Letting staff develop any level of strategic plans
8. Inadequate environmental assessment of future trends
9. Confusing budgeting with planning
10. Failure to think comprehensively about those HR programs and practices that will motivate the firm's employees to become a competitive business advantage.

Strategy Implementation Barriers

1. The culture of any organization is both its strength and its limitation.
2. The conflict the plan causes with the organization's political minefields.
3. Failure to continually communicate fully throughout the process of implementation.
4. In addition, failure to gather feedback on the plan's status, acceptance and motivational impact is like an "out of control satellite". Without feedback, midcourse corrections are rarely successful.
5. Despite the best intent of senior management, a crucial barrier to success is the fact that many organizations have two distinct and different cultures: management and nonmanagement! A clear understanding of the nonmanagement culture and their needs and desires is necessary to properly target the HR Plan. The title to a long-forgotten article makes the point: "If it's right for you, it's wrong for your employees!"
6. The correctness of an HR plan is subject to the traditions of the human resources field. Unfortunately, many of the traditional solutions in the HR field are ones formulated in a different era than the 1980's. While they may have met the unique needs of the employees of that 1940's-50's era, old guideposts are often the wrong solutions today (see Haines 5/1987 for specific examples). Proven research on what works in the field of human and organizational behavior is frequently ignored by HR and line executives, resulting in a strong negative impact on the success of the HR Plan.
7. Rewards systems are always crucial to the successful implementation of any plans and programs. Careful recrafting of all parts of a total rewards system (both financial and nonfinancial) to fit faithfully with all aspects of the four levels of strategic plans is absolutely essential. *This lack of fit is where most strategic management and implementation plans go awry.*

8. Not monitoring the progress of the plans on a regular basis.
9. HR policies, programs and practices are fragmented among different specialists.

Summary

This redefinition of HR Planning has the potential to be one of the ways an organization can develop its competitive business advantage. Recognition is coming slowly. Employees can drive the selection of both a Corporate and a Business Unit strategic plan. It is becoming more understood by senior management that their employees hold the keys to successful strategic management and implementation. This is regardless of the specific strategy chosen. Perhaps this is due to more and more firms choosing their competitive advantages in the employee-driven areas of (1) customer service, (2) cost efficiencies and productivity, (3) unique selling channels or (4) quality products. The one thing these four strategies have in common is "the dependency on meeting employees' needs in order to tap their full motivation and commitment to act" in support of these strategies. Employees can also support or block implementation of a well thought out strategic plan, and especially so in these four cases.

This redefinition of HRP is more an ideal than reality in most organizations today. However, it is still a vision for HR executives to strive for in order to be taken more seriously and successfully by senior executives. The latest data available indicates there are few organizations with fully developed five-year human resource plans. It is becoming clearer through Porter's research and case studies of the failures of People's Express and MCI Communications that price or costs alone do not result in a long-term competitive business advantages. They are only half-a-loaf; necessary, but not sufficient for long-term success.

While the concepts, perils and challenges of HR Planning are great for the HR professional, so are the potential rewards! By having the H.R. function represented when strategic direction is set, the organization is more likely to have a fully developed H.R. plan.

Acknowledgment

This chapter is adapted from a working paper developed with Dr. Steve Haines, La Jolla, California.

Human Resources Plan

	Last Year Actual	Next Year	Five Years
Culture Index			
Yearly People Development Audit			
Quality Circles (participation teams) implemented			
Turnover			
Performance/Reward System			
Benefits			
Compensation Levels			
Wellness			
Manpower Forecast			
Recruiting Objectives and Costs			
Succession Planning			
Affirmative Action			
Pro-Active Labor Relations			
Culture Index			
Measure of Skills Needed/100 Index			
Full Time/Temporary Employee Ratios			
Cross Training Index			
Literacy Rate			
Computer Literacy			
Legislation			

OBJECTIVES: <u>Huma n R sou ces</u>
OVERALL
RESPONSIBILITY:_____

STRATEGIES: <u>Pol i ies , La bo R el a ti s ,E x e u tv e D eve lop nt</u>
<u>Training</u>

START DATE:	ACTION STEPS:	DUE DATE:	RESPON- SIBILITY:	STATUS:

References
Chapter 10

Beckhard, R., Harris, R. *Organization Transition: Managing Complex Change.* Reading, MA: Addison-Wesley, 1977.

Berger, L. "Dispelling a Mystique: Practical Managerial Manpower Planning." *Personnel Journal,* June 1976, pp. 296-299.

Bolt, J. "Managing Resource Planning: Keys to Success." *Human Resource Planning,* 1982, pp. 185-195.

Burack, E. "Corporate Business and Human Resources Planning Practices: Strategic Issues and Concerns." *Organizational Dynamics,* 1984, pp. 73-87.

Burack, E. "Linking Corporate Business and Human Resource Planning: Strategic Issues and Concerns." *Human Resource Planning,* 1985, pp. 133-146.

Cascio, W. *Costing Human Resources: The Financial Impact of Behavior in Organizations.* Boston, MA: Kent Publishing, 1982.

DeSanto, J. "Work Force Planning and Corporate Strategy." *Personnel Administrator,* October 1983, pp. 33-36.

Devanna, M. A., Fombrun, C. J, & Tichy, N. M. *Human Resource Management: A Strategic Approach.* Unpublished manuscript. Columbia University, Graduate School of Business, New York. February 1, 1980.

Dyer, L. "Human Resource Planning at IBM." *Human Resource Planning,* 1984, 111-126.

Dyer, L. (Ed.). *Human Resource Planning: Tested Practices Five Major U.S. and Canadian Companies.* New York: Random House, 1986.

Dyer, L., Shafer, R., & Regan, P. "Human Resource Planning at Corning Glass Works: A Field Study." *Human Resource Planning,* 1982, 115-184.

Fiorito, J. "The Rationale for Human Resource Planning." *Human Resource Planning,* 1982, 103-104.

Fraze, J. "Displaced Workers: Okies of the 80's." *Personnel Administrator,* January 1988, pp. 42-56.

Galbraith, J. *Designing Complex Organizations.* Reading, MA: Addison-Wesley, 1973.

Galbraith, J. *Organization Design.* Reading, MA: Addison-Wesley, 1977.

Galbraith, J. (Speaker). *Organization Planning.* Imperial Corporation of America, San Diego, CA, November 1986.

Gould, R. "Gaining a Competitive Edge Through Human Resource Strategies." *Human Resource Planning,* 1984, pp. 32-38.

Hall, D., & Hall, F. "What's New in Career Management" (Reprint). *Organizational Dynamics,* Summer 1976, pp. 191-214.

Haines, S. *Organizational Rewards: Why Don't We Use What Works?* Speech presented at The Center for Effective Organizations, University of Southern California, Los Angeles, May 1987.

Haines, S. *Human Resources as a Competitive Business Advantage* (Doctoral Proposal). Temple University, Philadelphia, Pennsylvania, 1987.

Hennecke, M. "The "People" Side of Strategic Planning." *Training*, November 1984. pp. 25-31. *Human Resource Planning: Strategy Formulation and Implementation*. Minnetonka, MN: Golle & Holmes Consulting, 1984.

Janger, A. *The Personnel Function: Changing Objectives and Organization* (Report No. 712). New York: The Conference Board, 1977.

Kaumeyer, R., Jr. *Human Resources: A Critical Planning Issue*. Oxford, OH: Planning Executives Institute, 1984.

Kelleher, E., & Cotter, K. "An Integrative Model for Human Resource Planning and Strategic Planning." *Human Resource Planning*, 1982, pp. 15 & 16.

Leskin, B. *Human Resources Strategic Planning*. Paper presented at the meeting of CEO Sponsor's Group, Los Angeles: CA, May 5, 1984.

Mackey, C. "Human Resource Planning: A Four-Phased Approach. *Management Review*, May 1981, pp. 17-21.

Mahler, W., & Gaines, F, Jr. *Succession Planning in Leading Companies*. Midland Park, NJ: Author, 1984.

McFillen, J., & Decker, P. "Building Meaning into Appraisal" (Reprint). *The Personnel Administrator*, June 1978, 23(6).

Migliore, R. *MBO: Blue Collar to Top Executive*. Washington, D.C.: BNA Press, 1974.

Migliore, R. *An MBO Approach to Long Range Planning*. Englewood Cliffs, NJ: Prentice Hall, 1984.

Migliore, R. *Strategic Long Range Planning* (rev. ed.). Tulsa, OK: Western Printing, 1986.

Migliore, R., Spence, J., & Thurn, W. *Production Operations Management: A Productivity Approach*. Jenks, OK: J. Williams, 1987.

Miles, R., & Snow, C. "Designing Strategic Human Resources Systems." *Organization Dynamics*, 1983. pp. 36-52.

Mills, D. "Planning with People in Mind." *Harvard Business Review*, July-Augst 1985, pp. 97-105.

Nadler, D. *Feedback and Organization Development: Using data-based methods*. Reading, MA: Addison-Wesley, 1977.

Nkomo, S. M. *Strategic Planning for Human Resources—Let's get Started*.

Odiorne, G. (personal communication). Eckerd College, St. Petersburg, FL. August 31, 1987.

O'Toole, J. *Making America Work: Productivity and Responsibility*. New York: Continuum, 1981.

Peters, T., & Waterman, R., Jr. *In Search of Excellence: Lessons from America's Best-Run Companies*. New York: Harper-Row, 1982.

Peters, T., & Austin, N. *A Passion for Excellence: The Leadership Difference*. New York: Random House, 1985.

Pfeiffer, W. (Ed.). *Strategic Planning: Selected Readings.* San Diego, CA: University Associates, 1986.

Pfeiffer, J. W., Ph. D., J. D. *Power and Organizational Politics: Managing the Change Process.* La Jolla, CA: University Associates, 1987.

Porter, M. *Competitive Strategy.* New York: The Free Press, 1980.

Porter, M. *Competitive Advantage: Creating and Sustaining Superior Performance.* New York: The Free Press, 1985.

Porter, M. "From Competitive Advantage to Corporate Strategy." *Harvard Business Review,* May-June 1987, pp. 45-59.

Reid, D. "Human Resource Planning: A Tool for People Development." *Personnel,* March-April 1977, pp. 15-25.

Rhodes, D., & Walker, J. "Management Succession and Development Planning," (Reprint). *Human Resource Planning,* 1984, 7(4).

Rowland, K., & Summers, S. "Human Resource Planning: A Second Look." *Personnel Administrator,* December 1981, pp. 73-80.

Russ, C., Jr. "Manpower Planning Systems: Part II." *Personnel Journal,* February 1982, pp. 119-123.

Schein, E. "Increasing Organizational Effectiveness Through Better Human Resource Planning and Development," (Reprint). *Sloan Management Review,* Fall 1977, pp. 1-20.

Shaeffer, R. *Monitoring the human resource system.* Paper presented at The Conference Board's Division of Management Research. New York. April 20, 1976.

Strategic Planning for Human Resources. Cambridge, MA: Goodmeasure, 1982.

Ulrich, D. "Human Resource Planning as a Competitive Advantage." *Human Resource Planning,* 9(2), 1986, pp. 41-50.

Ulrich, D. "Strategic Human Resource Planning: Why and How." *Human Resource Planning,* 10, (1), 1987, pp. 37-56.

Walker, J. "Problems in Managing Manpower Change" (Reprint). *Business Horizons,* February 1970, pp. 63-68.

Walker, J. "Models in Manpower Planning" (Reprint). *Business Horizons,* April 1971, pp. 87-96.

Walker, J. *Evaluating the practical effectiveness of human resource planning applications.* Paper presented at the 20th International Meeting, Institute of Management Sciences, Tel Aviv, Israel, June 24-29 1973.

Walker, J. "Linking Human Resource Planning and Strategic Planning" (Reprint). *Human Resource Planning,* 1(1), 1978, pp. 101-111.

Walker, J. "Human Resource Planning: An Evolution" (Reprint). *Pittsburgh Business Review,* 47(1), March 1979, 2-8.

Waterman, R., Jr. *The Renewal Factor.* New York: Bantam, 1987.

Yankelovich, D. *New Rules.* New York: Random House, 1981.

Chapter 11
Strategic Management

The management team must guide the organization through the process of attaining the objectives outlined in the strategic plan. Part of the job is to stay within the philosophical and ethical boundaries of the purpose statement. Strategic management implies the management team will find the best uses for available resources. It will find the best culture for the organization to succeed and maintain that culture.

For example, one of my clients in Florida is a young aggressive computer service company. They have revenue and ROI objectives to double in next five years. Their mission statement reflects a strong commitment to ethics and integrity. Because of the creativity needed for new products and services the culture needed is one that encourages innovation. The president must balance the need for innovation with the need to control an expanding organization. The management philosophy must balance a business manager, secretaries, and telephone operator that work from 9:00 to 5:00 p.m., while R and D engineers and computer specialists work by inspiration.

Another part of strategic management is problem-solving. How do you handle the steady stream of major and minor problems? Years of helping other people solve problems has taught me a valuable lesson and approach. You must evaluate each situation in respect to its effect on where the organization wants to be in the long run. What people tend to think of as immediate severe problems needing top management attention often have little affect on long term success. In that case the problem gets delegated down into the organization.

One manufacturing client of mine has achieved steady growth and has successfully reached initial revenue and return on investment objectives. At a recent planning retreat as we worked on 1995 objectives, it became apparent to everyone that major and/or minor problems depended on the long-term targets. Doubling of revenues presented one set of problems. If the long-term objectives were to maintain the present revenue and probability base, that meant grappling with another set of problems.

A recent experience illustrates the point. My work and travel schedule keeps my calendar full 12 to 18 months in advance. Two Texas churches had been seeking my assistance. An east coast trip was cancelled at the last minute (environmental factor and assumption changed.) This created the opportunity for a fast two-day swing through San Antonio and College Station, Texas. *Objective* was set to work one evening and one day with each church. *Objective* for both was to work with their management team to develop a rough draft plan up through objectives and then confront the major problems they perceived would prevent them from reaching the long-term objectives. They, like all organizations I work with, used the worksheet in Appendix A. Through gathered information (which is environmental analysis), it was apparent that regularly scheduled airlines wouldn't meet the needed arrival and departure times. Private aircraft was the best way to go (strategy). The whole operation was based on the *assumption* there would be good weather. Every assumption needs a *contingency plan*. I mailed the worksheet in Appendix A, a video training tape and books ahead to both clients. Also, I discussed with a key person at each location what to do in case of delay.

Sure enough, we got about halfway to San Antonio and air traffic control closed Dallas-Ft. Worth airport due to weather conditions. They advised all small aircraft to land somewhere immediately. We did. We were on the ground for three hours. One simple phone call to the contact person, a fast review, and the meeting went on as scheduled. We flew in late that night after the weather cleared and had a very successful meeting. As we got set to leave San Antonio for the evening meeting in College Station, the same thing happened again...bad weather, one phone call, successful evening meeting, we flew in later when the weather cleared. I was away from home about 52 hours, traveled almost 2,000 miles, and helped two groups through the planning and problem identification process. The key point is to have a well thought out plan and then strategically to manage the plan.

If you have no plan, and you don't know what to manage. People rally around targets and directions. They need to know where the organization is going. It is top management's job to get them in on the plan.

Another key to problem solving is to develop at least three alternatives for each major and/or minor problem. All too often, not enough time is spent evaluating what the real problem is. Once the real problem is identified, then the various alternative courses of action must be determined.

Only by listing and discussing the alternatives can you set the stage to make the best choice of alternatives.

For example, on the trip to San Antonio we had a problem: bad weather. Another problem was the need to work with the client. Fortunately, with the contingency plan in effect the client's problem of getting the meeting going was minimized. The alternatives from that remote airport 60 miles from Dallas were:

1. Call my wife and have her drive to pick us up and drive all night to San Antonio.
2. Hire one of the workers there at the airport repair shop to drive us in an old pickup to Dallas for a commercial flight.
3. Fly back to Tulsa and take a commercial flight to San Antonio the next day.
4. Wait a few hours and see if the weather improved.

We chose the fourth alternative, arrived at San Antonio, had a good night's sleep, and worked the next day.

This problem-solving formula that, first of all, is based on where the organization is going, defining the real problem, and then developing all reasonable alternatives before making a choice has paid off in my work for years. This is what I call strategic management.

This problem-solving formula that, first of all, is based on where the organization is going, defining the real problem, and then developing all reasonable alternatives before making a choice has paid off in my work for years. This is what I call strategic management.

Another important aspect of strategic management is continuous improvement. Continuous improvement is driven by the philosophy in the purpose statement. The culture of the organization sets the tone for continuous improvement. Strategic management is the process and action of managing the strategic plan. If copies of the strategic plan are near-at-hand, have a few coffee stains with markings and notes then the plan is being strategically managed. If the plan is on the shelf gathering dust, this suggests managing the same old way.

Chapter 12
Appraisals, Rewards, and Reevaluation

This chapter presents the concepts of appraisal systems, rewards, revision of objectives, and reevaluation. The objectives of this chapter are to understand the factors involved in appraisal, to appraise last year's performance, and to determine appropriate rewards if objectives, both intrinsic and extrinsic, are met. Also, you should be able to defend the reasoning for including reevaluation in the Long-Range Planning/MBO process.

Appraisal

The last stage in MBO is to appraise the organization and each of its entities to determine if all objectives have been met. Have the measurable objectives and goals been accomplished? How far did actual performance miss the mark? Did the attainment of the objectives and goals support the overall purpose? Has the environment changed enough to change the objectives and goals? Have additional weaknesses been revealed that will influence changing the objectives of the organization? Have additional strengths been added, or has your position improved sufficiently to influence the changing of your objectives?

Has the organization provided its members with organizational rewards, both extrinsic and intrinsic? Is there a feedback system to help the members satisfy their high-level needs? Please notice how my brand of Long-Range Planning/MBO is easily revised. Notice the various objectives and the quarterly review. If there is a deviation, the problem is red-flagged and given attention. For example, when I was Dean of the School of Business, I reviewed the School of Business objectives and results with my boss at the end of each semester and at the end of the summer. If there is a major problem that would inhibit goal attainment, I let him know immediately.

Part of the appraisal process is the reward system. Most organizations do not directly tie objectives and results to pay. I believe this is a mistake. It is my feeling that almost all the performance appraisal systems in use in this country are a waste of time and actually contribute to negative results. Harry Anderson[1] recently reported on the problems.

A recent report by the Conference Board noted that over half of the 293 firms it surveyed had developed new systems within the past three years. But despite these efforts, the report concludes, "current systems are still widely regarded as a nuisance at best and a dangerous evil at worst." . . . The latest rage in appraisal systems is something called "management by objectives," or MBO, which is used by over half the firms surveyed by the Conference Board. Under this system, an employee and his supervisor periodically sit down to negotiate what the subordinate should accomplish by the end of the rating period. A salesman, for example, might agree to increase new orders for his product by ten percent, while a production engineer could agree to hold manufacturing costs even. The employee's performance is then measured by how well he has met his predetermined objectives.

I have been through that process many, many times after having been on both sides of the fence. All that rating of poise, getting along with fellow workers, and so on is not the basis of a reward system. It is the negotiated results contracted between the individual and his boss. The traditional factors can then be covered with appraisal. The appraisal process is something that is difficult to manage. To determine if the organizational reward system is working properly, ask any member this question, "What is the most satisfying thing you do?" If the respondent lists half a dozen items and his work is not included, then you have an organizational problem. People are seeking the satisfaction of the higher level needs of self-esteem, recognition, and autonomy. I have administered the questionnaire in Chapter 7 to more than fifty organizations. The top-ranked job goals have been achievement, recognition, and opportunity for independent thought and action. If the organization does not have the means of satisfying these higher level needs, organizational members will go outside the organization to have these needs met. When this happens, the outside areas of interest—Girl Scouts, PTA, church clubs, and so on—receive the major part of the enthusiasm, as well as the independent and innovative work of the organization member. His or her job, and the organization itself, receive only base efforts. An organization can sustain itself for quite a while in such a situation. The loss is hard to measure. What could have been accomplished if every organization member were receiving at least some of his or her satisfaction of high-level needs from within the organization and giving the resultant enthusiastic support to the organization?

I do not claim to understand this complex situation thoroughly, but I can make these observations:

1. Salary is largely a "dissatisfaction." If it is adequate, it tends to be a short-term motivator. If it is inadequate, it is a long-term problem and cuts down on innovative, enthusiastic support.
2. Most people feel they are worth more than they are paid.

3. A universal problem in all industries and organizations is how to give extrinsic rewards for performance.
4. Provision must be made for the person to satisfy higher level needs within the organization.
5. Loyalty has ranked and will continue to rank high as a factor in the appraisal process.

Odiorne lists and explains 33 rules in "MBO Special Report; Compensation."[2] A few of the more important are the following, using Odiorne's numbering:

2. Salary administration should be centered around accountability, not activity.
3. Write job objectives instead of job descriptions.
9. People who are committed to your organization are worth more than people who are not committed to it.
13. People who feel they are underpaid will behave like underpaid employees.
16. People who aren't meeting all of their regular ongoing and recurring responsibilities should not be given merit increases.
19. Bonuses should be paid only for beating an indicator.
23. Paying people below equitable market rates will assure you of an ironclad grip on marginal performance.
29. Fair pay does not motivate, but unfair pay demotivates.
31. The higher the person is in the organization, the more you pay for strategies and creative thinking.

Important for a proper appraisal system are the new legal trends and ramifications. Judges in several recent cases in California have looked hard at appraisal systems. They indicate that the appraisal system must be relevant and important to the job, not to some other standards such as personality or education. I can't think of anything safer, easier to understand, or more relevant than basing performance appraisal/pay/promotion on results achieved against agreed-on objectives.

Chuck Adams, when he was personnel manager for the City of Tulsa, developed an appraisal system with a system to rate and tie in rewards based on achieved results. It is well thought out. He has developed a point value that considers percentage of completion, effectiveness, and other factors that give an overall performance rating. This is then translated into a salary recommendation. I have, however, had difficulty with appraisals that are "numbers" and that are index-oriented.

Richard Jarvis, a financial executive with Red Cross and former Coordinator of Long-Range Planning at T. D. Williamson, Inc., used ideas he picked up from the Brunswick Appraisal System. He developed some innovative ideas of his own to better quantify the appraisal process.

Richard B. Higgins found in a recent study conducted among Fortune 1000 companies that those managers who were rewarded for their contributions to strategic planning believed they were doing a better job of planning, were more satisfied with their participation in the process, and were more positive about the results achieved by strategic planning. Simply stated, this tells us if we want good strategic planning, build it into the reward system.

Conclusion

After 25 years of organization consulting, it is my observation that those organizations that do the best job in the area of appraisal, rewards and reevaluation have a "more stable, higher motivated work force." A more productive people factor gives that organization a competitive edge.

Performance Appraisal: An MBO Approach

The keys to performance appraisal and salary administration are profit and performance. This discussion focuses on two factors: (1) appraisal and reward for individual performance, and (2) group bonus reward systems.

Figure 6-1 shows the various possible reward alternatives each individual faces. In the lower left-hand section A, the low performer in an organization whose objectives were not achieved would receive low pay and a low bonus. At the other extreme in Section C, the individual had achieved his objectives and the organization had achieved its objectives; the individual would receive high pay and a high bonus. Alternatives B and D represent other situations. In B, the individual achieves his objectives, yet the organization has modest success. Thus, he receives high pay and a medium bonus. Alternative D is a situation in which a person didn't do as well at achieving his individual objectives but the organization did well, and he would receive medium pay and a high bonus. The rest of the chapter discusses specific programs that contribute to individual rewards along with the group bonus reward.

Ideally, the organization meets its broad overall purpose and reason for being. Specific measurable objectives in key result areas are largely met on a constant, sustaining basis. This success is based on a management team that has the motivation, ability, and insight to manage the organization's resources. The individual manager meets or exceeds his specific, measurable, key result objectives.

194

Figure 6-1
Reward Opportunities

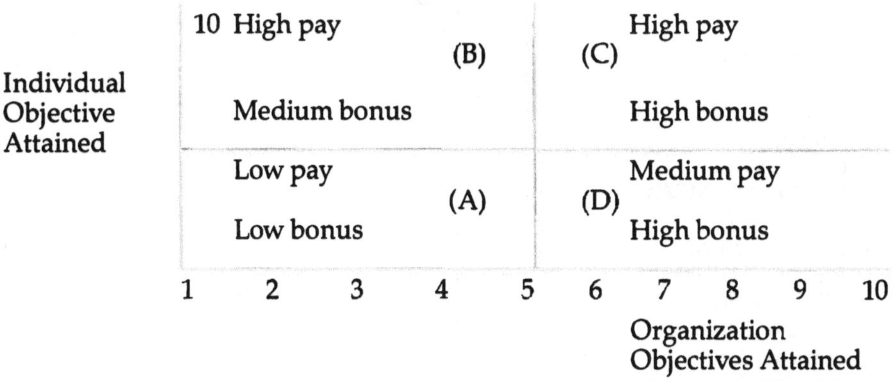

Individual Objective Attained	10 High pay (B) Medium bonus	(C) High pay High bonus
	Low pay (A) Low bonus	(D) Medium pay High bonus

```
        1    2    3    4    5    6    7    8    9    10
```
Organization
Objectives Attained

The successful organization rewards its contributors: stockholders, owners, managers, and employees. As a spinoff, it now contributes to society in its roles as taxpayer, employer, and so on. It encourages its suppliers to make long-term plans to meet its needs. The ripple effect of success works its way down.

The successful organization now must devote attention to rewarding its own managers and employees for their contributions. The organization's needs are met. Now, how does the *organization* meet the extrinsic and intrinsic needs of its *people?*

The extrinsic needs have always been more difficult to deal with. Few salary and bonus systems do well over the long run. The big question mark among MBO scholars, students, consultants, and executives is: "How do you combine MBO with salary administration?"

This chapter deals with that subject. In its simplest form, the person must be evaluated on how he or she performed against key objectives that were negotiated, thoughtfully considered, and obtainable. The objectives are usually scored on a scale from 5 to 10.

Figure 6-2
MBO Performance Appraisal Form Rating

	Excellent 5	Above Avg. 4	Avg. 3	Below Avg. 2	Poor 1	DISCUSSION NOTES
1. Operate within budget of $250,000 and cost per credit hour of $130	5					
2. Graduate 50 MBA's in May 1990	5					
3. Maintain enroll-ment of 300 FTE MBA students		4				
4. Publish in top 1/3 of the nation	5					
5. Average 35 aerobic points per week and reduce weight to 205			3			
	18	4	3			22 = Total
1. Use of LRP/MBO	5					
2. Developing people	5					
3. Contribution to morale	5					
4. Communication			3			
5. Creativity	5					
6. Emotional stability	5					
7. Job knowledge		4				
8. What kind of leader	5					
9. Problem Solver			3			
10. Public Image	5					
	35	4	6			

Average of objectives = 22   5 = 4.4
Average of other items = 45   10 = 4.5
Weighted average = (4.4 X 75%) + (4.5 X 25%) = 4.425.

The managers should also be evaluated. Then each year's pay increase should be based on performance of the 5 to 10 key performance objectives and the 10 criteria listed below:

1. Use of Long-Range Planning/MBO
2. Developing people
3. Contribution to morale
4. Communication
5. Creativity
6. Emotional stability
7. Job knowledge
8. Leadership style
9. Problem-solving ability
10. Public image/social responsibility

I have devised a method that takes already existing sets of objectives and turns them into appraisal forms. See Figure 6-2. The individual's regular performance objectives are listed at the top of the sheet, and their final outcome is given a rating of 5 for excellent through 1 for poor performance. The ten items previously listed are then rated according to the same system.

These ten items are not measurable, but they should be considered. I feel that the main criteria should be the results of how the managers performed as compared to what they negotiated as their performance objectives. Each objective at year-end would be rated excellent through poor on performance. Table 6-1 could be followed in determining the specific pay increases. Average the objectives and give them a 75 percent weight, and give the 10 nonmeasurable areas a 25 percent weight.

Table 6-1

Performance Level	Recommended Pay
1. Performance less than satisfactory (Has not met all minimum acceptable performance standards and objectives for the position. Point average below 1.5.	Zero percent increase
2. Performance meets minimum standards and objectives but not up to average. Point average 1.5 to 2.5.	Not more than 5 percent increase (0-5).

3. Performance meets at least average standards and objectives and may excel in some areas. Point average 2.5 to 3.5.

  Not more than 10 percent increase (5-10).

4. Performance is better than average overall and excels in a majority of standards and objectives for the position. Point average 3.5 to 4.5.

  Not more than 15 percent increase (11-15).

5. Performance is outstanding because it excels in all the objectives and conditions previously listed. Point average 4.5 to 5.0.

  Not more than 20 percent increase (16-20).

If the person has fared well against these expectations and the organization has done well, he or she should receive a salary boost commensurate with the performance. In today's economic climate, this would be a 12 to 20 percent increase in pay.

Next, let's consider another circumstance: the organization doesn't do as well but the individual performer posted a good record in all areas over which he has control. He should be paid by the same criteria. The organization has too much at stake to risk losing its high performers. Usually 20% of the people contribute 80% of the key results. Don't be niggardly with the 20%. The same rule of thumb, 12% to 20% pay increase, holds if the organization does poorly. The other 80% receive pay in the third 10% range.

In the third possible circumstance, the organization does poorly but the individual does very well. In this case, the high-performance individual is not in a position to expect the kind of organizational rewards listed in the first two circumstances. A mature management system should realize this. My best suggestion is that the same five performance levels above be recognized but that the pay scales be exactly half of what they normally would have been.

In the circumstance where the individual does poorly, it is my feeling that it doesn't make any difference what the organization did. The individual did not make the right kind of contribution and should not be rewarded. Rewarding for a poor performance is a guarantee to continue the same.

One complicating factor in this era of high inflation is what do you call a pay increase and what do you call an adjustment for inflation? I know of no organization that has completely solved that problem. In reality, even with the table above, this past year with inflation at 15%, if a top performer received 20%, in effect he is receiving only a net 5% reward for his performance. I believe the recommended pay percentages should be tied into the inflation rate. Theoretically, every organization should automatically modify its pay ranges based on the inflation level and then add the pay increase on top of inflation.

Bonus System

Working hand-in-hand with salary rewards based on individual achievement is the bonus system. This is nothing new of itself. But how does it work with MBO? If the organization meets certain understood, agreed-upon objectives and criteria, every organization member shares in the harvest. Objectives such as sales, profit, manufacturing efficiency, quality, and safety could be the bases. Criteria could be set for those deemed to be of importance based on the individual organization. The bonus system must be simple, straightforward, and understood.

The most important objective is profit. Good, solid, long-term-oriented profit is the golden word of capitalism. It's simple: no profit, no bonus. Other objectives can be a factor but only after profit objective is met.

The criterion for profit might be 15% before tax profit on sales. A pool is set up with 20% of all profit above the minimum criterion of 15% going into the pool. For example, a $40,000,000 sales company with $6,000,000 profit would have no bonuses. One company I am working with provides a nice working vacation at a popular resort area if the minimum criteria are met. Another idea would be to give some percentage such as 1% of all profits if the minimum criterion is met. However, a $7,000,000 profit would put $200,000 into a pool. If there were 500 employees, this would be a bonus of $400 per person. All employees share equally in this pool. The bonus is a non-budgeted item.

Another way the pool can be distributed is to give divisional managers shares of the pool to distribute as they see fit within their units. This method is of doubtful value because of the bias problem. This is one instance in which I advocate treating everyone on the team the same. The bonus is the team reward. If the team wins the league championship, it goes to the Superbowl and everyone shares equally in the reward. If you don't win the league championship (in this case 15% profit before taxes) you stay home and everyone gets the same thing . . . nothing.

Under this system, a person has an opportunity to get ahead on his own and is also rewarded for being a team player.

I still believe the most effective way to handle a bonus is to include everyone, including the management team, by setting up a bonus fund. The fund is not budgeted, but comes out of after-tax corporate profits based on an audited financial statement. Another alternative is that funds should be available for bonus distribution unless the corporate performance exceeds all of the following: a) 10% return on sales before taxes; b) 5% return on sales after taxes; c) 80% manufacturing efficiency; and d) 40% sales growth increase. The total fund available for distribution each year is not to exceed 10% of corporate after-tax net profit or 1% of sales. This sets some standards, is reasonably simple, and lets everyone in on the bonus if things go well. Another criterion is 20% of after-tax profit in excess of 8% gross revenue.

Again, pay particular attention to the 20/80 rules. Those 20% who contribute the 80% need to be rewarded. A rigid reward system that holds them back just encourages them to go elsewhere. The other 80% are not going anywhere anyway so don't spend as much time worrying about them.

Incentives are finding a renewal. More and more organizations are looking at financial rewards. Despite the difficulties, incentives are growing in popularity. A survey of 2,000 companies conducted by Mercer Meidinger Hansen showed that 25 percent granted stock options or other incentives to middle- or lower-level employees who formerly were excluded from such plans. New participants most often got stock options, followed by annual incentives, usually in the form of one-time bonuses. Many of my clients are using a wide range of profit-sharing and other production/quality incentives.

Dr. Ken Matejka, in the Spring 1979 edition of the Arkansas Business Review, suggests the employee's rating of his boss. He lists 17 ways a person could rank his boss. His intention was to determine how people would feel about rating those items. After conferring with Dr. Matejka, we agreed a scale could be developed and the appraisal process would be a two-way street. The manager might need to have all the evaluations be done anonymously. A suggested form is listed on the next page.

Boss Evaluation

Evaluative Questions	Low/ Poor 1	Below Average 2	Average 3	Above Average 4	High/ Excellent 5
1. Depth of knowledge about work.					
2. Awareness of recent developments in his field.					
3. Ability to help subordinates answer questions or solve problems.					
4. Ability to get people to accept ideas on what should be done.					
5. Willingness to adapt to new ideas and innovations.					
6. Ability to motivate subordinates.					
7. Interest in subordinates' welfare.					
8. Ability to provide an opportunity for subordinates to pursue their own ideas.					
9. Tolerance and respect for subordinates' opinions.					
10. Fairness and lack of personal prejudice.					
11. Attitude toward subordinates in terms of help, encouragement, advice, and friendliness.					
12. Ability to present oneself in a clear and organized manner.					
13. Interest and enthusiasm for job.					
14. Ability to communicate ideas and directives.					
15. Ability to listen well.					

16. Willingness to encourage two-way communication.

17. Your overall opinion of him as a supervisor/manager.

OVERALL MEAN

Following is a quick review of what has been covered. Examples of basketball, the situation I found at Continental Can in 1967, and a real estate business are given.

	Basketball	1967-68 Continental Can	Real Estate Company
Purpose	Have prestigious, well-recognized, program	Survival and profit in the packaging business	Profit and survival in local ethical real estate business
Environmental Analysis	Statistics and analysis of other teams	Pork prices, trends in new packages	Housing starts up
Strengths and Weaknesses	Good shooters, weak bench,	Knowledgeable managers, poor organization	Experienced salesman new coach
Assumptions	Rules will stay the same	Demand for ham stays same. No governmental controls.	No labor strike
Objectives and Goals	Win NCAA by 1995, recruit 7-foot all-American high school player in 1991. Win 20 games 1991-92	Cut M.E. efficiency loss of - 17% by April 1968 to break even	Profit/sales of 10% in first quarter
Strategy	Have disciplined offense	Go after the fruit packers, government business	Heavy emphasis in southeast sections
Long-Range Plan	Schedule 15 teams in the top 10 over next 5 years	Relocate department in stages over next 5 years	Build new home office in southeast
Short-Range Plan	Visit high school of top 10 choices, visit parents, basketball camp in summer	Follow the MBO plan for the year and the budget	Ask for home-office bids in first quarter
Appraisal Recycling	22-6, recruiting questionable	Ran 10 straight weeks in black April 15, 1968	(See how you do each quarter)

Review, Checklist of
Long-Range Planning/MBO

I. Purpose
   A. What is "reason for being," your "mission," why needed, customers served, needs met in marketplace, scope of the endeavor; nationwide, local, ethics, profit, or nonprofit.

II. Environmental Analysis
   A. Pulse
   B. Present or past
   C. Industry surveys
   D. Studies of future done now.

III. S & W (usually internal)
   A. Human
   B. Facilities/equipment
   C. Patents/resources natural
   D. Financial

IV. Assumptions
   A. You have no control over
   B. Extend environmental analysis
   C. Usually external

V. Objectives and Goals
   A. Specific, time frame, measurable in key result areas. Note all rules for objectives.

VI. Strategy
   A. Thinking stage
   B. Where and how to commit resources
   C. Timing D. Pricing policy

VII. L.R.P.
   A. Doing something in future
   B. Build, hire, fire
   C. Keep out results
   D. Develop pro forma income/balance sheets
   E. Sales forecast
   F. Use action words

VIII. S.R.P.
   A. What to do this year, this quarter
   B. Oriented statements

    C. First year of 5-year plan
    D. Use action words
    E. Zero-base budgeting

ASSIGNMENT:

Now, on a separate piece of paper, develop an in-depth long-range plan. Review the material presented and the notes you made at each subset. Use the checklist on the previous page to be sure you have each of the planning process stages set correctly.

Finish the book now for advice and discussion on the planning and MBO process.

Notes

[1]Harry Anderson
[2]George Odiorne, "Mbo Special Report: Compensation," MBO Press.
[3]Richard B. Higgins, "How Well Are We Rewarding Our Managers for Strategic Planning?" Journal of Business Strategy, Winter 1981.

Chapter 13
Measuring SLRP/MBO Effectiveness
Using Questionnaire

This chapter discusses how an organization can use an attitude instrument. A method for evaluating the extent of SLRP/MBO in an organization and its perceived effectiveness will be described. Also included will be a discussion on how to use the questionnaire results to get a commitment. I have tested and successfully used this particular method, involving the use of a questionnaire with discussion and feedback sessions, in many organizations under many conditions. (If you wish to refer to an excellent compendium of other methods for determining organizational climate, effectiveness, and worker attitudes, see the recent book by Fred Rudge, *The Key to Increased Productivity: A Manual for Line Executives.*[1])

I developed a structured questionnaire to determine perceptions about certain factors in the organizational climate. In its initial form, it was used in a study of twenty-seven organizational entities in 1973-74, providing a valuable pretest of the questionnaire and that method of data collection.

After the original study of the twenty-seven entities, the questionnaire was again pretested in two organizations, and the participants were asked to comment on its clarity. A number of suggestions were made, many of which were incorporated into the final draft of the questionnaire.

The questionnaire was then used to evaluate fourteen organizations in the fall of 1974. The questionnaire is presented on page 208. The questionnaire was updated and used again in 1975-76 in various other organizations. Another refinement was made in the fall of 1977.

A factor-analysis comparison was made on fifty-four of the appropriate questionnaire variables.[2] One of the basic reasons for using factor analysis is its data-reduction capability, and another objective of factor analysis is the exploration and detection of patterning of variables.[3] The categories to be tested were: defined duties, goals, supervision, control, performance evaluation, job satisfaction, recognition, communication, planning, and pay. The fifty-four questionnaire variables which came from questions 2, 3, 5, 7, 8, 9, 11, 12, 13, 14, and 15 were designed to measure these categories.[4] Through the use of factor analysis, the original ten categories were reduced to three.

These three categories are statistically proven for valid comparison within an organization. The same categories can be used to compare one company with another.

In each of the categories, an index was developed to measure the category. The factor analysis for each of the categories defined indicated that a number of questions in the questionnaire were grouped together. Each of these questions received a response from each manager that was given a score from 1 for low to 5 for high. All of the managers' responses were combined to develop a mean response for each question. The index for an entity of study was developed by averaging the mean of each question to create a category. The index ranged from 1 for low to 5 for high.

The questionnaire derived these categories through factor analysis:

Extent of planning. This factor measures the extent of the manager's personal planning and the extent to which he perceives his contribution is needed by his boss when his boss makes his own plans. Responses to alternatives a and b of Question 9 were used for this index. Following the statement, "In terms of planning," these sentence endings were listed to be ranked:

a_____I make a total plan as a road map to go by each year.
b_____my contribution is needed in making my boss's plans.

Column headings for the respondent's answer ranged from "no, never," through "seldom," "sometimes," "almost always," and "yes, always."

Selected effects of the planning and control system. This factor is a measure of the perceived effect of the organization's planning and control system on planning, recognition, expected job performance, and feedback. Alternatives a, c, and e of Question 7, and Question 12 were used for this index. Question 7 stated, "The planning and control system of management in my organization has accomplished the following in the past few years." The responses which addressed this factor were:

a_____has given me more opportunity for personal recognition.
c_____ has helped me to know what is expected of me.
e_____has made for better planning.

Response choices were mixed. Question 12 stated, "I would describe the feedback of performance in this organization as . . ." and asked the respondent to rate feedback on a scale from 1 for poor to 5 for excellent.

Performance: Measurements and Rewards. This factor is a measure of how performance is evaluated and how it affects pay, promotions, and recognition. Question 3 stated:

In this company:
a____pay is based on performance;
b____promotions go to those who deserve them;
...
j____I am recognized for doing good work.

Column headings ranged from "strongly disagree," through "disagree," "undecided," "agree," and "strongly agree." The respondent checked the column that most clearly reflected his feelings. One of the variables to be rated from Question 2 was: "I feel I would be more effective on the job if I had (. . .g____)a better conception of how my boss evaluates my work." Question 15 asked the respondent to rate the organization's performance-appraisal system on a scale from 1 for poor to 5 for excellent.

Communication. The questionnaire did not contribute a category that would measure communication. The following questions have been devised by Dennis, Richetto, and Wiemann[5] for measuring communication:

1. How well informed does your organization try to keep employees on matters important to employee interests?

   a____fully informed.
   b____fairly well informed.
   c____somewhat informed.
   d____practically no effort is made to keep employees informed.

2. To what extent can employees have faith that the information put out by management gives a true picture?

   a____information put out is always believable.
   b____information put out is usually believable.
   c____information put out is seldom believable.
   d____information put out is never believable.

3. How satisfied are you with your face-to-face communication with your supervisor (superior) about your job needs?

   a____very satisfied.
   b____fairly satisfied, but there is room for improvement.
   c____somewhat satisfied and wish it could be improved.
   d____not at all satisfied.

4. Which one of these statements would you say reflects the attitude of management in getting information from employees?

   a____they are very interested in what employees have to say.
   b____they are fairly interested in employees' opinions.
   c____they are somewhat interested in employees' opinions.
   d____they have practically no interest in employees' opinions.

5. How would you describe the overall atmosphere existing in your organization for open and free exchange of information and ideas?

    a____excellent—people feel free to say how they feel.
    b____good—but people don't have complete freedom to exchange information and ideas.
    c____fair—because people have to watch what they say to whom.
    d____poor—because you never know when what you say can get you into trouble.

6. How well do individuals in different departments (work groups) share information for the purpose of coordinating their job efforts?

    a____very well—because there is a free exchange of information among departments (work groups).
    b____good—but sometimes differences and disagreements arise among departments (work groups) that could be prevented.
    c____fair—because differences and disagreements often prevent information exchange.
    d____poor—because "empire-building" and other problems result in little communication among departments (work groups).

The authors commented: "These six questions can aid the communication specialist in pinpointing a problem area (or areas) that may be contributing to a low communication satisfaction rating or to an unhealthy communication climate. And our research suggests that if an organization's internal communication system is in need of some overhaul, the areas of immediate concern will probably surface in employees' responses to these six items."[6] I added a fifth choice on each of these. Note Question 5 on the questionnaire.

Goals. A list of eight job goals is presented for ranking in Question 1 of the questionnaire at the end of this chapter. The order in which the job goals appear was determined by random numbers. The goals to be ranked as they were presented on the questionnaire are as follows:

    a____satisfying my boss's expectations
    b____prestige and status
    c____job security
    d____opportunity for independent thought and action
    e____higher salary, more benefits, or both
    f____recognition for good performance
    g____promotion to a better job
    h____personal growth and development

The same list of job goals is presented again in Question 4, where the managers rank how they perceive their bosses would rank their (the managers') job goals, and in Question 6, where managers rank how they perceive their immediate subordinates' goals.

The Kendall rank correlation test can be made to determine whether there was agreement among the managers' rankings of the goals and how they perceived their bosses and subordinates would rank their goals. This can give an organization a quick, clear picture of perceived goal congruence among organization levels. A level of significance of .05 is set as the criterion.[7] The test also can be (and has been) made to see if there is a difference between the job goals of managers using and not using MBO. My research of more than 500 managers and 50 organizations has indicated little significant difference exists in job goals between managers using and those not using MBO.

The significant point here is that all managers have the same needs. A longitudinal study from 1974 to 1977 which I am submitting to the Academy of Management indicated about the same conclusions over time. So far, all groups have ranked recognition and personal growth at the top. In most cases they see their bosses giving a different priority to their goals.[8]

Any study of an organization based on answers to questionnaires has certain built-in limitations. Every researcher is aware that words have different connotations to different persons. The time of day a person answers a question may influence his answer — when he is fresh and energetic his feeling may be different from that when he is fatigued or worried. A researcher soon learns how difficult it is to keep answers free from bias. On the other hand, some people may put down what they think is the "right" answer, instead of expressing their honest convictions. These factors all prevent complete objectivity in drawing conclusions from answers to questionnaires. Thus the researcher makes every effort to ensure that the questions are as foolproof as careful wording can make them. This means that they are easy to understand, simple to answer, and are sharply focused so as to assure precise and accurate answers and not broad, vague generalizations.

Example of Extent of Planning

The following is an example of how indexes can be used to compare divisions, sections, departments, or companies.[9] A study of five banks determined that they were using varying degrees of MBO. Table 1 presents the perceived extent of MBO use.[10]

Table 1

Use of MBO in the five banks as indicated by index number

Extent of MBO	Bank	Index of MBO
High	2	4.0
Middle	1	3.6
	6	3.5
Low	5	3.1
	4	2.6

The extent-of-planning index was developed from responses concerning the amount of planning done by each individual manager and the contribution needed for his boss's plans. Banks that used a higher degree of MBO also showed a higher planning index than those not using MBO. There was a direct positive relationship between the extent to which MBO was used in the banks and the extent-of-planning index among the banks studied.

The highest MBO bank, Bank 2, had a 4.29/5.00 index; the mid-MBO banks, Banks 1 and 6, had indexes of 3.84/5.00 and 4.06/5.00; while the low-MBO banks, Banks 5 and 4, had indexes of 3.69/5.00 and 3.03/5.00, respectively. There is a direct, positive correlation between the extent of use of MBO in the banks and the extent-of-planning index. Figure 1 presents the results comparing the banks individually.

This same type of comparison can be made within an organization. Divisions, departments, and so forth can be compared. Admittedly, this is not as precise as comparing concrete dollar figures such as profit and loss or sales. For example, this method does give management the opportunity to evaluate heretofore unmeasurable areas. Statistical, computerized validation assures confidence in the results. This study was done in 1974. I did another study in 1977 and reported to bank management the perceived changes in the extent of planning over the 3 year period. For example, Bank 2 had an index of 4.0 in 1974 and dropped to 3.2 in 1977. An example of how the computer displays the results for a typical question (in this case, Question 2 of the questionnaire) is presented after the questionnaire at the end of the chapter.[11]

How to Use the Questionnaire

One good use of the questionnaire and the computer display of data following it is for problem evaluation. My first step with any organization considering MBO is to evaluate individual perceptions with this questionnaire. The results show the major perceived problems. The second step is to put the individuals into problem-solving work teams. The team first verifies that a problem exists and then evaluates whether or not SLRP/MBO can solve this problem. If the group has not had MBO training, I go ahead with a training session. After the training, the groups evaluate to see if they feel MBO will help them. After careful analysis and discussion, the answer to this date has always been yes. The group can see where they ranked their individual goals. I then ask them to evaluate honestly to see if MBO can help them with their personal goals. The response has always been positive. The secondary objective of this strategy is to help the group evaluate and determine that MBO will help them.

Then, and only then, should the organization continue the MBO installation. If the management team is not committed to a thorough involvement with MBO, there can be no guarantee of success.

It is apparent that a company/organization could evaluate the extent of planning and other variables over a time period to determine if there was improvement or change. I did such a study for six banks and reported changes over a three-year period from 1974 to 1977. Although the results are confidential, one bank went from 3.6 to 3.1 on the extent-of-planning index. This indicated some drop in the planning area.

On the following pages is the questionnaire I developed for use in evaluating the extent of SLRP/MBO in an organization and its perceived effectiveness. It is the same questionnaire that generates the results for a new concept I am developing called the "Management System Balance Sheet." A discussion on the balance sheet follows the questionnaire.

CORPORATE CULTURE QUESTIONNAIRE

CODE
[1-3]

Please give your honest opinion to each question. There are no right or wrong answers. Your opinion is what is important. Your cooperation in filling out the questionnaire is appreciated.

____ I. From the list below please rank these job goals in the order of importance *to you*. (Put a #1 beside your first choice, a #2 beside your second choice, and so on to #8.)

[4] A.___ Satisfying my boss' expectations
[5] B.___ Prestige and status
[6] C.___ Job security
[7] D.___ Opportunity for independent thought and action
[8] E.___ Higher salary, more benefits, or both
[9] F.___ Recognition for good performance
[10] G.___ Promotion to a better job
[11] H.___ Personal growth and development.

II. I believe I would be more effective on the job if I had: (circle the NUMBER to indicate answer)

			not at all	slight- ly	moder- ately	consid- erably	very much so
[12]	A.	More job training	1	2	3	4	5
[13]	B.	Better supervision	1	2	3	4	5
[14]	C.	More control over my subordinates	1	2	3	4	5
[15]	D.	Greater personal commitment to produce more	1	2	3	4	5
[16]	E.	More clearly defined job description and duties	1	2	3	4	5
[17]	F.	More freedom to use my own judgment	1	2	3	4	5
[18]	G.	Better conception of how my boss evaluates my work	1	2	3	4	5
[19]	H.	Clearer goals to work toward	1	2	3	4	5
[20]	I.	Better understanding of organization's purpose or mission	1	2	3	4	5
[21]	J.	Better resources (facilities, equipment, tools, etc.) to work with	1	2	3	4	5
[22]	K.	Better team to work with	1	2	3	4	5

III. I believe that: (circle the NUMBER to indicate answer)

			Strongly Disagree	Disagree	Neutral	Agree	Strongly Agree
[23]	A.	My pay is based on my performance	1	2	3	4	5
[24]	B.	My promotion(s) was deserved	1	2	3	4	5
[25]	C.	I am unhappy with my job	1	2	3	4	5

---

[26]	D.	My anxiety of my manager(s) is high	1	2	3	4	5
[27]	E.	My fringe benefits are poor	1	2	3	4	5
[28]	F.	My morale is low	1	2	3	4	5
[29]	G.	My suggestions are listened to	1	2	3	4	5
[30]	H.	I am free to make improvements on the job	1	2	3	4	5
[31]	I.	My capabilities are fully utilized	1	2	3	4	5
[32]	J.	I am recognized for good work	1	2	3	4	5
[33]	K.	The organization is interested in my welfare	1	2	3	4	5
[34]	L.	Two-way communication is present	1	2	3	4	5
[35]	M.	My supervisor cares about my personal needs	1	2	3	4	5
[36]	N.	I conform to accepted professional standards of conduct	1	2	3	4	5

IV. I believe my immediate boss would rank my job goals in this order: (Put a #1 beside your first choice, a #2 beside your second choice, and so on to #8.)

[37] A.___ Satisfying my boss' expectations
[38] B.___ Prestige and status
[39] C.___ Job security
[40] D.___ Opportunity for independent thought and action
[41] E.___ Higher salary, more benefits, or both
[42] F.___ Recognition for good performance
[43] G.___ Promotion to a better job
[44] H.___ Personal growth and development

V. In this organization: (circle the NUMBER to indicate answer)

			Strongly Disagree	Disagree	Neutral	Agree	Strongly Agree
[45]	A.	Employee's pay is based on performance	1	2	3	4	5
[46]	B.	Promotions are given to those who deserve them.	1	2	3	4	5
[47]	C.	Employees are unhappy with their job	1	2	3	4	5
[48]	D.	The anxiety of managers is high	1	2	3	4	5
[49]	E.	Employee's fringe benefits are poor	1	2	3	4	5
[50]	F.	Employee's morale is low	1	2	3	4	5
[51]	G.	Employee's suggestions are listened to	1	2	3	4	5
[52]	H.	Employees are encouraged to make improvements on the job	1	2	3	4	5
[53]	I.	Employee's capabilities are fully utilized	1	2	3	4	5
[54]	J.	Employees are recognized for good work	1	2	3	4	5

[55]	K.	The organization is interested in the employee's welfare...............	1	2	3	4	5
[56]	L.	Two-way communication is present..........	1	2	3	4	5
[57]	M.	Supervisors care about employees' personal needs	1	2	3	4	5
[58]	N.	Employees conform to accepted professional standards of conduct....	1	2	3	4	5

Check *one* response for each of the following questions:

[59]   VIa.   How well does your organization keep employees informed on matters important to employee interests?

( )[1] Practically no effort is made to keep employees informed
( )[2] Tries to keep us somewhat informed
( )[3] Tries to keep us moderately informed
( )[4] Tries to keep us usually informed
( )[5] Tries to keep us always informed

[60]   VIb.   To what extent can employees have faith that the information distributed by management is believable?

( )[1] Information distributed is practically never believable.
( )[2] Information distributed is somewhat believable.
( )[3] Information distributed is moderately believable.
( )[4] Information distributed is usually believable.
( )[5] Information distributed is always believable.

[61]   VIc.   How satisfied are you with your face-to-face communication with your supervisor (superior) about your job needs?

( )[1] Not at all satisfied
( )[2] Somewhat satisfied
( )[3] Moderately satisfied
( )[4] Usually satisfied
( )[5] Always satisfied

[62]   VId.   Which one of these statements would you say reflects the attitude of upper management in getting opinions/information from employees?

( )[1] They have practically no interest in employees' opinions/information.
( )[2] They are somewhat interested in employees' opinions/information.
( )[3] They are moderately interested in employees' opinions/information.
( )[4] They are usually interested in employees' opinions/information.
( )[5] They are always interested in employees' opinions/information.

[63]   VIe.   How would you describe the overall atmosphere existing in your organization for open and free exchange of information and ideas?

( )[1] Poor
( )[2] Fair
( )[3] Average
( )[4] Good
( )[5] Excellent

[64] VIf. How well do persons in different departments (work groups) share information for the purpose of coordinating their job efforts?

( )¹ Poor
( )² Fair
( )³ Average
( )⁴ Good
( )⁵ Excellent

VII. From the list below, please rank how you believe the *persons directly reporting to you* would rank their goals: (Put a #1 beside your first choice, a #2 beside your second choice, and so on to #8.)

[65]   A.___   Satisfying my boss' expectations
[66]   B.___   Prestige and status
[67]   C.___   Job security
[68]   D.___   Opportunity for independent thought and action
[69]   E.___   Higher salary, more benefits, or both
[70]   F.___   Recognition for good performance
[71]   G.___   Promotion to a better job
[72]   H.___   Personal growth and development

VIII. I have heard of the terms management by objectives (MBO), strategic planning, and/or accountability management, and know what they are: (CIRCLE ANSWER).

Strongly Disagree	Disagree	Neutral	Agree	Strongly Agree
1	2	3	4	5

[73]

IX. The planning and control system of management (Strategic Planning or something like it) in my organization has accomplished the following in the past few years: (CIRCLE ANSWER).

		not at all	slight-ly	moder-ately	consid-erably	very much so
[74]	A. Gives me more opportunity for personal recognition	1	2	3	4	5
[75]	B. Has increased enthusiasm on the job	1	2	3	4	5
[76]	C. Has helped me know what is expected of me ..	1	2	3	4	5
[77]	D. Has reduced the need for tight personal control ...	1	2	3	4	5
[78]	E. Has resulted in better planning	1	2	3	4	5
[79]	F. Has contributed to better teamwork	1	2	3	4	5
[80]	G. Promotion is now based on performance	1	2	3	4	5

X.
[1-3] In which of the following ways could our planning and control system of management be improved? (CIRCLE ANSWER)

			not at all	slight-ly	moder-ately	consid-erably	very much so
[4]	A.	More top-management support	1	2	3	4	5
[5]	B.	Less influence by outside departments	1	2	3	4	5
[6]	C.	System should be more widely encouraged and promoted	1	2	3	4	5
[7]	D.	Better feedback of results	1	2	3	4	5
[8]	E.	Bring in outside consultant	1	2	3	4	5
[9]	F.	More formalized planning system	1	2	3	4	5
[10]	G.	Reduce the amount of paperwork	1	2	3	4	5
[11]	H.	Promotions and pay should follow achievement	1	2	3	4	5
[12]	I.	Increase opportunity to discuss and negotiate job and personal goals with my boss	1	2	3	4	5
[13]	J.	More time is needed to implement such a system	1	2	3	4	5
[14]	K.	More clearly defined purpose	1	2	3	4	5
[15]	L.	Make goal setting easier	1	2	3	4	5

XI. In terms of planning: (Circle the number to indicate answer.)

			never	seldom	some-times	usually	always
[16]	A.	I make a total plan as a road map to go by each year	1	2	3	4	5
[17]	B.	My contribution is needed in making my boss's plans	1	2	3	4	5
[18]	C.	We really strive to follow yearly plans	1	2	3	4	5

[19] XII. Check (✓) all of those items listed (A through D) which are applicable for you.

A.___ Performance and personal objectives are set for the coming year.
B.___ These objectives are submitted to your boss, discussed and negotiated, and then you are held accountable for achieving.
C.___ Progress toward meeting the objectives is reviewed periodically.
D.___ At year-end actual performance is compared with objectives.

_____ TOTAL CHECKS (✓) (ENTER ZERO IF NO CHECKS)

Circle the number that most closely describes your feelings on Questions XIII-XXX.

[20]	XIII.	An organization should use the type of management described in Question XII (Items A through D)	**Strongly Disagree** 1	**Disagree** 2	**Neutral** 3	**Agree** 4	**Strongly Agree** 5
[21]	XIV.	I would rate the effectiveness of our entire management team as:	**Poor** 1	**Fair** 2	**Average** 3	**Good** 4	**Excellent** 5
[22]	XV.	I would rate the communication in our organization as:	**Poor** 1	**Fair** 2	**Average** 3	**Good** 4	**Excellent** 5
[23]	XVI.	I would rate the planning in our organization as:	**Poor** 1	**Fair** 2	**Average** 3	**Good** 4	**Excellent** 5
[24]	XVII.	I would rate the performance-appraisal system in this organization as:	**Poor** 1	**Fair** 2	**Average** 3	**Good** 4	**Excellent** 5
[25]	XVIII.	I have a firm sense of direction and values for my life.	**Strongly Disagree** 1	**Disagree** 2	**Neutral** 3	**Agree** 4	**Strongly Agree** 5
[26]	XIX.	I believe I am accepted as part of the "team" in this organization.	**Strongly Disagree** 1	**Disagree** 2	**Neutral** 3	**Agree** 4	**Strongly Agree** 5
[27]	XX.	Feedback in this organization is:	**Poor** 1	**Fair** 2	**Average** 3	**Good** 4	**Excellent** 5
[28]	XXI.	People have the opportunity to be involved in the decision making process.	**Strongly Disagree** 1	**Disagree** 2	**Neutral** 3	**Agree** 4	**Strongly Agree** 5
[29]	XXII.	I believe our organization is open to change.	**Strongly Disagree** 1	**Disagree** 2	**Neutral** 3	**Agree** 4	**Strongly Agree** 5
[30]	XXIII.	People in our organization widely share the same philosophy.	**Strongly Disagree** 1	**Disagree** 2	**Neutral** 3	**Agree** 4	**Strongly Agree** 5
[31]	XXIV.	I believe the work environment of our organization is:	**Very Neg.** 1	**Neg** 2	**Neutral** 3	**Agree** 4	**Very Agree** 5

			Strongly Disagree	Disagree	Neutral	Agree	Strongly Agree
[32]	XXV.	I believe this organization offers sufficient job training for employees.	1	2	3	4	5
[33]	XXVI.	People in this organization share a common set of moral principles.	1	2	3	4	5
[34]	XXVII.	I am pleased with the opportunities I have to be promoted in this organization.	1	2	3	4	5
[35]	XXVIII.	There are leaders in this company who symbolize the values and beliefs of this organization.	1	2	3	4	5
[36]	XXIX.	Your company does its fair share to support community projects.	1	2	3	4	5
[37]	XXX.	Management values the employees of the company.	1	2	3	4	5

XXXI. In your opinion:

			Strongly Non-Favorable	Non-Favorable	Neutral	Favorable	Strongly Favorable
[38]	A.	How do city, state and federal government officials feel about the company	1	2	3	4	5
[39]	B.	How do suppliers feel about the company	1	2	3	4	5
[40]	C.	How do your neighbors and friends feel about the company .	1	2	3	4	5
[41]	D.	How does the press (T.V., radio, newspapers, etc.) feel about the company	1	2	3	4	5

[42] XXXII. Into which marital category do you fit?

( )^1 Single   ( )^3 Widowed
( )^2 Married   ( )^4 Separated or divorced

[43] XXXIII. Into which age category do you fit?

( )^1 Under 25   ( )^4 45-54
( )^2 25-34   ( )^5 55-64
( )^3 35-44   ( )^6 65 and older

[44] XXXIV. What is the highest level of education you have obtained?

( )^1 Didn't complete high school   ( )^4 College graduate
( )^2 High school graduate   ( )^5 Some graduate work
( )^3 Some college   ( )^6 Graduate degree holder

[45] XXXV. Into which race category do you fit?

( )^1 American Indian   ( )^4 Caucasian
( )^2 Asian   ( )^5 Other, please specify:
( )^3 Black   _____

[46] XXXVI. What is your sex?

( )¹ Female   ( )² Male

[47-48]XXXVII. What is the name of your department? (OPTIONAL)

QUESTIONS USED TO DEVELOP MSBS
AND CORPORATE CULTURE INDEX.

Refer back to Question 2 on the questionnaire. The information displayed below is how it looks after computer analysis. It displays the number of people and percent who responded to each possible questionnaire response. For example, on Question 2A, a total of 8, or 20.5%, indicated "not at all" when asked if they would be more effective with more job training.

Table II

Sample computer display of questionnaire results (question 2) from 39 managers in a unit

2. I WOULD BE MORE EFFECTIVE WITH	NOT AT ALL		SLIGHTLY		MODERATELY		CONSIDERABLY		VERY MUCH SO		AVERAGE
A) MORE JOB TRAINING	8	20.5%*	15	38.5%	12	30.8%	1	2.6%	3	7.7%	2.4
	25	16.1%	42	27.1%	60	38.7%	16	10.3%	9	5.8%	2.6
B) BETTER SUPERVISION	17	43.6%	17	43.6%	3	7.7%	2	5.1%	0	0.0%	1.7
	59	38.1%	66	42.6%	16	10.3%	7	4.5%	4	2.6%	1.9
C) MORE CONTROL OVER SUBORDINATES	22	56.4%	12	30.8%	4	10.3%	0	0.0%	0	0.0%	1.5
	72	46.5%	44	28.4%	26	16.8%	6	3.9%	2	1.3%	1.8
D) GREATER PERSONAL COMMITMENT	16	41.0%	11	28.2%	8	20.5%	4	10.3%	0	0.0%	2.0
	51	32.9%	49	31.6%	34	21.9%	14	9.0%	5	3.2%	2.1
E) MORE CLEARLY DEFINED DUTIES	14	35.9%	12	30.8%	8	20.5%	4	10.3%	1	2.5%	2.1
	54	34.8%	46	29.7%	33	21.3%	14	9.0%	5	3.2%	2.1
F) MORE FREEDOM TO USE OWN JUDGMENT	10	25.6%	12	30.8%	4	10.3%	5	12.8%	8	20.5%	2.7
	49	31.6%	50	32.3%	19	12.3%	18	11.6%	17	11.0%	2.3
G) BETTER EVALUATION OF WORK	10	25.6%	14	35.9%	8	20.5%	3	7.7%	4	10.3%	2.4
	33	21.3%	41	26.5%	34	21.9%	27	17.4%	18	11.6%	2.7
H) CLEARER GOALS TO WORK TOWARD	7	17.9%	11	28.2%	9	23.1%	9	23.1%	3	7.7%	2.7
	24	15.5%	42	27.1%	42	27.1%	31	20.0%	14	9.0%	2.8

*The top line for each subquestion (e.g., 2A, 2B, etc.) is the individual unit response. The second line represents the total organization response to the same question.

Management System Balance Sheet

In 1974, I developed the questionnaire as the initial step in an effort to develop an instrument that would help managers appraise their management systems. The questionnaire's 78 questions covered a wide range of areas, including personal goals, performance appraisal, job goals, perception of job satisfaction, training, planning, communication, and feedback. I have administered the questionnaire to some 3,000 persons during the past six years. These persons represent several professions, occupations, and businesses—banking, manufacturing, oil companies, pipelines—down to middle and lower management. Six banks were studied in 1974 and again in 1977.

It was interesting to note how the perceptions in these management systems changed in 3 years. In 1976, the thought occurred to me that a balance sheet could be designed that would reveal both the assets and liabilities of the management system at a particular time. Considerable study followed in human resource accounting. The main thrust has been to put a dollar value on the human resources of the organization.

This work differs from the human resource accounting model in that we are working with perceptions of the management system, whereas the normal resource accounting method has tried to relate dollars to the human assets in a firm.

In the fall of 1979, Ann Tittle Muller, an ORU graduating senior in the School of Business, became interested in the project. She had demonstrated skills in computer programming, as well as creative thinking, and seemed a natural to help develop the management-system balance sheet.

In the summer of 1980, Neal Bratshun took an interest in the project and has done a study with a number of organizations to validate and learn more about the concept.

In my career as a manager, professor, and consultant, I have long observed and been interested in the cyclic changes in management systems. My career with Continental Can Co. involved moving from plant to plant and building management systems to seek out and correct problem situations. I was in on the ground floor of the turnaround of several Continental Can plants, including St. Louis, Chicago Stockyards, and the Indiana-Elwood plant. I noticed in each of these situations how the management systems improved from states of confusion, poor planning, lack of direction, and poor communication, into highly proficient organizations that met both the financial needs of the corporation and the individual needs of the people involved. What I could see then and more clearly now is a need for a system that would enable an organization to annually assess its balance sheet financially, as all corporations and organizations are now doing, as well as assessing the status and perception of the management system.

Needed is a "thermometer" that can be read so that management can see what is happening in its own management system. We need the ability to check the "pulse" of the organization at any given moment. The Management System Balance Sheet will afford management that opportunity. We want to be able to compare what the "pulse" or the "thermometer reading" was over a period of time so that we can make projections and corrections in the future. The management system can ascertain if progress is being made in a particular problem area.

It should be noted that the original management questionnaire in 1974 enabled organizations to pinpoint specific problem areas such as communication, job satisfaction, and performance appraisal. Now they can see the progress that has been made over time in any of these problem areas.

The questionnaire previously presented is the basis of the management—system balance sheet. Questions from that questionnaire have been sorted into the following categories:

1. Goals
2. Planning
3. Planning effectiveness
4. Morale
5. Performance appraisal system
6. Performance reward system
7. Freedom/supervision balance
8. Communication
9. Job satisfaction

Planning and Communication have been scientifically validated through factor analysis. All other categories were developed by both Ann Tittle Muller and me, based on what we thought made sense. We are assuming that the other seven categories measure what we intended to measure.

The responses of organization members are combined to come up with the categories mentioned.

Category	Questions Used
I. Goals	
A. Normality of goals	1, 4, 6
B. Clarity of goals	2h
II. Planning	
A. MBO	7, 11

	B. Quality of planning	8, 14
	C. Extent of planning	9, 10
III.	Planning effectiveness	7a-7d, 7f, 7g
IV.	Morale	2d, 3c, 3d, 3f, 7b
V.	Performance appraisal	2g, 2e, 7c, 15
VI.	Rewards	3a, 3b, 3j, 7a, 7g, 8h
VII.	Freedom/supervision balance	2b, 2c, 2f, 3h, 7d
VIII.	Communication	3g, all of 5, 8i, 13
IX.	Job satisfaction	2a, 3e, 3h, 3i, 3k

Note that each question on the questionnaire may be used once, twice, or not at all. The methodology section more clearly explains this process.

Each category has a measurement in the range -2.0 to +2.0. If the measurement is 0.0 or greater, then the category is considered an asset. If the measurement is less than 0.0, then the category is considered a liability. Since there are nine categories, the best reading an organization could possibly receive is +18.0. The worst reading an organization could possibly receive is -18.0.

The questionnaire is given to organization members. After the planning/MBO process is introduced, the questionnaire is given again. At this point top management can see if Long-Range Planning/MBO is actually improving the management system.

To determine the actual validity of the Management-System Balance Sheet, two specific organizations were studied over a period of time to see if the idea is viable. Both organizations had a set of questionnaires administered when I went to work on their planning and MBO systems. Both organizations had problems. I was called in as a consultant to help develop plans, priorities, and strategies to improve their situations. The second set of questionnaires was administered approximately a year after the long-range-planning system had been installed. In both cases, dramatic changes had taken place in all traditional measurement areas, including profits, performance, efficiency, and other financial criteria. In the case of a manufacturing company, it had gone from four years of barely breaking even to a healthy profit profile and a 25% increase in productivity.

A hotel complex had gone from the cashflow problems of a rapidly expanding organization, construction, remodeling delays, and rapidly approaching financial problems, into a reasonably well-organized, on-schedule system. Two specific financial crises were handled while Long-Range Planning/MBO was being instituted.

The changes in the perceived effectiveness of the management system are displayed. The management-system assets and liabilities for both the manufacturing and the hotel complex showed improvement in most categories. Tables III, IV, and V demonstrate the Management System Balance Sheet. Table I shows the management-system balance sheet for the manufacturing company as of September 1979.

Table III
Manufacturing Before Long-Range Planning/MBO

Assets

Planning effectiveness	+0.0
Morale	+0.2
Freedom to work	+0.6
Communication	+0.0
Job satisfaction	+0.2
Total assets	+1.0

Liabilities

Goals	-0.9
Planning	-0.7
Performance appraisal	-0.7
Performance reward	-0.2
Total liabilities	-2.5

This shows the need for an improvement index of -1.5.

Table IV shows the manufacturing management system balance sheet as of April 1980.

Exhibit II
Manufacturing After Long-Range Planning/MBO

Assets

Goals	+0.6
Planning	+0.1
Planning effectiveness	+0.5
Morale	+0.3
Performance appraisal	+0.1
Performance reward	+0.0
Freedom to work	+0.6
Communication	+0.3
Total assets	+2.5

Liabilities

Job dissatisfaction	-0.2
Total liabilities	-0.2

The balance sheet indicates significant changes were made in the management system at the manufacturing company after introduction of

Long-Range Planning/MBO.

Liabilities improved from -2.5 to -0.2 and assets went from +1.0 to +2.5 or overall improvement of -1.5 to +2.3. The top management team made these statements to verify the results of the Management System Balance Sheet.

The entire top-management team responded to the question, "What has this Planning/MBO system done for the company?" Some of their responses were:

1. Better communication and teamwork. Cooperation on every one's part to work together as a team.
2. The system has achieved a procedure whereby all the management people of … manufacturing company are now included in the overall planning and objectives of the company. There is a more open communication and understanding of proper management techniques.
3. It has pulled department heads and managers together for more constructive planning, better planning, more input from people and ideas.
4. Has allowed each department a means of planning and evaluating itself.
5. Got every manager working smarter and requesting help in achieving his goals.
6. It has given everyone a course to follow and a feeling of being part of a winning team.

These comments tend to support and validate the gains shown by the Management System Balance Sheet.

In the hotel situation, the first questionnaire was given in July 1979. The Management System Balance Sheet for the hotel is listed in Table V.

Table V
Hotel Before Long-Range Planning/MBO

Assets

Freedom to work	+0.1
Total assets	+0.1

Liabilities

Goals	-0.6
Planning	-0.5
Planning ineffectiveness	-0.2
Low morale	-0.6
Performance appraisal	-0.7
Performance reward	-0.6

Communication	-0.2
Job dissatisfaction	-0.4
Total liabilities	-3.8

Notice that the liabilities far outweighed the assets. This difference we call improvement needed, which is a factor of -3.9.

The Management System Balance Sheet of the hotel as of January 1980 is listed in Table VI.

Table VI
Hotel After Long-Range Planning/MBO

Assets

Goals	+0.2
Planning	+0.0
Planning effectiveness	+0.4
Performance appraisal	+0.0
Performance reward	+0.2
Freedom to supervise	+0.0
Communication	+0.2
Job satisfaction	+0.2
Total assets	+1.2

Liabilities

Low morale	-0.3
Total liabilities	-0.3

Significant changes were made in the hotel complex after the introduction of Long-Range Planning/MBO.

Improvement factor went from -3.9 to +0.9 through the implementation of Long-Range Planning/MBO.

Both the manufacturing and hotel improved after strategic planning/MBO was introduced. The two control organizations had no change in their balance sheets over the same period of time.

References
Chapter 13

[1]Washington, D.C.: The Bureau of National Affairs, Inc., 1977. In addition to an excellent discussion of productivity problems and solutions, case histories, and facsimiles of material used by many companies, Rudge's book includes four of his specially designed "audits"—questionnaires directed to specific segments of the worker population.

[2]The SPSS factor-analysis computer program was set up and run with the assistance of James E. Dunn at the University of Arkansas. For more information on factor analysis, refer to the article, "Understanding Factor Analysis," by R. J. Rummell, Journal of Conflict Resolution, December 1967, pp. 445-448.

[3]Dale H. Bent, Norman H. Nie, and C. Hadle Hull, SPSS, New York: McGraw Hill, 1970, p. 209.

[4]The objective for each question in the questionnaire is apparent. Stephen J. Carroll, Jr., and Henry L. Tosi, Jr., describe an intensive study of MBO in their book *Management by Objectives: Applications and Research*, New York: Macmillan, 1973, pp. 21-46 and Appendix A, pp. 149-161.

[5]Harry S. Dennis III, Gary M. Richetto, and John Wiemann, "Articulating the Need for an Effective Internal Communication System: New Empirical Evidence for the Communication Specialist," paper delivered to the 1974 annual convention of the International Communication Association, New Orleans, La.

[6]*Ibid.*

[7]Sidney Siegal, *Nonparametric Statistics for the Behavioral Sciences*, New York: McGraw Hill, 1956, pp. 213-239. See also Charles T. Clark and Lawrence L. Schkade, *Statistical Methods for Business Decisions*, Cincinnati: Southwestern Publishing Co., 1969, pp. 570-571.

[8]R. Henry Migliore, "A Three-Year Longitudinal Study of Goal Priority in the Banking and Selected Manufacturing Industries," an unpublished manuscript, 1978.

[9]R. Henry Migliore, "A Study of Management by Objectives in the Banking and Selected Manufacturing Industries" (Ph.D. dissertation, University of Arkansas, 1975).

[10]Dr. Bruce Kirchhoff has developed a method to determine the extent of use of MBO in an organization. Bruce A. Kirchhoff, "A Foundation for the Measurement of the Extent of Use of Management by Objectives," (Ph.D. dissertation, University of Utah, 1972).

[11]The computer program was written with my help by David Down in 1973 for a study on productivity sponsored by the Faculty Senate Research Fund.

Chapter 14
Applying SLRP/MBO in the
Mid-size Organization

I have had the opportunity to assist, advise, and install strategic planning/MBO systems in a wide variety of organizations over the past decade. Included in this number are major corporations, a large number of nonprofit organizations, and of late, a number of medium-sized organizations. The last two years I have worked with hundreds of small businesses. The strategic planning system developed and used in the organizations is the one introduced in this book.

A discussion follows on how this management system was introduced, used, and its ultimate results in three medium-sized organizations. The organizations discussed are:

1. Cross Manufacturing — A manufacturing company that sells hydraulic equipment to farm equipment companies.
2. T. D. Williamson, Inc. — A major product and service company for the pipeline industry.
3. A nonprofit association — An association with a major hotel/motel subsidiary.

Although not discussed here, the same general procedure described was used in the Colowyo Coal Co., Intregal Corp., Hydrus Corp., Back-to-the-Bible Broadcast, First United Methodist Church, Tulsa, Department of Parks and Recreation, Tulsa, General Information Systems, Inc., and a number of other organizations. The implementation, use, and review seem to have worked well in all of those organizations.

The chapter is divided into the following categories; SLRP/MBO Introduction, The Use of SLRP/MBO, and Results.

SLRP/MBO Introduction

In Cross Manufacturing Company and the nonprofit association, I was assigned to introduce the strategic planning MBO system. The management questionnaire was administered to determine the assets and liabilities in the management system. This helped to understand the management system and provided a discussion tool for the managers to be able to discuss the merits of their own management system. In both those organizations, a teaching/working seminar helped the participants know the intricate parts of the nine-step planning system. The top two levels of management participated in both of those seminars.

In the third organization, T. D. Williamson, Inc., the strategic planning system was started by the late Ed Green. He had set up the planning system and it was functioning very well when I became involved with the company as a member of the Board of Directors. A. B. Steen, President; Richard Jarvis, then Director of Planning; and I assessed the planning system in 1978. We found weaknesses to be:

1. The planning system was not being used to its full extent.
2. The planning system did not tie into the reward system.
3. Not enough people were involved in the planning system.
4. Some decentralized entities were using MBO to a greater degree than others.

The Use of SLRP/MBO

In all three organizations, the same general and chronological cycle was either started or continued. Before the budget year began, all managers met to develop both short- and long-term objectives. These objectives were arrived at after a thorough look at the organization's purpose, mission, environment, strengths, weaknesses, and assumptions. These objectives were then reviewed on a quarterly basis. At Cross Manufacturing and the hotel complex, every other review session was a group review session. Each operating and staff manager would present his objectives and results to the total group. In all of these quarterly meetings, I participated and was leader of the program.

During at least one meeting per year, and in most cases two meetings, these review sessions were held between the president of the corporation and the individual management or department heads. This gave each manager at the second level in the organization an opportunity each year to have his progress reviewed both in a group with his peers present and individually for a more candid discussion with his boss. T. D. Williamson, Inc., holds the same quarterly meetings under the able leadership of A. B. Steen.

After the first year, the subject of strategy was developed both in Cross Manufacturing and the nonprofit organization as well as most of the other organizations listed. I have found that it is difficult to identify strategies to achieve the objectives stated during the first year. During the second year, however, the whole idea of strategic thinking and the development of stated strategies to be placed in the planning book is very appropriate. Of all the companies I have worked with over the past 10 years, T. D. Williamson executives seem to best understand and use the strategic concept.

I lead a two-day planning session that focused strictly on strategies to meet the corporative objectives. This was appropriate timing, because T. D. Williamson had been operating on a similar planning system for a number of years. With other parts identified, the managers could emphasize strategy.

In each organization that I have worked with, there must be an in-house person who directs and is the liaison person for the process. John Cross has done that job very well with Cross Manufacturing; Christopher Kenna has filled that position with the nonprofit organization; and Richard Jarvis did that job for T. D. Williamson, Inc. This person manages the process but in no way takes over the authority from top management to run the program. The liaison person must be innovative and help adapt the planning process to the individual organization. The chief executive officer must be interested, present, and see this as his planning system that is coordinated by the director of long-range planning, and receives advice and training from me, the major consultant. Any other breakdown of responsibilities will make the whole process unsuccessful. The chief executive officers of all these organizations support, emphasize, and take part in this planning process.

Results

In all three organizations, there appear to be positive results. Again, with T. D. Williamson under the direction of Ed Green, the solid backing of then President T. D. Williamson, Jr., and the new president, A. B. Steen, and the coordination of Richard Jarvis, they had a fine planning management system going before I became involved. My involvement with the review process and emphasis on strategy and moving the process down to the next level of management seem to have paid dividends.

At the nonprofit organization, with the massive expansion going on, it provided the opportunity for better coordination during a time of rapid growth.

I developed a concept called a Management System Balance Sheet before long-range planning was introduced. Table VIII shows the initial nonprofit organization's Balance Sheet.

At the nonprofit organization, the first questionnaire was given in July 1979.

Table VIII
Nonprofit Association Before Long-Range Planning/MBO

Assets

Freedom to work	+0.1
Total assets	+0.1

Liabilities

Goals	-0.6
Planning	-0.5
Planning ineffectiveness	-0.2
Low morale	-0.6
Performance appraisal	-0.7
Performance reward	-0.6
Communication	-0.2
Job dissatisfaction	-0.4
Total liabilities	-3.8

Notice that the liabilities far outweighed the assets. This difference we call improvement needed, which is a factor of -3.9.

After MBO was introduced, Table IX shows its balance sheet. You will note it had improvement in all areas.

The Management System Balance Sheet as of January 1980 and June 1980 is listed:

Table IX
Nonprofit Association After Long-Range Planning/MBO

Assets

	January 1980	June 1980
Goals	+0.2	+0.0
Planning	+0.0	+0.0
Planning effectiveness	+0.4	+0.0
Performance appraisal	+0.0	+0.0
Performance reward	+0.2	+0.0
Freedom to supervise	+0.0	+0.6
Communication	+0.2	+0.1
Job satisfaction	+0.2	+0.1
Total assets	+1.2	+1.9

Liabilities

	January 1980	June 1980
Low morale	-0.3	-0.0
Total liabilities	-0.3	-0.0

Note the +5.0 improvement factor from -3.9 to +4.6 to +5.0. The initial balance sheet for Cross Manufacturing is shown in Table X.

Table X
Manufacturing Before Long-Range Planning/MBO

Assets

Planning effectiveness	+0.0
Morale	+0.2
Freedom to work	+0.6
Communication	+0.0
Job satisfaction	+0.2
Total assets	+1.0

Liabilities

Goals	-0.9
Planning	-0.7
Performance appraisal	-0.7
Performance reward	-0.2
Total liabilities	-2.5

This shows the need for an improvement index of -1.5.

Table XI shows the manufacturing management-system balance sheet as of April 1980.

Table XI
Manufacturing After Long-Range Planning/MBO

Assets

Goals	+0.6
Planning	+0.1
Planning effectiveness	+0.5
Morale	+0.3
Performance appraisal	+0.1
Performance reward	+0.0
Freedom to work	+0.6
Communication	+0.3
Total assets	+2.5

Liabilities

Job dissatisfaction	-0.2
Total liabilities	-0.2

The balance sheet indicates that significant changes were made in the management system at the manufacturing company after the introduction of Long- Range Planning/MBO.

Liabilities improved from -2.5 to -0.2 and assets went from +1.0 to +2.5 or overall improvement from -1.5 to +2.3. The top management team made these statements to verify the results of the Management System Balance Sheet.

The entire top-management team responded to the question, "What has this Planning/MBO system done for the company?" Some of their responses are:

1. It has fostered better communications and teamwork. Cooperation on everyone's part to work together as a team.
2. The system has achieved a procedure whereby all the management people of ... manufacturing company are now included in the overall planning and objectives of the company. There is a more open communication and understanding of proper management techniques.
3. It has pulled department heads and managers together for more constructive planning, better planning, more input from people and ideas.
4. It has allowed each department a means of planning and evaluating itself.
5. It has taught every manager to work smarter and to request help in achieving his goals.
6. It has given everyone a course to follow and a feeling of being part of a winning team.

These comments tend to support and validate the gains shown by the Management System Balance Sheet.

Table XII
T.D. WILLIAMSON, INC.
MANAGEMENT SYSTEM BALANCE SHEET

ASSETS	JUNE 1979	JAN 1981
Goals	+0.79	+ .82
Planning	+0.97	+ .88
Planning effectiveness	+0.52	+ .26
Morale	+0.75	+ .32
Performance appraisal	+0.54	+ .49
Performance reward system	+0.36	+ .17
Supervision balance	+1.01	+ .79
Communication	+0.66	+ .62
Job satisfaction	+0.75	+ .43
TOTAL ASSETS:	+6.35	+4.78

LIABILITIES

TOTAL LIABILITIES: +0.00   +0.00

Of the for-profit organizations tested to date, T.D. Williamson, Inc., has shown the best consistent balance sheet. Its results are in Table XII. It has a sophisticated planning system that has been in place since 1976. Back to the Bible Broadcast has had the most consistent scores over the past 10 years. Note their results in Tables XIII and IV. It is assumed that the planning system has contributed to the good balance sheet results.

Table XIII

Back to the Bible Broadcast
MANAGEMENT SYSTEM BALANCE SHEET

ASSETS	TOTAL	August 1986 DIRECTOR	SUPERVISOR	MANAGER
Goals	0.98	1.08	1.15	1.13
Planning	0.95	1.17	0.91	0.93
Planning Effectiveness	0.42	0.79	0.33	0.40
Morale	0.62	0.75	0.75	0.41
Performance Appraisal	0.95	1.08	1.06	0.78
Supervision Balance	1.00	1.30	1.07	0.85
Communication	0.82	1.00	0.80	0.77
Job Satisfaction	0.88	1.07	0.94	0.75
Performance Reward System	0.34	0.71	0.24	0.35
TOTAL ASSETS	6.96	8.95	7.25	6.37
LIABILITIES	——	——	——	——

Table IV

Back to the Bible Broadcast
Using Strategic Planning/MBO

MANAGEMENT SYSTEM BALANCE SHEET

ASSETS	OCT 1980	FEB 1981	NOV 1981	DEC 1982	JULY 1985	JULY 1986	JULY 1987
Goals	+0.60	---	+0.59	+0.67	.89	.98	1.08
Planning	+0.27	+0.00	+0.52	+0.84	.71	.95	.92
Planning Effectiveness	+0.04	+0.17	+0.20	+0.50	.24	.42	-0.01
Morale	+0.23	+0.83	+0.11	+0.32	.53	.62	.94
Performance Appraisal	+0.00	+0.33	+0.12	+0.44	.76	.95	.78
Supervision Balance	+0.64	+0.67	+0.53	+0.59	.96	1.00	.85
Communication	+0.46	+0.36	+0.25	+0.64	.75	.82	.67
Job Satisfaction	+0.37	+0.48	+0.55	+0.63	.79	.88	.33
Goals	---	-0.43					
Performance Reward System	-0.05	-0.41	-0.16	+0.34	+.16	+.34	.33
TOTAL ABILITIES MINUS TOTAL LIABILITIES	+2.56	+2.00	+2.71	+4.97	+5.79	+6.96	+5.89

234

Chapter 15
Corporate Culture Index
A Base for Strategic Planning and Management

The culture of an organization is important to its life, contribution to society, and survival.

The opportunity to recognize and measure culture gives organization leaders the ability to understand and to better manage. A Corporate Culture Index has been developed.

The instrument to measure culture was given to businesses, hospitals, and churches. It was determined that a Corporate Culture Index could be developed for all those that participated.

What Is Corporate Culture?

A good definition of organizational culture was provided almost four decades ago by Eliott Jacques:

"The customary or traditional ways of thinking and doing things, which are shared to a greater or lesser extent by all members of the organization and which new members must learn and at least partially accept in order to be accepted into the service of the firm."[1]

The culture of an organization is generally viewed as a complete set of beliefs, ethics, values, ideologies, assumptions, and symbols. Culture is defined as "the totality of socially transmitted behavior patterns, arts, beliefs, institutions, and all other products of human work and thought characteristic of a community or population."[2] Another definition is "basic and enduring values and beliefs which are widely held throughout the organization. These values and beliefs comprise the content of an organization's culture and are common understandings which are frequently taken for granted and which are reinforced by stories, symbols, rituals, and language systems. Intangible and unseen but known, these values and beliefs are distinguished from the concrete or visible manifestations of culture."[3]

Most researchers conclude that corporate culture ascribes to the beliefs, principles, and behavior patterns that come together to shape the central individuality of each organization. Tulsa University professor, Donald D. Bowen, commented in a newspaper interview that corporate culture "includes a company's dress code, philosophy, public functions, communications, material goods, and physical environment."[4]

Edgar Schein of Massachusetts Institute of Technology states that it is an incomplete notion that "culture is only a set of shared meanings that make it possible for members of a group to interpret and act upon their environment."[5]

A culture is a template of basic assumptions that a particular group has invented, discovered, or devised in learning to deal with its problems of external adaption and internal integration. This template has worked well enough to be considered valid; therefore it is taught to new individuals in the organization as the correct way to think, feel, and perceive in accordance with other problems.[6]

The corporate culture of an organization can be analyzed at many different levels. The "visible artifacts" or the developed environment of the company are its manner of visible or audible behavior patterns, unspoken doctrine, architecture, technological level or current modernity, employee orientation, materials, public documents, characters, credo statements, or even books of discipline. This level of cultural analysis is difficult data to evaluate because it is easy to find and difficult to interpret. Descriptions can be given on how behavior patterns are discernible among the members, but it is common not to be able to know the true reason why the organization acts the way it does.[7]

Typically speaking, all organizations have some set of values that guide their behavior (second box in Chart 1). As a result of the elusive nature of an innate value system, it is difficult to observe values directly. This forces organizations to research their character documents, doctrines or interview key personnel to glean any concrete information. The problem with this "value" information is that it is only a personal perception of why they behave the way they do, rather than the true motivation which is generally cloaked or unconscious.

To get to the root of culture, this concealed or unconscious motivation behind the outward behavior must be discovered. These learned values are forces behind the decision-making process. The decision made is based on an assumption which is soon frequently forgotten. Assumptions which are taken for granted are very powerful, ingrained characteristics. Power renders assumptions less debatable or adjustable than given values. Some examples of such assumptions would be, that schools should educate, businesses should be profitable, medicine should prolong life, and churches should be religious. These are assumptions even though they are often considered values.

Controlling values can be divided into: (1) ultimate, non-debatable, taken-for-granted values, for which the term "assumptions" is more appropriate; and (2) debatable, overtly espoused values for which the term "values" is more applicable (see Chart 1).[8]

There are different positions taken on the cohesiveness of organizational culture. Many scholars believe that a strong culture with a "well-defined set of guiding beliefs" is better than a weak culture that has less of a bonding nature. "Not only do individual businesses have strong cultures, but links among business, the banking industry, and the government are also cultural and very powerful. Japan, Inc., is actually an expansion of the corporate culture idea on a national scale."[9]

Organizations have ingrained cultures. It is believed that a strong culture denotes agreement among the members of the organization. Also, strong culture promotes cohesion of all those who wish to be an active part of the organizational structure or membership body. The extent of the bond and harmony that remains among the values and ideologies, is a measure of the internal fit or attachment that characterizes the culture. Chart 2 shows the different factors in the organization in relation to the main objective of performance. Failing to practice consistency within the structure can provide a degree of incompatibility among individual groups with regard to the values of the espoused culture.

A survey of chief executive officers revealed that most believed that organizational cultures are real, and that strong cultures contribute to corporate success. Forty percent said they believed strongly enough to try to "deal with culture in a serious manner."[10]

CHART 1

THE LEVELS OF CULTURE AND THEIR INTERACTION

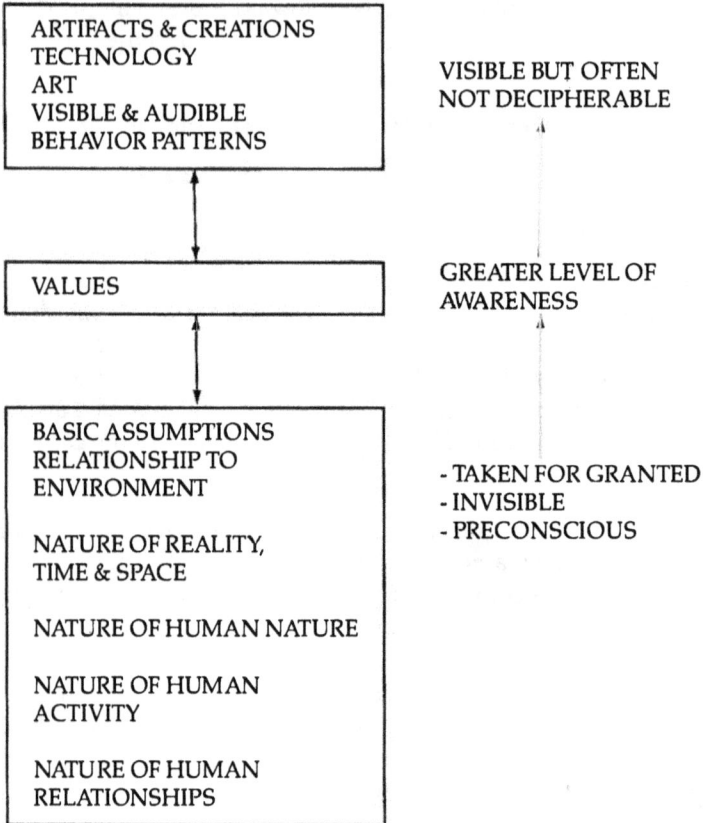

```
┌─────────────────────────────┐
│ ARTIFACTS & CREATIONS       │        VISIBLE BUT OFTEN
│ TECHNOLOGY                  │        NOT DECIPHERABLE
│ ART                         │
│ VISIBLE & AUDIBLE           │
│ BEHAVIOR PATTERNS           │
└─────────────────────────────┘

┌─────────────────────────────┐
│ VALUES                      │        GREATER LEVEL OF
└─────────────────────────────┘        AWARENESS

┌─────────────────────────────┐
│ BASIC ASSUMPTIONS           │        - TAKEN FOR GRANTED
│ RELATIONSHIP TO             │        - INVISIBLE
│ ENVIRONMENT                 │        - PRECONSCIOUS
│                             │
│ NATURE OF REALITY,          │
│ TIME & SPACE                │
│                             │
│ NATURE OF HUMAN NATURE      │
│                             │
│ NATURE OF HUMAN             │
│ ACTIVITY                    │
│                             │
│ NATURE OF HUMAN             │
│ RELATIONSHIPS               │
└─────────────────────────────┘
```

CHART 2

CULTURAL INFLUENCE

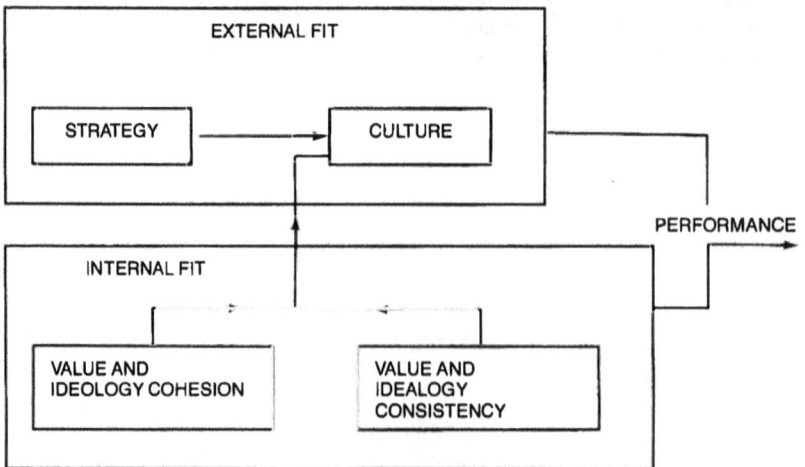

```
┌──────────────────────────────────────────────┐
│ EXTERNAL FIT                                   │
│                                                │
│  ┌───────────┐         ┌───────────┐           │───────┐
│  │ STRATEGY  │────────▶│  CULTURE  │           │       │
│  └───────────┘         └───────────┘           │       │
│                                                │       │──▶ PERFORMANCE
└──────────────────────────────────────────────┘       │
┌──────────────────────────────────────────────┐       │
│ INTERNAL FIT                                   │       │
│                                                │───────┘
│  ┌───────────────┐      ┌───────────────┐      │
│  │ VALUE AND     │      │ VALUE AND     │      │
│  │ IDEOLOGY      │      │ IDEALOGY      │      │
│  │ COHESION      │      │ CONSISTENCY   │      │
│  └───────────────┘      └───────────────┘      │
└──────────────────────────────────────────────┘
```

Development of Corporate Culture Index

An index is developed to measure corporate culture. By definition, it is illusive at best with every organization being unique and having a culture all its own. After working with a wide range of public and private companies, (government-related, nonprofit and ministry/church related), the differences can be quickly detected.

A basic assumption when developing an index is that you know what to measure and how much weight to put on each factor involved. For research purposes and this paper, the following categories were determined as important in measuring the culture in an organization:

1. Goals	11. Values
2. Planning	12. Training
3. Planning Effectiveness	13. Unique
4. Morale	14. Social
5. Performance Appraisals	15. Ethics
6. Rewards	16. Leader
7. Freedom	17. Interaction
8. Communication	18. Benefits
9. Job Satisfaction	19. Perception
10. People	20. Environment

The measurement method is designed to create a negative and positive opportunity for each category. If the culture is very favorable, it will have a higher positive score. If poor culture, it will be a lower score. The index is the combined measurement of the positive minus the negative scores.

No attempt is made to determine if upper management is satisfied with its culture index. It is beyond the scope of this paper to suggest that culture affects the bottom line in key result areas. In contrast, the Strategic Planning Institute's PIMS model suggests, for example, that market share has the largest impact on normal profit. There is no proof today that culture directly affects normal profit, although opinions might suggest it does.

It can be seen that the total Corporate Culture Index score (CCI) is close in regard to a possible high of 100 or low of 20. Company Two scores the highest with a score of 61.3. Figure 2, page 17, Ministry One, is next, with a score of 57.9, and Company One, follows with a score of 54.5. (See Figure 1 and Figure 3 on page 16 and page 18.) A closer examination of the 20 categories is needed to provide more information as to how the organization has performed in comparison with others. An example of this could be shown in the area of planning effectiveness of Company One and Ministry One with scores of 1.6 and 1.7 respectively, contrasted with Company Two's score of 3.0. This can even be further broken down on the MSBS score (also part of total CCI questionnaire): Company One, Ministry One, and Company Two are -0.76, -0.80, and .43, respectively. The scope value is incidental in these cases, the performance among them is what is important. An understanding of what these scores mean is made intelligible by evaluating the questionnaire. (A sample is in Appendix B. Figure 4 on pages 19 and 20 give sample questions asked into the 20 different areas.) Planning effectiveness (question three) is section IX(a-d), IXf, and IXg. Question IX,a, for example, specifically deals with the strategic plan being followed. It gives more opportunity for personal recognition: (1) not at all, (2) slightly, (3) moderately, (4) considerably, and (5) very much so. Has the employee had the opportunity to satisfy his higher level needs? This specific example of planning effectiveness is segmented in possible response scores. As noted, rankings one through five give a value to the particular area investigated. When compiled, the other 19 areas are formulated in a similar fashion of questions and valued responses to create the possible CCI score of 100. Pursuing these inner drives and motivations is necessary to understand the employees' fulfillment. Performance is always the concern of the task-orientated organization; to understand and utilize the most from the staff that really wants to be part of the team.

As additional information becomes available, the telltale sign of performance on the CCI score will provide an index of possible achievement. This, in comparison with other businesses, profit or nonprofit, of the same nature, can be evaluated on how they are progressing internally. The staff of the organization then can understand that perhaps they are, nationally speaking, doing well, but that there are weak areas that need improvement, or that nationally their performance is below par in most areas, and this signifies the need for change.

The next task is to develop an index with a large data base to provide organizations with enough information to accurately assess where they are and where they could be within their own given situation.

Conclusion

It is important to identify and measure the culture of an organization. A culture index has been developed so that each participating organization can measure its culture against others. In each of the 20 categories, each organization can make comparisons. Especially important at this time is how the organization is perceived by the outside community. Scores in these categories indicate a need for serious self-examination followed by planned public relations plans on how to bolster that negative image. Low scores on how the organization is being managed, and high turnover of employees dictate a need to look at how the planning and management system operate. Closer examination of an organization's culture could assist it to adapt and be more effective.

A total of 30 organizations were tested. The Management System Balance Sheet and Corporate Culture Index were calculated for each organization. Top management was presented the data in each case. The conclusion was that the MSBS and CCI did, in fact, measure perceptions of how the organization was managed and give an accurate measure of culture.

A consultant with McKinsey and Company has stated that to manage successfully, a company must (1) decide what kind of culture is needed in the organization, (2) evaluate the existing culture to determine where gaps exist between the actual and desired cultures, (3) decide how to close these gaps, and (4) repeat the entire process periodically.[11] The CI as developed gives managers the four options. The management team could determine what the score in each of the 20 categories should be. They could evaluate where they are with the CI. Then an action plan could be developed to close the gap. Both the MSBS and CI can be measured periodically to keep culture where it should be.

Blake and Mouton state that Corporate Culture is "the attitudes, beliefs, and values of its people along with traditions, precedents, and past practices of the organization comprise that organization's culture, its way of doing business. It may be integrated around values of achievement and excellence, woven around seniority and benefits, or may reveal disinterest, apathy, and hopelessness. It significantly influences how people apply or withhold their energies. To attempt to change a firm which is ineffective or marginally effective into a highly effective one despite its culture, at the worst is likely to be futile and at the best, of limited success. It may even generate stronger negative attitudes and deeper resistances and produce a worse corporate performance than formerly existed."

Blake and Mouton believe that culture does have an effect on how the organization is managed. They continue, "Corporate culture results in organization work which is:

Completely Sound: attitudes, values, and beliefs, and traditions, precedents, and practices which currently influence corporate members have the effect of stimulating efforts to produce, achieve, and accomplish; excellence is a value throughout the corporation; it has a strong and constructive impact on short term operations and long term planning.

Almost Completely Sound

Quite Sound

Moderately Sound

As Sound As Unsound: corporate culture contains some positive elements which promote productive effort and accomplishment, but others which restrict people from applying their energies so as to further excellence; tradition, "the company way," and "how things were done in the past" tend to stifle approaches based upon actualities; "status quosim" is a key to understanding attitudes, efforts, and actions.

Moderately Unsound

Quite Unsound

Almost Completely Unsound

Completely Unsound: traditions, precedents, and practices, expectations, beliefs, and values bear little relationship to productive achievement or profit seeking; apathy and indifference are in the warp and woof of the culture; militant resistance and antagonism toward the corporation are evident.[12]

Using the culture Index, the CI provides a measure to monitor and improve performance. Last year at my annual physical exam, my blood pressure was 160/100. That was a measure of a present condition. I had to develop objectives and strategy to improve an unfavorable score. A few months ago at this years physical, the blood pressure was 120/80. Why the improvement? I knew the score and took action. A number of organizations use the CI to monitor the planning, management and control system.

Figure 1

SUMMARY OF M.S.B.S. - COMPANY ONE

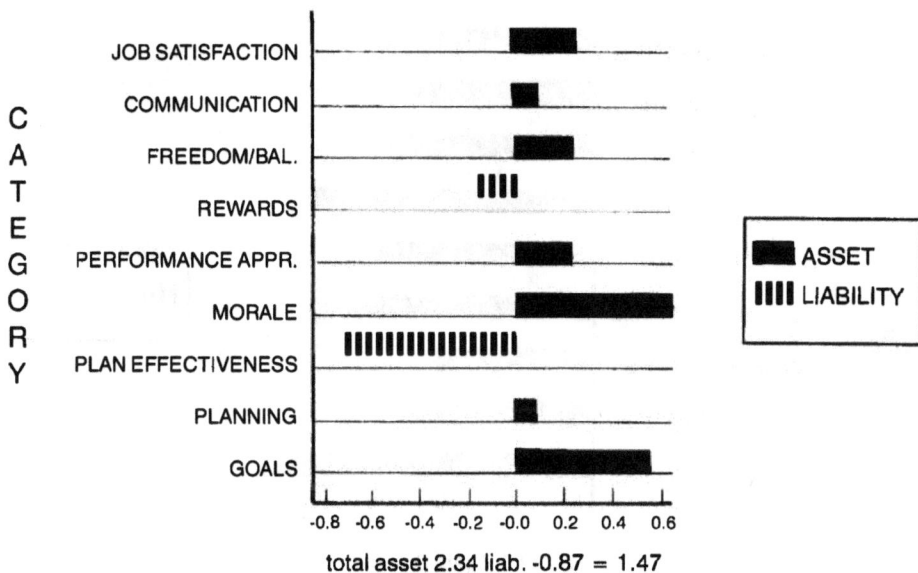

total asset 2.34 liab. -0.87 = 1.47

SUMMARY OF C.C.I. - COMPANY ONE

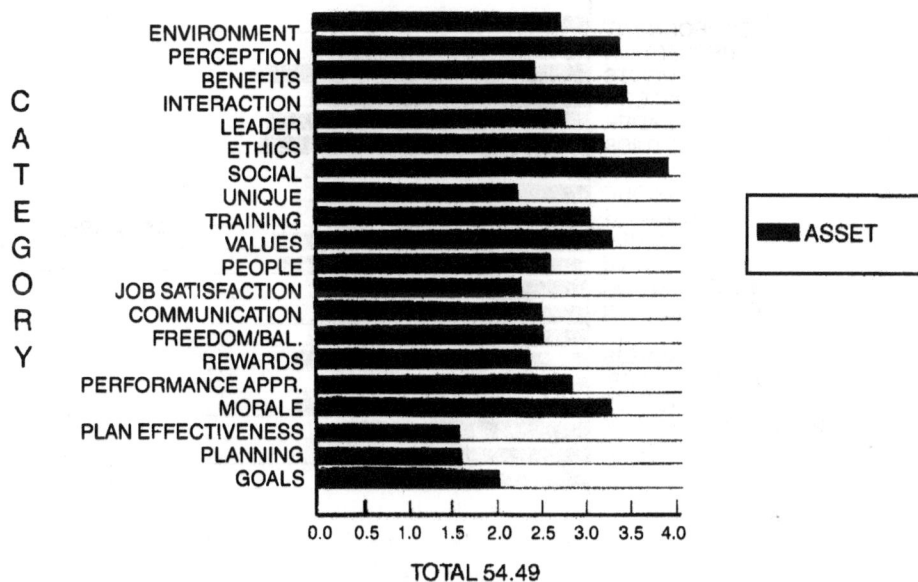

TOTAL 54.49

Figure 2

SUMMARY OF M.S.B.S. - COMPANY TWO

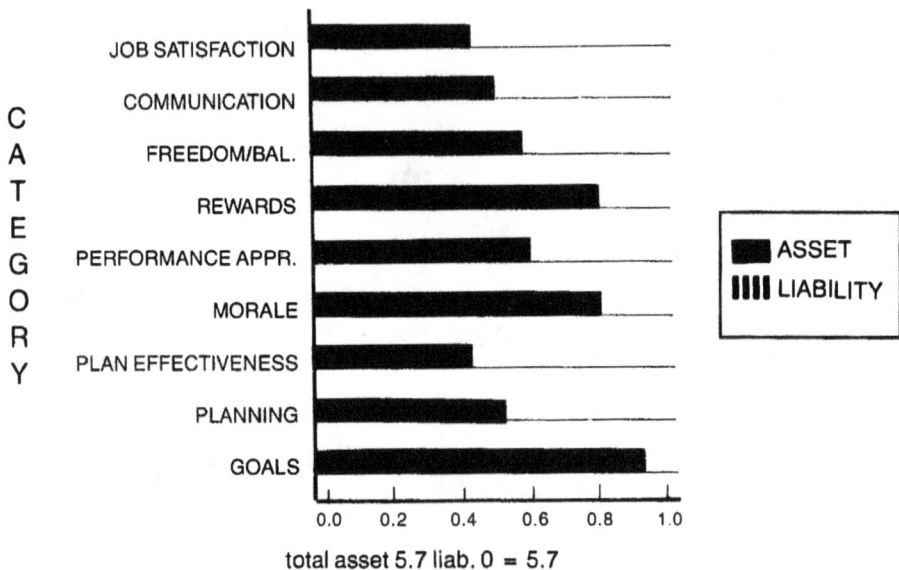

total asset 5.7 liab. 0 = 5.7

SUMMARY OF C.C.I. - COMPANY TWO

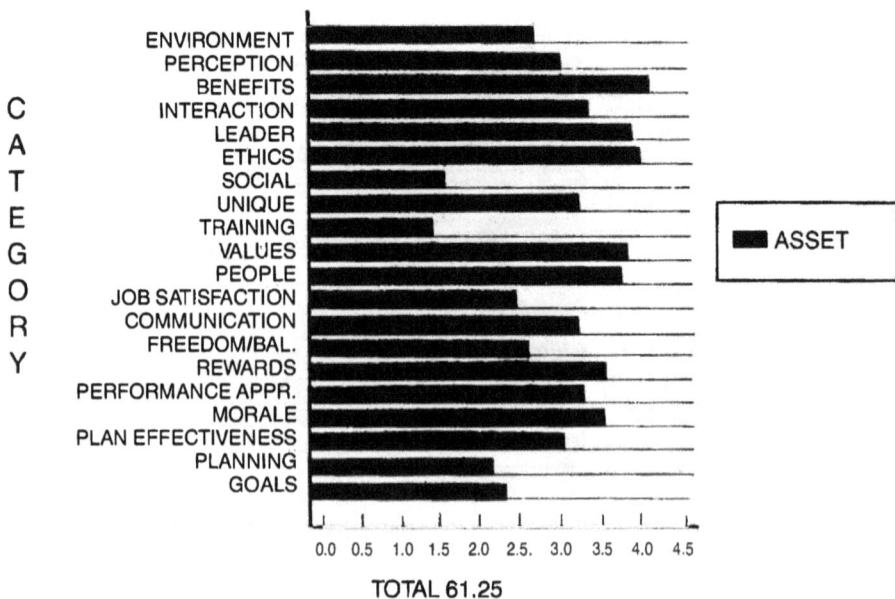

TOTAL 61.25

Figure 3

SUMMARY OF M.S.B.S. - MINISTRY ONE

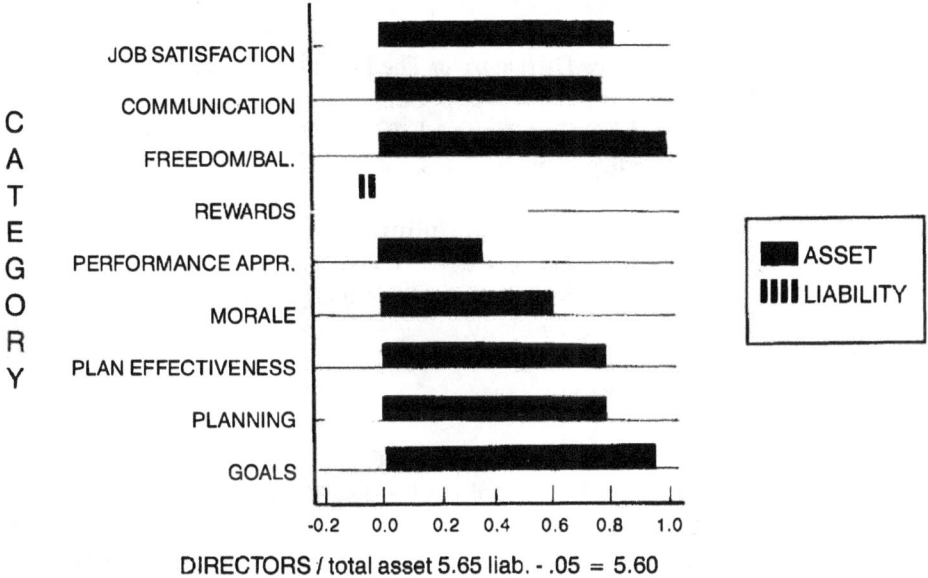

DIRECTORS / total asset 5.65 liab. - .05 = 5.60

SUMMARY OF C.C.I. - MINISTRY ONE

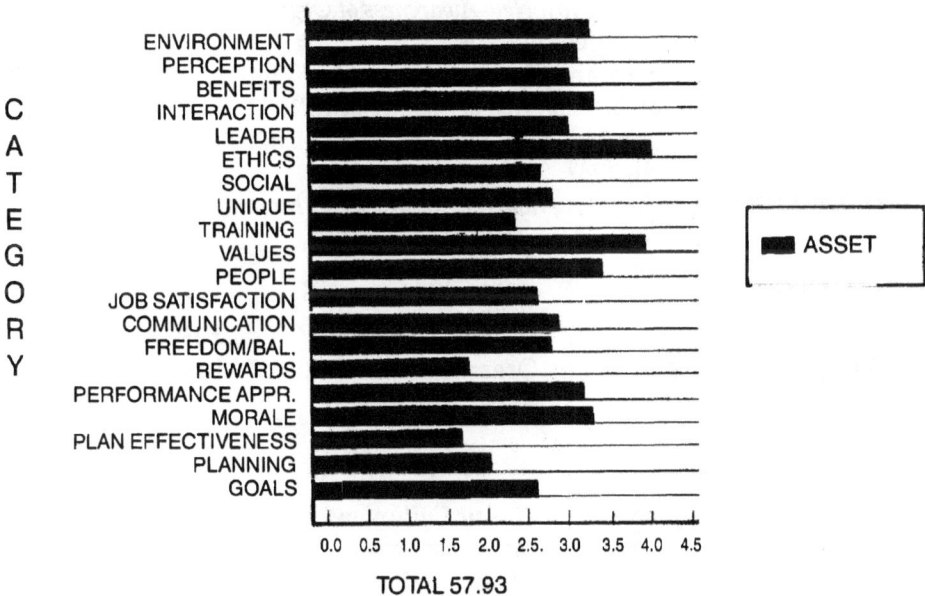

TOTAL 57.93

ENDNOTES

[1]Jacques, Eliott, *The Changing Culture of a Factory,* London: Tavistock Institute, 1951, p. 251.

[2]*The New American Heritage Dictionary of The English Language,* Boston, MA: Houghton Mifflin Company, 1978, p. 321.

[3]Byles, Charles M. and Keating, Robert J., *Strength of Organizational Culture and Performance: Strategic Implications,* Stillwater, OK: Oklahoma State University.

[4]Bowen, Donald D., "A Company's Culture Can Affect Its Performance," Tulsa, OK: *Tulsa Business Chronicle.*

[5]Sheen, Edgar H., *Coming To a New Awareness of Organizational Culture,* Massachusetts Institute of Technology.

[6]Ibid.

[7]Ibid.

[8]Ibid.

[9]Dean, T.E., and A. A. Kennedy. *Corporate Cultures: The Rites and Rituals of Corporate Life.* Reading, MA: Addison-Wesley, 1982, p. 5

[10]Gardner, M., "Creating A Corporate Culture for the Eighties," *Business Horizons,* January/February 1985, pp. 59-63. For some of the problems involved in creating a culture, see A. L. Wilkins and N. J. Bristow, "For Successful Organizational Culture, Honor Your Past," Academy of Management Executive, August, 1987, pp. 221-229.

[11]Sheen, Edgar H., *Coming to a New Awareness of Organizational Culture,* Massachusetts Institute of Technology.

[12]Arogyaswany, Bernard and Byles, Charles M., "Organizational Culture: Internal & External Fits," *Journal of Management,* 1987, Vol. 13, No. 4.

[13]Migliore, Henry R., and Neal Bratschun, *Using Management System Balance Sheets,* March/April, 1987.

[14]Wright, J.P., *On a Clear Day You Can See General Motors,* Gross Point, MI: Wright Enterprises, 1979, p. 149.

[15]Ibid., p. 215.

[16]Ibid.

[17]"Paradise, Corporate Style," *Business Month,* July/August 1988, p. 47.

[18]Baker, Edwin L., "Managing Organizational Culture," *Management Review,* July 1980, pp. 8-13.

Source

1. Denison, Daniel R. *The Climate Culture and Effectiveness of Work Organizations: A Study of Organizational Behavior and Financial Performance,* Ann Arbor, Mich: University of Michigan, 1982.

Chapter 16
Conclusions and Recommendations

CONCLUSIONS

This book has told the story of the successful application of a system of management. I chose the title Strategic Long-Range Planning/MBO to describe this philosophy. You can see that this description is greatly expanded beyond the traditional definition. I feel strongly that this philosophy must include many steps before objectives are set. The key word then becomes management through the use of objectives in an orderly long-range planning system.

I stood with a consulting friend at a long drawn-out social gathering. An acquaintance introduced his wife and she shared about her new job with a new business being started in Tulsa. With nothing else to talk about, we discussed the things that would guarantee failure. The list included: *don't* do a feasibility study to see if another station was needed; *don't* develop a strategic plan; *don't* ask advice from anyone, go on the air immediately; *don't* develop a marketing plan, hire salespersons with no defined criteria; *don't* have a target market, forget any kind of market research to find out the listening preference; *don't* analyze the competition. Someone must have heard our conversation because all these things were done. The company has been a lost cause from the start.

As we know, 50 percent of small businesses fail the first year and 80 percent by year five. I am continually baffled at how many businesses/churches/organizations are started this way.

I have managed successfully using objectives since 1964. From those days in manufacturing on the third shift with Continental Can Company to its present use with scores of clients.

Students have learned my brand of Long-Range Planning/MBO and have used it in a wide range of occupations. They report successful experiences ranging from a chaplaincy in the Navy to management of a food service, proving that this philosophy can be learned and used by others.

I sincerely hope that this book will help management deal successfully with its most important resource—PEOPLE.

This book has attempted to make the following points:

1. There is a systematic, logical way to develop a long-range plan.
2. MBO has evolved into a long-range strategic planning system.
3. Everyone can be and should be involved in the planning process.
4. We do have a productivity problem in the United States.
5. Many organizations have had successful experiences with MBO.
6. Some organizations have had unsuccessful experiences, however,
7. Unsuccessful applications can be traced to a few well-defined causes.
8. MBO is more successful as a system of management when it is implemented from the top down rather than by a staff function such as personnel.
9. Planning and a management style based on person-oriented theory are derivatives of successful MBO applications.
10. MBO is applicable at the lowest levels of the organization.
11. The theoretical contributions from most academic scholars support MBO theory.
12. Commitment and self-control are the keys to MBO success.
13. There is a proper way to write meaningful objectives.
14. The perceived extent and effectiveness of MBO can be quantified.
15. I have successfully implemented the Long-Range Planning/MBO philosophy discussed in this book in the following settings: railroad, coal mine, oil company, church, government, and education.

My experience with and study of this brand of management and MBO lead me to make these observations:

1. MBO is not a current fad but has evolved with our country's industrialization.
2. MBO is not a staff program, but rather a top-to-bottom philosophy of management.
3. Every organization and each decentralized entity within an organization should adapt MBO to its own needs.
4. Goals must be negotiated to as high a degree as possible.
5. Periodic reviews are a must.
6. Both extrinsic and intrinsic rewards must be obtainable to as high a degree as possible for the individual and/or the group he works in.
7. There are methods for setting, reviewing, and updating MBO that require minimum paperwork.
8. Organizations must use consultants who have insight into the fundamentals of MBO, not merely a preconceived format.
9. MBO has applicability from top levels right down to the blue- and white-collar levels.
10. If you start using MBO, begin benefiting from its use, and then stop, a big dropoff in morale will result.
11. We have a problem in equating objective attainment with extrinsic

rewards.

There is an indication that MBO is not perceived to be doing enough in the area of measurement of performance and rewards. It would appear that if MBO is to have a long-term effect, providing a positive motivational climate, a fair and concise means of measuring and rewarding performance must be used. I suspect, based on observations over the last decade, that the major problem to be overcome is that of tying the extrinsic rewards—pay, bonuses, and so forth—to performance. This program area offers the opportunity for research to gain more insight into the problem.

RECOMMENDATIONS

An organization thinking about instituting a Long-Range Planning/ MBO program should consider the following points:

1. The decision to implement this management philosophy should not be made in haste.
2. To the extent possible, it should receive management support.
3. It is strongly recommended that some type of training session take place in a neutral environment.
4. An outside resource person is needed to get the program started.
5. A person from the organization should be assigned to work with the consultant so that he can take over as the in-house expert.
6. Each organization must find the best way for its people to set objectives.
7. Each organization should come up with its own best method for handling feedback and reviews.
8. Be prepared to expose your management team to new ideas and new ways of approaching managerial problems.
9. Ways should be found to involve all employees in some decision-making.
10. Performance reviews must be conducted at regular, scheduled intervals.
11. Be prepared to spend time and hard work keeping the program viable, especially in the first six months.
12. Every organization and each decentralized entity in a decentralized organization can adapt MBO to its organization.
13. Goals must be negotiated to as high a degree as possible, rather than imposed unilaterally by management.
14. Periodic reviews are a must, and must be done by the boss.
15. Both extrinsic and intrinsic rewards must be obtainable to as high a degree as possible for the individual and the group he works in.
16. Use methods for setting, reviewing, and updating MBO that require minimum paperwork.

17. Don't let a staff department dominate your program.
18. Set up a schedule and timetable for strategic planning.

One of the most important features of this Strategic Planning Process is that the top-management team agree on a strategic plan which, by its very nature, establishes the overall direction for the organization. Because of this involvement by all members of the management team, a consensus is reached through study and compromise.

Another important requirement is that the organization subunits then go through the very same process and get the same result—the same kind of involvement and consensus out of its organization members.

Still another important requirement is that the chain reaction of involvement go down into the organization all the way to its lowest levels. Theoretically, the process of identifying the targets and objectives, responsibilities, and follow-up needed go right down to the janitor. The net effect of this planning system is that everyone in the organization is tied to the overall purpose and plan. The system of feedback and review makes everyone aware of what is going on and serves as a scorecard of the organization's progress toward its goals. The individual organization members have an opportunity to satisfy their higher-level needs for involvement, recognition, and individual development. Once a person sees that his personal goals are being met, both the intrinsic and extrinsic rewards, he is tied more closely to the organization's goals. The result is a chain reaction with the organization being able to adapt to changing times, objectives being met, persons tied to the organization, their needs being met, and a good, healthy organization serving the needs of everyone involved.

At the root of this Strategic Planning System is the fact that the top corporate team and the highest levels set the organization's direction. The firm is not driven by the marketing plan, finance plan, or perhaps the production plan as is often the case in many organizations. Marketing, production, and finance develop their plans after the overall plan is set. Marketing does the normal forecasting, situation analysis, product development, and other things that go into a strategic plan. A recent book by Dr. Robert Stevens discusses how a strategic marketing plan fits in with the overall company plan.[1]

The financial plan must have projections of income statements, balance sheets, and cash budgets to show how the organization will progress financially through the time period of the plan. The manufacturing plan, similarly, must be geared to producing products called for in the marketing plan, intricately interwoven with the financial plan to be able to update capital equipment needed and interacting with the people plan to be sure that organization members are there to ensure production of the plan.

The people plan then must take into account all the needs of the people to man and manage the organization. It must concern itself with factors all the way from executive compensation, bonus plans, retirement, insurance policies and procedures, down to scheduling vacations.

At this point, it is well to mention budgets. Strategic plans should be the central managing entity of organizations, with the budget being the allocation and review arm that ensures execution of the strategic plan.

Capital budgets can be approved within dollar limits over the five-year scope of the strategic plan, with the normal capital budgeting approval procedure used to justify individual projects within that overall approved capital budget.

Of critical importance is the timing of the steps in the strategic planning process. The following sequence is being used by a number of organizations and has proved successful.

Note there is a constant overlap. By July, top management is already projecting another year into the future and dropping the current year in the five-year strategic plan.

This does not mean they are not conscious of the current year; they are, and must manage, control, and make key decisions to finish out the current year. What top management is doing is constantly pushing the planning horizon, looking through the clouds, and providing direction for the organization in an organized manner.

Although this sequence of events seems rigid, it puts the organization in a position to make fast, logical decisions. All members of management are familiar with the approved strategic plan. When new opportunities present themselves or a crisis appears, the organization must be in a position to react quickly. The strategic plan is the focal point of this reaction.

For example, during the oil embargo crisis in 1974, I was interviewing one of Frontier Airlines' middle managers on how he used MBO. A phone call came in from his boss at the corporate office. During the next hour the manager I was interviewing completely renegotiated the plan and objectives for his responsibility area. An environmental factor, the oil embargo, affected the operation of the company. An assumption that there would be adequate fuel to run the airline had to be changed. Top management of Frontier made new plans and started renegotiating plans with the next level down. A subtle but important thing happened. The man I was interviewing had complete input into how plans, schedules and operations would be changed in his responsibility areas. He was in on the decisions and when the conference call was completed, was set to react immediately with enthusiasm. I stayed the rest of the day watching a top-level manager use MBO to perfection. Everyone down to the people selling tickets knew the new game plan in a matter of hours.

The key ability to react was the strategic plan. On both ends of the phone were Frontier executives looking at the same plan and literally making changes and agreeing on them with notations on their plans. The discussions were confirmed with memos.

How many times have we seen organizations meet a critical crossroad, a few managers make a decision and say "let's go this way," and throw the entire organization into chaos? The organization does not know how to react, where to go, or what to do. Everyone is second-guessing the decisions. The organization then slowly reacts to the new changes.

The strategic planning/MBO system outlined in this book creates a management climate to react to change. I have every reason to believe that the strategic planning process discussed in this book will work in every kind of profit and nonprofit organization. To date, I have assisted more than 500 organizations in using the Strategic Planning and Management Process.

As we enter the 21st Century there are great opportunities for the business firm. Many will prosper. Not all will survive into the 22nd Century. The principles and philosophy of this book can contribute to the success and survival of the organization.

Work Sheets

Overall Plan
Strategic Planning and Management Work Sheet

OUTLINE

I. PURPOSE

    A. What is your vision, your reason for being, your mission, why you are needed, customers served, needs met in community, scope of the endeavor: nationwide, local, accountability, profit or nonprofit?

II. ENVIRONMENTAL ANALYSIS

    A. What is the direction of your industry, your SIC Code?

    B. Who are your primary competitors?

    C. What are international, national, regional, and local statistics as they relate to your business; interest ratios, unemployment, etc.?

    D. Who are your primary customers?

        A.

III. Strengths & Weaknesses (usually internal)

    A. Human Resources/People

    B. Facilities/Equipment

    C. Patients/Resources Natural

    D. Financial

    E. Other

IV. ASSUMPTIONS

    A. You Have No Control Over

    B. Extend Environmental Analysis

    C. Usually External

        1.

        2.

        3.

V. OBJECTIVES AND GOALS

Specific, time frame, measurable in key result areas

KEY RESULT/OBJECTIVES/TARGETS

AREA   OBJECTIVES

	Last Year	This Year	Next Year	Five Years
1. Sales/Total Revenue/Size				
2. Market Share				
3. Return; ROA, ROS, ROI				
4. Quality/Customer Service				
5. Human Resources/People				
a. Turnover Rate				
b. Total Work Force				
c. Training Hours/Employees				
d. Safety				
6. Productivity				
7. Public Responsibility/Ethics				
Other				
8. Other				

Now for each objective, use this format to develop specific objectives, strategy and action.

Key Result Area

Objective

Strategy to achieve objective:

  1.

  2.

  3.

What do I have to do to make it happen:

1.

2.

3.

VI. STRATEGY (General Overall Strategies)

   A. Thinking Stage

   B. Where and How to Commit Resources

   C. Timing

   D. What have to do to achieve objectives

      1. Sales/Total Revenue

      2. Market Share

      3. Return; ROA, ROS, ROI

      4. Some Measure of Efficiency and/or Productivity

      5. Quality/Customer Service

      6. People/Training/Human Resources/Morale

      7. Public Professional Responsibility

      8. Other Key Result Strategies

VII. OPERATIONAL PLAN

   A. Getting Work Accomplished/What Must Be Done in Short Term

   B. Develop Overall Budget and Support Budgets to Accomplish Overall Plan.

   How much is needed during operational year to accomplish objectives?

      1. Overall Budget $_____   ____

      2. Marketing Budget $_____   ____

      3. Production Budget $_____   ____

      4. HR Budget $_____   ____

      5. Staff Support Budgets $_____   ____

   C. Capital Budget is Revised and Developed Yearly

VIII. REWARD/PERFORMANCE APPRAISAL

A. What team and individual review/reward system/bonus/salary needed

B. Review of Performance/Schedule overall and support review dates

IX. ISSUES/PROBLEMS

A. Major

B. Minor

X. ANALYSIS

A. How do you measure cultures

XI. ALTERNATIVE SOLUTIONS

A. List of Alternatives

   1.

   2.

   3.

B. Pros/Cons of each

C. Problems/opportunities associated with each.

   1.

   2.

   3.

XII. RECOMMENDED COURSE OF ACTION

A. Alternative Selected and Why It Was Selected

B. Expected Benefit of This Recommendation

C. What Effect Will This Recommendation Have on Performance Income and Balance Sheet Statements

SET UP WAY TO MONITOR HOW YOU ARE DOING AND A WAY
TO CREATE ACTION

An action plan for each objective area should be developed. The
action plan objectives, strategies, and operational plans into perspective
with each other and helps you develop the inter-relationship between
the phases. It helps goals come to life with appropriate action.

ACTION PLAN

OBJECTIVE:

STRATEGIES:

    D.

    E.

    F.

    G.

    H.

Action Plan

Person Responsible

Start Date

Date Completed

Strategic Marketing Plan to Support the Organization's Overall Basic Plan

OUTLINE

The organization's overall strategic plan is developed according to the following format. The Marketing Manager, as part of the organization's top management team, has played a vital and integral role in developing this overall plan.

1. Purpose

    a. What is your "reason for being," your "mission," why products and/or services are needed, customers and/or people served, needs met in marketplace, and scope of the endeavor?

    b. Nationwide and/or local, ethics, profit, or nonprofit.

2. Environmental Analysis

    a. Pulse

    b. Now or past

    c. Industry surveys

    d. Completed studies of future done now

3. S & W (usually internal)

    a. Human

    b. Facilities/equipment

    c. Patents/resources natural

    d. Financial

4. Assumptions

    a. Have no control over

    b. Extend environmental analysis

    c. Usually external

5. Objectives and Goals

Specific time frame, objectives, and goals including specific time frames measurable in key result areas. Note all rules for objectives in Migliore's book Strategic Planning and Management.

6. Strategy-Two to three strategies for each objective: Thinking stage, Where and how to commit resources, Timing, Pricing policy

7. Issues/Problems-What are the major/minor problems facing the organization that would prevent it from achieving its objectives?
    a. Major
    b. Minor

8. Analysis
    a. Industry/competitive/organizational situation analysis
    b. Functional; marketing, financial accounting, management, production, and people

9. Alternative Solutions
    a. List of alternatives
    b. Pros/cons of each

10. Recommended Course of Action
    a. Alternative Selected
    b. Justification

Now that strategic direction has been set, problems identified, and an overall course of action set, and the marketing manager has contributed to the plan, then and only then can the marketing plan be started. The marketing and public relations plans are developed hand-in-hand. Each contributes to the other's success. Using the same philosophy and basic team principle, the marketing plan is developed. All staff/line managers that report to the Marketing Manager play an active role in the development of the marketing plan. The Marketing Manager and others then concentrate on a marketing plan that will support the overall organization.

Marketing Plan

11. Purpose of Marketing Function:

12. Environmental Factors Specific to Marketing:
    a. Market Analysis
    b. Customer Analysis
    c. Competitive Analysis/Benchmarking
    d. Opportunity Analysis
    e. Market Research

13. What products do you expect to be best opportunity in year 2000?
    a.
    b.
    c.
    d.
    e.

14. Which products will decline and/or present a problem to remain in competition by year 2005?

15. Put yourself in your customers' shoes. Why are they buying from you?

16. What is your competition doing that could be a threat?

WHERE DO PRODUCTS/SERVICES/PROGRAMS FIT PRODUCT LIFE CYCLE?

10

MATURE

INTRODUCTION   DECLINE

1   R&D

HOW DO PRODUCTS/SERVICES/PROGRAMS FIT PERFORMANCE/ POTENTIAL MATRIX?

        10

E

C

N

A

M

R

O

F

R

E

P

Cash Cows

Stars

Dogs

Problem Child

1   POTENTIAL   10

WHAT IS PRESENT CONTRIBUTION TO ACHIEVING THE
PHILOSOPHY STATED IN THE MISSION STATEMENT PER
PRODUCT LINE/SERVICES/PROGRAMS?

Product/Service A

Product/Service B

Product/Service C

Where do all (or most) of products fit product life cycle?
List: A.

       B.

       C.

       D.

       E.

       F.

       G.

       H.

       I.

       J.

WHAT IS EXPECTED CONTRIBUTION TO PROFIT PER PRODUCT
IN FIVE YEARS IF YOU STAY WITH PRESENT PRODUCT/SERVICE/
PROGRAM MIX?

Product/Service A

Product/Service B

Product/Service C

17. Marketing Strengths and Weaknesses

18. Marketing Assumptions

18.

19. Major Marketing Objectives should consider sales, profitability, and customer.

OBJECTIVES

Last Year Actual

Next Year

5 Years

Sales
Total Sales/Revenue
Net sales per dollar of net worth
Net sales per dollar of total assets
Net sales per dollar of net working   capital
Net sales per dollar of depreciated   fixed assets

Market Potential
Percent regional market share
Percent local market share
Percent product in introductory   stage
Percent product in maturity stage
Percent product in declining stage

Marketing Research

Usually on a project basis

Sales Management

Revenue per territory

Quotas/objectives for sales teams

Quotas/objectives per person

Customers

Satisfaction

On time delivery

20. Marketing Strategy

WHAT IS OPTIMUM PRODUCT/SERVICE/PROGRAMS MIX?

%

PRESENT   5 YEARS

WHAT PRODUCTS/SERVICES/PROGRAMS SHOULD BE ADDED
TO PRESENT PRODUCT MIX?

WHAT PRODUCTS/SERVICES/PROGRAMS SHOULD BE DROPPED
FROM PRESENT PRODUCT MIX?

HOW DO YOU REACT TO A RAPIDLY CHANGING MARKET PLACE?

WHAT OPPORTUNITIES ARE AVAILABLE DUE TO CHANGES?

21. Marketing Action Plan

22. Monitoring and Control
    a. Performance Analysis
    b. Customer Data Feedback

SALES MANAGEMENT PLAN

Now that the marketing plan is developed, it is time to develop a sales management plan. Ideally, managers and salesmen have been in on developing the marketing plan. It is important that those who execute the plan are in on the plan. The task is to develop a sales management plan, which in effect executes the marketing plan.

Sales Management Plan

23. Organize sales force

24. Select sales force

25. Train sales people

26. Motivate

27. Set quotas, goals, objectives for total sales effort down to individual salesperson.

28. Compensation plan that encourages performance

29. Evaluate progress

Objectives: Marketing

Overall Responsibility:

Strategies: Product, Market Position, Distribution Channel and Pricing

Start Date

   Action Steps

Due Date

Responsibility

Status

Objectives: Research and Development

Overall Responsibility:

Strategies: Percentage of products in what stage of research

Start Date

   Action Steps

Due Date

Responsibility

Status

Set Up Way to Monitor How You Are Doing and a Way to Create Action.

An action plan for each objective area should be developed. The action plan objectives, strategies, and operational plans into perspective with each other and helps you develop the inter-relationship between the phases. It helps goals come to life with appropriate action.

ACTION PLAN

OBJECTIVE:

STRATEGIES:

A.

B.

C.

D.

E.

ACTION PLAN

PERSON
RESPONSIBLE

START
DATE

DATE
COMPLETED

STRATEGIC MARKETING PLAN TO SUPPORT THE ORGANIZATION'S OVERALL BASIC PLAN

OUTLINE

The organization's overall strategic plan is developed according to the following format. The Marketing Manager, as part of the organization's top management team, has played a vital and integral role in developing this overall plan.

30. Purpose

   a.   What is "reason for being," your "mission," why products and/or services are needed, customers and/or people served, needs met in marketplace, and scope of the endeavor.

   b.   Nationwide and/or local, ethics, profit, or nonprofit.

31. Environmental Analysis

   a.   Pulse

   b.   Now or past

   c.   Industry surveys

   d.   Completed studies of future done now

32. S & W (usually internal)

    a. Human

    b. Facilities/equipment

    c. Patents/resources natural

    d. Financial

33. Assumptions

    a. Have no control over

    b. Extend environmental analysis

    c. Usually external

34. Objectives and Goals

Specific, time frame, objectives, and goals including specific time frames measurable in key result areas. Note all rules for objectives in Migliore's book Strategic Planning and Management.

35. Strategy-Two to three strategies for each objective: Thinking stage, Where and how to commit resources, Timing, Pricing policy

36. Purpose

    a. What is "reason for being," your "mission," why products and/or services are needed, customers and/or people served, needs met in marketplace, and scope of the endeavor.

    b. Nationwide and/or local, ethics, profit, or nonprofit.

37. Environmental Analysis

    a. Pulse

    b. Now or past

    c. Industry surveys

    d. Completed studies of future done now

38. S & W (usually internal)

    a. Human

    b. Facilities/equipment

  c. Patents/resources natural

  d. Financial

39. Assumptions

  a. Have no control over

  b. Extend environmental analysis

  c. Usually external

40. Objectives and Goals

Specific, time frame, objectives, and goals including specific time frames measurable in key result areas. Note all rules for objectives in Migliore's book Strategic Planning and Management.

41. Strategy-Two to three strategies for each objective: Thinking stage, Where and how to commit resources, Timing, Pricing policy

Startegic Human Resource Plan to Support The Overall Basic Company Plan

The overall strategic plan is developed according to the following format. The human resource manager, as part of the organization's top management team, has played a vital and integral role in developing this overall plan.

1. Purpose

    1. What is your "reason for being," your "mission," why products are needed, customers served, needs met in marketplace, and scope of the endeavor?

    2. Nationwide and/or local, ethics, profit, or nonprofit

2. Environmental Analysis

    1. Pulse

    2. Present or past

    3. Industry surveys

    4. Completed studies of future down now

3. S & W (usually internal)

    1. Human

    2. Facilities/equipment

    3. Patents/natural resources

    4. Financial

4. Assumptions

    1. Have no control over

    2. Extend environmental analysis

    3. Usually external

5.   Objectives and Goals

Specific time frame, objectives, and goals including specific time frames measurable in key result areas. HR needs to know especially size because there is a direct correlation with the number of people needed.

6.   Strategy-Two to three strategies for each objective
    1.   Thinking stage
    2.   Where and how to commit resources
    3.   Timing

Now that strategic direction has been set and the human resource manager has contributed and bought into the plan, then and only then can the human resource plan be started. Using the same philosophy and basic team principle, the human resource plan is developed. All staff/ line managers that report to the human resource manager play an active role in the development of the human resource plan.

The human resource manager and others then concentrate on a human resource plan that will support the overall organization.

HUMAN RESOURCE PLAN

Purpose of Human Resource Function:

Environmental Factors Specific to Human Resource:

Human Resource Strengths and Weaknesses:

Human Resource Assumptions:

OBJECTIVES

Actual Last Year	Next Year	Five Years

Manpower Forecast

Full-time/Temporary Employee Ratios

Total Labor Cost

Yearly People Development Audit

Hours Training per Employee/Year

Actual Last Year	Next Year	Five Years

Quality Circles (participation teams)

Turnover Rate

Performance/Reward System

Benefits

Compensation Levels

Actual Last Year	Next Year	Five Years

Wellness

Recruiting Objectives and Costs

Succession Planning

Affirmative Action

Pro-active Labor Regulations

Actual Last Year	Next Year	Five Years

Culture Index

Measure of Skills Needed/100 Index

Cross-training Index

Literacy Rate

Computer Literacy

HR Audit

OBJECTIVES (PEOPLE)

	Actual Last Year	Next Year	Five Years

Manpower Forecast

Administration

Faculty

Full Time

Staff

OBJECTIVES (PEOPLE)

	Actual Last Year	Next Year	Five Years

Full Time

Temporary

Turnover Rate

Training

Budget for Total Labor

Strategies to meet objectives

Action PlanCWho does what/when?

Strategic Financial Plan to Support The Firm's Overall Basic Company Plan

Outline

OVERALL ORGANIZATION PLAN

The organization's overall strategic plan is developed according to the following format. The chief financial officer, as part of the organization's top management team, has played a vital and integral role in developing this overall plan.

I. Purpose
    A. What is your "reason for being," your "mission," why products are needed, customers served, needs met in marketplace, and scope of the endeavor.
    B. Nationwide and/or local, ethics, profit, or nonprofit.

II. Environmental Analysis
    A. Pulse
    B. Present or past
    C. Industry surveys
    D. Completed studies of future done now

III. Strengths & Weaknesses (usually internal)
    A. Human
    B. Facilities/equipment
    C. Patents/resources natural
    D. Financial

IV. Assumptions
    A. Have no control over
    B. Extend environmental analysis
    C. Usually external

V. Objectives and Goals
    A. Specific, time frame, objectives, and goals including specific time frames measurable in key result areas. Note all rules for objectives.

VI. Strategy - Two to three strategies for each objective
    A. Thinking stage
    B. Where and how to commit resources
    C. Timing
    D. Pricing policy
            Sales/Marketing
            Manufacturing

Financial
Facilities: People/training/morale/public responsibility

The chief financial officer and others then concentrate on a financial plan that will support the overall organization.

Financial Plan

Purpose of Finance Function:

Environmental Factors Specific to Finance:

Financial Strengths and Weaknesses

Finance Assumptions:

Major Finance Objectives: Pick a minimum of three to five key financial ratios/figures for objectives. They can be the same as overall firm's financial objectives. Note suggested list on next page.

Minor Financial Objectives: List the range that other important ratios should remain. Note suggested list on next page.

FINANCIAL

SALES

	Last Year Actual	1990	1996
Return on Investment			
1. Net profit after taxes/net worth			
2. Net profit after taxes/total assets			
3. Net profit after taxes + depreciation + noncash expense/total assets			
Return on Sales			
1. Net sales per dollar of net worth			
2. Net sales per dollar of total assets			
3. Net sales per dollar of net working capital			
4. Net profit after taxes/net sales			
5. Cost of sales per dollar of inventory			
6. New sales per dollar of depreciated fixed assets			
Financial Leverage			
1. Debt/Equity Ratio			
2. Total Debt/Total Assets			
3. Times Interest Earned			
Current Ratio			
1. Current assets to current liabilities			
2. Cash and receivables to current liabilities			
3. Cash and equivalent to current liabilities			
4. Current liabilities to net worth			
5. Acid-Test Ratio (current assets-inventory)/ (current liabilities)			
Activity			
1. Inventory Turnover			
2. Accounts Receivable Turnover			
3. Average Collection Period			
4. Total Asset Turnover			
5. Fixed Asset Turnover			
Market Ratios			
1. Earnings per share			
2. Dividend per share			
3. Dividend payout ratio			
4. Book value per share			
5. Price/earnings ratio			
6. Dividend yield			

Strategic Production Plan to Support The Firm's Overall Basic Company Plan

Outline

The organization's overall strategic plan is developed according to the following format. The Production Manager, as part of the organization's top management team, has played a vital and integral role in developing this overall plan.

I.   Purpose
    A. What is your "reason for being," your "mission," why products are needed, customers served, needs met in marketplace, and scope of the endeavor.
    B. Nationwide and/or local, ethics, profit, or nonprofit.

II.   Environmental Analysis
    A. Pulse
    B. Present or past
    C. Industry surveys
    D. Completed studies of future done now.

III. S & W (usually internal)
    A. Human
    B. Facilities/equipment
    C. Patents/natural resources
    D. Financial

IV.   Assumptions
    A. Have no control over
    B. Extend environmental analysis
    C. Usually external

V.   Objectives and Goals
    A. Specific, time frame, objectives, and goals including specific time frames measurable in key result areas. Note all rules for objectives.

VI.   Strategy - Two to three strategies for each objective
    A. Thinking stage
    B. Where and how to commit resources
    C. Timing
    D. Pricing policy
       Sales/Marketing
       Manufacturing
       Financial

Facilities: People/training/morale/public responsibility

VII. Issues/Problems
    A. Major
    B. Minor

VIII. Analysis
    A. Industry/competitive/company situation analysis
    B. Functional; marketing, financial accounting, management, production, and people

IX. Alternative Solutions
    A. List of alternatives
    B. Pros/cons of each

X. Recommended Course of Action
    A. Alternative Selected
    B. Justification

Now that strategic direction has been set and the production manager has contributed and bought into the plan, then and only then can the production plan be started. Using the same philosophy and basic team principle, the production plan is developed. All staff/line managers that report to the production manager play an active role in the development of the production plan.

The production manager and others then concentrate on a production plan that will support the overall organization.

Production Plan

Purpose of Production Function:

The production function is essentially the implementation of the firm's overall strategy.

The production function mobilizes varied resources to put the firm's strategies in motion.

Environmental Factors Specific to Production:

I. The production function implements the total strategy; production greatly affects the attainment of the other functional plans. Therefore, the production function operates within an environment of subtle internal pressures from other functional areas.

II. The production function operates within an environment of standards and measures
    1) the never-ending hourglass

2) measuring process parameters on a continuing basis
3) input vs. output of each production factor

III. Includes latest information of what is going on in production/ operation

Production Strengths and Weaknesses:

1) Having in place a complete set of standards and benchmarks for each
   a) operation
   b) process
2) Having in place a seasoned, well-trained work force

Conversely, the lack of either of the above universal strengths would constitute a weakness in the production function.

Production Assumptions:

There are several generic assumptions that we often take for granted; however, we need to list them because the consequences of their not occurring could be severe.

1) All required production factors will be available as needed at current, or near current, prices.

2) All completed production will be distributed to end users and liquidated to cash on a timely basis.

OBJECTIVES

	Last Year Actual	1990	1996

MANUFACTURING/PRODUCTIVITY

Total Output = labor + materials + energy + capital + miscellaneous input

Number projects completed
Number projects scheduled

Units produced
Hours worked

Sales
Employee

Labor Productivity

1. Items produced per employee
2. Quantities produced per employee-hour
3. Labor Index = $\dfrac{\text{equivalent employee-hours of output} \times 100}{\text{actual total employee-hours}}$

4. Labor Prod. Index = $\dfrac{\dfrac{\text{price weighed output (period 2)}}{\text{total labor costs (period 2)}}}{\dfrac{\text{price weighed output (period 1)}}{\text{total labor costs (period 1)}}} \times 100$

Materials Productivity
1. Output per constant dollar of total material cost

Energy Productivity
1. Output per energy consumer (BTU's)

2. Energy Productivity Index = $\dfrac{\dfrac{\text{output}}{\text{BTU (constant period)}}}{\dfrac{\text{output}}{\text{BTU (base period)}}} \times 100$

OR

Energy Productivity Index = $\dfrac{\dfrac{\text{output in current period}}{\text{output in base period}}}{\dfrac{\text{BTU in current period}}{\text{BTU in base period}}} = \times 100$

Capital Productivity
1. Quantity of output per quantity of capital input

OBJECTIVES

	Last Year Actual	1990	1996

MANUFACTURING/PRODUCTIVITY CONT.

2. Capital productivity

$$= \frac{\text{quant. of output}}{\text{quant. of capital of input}} = \frac{\text{units produced/day}}{\text{units inventory}} =$$

$$\frac{\text{units produced/day}}{\text{machine (process unit)}}$$

People
1. Manhours worked without lost time from accidents.
2. Various other safety objectives.

Quality
1. Zero defects.
2. Acceptance rates vs. various sampling plans.

Church/Ministry
Strategic Planning and Management
Work Sheet

I. Purpose

What is "reason for being," your "mission," why needed, customers served, needs met in marketplace, scope of the endeavor; nationwide, local, ethics, profit, or nonprofit.

Where there is no vision, the people perish: but he that keepeth the law, happy is he.

Proverbs 29:18

And it shall come to pass afterward, that I will pour out may spirit upon all flesh; and your sons and your daughters shall prophesy, your old men shall dream dreams, your young men shall see visions . . . .

Joel 2:28

II. Environmental Analysis

It is the glory of God to conceal a thing: but the honour of kings is to search out a matter.

Proverbs 25:2

III. S & W (usually internal)

  A. Human

  B. Facilities/equipment

  C. Programs

  D. Financial

But he that knew not, and did commit things worthy of stripes, shall be beaten with few stripes. For unto whomsoever much is given, of him shall be much required: and to whom men have committed much, of him they will ask the more.

Luke 12:48

That the man of God may be perfect, thoroughly furnished unto all good works.
2 Timothy 3:17

IV. Assumptions

    A. You have no control over

    B. Extend environmental analysis

    C. Usually external

        1.

        2.

        3.

V. Objectives and Goals

    Specific, time frame, measurable in key result areas

	Actual Last Year	Next Year	Five Years
1. Attendance			
2. Membership			
3. Building			
4. Missions			
5. Facilities			
6. Programs			
7. Financial			
8. People			

Let all things be done decently and in order.
I Corinthians 14:40

Then the King said unto me, For what dost thou make request? So I prayed to the God of heaven.
Nehemiah 2:4

VI.   Strategy Two to three strategies for each objective
    A. Thinking stage
    B. Where and how to commit resources
    C. Timing

Neither do men light a candle, and put it under a bushel, but on a candlestick;
and it giveth light unto all that are in the house.
Matthew 5:15

VII. Problems

Major
Minor

VIII. Analysis

IX.   Alternatives
    A.
    B.
    C.

X. Recommendations

XI. Operational Plan
    A. Getting work accomplished
    B. Budget

Let all things be done decently and in order.
I Corinthians 14:40

Study to shew thyself approved unto God, a workman that needeth not to be ashamed, rightly dividing the word of truth.

2 Timothy 2:15

For which of you, intending to build a tower, sitteth not down first and counteth the cost, whether he have sufficient to finish it?

Luke 14:28

XII.   Reward/Performance Appraisal

    A.   Agreed upon objectives

    B.   Review of Performance

Now he that planteth and he that watereth are one: and every man shall receive his own reward according to his own labour.

I Corinthians 3:8

ACTION PLAN

    Objective:

    Strategy:

    Action Plan

    Person Responsible

    Start Date

    Date Completed

Nonprofit Overall Plan
Strategic Planning and Management
Work Sheet

OUTLINE

I. PURPOSE

    A. What is "reason for being," your "mission," why needed, customers served, needs met in community, scope of the endeavor: nationwide, local, accountability.

II. ENVIRONMENTAL ANALYSIS

    A. Pulse-What's going on now?

    B. Now or past

    C. Studies of future done now

III. S & W (usually internal)

    A. Human/People

    B. Facilities/Equipment

    C. Financial

Cash Ratio (cash and cash equivalents/current liabilities); Current Ratio (current assets/current liabilities); Donation Ratio (total donations/total revenue); Return on Assets (total revenue/total assets); Debt to Assets Ratio (total liabilities/total assets); Net Operating Ratio (excess of income over expenses/total revenue); Fund Balance Reserve Ratio (total fund balance/total expenses); Cash Reserve Ratio (total cash/total expenses); Program Expense Ratio (total program expenses/total expense); Support Services Ratio (total support serves expenses/total expenses); Net Surplus/Deficiency (total income less total expense)

    D. Other

IV. ASSUMPTIONS

    A. You have no control over

    B. Extend environmental analysis

    C. Usually external

        1.

        2.

        3.

V. OBJECTIVES AND GOALS

Specific, time frame, measurable in key result areas

Actual Last Year	Next Year	Five Years

    1. People Served, Attendance, a Count of People Worked with

    2. Budget/Revenues/Cash Generated

    3. Services Rendered

    4. Some Measures of Efficiency and/or Productivity

    5. People/Training/Human Resources

    6. Some Measure of Accountability

    7. Other Key Result Areas

VI. STRATEGY (two or three strategies for each objective)

    A. Thinking stage

    B. Where and how to commit resources

C. Timing

    1. People Served, Attendance, a Count of People Worked with

    2. Budget/Revenues/Cash Generated   3. Services Provided

    4. Some Measures of Efficiency and/or Productivity

    5. People/Training/Human Resources

    6. Some Measure of Accountability

    7. Other Key Result Areas

VI. ISSUES/PROBLEMS

    A. Major

    B. Minor

VII. ANALYSIS

Analysis of Situation

VIII. ALTERNATIVE SOLUTIONS

    A. List of Alternatives

        1.

        2.

        3.

    B. Pros/Cons of eachCproblems/opportunities associated with each.

IX. RECOMMENDED COURSE OF ACTION

    A. Alternative selected

    B. Expected benefit of this recommendation:

SET UP WAY TO MONITOR HOW YOU ARE DOING AND A WAY TO
CREATE ACTION

An action plan for each objective area should be developed. The
action plan objectives, strategies, and operational plans into perspective
with each other and helps you develop the inter-relationship between
the phases. It helps goals come to life with appropriate action.

ACTION PLAN

OBJECTIVE:

STRATEGIES:
    A.
    B.
    C.
    D.
    E.

Action Plan

Person Responsible

Start Date
Date Completed

Golf Club/Course
Strategic Planning and Management
Work Sheet

I.   Purpose of Golf Club/Course

What is "reason for being," your "mission," why needed, who is served, needs met, scope of the club/course, national, regional, local, ethics.

II. Environmental Analysis

    A. Pulse players per day

    B. Now or past number of players last two years

    C. Surveys growth of game %'s

    D. How many courses in area

III. S & W (usually internal)

    A. Human

    B. Facilities/Equipment

    C. Patents/Resources natural condition of grounds

    D. Financial

IV. Assumptions

    A. You have no control over

    B. Extend environmental analysis

    C. Usually external

        1.

        2.

        3.

V.   Objectives and Goals

Specific, time frame, measurable in key result areas

VI. Strategy Two to Three Strategies for Each Objective
   A. Thinking stage
   B. Where and how to commit resources
   C. Timing

VII. Operational Plan
   A. Getting work accomplished
   B. Budget

VIII. Reward/Performance Appraisal
   A. Agreed upon objectives
   B. Review of performance

IX. Problems
   A. Major
   B. Minor

X. Analysis
   A. Situation
   B. Functional; financial, accounting, management, people

XI. Alternative Solutions
   A. List of alternatives
   B. Pros/Cons of each
      1.
      2.
      3.

XII. Recommended Course of Action
   A. Alternative selected
   B. Justification

I. Purpose of Golf Club/Course

What is "reason for being," your "missions," why needed, customers served, needs met in marketplace, scope of the club/course, national, regional, local, ethics, profit, or nonprofit.

II. Environmental Analysis
   A. Pulse What's going on now?

      1. Players per day this year

      2. Players per day past two (2) years

   B. Now or past

      Growth of game

   C. Industry surveys

      What's going on?

   D. Studies of future done now

      What is predicted for future?

III. S & W (usually internal)
   A. Human

      1. Staff personality

      2. Reputation

      3. Knowledge of game

   B. Facilities/Equipment

      1. Range

      2. Course

      3. Greens

      4. Carts

   C. Patents/Resources natural

   D. Financial

      Analyze all ratios

IV. Assumptions
   A. You have no control over

   B. Extend environmental analysis

C. Usually external

1. Weather days to be played

2. Population growth of area

3.

V. Objectives and Goals

Specific, time frame, measurable in key result areas. Note all rules for objectives in Chapter VIII. Note next four pages.

	Actual Last Year	Next Year	Five Years

SALES

Total merchandise sales/total green fee and carts revenue

Net sales per dollar of net profit usually $1.00 per round is your net profit income

Net sales per dollar of total assets

Net sales per dollar of net working capital

Cost of sales per dollar of inventory

Net sales per dollar of depreciated fixed assets

Bottom line

MARKET POTENTIAL

Percent regional market share

Percent local market share

PRODUCTIVITY

Number of employees per rounds played

FINANCIAL

Return on Investment

1. Net profit after taxes/net worth

2. Net profit after taxes/total assets

3. Net profit after taxes + depreciation + noncash expense/total assets/bottom line

Return on Sales

1. Net sales per dollar of net worth

2. Net sales per dollar of total assets

3. Net sales per dollar of net working capital

4. Net profit after taxes/net sales

5. Cost of sales per dollar of inventory

6. New sales per dollar of depreciated fixed assets

Financial Leverage

1. Debt/equity ratio

2. Total debt/total assets

3. Times interest earned

Current Ratio

1. Current assets to current liabilities

2. Cash and receivables to current liabilities

3. Cash and equivalent to current liabilities

4. Current liabilities to net worth

5. Acid-test ratio (current assets-inventory)(current liabilities)

Activity

1. Inventory turnover

2. Accounts receivable turnover

3. Average collection period

4. Total asset turnover

5. Fixed asset turnover

FACILITIES
  Yearly safety check
    Annual energy audit
      Electric or gas

PEOPLE/TRAINING/MORALE
  Yearly people development audit
  Hours training per employee/year
  Quality circles (participation teams)   implemented
  Turnover
  Performance/reward system
  Benefits
    Compensation levels
  Wellness
  Manpower forecast
  Recruiting objectives and costs
  Succession planning

PUBLIC RESPONSIBILITY
  Sponsor Junior Achievement Co.
  Pay all taxes, wages, and bills
  Contribute to civic projects
  Meet OSHA safety requirements

VI. Strategy Two to Three Strategies for Each Objective
    A. Thinking stage
    B. Where and how to commit resources
    C. Timing
    D. Pricing policy
    E. Sales/Advertising
        1. Where and when to commit
        2. Timing
        3. Pricing policy

    F. Financial bottom line

       1. Where and how to commit

       2. Timing

       3. Pricing policy

    G. Financial (strengths)

       Pricing policy

    H. People/Training

    I.   Morale

    J.   Public responsibility

VII. Operational Plan

    A. Get work accomplished

    B. Budget

       1. Golf shop

       2. Course

VIII. Issues/Problems

    A. Major

    B. Minor

IX. Analysis

    A. Industry/Competitive/Course situation analysis

    B. Functional; marketing, financial accounting, management, production, people

X. Alternative Solutions

    A. List of alternatives

    B. Pros/cons of each problems/opportunities associated with each

       1.

       2.

       3.

XI. Recommended Course of Action

    A. Alternative selected

    B. JustificationSet up way to monitor how you are doing and a way to create action.

    An action plan for each objective area should be developed. The action plan objectives, strategies, and operational plans into perspective with each other and helps you develop the inter-relationship between the phases. It helps goals come to life with appropriate action.

ACTION PLAN

OBJECTIVE:

STRATEGIES:

    A.

    B.

    C.

    D.

    E.

ACTION PLAN

PERSON
RESPONSIBLE

START
DATE

DATE
COMPLETED

Case Studies

Case Study
Things Got Out of Whack

Ken Brasfield was a computer design specialist. He was busy working on the final stages of the installation of a sophisticated computerized system. Frank Roma was in charge of the overall project. His title was Project Manager in a Matrix organization scheme. Roma had negotiated a deadline for installation which was ten days away. The sales contract provided for a severe price penalty in case the firm wasn't ready. The firm had to have their part of the job done when the company delivered the equipment and brought its service personnel into town.

The General Manager, Jim Jones, had been there 18 months. He was easy going, loved to do public relations work, and stay in touch with customers. He ignored the business of the firm. He stayed clear of any strife or problem-solving.

Ken Brasfield's immediate boss was Chuck Creekmore, Vice President of Finance. Roma also reported to Creekmore. Last night, Ken Brasfield phoned Mr. Creekmore and told him that he was quitting immediately. He had had all he could take from Roma, and he had decided to leave the firm. Ken told Mr. Creekmore that Roma had been "breathing down his neck" continuously, and pressuring him needlessly to get the job completed. Ken assured Mr. Creekmore that he had been doing his best, but that in a sophisticated installation of this sort, many things create problems and interfere with getting quick results. Ken said that he didn't attempt to explain the problems to Roma, because in Ken's words, "Roma knows next to nothing about the intricate nature of the problems involved." The "straw that broke his back" was a threat from Roma to lock him in the building until the installation was operable even if he had to bring him his food. Ken said he realized that Roma did not intend to do this, but saying this after everything else he had done, was too much to take. In Brasfield's view, Roma was a Theory Triple X Manager, all the way!

Mr. Creekmore wondered what to do. Mr. Creekmore knew that people with Ken's skills were hard to find. Particularly at this stage of the project, it would be next to impossible to get a replacement employee who could come in to pick up the installation where Ken Brasfield had left off and complete the projection time. Mr. Creekmore understood the meaning of a penalty for late delivery.

Out of Whack Case

The next morning, Mr. Creekmore decided to meet with Frank Roma to discuss the situation.

I.   What are the major and minor problems?

II.   Analyze the case.

III. Develop alternative solutions. What are the pros and cons of each alternative?

IV.   Which alternative is best?

V.   What should Brasfield have done at the beginning of the assignment?

VI.   If you were Roma's boss what would you do?

VII. How could this situation have been avoided in the first place?

My suggestion is the continual use of this case and the 7 step approach. The case helps illustrate the methodology. Any group can work through it in a non-threatening manner. I use it to set the stage for real company problems. After the group goes through the exercise then assign a real problem in the organization.

My experience is that it is a big mistake to start any work session with "what's our problem." All you do is run around in circles. The "out of whack" case helps create a mind set. It also gets the group more relaxed.

CROSS MANUFACTURING OVERLAND PARK, KANSAS

"John, you need to earn a red badge of courage" said Henry Migliore driving across Kansas with John Cross and his wife Patrice in 1980. John had graduated from ORU in 1979 with a BS degree in Management. John would be graduated with an MBA from Arizona State University in Tempe, Arizona in 1982. John is the son of Jim Cross, founder of Cross Manufacturing, Inc. in Lewis, Kansas. John was returning to work in the family business. The conversation in the car on a pleasant day had wondered through a number of trivial topics. Migliore's comment just came out of the blue.

Migliore had been a consultant for a number of family businesses for almost 20 years. The family business has been the cornerstone of the American economy. It provides the opportunity for the family to contribute to society. It provides members of the family a career opportunity.

Every family business confronts both the opportunities and problems of weaving family members into the organization. Migliore had tutored a number of younger family members in a wide variety of small family businesses.

The comment on the "red badge" got everyone's attention. Migliore had seen the difficulty of this transition from college into the company. One strategy is to work for another company and then come back to the family business. In this case, John and Patrice wanted to come right into the company. Nothing was resolved as they continued the trip to a company meeting. Little did this threesome know what was on the horizon. After years in existence, Cross Manufacturing would find itself in bankruptcy. The survival of the company was in doubt. At age 24, John Cross was given the charge to lead Cross Manufacturing out of bankruptcy in 1982. The rest is history. John and Patrice Cross earned their "red badge of courage".

On June 25, 1998, John was awarded the prestigious *Ernest and Young Entrepreneur of the Year Award* in the turnaround category. In June 1999, Cross Manufacturing celebrated its 50th anniversary.

In a meeting in Overland Park, Kansas, July 2000, Dr. Migliore asked John and Patrice "What is next for Cross Manufacturing? How big should the company be in the year 2005? How will the company for example, respond to the challenge of a cylinder being produced in China at a cheaper cost that can be sold in the U.S. markets at a much cheaper price?" What would you recommend?

Appendix --   *The Cross Times,* 1998.   Cross Technical Corner (p.34)
              June 1991.

              Walking in Integrity

              Excellence, Fall 97 / Winter 98

              Selected pages from Cross 50th Anniversary calendar

              Notes from R. Henry Migliore

CROSS MANUFACTURING
STRATEGIC PLAN OUTLINE

Cross Manufacturing has used and continues to use a planning, management, and control system. The overall Cross plan follows this general outline.

I. Executive Summary

II. Purpose

III. Environmental Analysis

IV. Strengths and Weaknesses

V. Assumptions

VI. Objectives

VII. Strategy

VIII. Problems/Alternatives/Action/Rewards/Summary

6666666666

IX. Support Plans

1) Marketing
2) Purchasing/Materials
3) Engineering/Capital Equipment Budget
4) Finance
9) Environmental/Health/Safety

5) Hays
6) Lewis
7) Pratt
8) Quality

X. Appendix

1) Culture Study
2) Last Year's Executive Summary
3) Action Plans
4) Articles
   Almanac of Financial Ratios
   Predicasts Forecasts
   Standard and Poor's surveys

INDUSTRY AVERAGES (SIC CODE 3593)

(# of times ratio is to one) %			D&B 1998 ratios for 3593
Return on Sales	=	3.1	4.4
Current Ratio	=	2.6	2.1
Quick Ratio	=	1.5	1.1
Net Sales to Net Working Capital	=	7.2	5.8
Coverage Ratio	=	1.8	N/A
Asset to Sales	=	47.6	51.4%
Total Liability to Net Worth	=	2.1	115.0%

Major Competitors:

1) <u>Eaton:</u> In fluid power 58 years.

2) <u>Energy Mfg.</u>: Customer satisfaction through high quality products is the driving force for this company

3) <u>Prince</u>

4) <u>Vickers/Dana Corp.</u>: Driving force to couple fluid power with intelligent technology; to improve machine capabilities, and operator comfort. They want to lead the industry in the design of new technology.

5) <u>Parker Hannifin</u>: Ranked #1 in sales in the fluid power cylinders and actuators division.

6) <u>Hydroline</u>

7) <u>Monarch</u>

Key Customers:

Soo Tractor

Great Bend Manufacturing

Tru-Part

Sunflower

Deere and Company

OVERALL OBJECTIVES
(Illustrative - Not Actual Values)

OBJECTIVES

	PAST PERFORMANCE		CURRENT	NEXT YEAR	FIVE YEARS
SALES	28.0	31.0	33.0	35.0	50.0
GROSS MARGIN	25.2%	26.3 %	27%	28%	30%
ON-TIME DELIVERY	85.6%	86.5%	90%	94.5%	98.5%
INVENTORY TURNOVER	5.7	6.0	6.0	7.0	8.0

A number of key strategies Cross has and continues to use include:

1) Honor the Lord in all we do.
2) Create the kind of work place that makes Cross Mfg. the employer of choice in Central Kansas.

3) Provide a high quality product that creates value for the customer.
4) Stay in hydraulic and farm equipment industry.
5) Maintain strong finished goods standard stocking program.

Cross Manufacturing has had a Strategic Planning philosophy and process for over 20 years. These are representative statements taken from actual Cross Support Plans.

ENGINEERING MISSION STATEMENT

The Engineering Department is a staff function which provides professional and technical services of an engineering nature for all Cross product lines and provides research and development studies, analysis and development programs, as required to meet the overall company objectives.

To glorify God by reflecting Christ in our assigned tasks or projects, and follow basic Biblical principles of honesty, integrity, honor others, be dependable, fair, patient, and consistent. Treat all fairly, and maintain a safe, ethical, and discrimination-free work place.

Product Engineering Strategies

1. Staff the Engineering department adequately with a competent and experienced staff.

2. Procure pattern equipment for the new high pressure tie bolt cylinder.

3. Conduct search for a new corrosion resistant coating that will be environmentally acceptable.

Manufacturing Engineering Strategies

1. Ensure an experienced staff is always in place.

2. Conduct a study to determine a less labor intensive process to finish inside dia. of 2" dia. and under tubes.

3. Develop a program to reduce the solvents unused in the plant for cleaning paint related equipment.

4. Study methods and procedures to reduce cost of pump and motor line with focus on gears.

Prototype Department Strategies

1. Maintain an experienced and dedicated staff with full engineering support.

2. Maintain delivery lead times.

3. Provide a high quality prototype.

FINANCE MISSION STATEMENT

It is the purpose of the Financial Department to interpret operations, past, present, and future, in terms of funds, profits, and financial condition. We will be available to work with all plants and other departments involving any problems they may encounter with the system as it relates to our charge.

We will glorify God by reflecting Christ in every business transaction, i.e. follow basic Biblical principles: honesty, integrity, honors others, be dependable, fair, patient, consistent: treat suppliers, employees, and customers fairly, and act in a professional manner at all times.

Finance Strategy

1. Prepared job descriptions for accounts payable clerk and credit manager jobs. When experienced, the employees can perform this work during normal working hours with adequate time available for problem solving, thus reducing overtime.

2. Internal controls over the company assets are designed to provide adequate safeguards.

3. Audit trails and procedures pertaining to support documents have been established to provide "tracks/edits" for verifying the validity of transactions.

4. Training programs scheduled each year to provide necessary training to perform to job description.

MARKETING MISSION STATEMENT

It is the purpose of the Marketing Department to market all our products to increase sales and income. We will be available to work with all plants, departments, and vendors to meet the customers' needs.

We will glorify God by reflecting Christ in every business transaction, i.e. follow basic Biblical principles of honesty, integrity, honors others, be dependable, fair, patient, consistent: treat suppliers, employees, and customers fairly, and act in a professional manner at all times.

Marketing Strategy

A. Customer Service

1. Maintain actual versus forecast level and plan build schedules on all standard stock items.

2. Continue to maintain adequate levels of valve finished goods inventory. Establish standard finished goods inventory for cylinders, pumps and motors.

B. Sales Growth and Profitability

1. Utilize Market Place CD ROM to establish listings for prospective mailings.

2. Continue to improve product awareness with customers by publishing Communicator newsletter.

3. Advertising focuses on new products with ads and press releases.

MATERIAL CONTROL MISSION STATEMENT

The Materials Control department will seek to purchase materials effectively and timely for Cross Manufacturing, Inc. with top quality dependability at competitive pricing to meet customer/production demands.

We will glorify God by reflecting Christ in every business transaction, i.e. follow basic Biblical principles of honesty, integrity, honors others, be dependable, fair, patient, consistent: treat suppliers, employees, and customers fairly, and act in a professional manner at all times.

Material Control Strategy

1. Be more customer focused, company wide including more visits to suppliers locations and continuously assessing and striving to better Cross material needs and requirements to meet customer demands.

2. Be more teamwork focused, company wide. Including more visits to plant locations. Continuously assessing and striving to better Cross communication and requirements to meet plant demands.

3. Improve purchasing methods by further exploring blanket order contracts, further utilizing Vendor schedules, and conduct study on EDI.

B. Quality

1. Continue implementation and use of ISO9001 Policies and Procedures.

2. Continue to keep suppliers and Quality Assurance manager informed of request for credit data and percentages.

C. Financial Results

1. Continue cycle counting program in FY2000. Achieve sufficient accuracy levels to avoid having to take physical inventories in the future.

2. Keep up-to-date records on cycle counting variances by month/ warehouse and analyze variance explanations.

SAMPLE CROSS MANUFACTURING PLANT OBJECTIVES

(Illustrative - Not Actual Values)

A. Customer Service

1. Maintain on-time delivery ≥ targets

Last Year	Current Year	Next Year	Five Years
86.5	90.0%	94.5%	98.5%

2. Reduce customer complaints by 20% this year.

Last Year	Current Year	Next Year	Five Years
N/A	20%	15%	10%

3. Maintain competitive delivery lead-times.

B. Quality

1. Reduce Cost of Quality by at least 10% each year (sales & interplant).

Last Year	Current Year	Next Year	Five Years
72K/2.5%	71K/2.1%	59K/1.6%	42K/1%

2. Be ISO9000 certified by September 2000.

C. Financial Results

1. Operate within budget.
2. Improve consolidated gross margin percentage to ≥ targets:

Last Year	Current Year	Next Year	Five Years
26.3%	27.5%	28.0%	30.0%

3. Maintain capital spending within budgeted levels each year.

Last Year	Current Year	Next Year	Five Years
$132,550	$175,512	$197,353	$229,500

4. Inventory turnover ≥ targets.

Last Year	Current Year	Next Year	Five Years
6.0	6.0	7.0	8.0

D. Productivity

1. Increase productivity from 82% to 95% within 5 years.

Last Year	Current Year	Next Year	Five Years
82%	86%	88%	95%

E. Material Control

1. Operate within Material Control budget.

Last Year	Current Year	Next Year	Five Years
$53,000	$83,000	$90,000	$101,000

F. Human Resources

1. Maintain a labor turnover rate below 10%.

Last Year	Current Year	Next Year	Five Years
20.5%	17.0%	10.0%	2% or 5%

G. Loss Control/Safety

1. Maintain full compliance with applicable laws and regulations.
2. Reduce lost time of accidents by 50%.

Last Year	Current Year	Next Year	Five Years
9	14	7	0

Question

How big should Cross Manufacturing be? What is the right size for Cross Manufacturing?

Alternatives Facing Cross

1) Double size to 45-50 million with internal growth

2) Double size to 45-50 million with external growth

3) Stay in 25-30 million range

Recommended Course of Action

Alternative 3 - Steady, slow profitable growth is course of action current Cross Management now chooses. What is your recommendation?

REWARD

Inventory Turnover	≥	target
Gross Margin	≥	margin % target
Net Sales	≥	sales target

Year 2000 meeting in semi-exotic resort and group bonus system plus individual reward.

CONTINENTAL CAN
CASE STUDY

BACKGROUND

PART I

PART II

MAJOR PROBLEMS

Lack of planning/ Organization/ Coordination

Poor Performance

MINOR PROBLEMS

Equipment Breakdowns/High repair costs

Safety

Morale

Sabotage

Projects

Crowded Conditions

Production Control/ Scheduling

Repair Costs

New Product Introduction

Marketing

Accounting

Ethics

Integration

People

Chicago Stockyards Case Study, 1968
Part I

Background:

Continental Can Co.'s Chicago Stockyards Plant is located in Chicago's near southside at 39th and Pershing, directly across the street from the infamous Chicago stockyards. The cattle and hog stockyards grew with the city of Chicago in the early 1900's. Livestock from all over the United States was shipped to Chicago to be traded or slaughtered. Major companies built slaughter houses in the stockyards area. It was obvious, then, that it would be a wise move to have a can manufacturing plant as close to the packers as possible. This was the original purpose of the Continental Can Chicago Stockyards Plant; to supply cans for the meat industry, the main market being in the South Chicago packers area.

During World War II, the stockyards and the can plant both flourished.

Many ethic women in the neighborhood went to work in the can plant, performing many of the jobs traditionally done by men only in Continental Can's other 165 manufacturing plants. It was unheard of in St. Louis and other plants for women to be press feeders for example. At the Stockyards Plant 90 percent of the press feeders were women. The main reason was that during World War II there weren't enough men to do the jobs.

On the west side of the plant was a Polish neighborhood. Some 40 percent of the workers were of Polish descent. Most of them would walk to work. An intense amount of pride and loyalty prevailed among the Polish. They performed a good day's work for a good day's pay. The neighborhood was clean and well kept. A high sense of pride was always evident.

Surrounding the Continental plant were the Stockyards to the south, the Polish neighborhood to the west, the African American people living to the east, and to the north was the Irish neighborhood.. Almost 20 percent of the work force at the plant was comprised of African Americans, with the remaining 80 percent being caucasian. The caucasians had migrated from the hills of Missouri, Oklahoma, Arkansas, Tennessee, and Kentucky.

The Polish group were willing workers, and easy to manage. The African American were despondent because of their social barriers, lack of education, and job understanding,. The management of the group of employees who had migrated from the hills has been an issue in every industrial setting in which I have been involved, because of their low social ethic and work tradition . These three groups, because they shared a common need for employment, found themselves working together.

A number of trade unions were involved with the approximately 1,200 workers The United Steel Workers represented the bulk of the group . The machinist group represented the groups in the machine shop. Electricians were hired through an outside service, and did not actually belong to our work force. A general prosperity had prevailed in the stockyard area through about 1965.

As the country and rail system developed, the meat packers began moving closer to the other railheads at the point of delivery of the cattle, starting the general decline for the Chicago meat packers and Continental Can built a big can plant in Omaha to service that market. That and other business was lost by the stockyards plant.

With continued decline, survived of the plant was a problem. The plant ran at about three-quarter capacity through the middle 1960's. All Continental Can plants were generally organized according to the following organizational structure.

John Prieto was brought into the plant as plant manager early in 1968. -The plant was not running efficiently and was not earning up to its potential. The division headquarters was faced with options whether to close the plant down and transfer the business to other Chicago area plants, or try to make the plant profitable. The organizational structure had been depleted and was running with less than a full management team, as the decision was made from the top on the future of the plant.

Prieto was given the decision and the opportunity to hand pick four or five managers throughout the company to come in and put the plant back on its feet.

In late summer 1967, I began talking with Prieto about coming in and taking over press manufacturing. At the time I was Chief Industrial Engineer of the Elwood Industrial Plant In early October, I took the position, and arrived to take over in mid-October 1968. When I arrived, the press department had been running leaderless for approximately four months. Scarcely any organizational structure existed.

The press department was the plant's largest manufacturing entity. The plant was a multi-story, ancient building. Press manufacturing was done on three floors. Each was a separate, distinct entity. About 30 complete production lines were on the first floor . The second floor housed the production equipment for supplying cans for packing ham ends. Some 40 production lines that made tops for various other sizes of meat products such as Spam, etc., were on the third floor. Seven management personnel and 30 lead men managed this operation. When they came to work, they informally checked what had to be done and managed the operation on a day-to-day basis.

The department had long been running in the red. Various acts of sabotage had been committed on the third shift. The first shift would come in to find equipment out of adjustment, wrenches left in dies, and compound mixtures diluted. Spoilage was running at almost double the standard rate.

Since the plant's future had been in question over the past 10 years, each project or added piece of equipment was put on a temporary basis. The wiring for the second floor ham lines had been temporarily put in more than 10 years before and was still considered temporary when I arrived. The work conditions were extremely dirty around the first-floor production lines. The production control department scheduled change-overs and shipment at will, with little coordination with the manufacturing entity.

I was to discover later that the accounting system was often incorrect and haphazardly handled. For example, I traced down, one month, the spoilage charged to the department, and found that almost $1,000 of spoilage had been charged to the manufacturing operation owing to an accident at a customer's plant in Henderson, Ky.

Some cost accountants had charged the spoilage into the press manufacturing spoilage account just because it happened that it was the ends that had been spoiled. The department had earned the distinction of leading the entire company in 1967 in repair costs. The costs for repairing, mending, and installing broken and worn parts was about $250,000. Worker morale was very low. A high degree of frustration and a lack of sense of accomplishment were apparent.

When I agreed to take the job, I was given almost free rein, the only condition that I made upon accepting it. I was confident and didn't want someone constantly looking over my shoulder at every move I made. Prieto and Dick Griffith were startled when I made this a condition of accepting of the job, but agreed to my terms.

What would you do if you were in my shoes.

CONTINENTAL CAN PART II

The first thing I did upon taking over the head of press manufacturing was to get a grasp of what was going on and earn the people's confidence. I talked informally with as many people as I could those first few weeks. I took each management member out to dinner and spent time listening and explaining my managerial philosophy. Late in October I set up a general machine-cleaning and housekeeping project. The objective was more than just cleaning house; it was making a psychological impact. A new management regime was beginning. I brought in each production-line head. The objective of that first weekend was to get the key management team, the lead men, and the maintainers who headed each production line, tuned in to a new management philosophy; We spent that full Saturday having each maintainer go thorough and check out his production equipment, cleaning up the main working parts, and generally making sure his work area was well organized and presentable. I moved from man to man, generally encouraging, communicating, and listening, and in the best way I knew how, letting the team know that we were moving ahead. This program was well received. Incidentally each maintainer received time-and a half-for his day's work.

The next week I added four men to the third-shift crew to begin a methodical painting of the equipment. The lifeblood of the manufacturing organization is its equipment. It goes back to the philosophy of the Golden West that your horse is your most important asset, and you'd better take care of it. Having established a professional attitude, we addressed what I considered to be the major problems. (This assessment came from input of all involved.) By early November we identified: (1) lack of planning, organization and clearly established objectives; (2) high equipment breakage and repairs; (3) poor manufacturing efficiency; (4) a poor attitude, and a poor co-ordination with other plant departments, especially production control.

The following is a list of problems and how we dealt with them:

Problem 1- Poor Organization/Planing/Coordination

We organized the department into two subunits. The first floor was organized into a department called round press. The second and third floors were combined and called the oblong press department. A manager from the ranks was put in charge of both of those departments. Each of these department heads reported to me.

An overall plan was developed with support plans.They had foremen and lead men reporting to them.

Problem 2 - Equipment Breakage and High Repair Costs.

One cause of a high incidence of breakage was the lack of training and the attitude on the part of the maintenance personnel. The general cleanup was the start of solving this problem. A training program was set up for every maintainer in the department. Part of the program was to develop a properly functioning maintenance program. The heads of both round and oblong press were given the assignment to develop the program. Company engineers had developed proper preventive-maintenance programs used companywide, but they were not being used properly in this instance. We developed the procedures to implement this program, along with workable modifications. A check -maintenance and running-maintenance program was established. Monthly problem-solving meetings with the maintainers helped to identify the problem and get these programs going. An excellent training director in the work force taught the maintainers and brought them up to date on proper preventive checks and running maintenance. We also had special training sessions on equipment adjustment and proper die-setting procedures. Goals and objectives were negotiated with the maintainers on the expected level of performance for the 1968 budget year. We set an objective: Cut repair costs in half in 1968.

Problem 3 - Safety

I set up a safety and housekeeping committee. A member of management, a union member, a rank-and-file blue-collar worker, and I would make a monthly safety tour. The purpose here was twofold: (1) let the people know that I cared about them and their welfare; and (2) cut down on the high accident rate. Each month, as we made this tour, we would carry work orders with us on a clipboard and either I or the management team member would make out the work orders to repair broken conduit, exposed lines, or improperly set guards. This was strongly emphasized. Goals on the accident rate were set in monthly group meetings. It was at this same time that Prieto set up a plant-wide goal to work a million man-hours successfully. Prieto purchased a home first-aid kit for every employee in the plant to encourage success.

Problem 4 - Morale

Attitudes began to change as the workers began to sense that work could be organized and the department run efficiently. The Polish people were quick to respond to and support my new regime. The blacks maintained a "let's wait and see" attitude. To my knowledge, I was not discriminatory and gave them no reason not support me. One of the key black leaders came in during the early months and paid me what turned out to be a pretty fair compliment. He said that I was consistent, "that I was equally tough on everyone. " When the job was not done correctly.

During those early months we fired 28 persons. We had people working for us who had posted bond for murder, were dope addicts, and were basically non-productive malcontents. Most had not completed their apprenticeship in the union and were fairly easy to discharge without stiff union opposition. The Polish workers seemed to like this because they didn't like the people who were fired. They were dismissed because of nonperformance, not because of race, color, or creed. We put heavy pressure on nonproducers.

The management team was introduced to MBO, which wasn't particularly accepted in the early stages. Late in 1967, as we were having difficulty getting goals set, I called the management team together. On a Saturday morning I basically gave them the option of staying on the job with MBO or being put into some other activity. It was obvious that I was out of patience and meant business. I believe I finally won their confidence and we moved forward. We set up what would be considered a standard, blue-collar MBO program as outlined in my book, *MBO: Blue Collar to Top Executive.*

Each manager and foreman had his particular objectives to work toward. The objectives and goals were clearly identified and communicated to the work force. The standard communication feedback procedures were supplied to workers as we moved toward attainment of the goal. The actual 1970 press manufacturing plan is shown in Appendix A.

As efficiency improved, repairs declined, and the general organization started moving forward, I started an intense motivational campaign aimed at running in the black for the first time. It was a subject that was brought up frequently. What I wanted was to let people gain self-confidence in their own ability and in my ability to manage effectively. It was, in effect, a struggle for the credibility of our new management regime.

That was the year Joe Namath had predicted that the Jets would beat the Colts in the Super Bowl. I used the Namath example again and again saying that we would run in the black within six months. Mid-April, then, was published as the goal. Since the organization hadn't run in the black for years, that idea was not taken seriously by about half the people in the organization. As we began to get close, we were impatient to finally get our toe over the line to establish momentum. By early February, I thought we were close enough for me to juggle the books and create our first black week that month. I had giant 8 by 5-foot congratulatory letters printed to hang on the bulletin board, developed documents, and laid out a celebration plan for the third week in February. We were legitimately close that second week, but not really close enough to run in the black.

As I recall, a legitimate variable cost statement would have shown about a 5 percent red statement. I charged out various hours to preventive maintenance, training, and other activities so that we would run 1 percent in the black. The only other person aware of this bit of chicanery was Wanda, the production reporter. She had been on the same job for 45 years, and was a warm friend. We had a giant celebration, bought coffee and rolls, and in effect, took credit for a big victory. The organization was so big that an individual member couldn't necessarily know that his production line hadn't run that much better. I suppose they assumed that the other production lines did.

What that did was ignite the fuse I had been looking for. We started a string of 10 straight legitimate black weeks. Those 10 weeks were like an old time Oklahoma football season. Everyone in the company heard of the accomplishment and called, wrote, and visited. I passed the glory on to the people and they loved it.

Soon managers from other press departments were visiting to learn how we turned the operations around.

Problem 5 -Sabotage

Sabotage on the third shift got so bad by mid-1968 that we hired a private investigator. He went to work on the third shift and assumed an identity with the workers on the third shift. He got in with the "gang". He reported the incidents and collected evidence for us. We learned that two employees were the ring leaders in this particular action. We gathered the evidence and worked closely with Industrial Relations. We determined we had a case good enough to warrant discharge. I came in with the assistant plant manager, Frank Sudholt, on the third shift during the summer, and we suspended both employees. The union obviously backed the employees. We began the long struggle through the various grievance stages, and it appeared the case was going to arbitration.

As arbitration neared, we began to run into problems with the investigative firm. In arbitration the actual witnesses are subpoenaed and brought before the arbitrator. The detective agency reminded us that it had contracted to supply information, but would not interpret that contract to mean that their man would have to go on the witness stand. Obviously reprisals were feared, and of course the detective's identity would be revealed. We then realized that our case would not stand up in arbitration.

By refusing to arbitrate, we had to fully reinstate both employees at full pay and benefits. This was painful, but one must play by the rules. This naturally had an effect on morale, but not overwhelmingly. We did, however, stop the sabotage and the third shift became more productive.

For me it was a bitter defeat. As a former high school and college athlete, winning is ingrained in my spirit. As it turned out perhaps we lost the battle but won the war. There was an overwhelming show of support from the workforce. The honest, hardworking people were glad to see that someone would take a tough stand.

Problem 6 - Projects

The opportunities and problems that began to face us in the summer of 1969 included the handling of research-and-development projects. Continental Can's Central Can Making R & D Center was at nearby 69th at Racine . All projects must be brought into full manufacturing through a series of phases. The research and development personnel must work closely with a manufacturing unit. Our plant was nearby and the lack of full capacity made it ideal for R & D to experiment on our equipment. As long as there were not many projects, it became a good means of making money (there would be a dollar transfer of credit for supplying labor and a contribution to overhead for using our equipment).

What happened, however , in the summer of 1969, was that we ended up with the following projects: (1) an airline's new coffee can, (2) the cheese can for U.S. soldiers in Vietnam, and (3) the new equipment and manufacturing techniques for making easy-open coffee, nut, and tobacco cans. This research overload became a big problem. We got so many projects going that we tied up too many key people during the summer vacation months, and it made normal manufacturing efficiency. Note the graph.

Problem 7 - Crowded Conditions

Part of the management-by-objectives goal-setting system gave us the opportunity to move ahead on numerous improvement projects. We negotiated objectives and agreements with production control and the maintenance shop to shut down the second-floor ham equipment to complete the temporary wiring. We also set goals and began moving some of the second-floor equipment to the first floor. Unfortunately, this was the only place there was room to move that equipment. An engineering consulting report had indicated that the second floor would not support the heavy equipment and constant pounding much longer. We were faced with the expensive necessity of a complete reorganization of the equipment lay-out. After much hard work, we developed a plan for the relocation of this equipment, and began that project through 1969. An employee commit-tee made recommendations to the consulting firm and our management on the new lay out. They had many fine ideas and one women found an apparent flow in the plant that was corrected. That project had been half completed by the time I left in August 1970.

Problem 8 - Production-Control Scheduling

I had learned, as a staff head responsible for industrial engineering and long range planning at the Elwood Industry plant, some of the natu-ral hedging that takes place in production control. Production control is responsible for warehousing costs, and a long production run increases the department's cost. Production control naturally aspied to keep the production run short and make direct shipments to the customers, thereby keeping product out of the warehouse. We cut the line change-overs in half at Elwood when we forced production control to establish goals and guidelines to maintain delivery and keep warehousing costs at a minimum.

I became actively involved in the setting of objectives with produc-tion control to avoid being forced into to many unnecessary changeovers. Each changeover would required 8 to 20 hours to get the line back into production. The industrial engineering standard for a die change, for example, gave the department credit for about 3.5 hours. The curlers and other equipment gave it about 6 line hours and perhaps 15 to 18 man-hours. Only through the generation of standard line-hours could we earn spoilage materials and other dollars. To compound this changeover problem, we have found that many of the smashed dies came through the improper setting. What does this mean? We were exchang-ing a few dollars in warehousing costs for the tremendous expense of actual production downtime, repair costs, and repair material generated through increased frequency of die-change problems.

As every experienced person in manufacturing knows, a production line never comes out of change hour on schedule. This many increased changeovers and was an even bigger problem, than it appeared on the surface. We were able to get the line changeover cut down. This also help reduces repair costs.

Problem 9 - Repair Costs

As stated earlier, the first stage of halving the $250,000 repair costs was the maintainer-training program. Through increased worker skills we hoped to reduce broken equipment and downtime. We also instututed a rigorous preventive-maintenance program on the equipment. We did not use sophisticated methods to determine frequency of preventive maintenance, but gathered an information base that indicated how often preventive maintenance should be pulled on the equipment.

For example, the Minster presses required a preventive maintenance check once every seven days. I had learned through my experience that the nesting pins would likely have a high frequency of breaking between the eighth and the tenth day. When the nesting pins broke, anywhere from $10,00 to $50,000 damage would be suffered. Preventive maintenance obviously cost one full day's production on each piece of equipment every seventh day, but it had a tremendous effect on repair costs. In the long run, we got as much production time as before when the machine would be broken down and being repaired at the same time.

The equipment needed preventive-maintenance checks according to a set schedule. Goals and objectives were established. The following pictures shows the method of scheduling and feedback. Notice the ugly wolf picture in the corner. This exemplified my attitude toward the preventive-maintenance and maintenance programs. It basically boiled down to : If you don't want to tangle with the bull, (me) you'd better get your preventive maintenance done. The next procedure was to device a setup when installing a die. Note the copy of the actual form used on the following page.

I worked with the foremen and the maintenance men so that they could develop this procedure. I knew what had to be done, but realized that if I developed it, they would never do it. I let them developed it and then challenged them to make it work. As a result, in 1969 we cut repair costs down to $110,000.

Problem 10 -People problems

Although the management team functioned much better, we still had problems. The basic attitude of most of the management team was a very strong "Let's see what happens". I had the opportunity to bring two new men on board. They were both younger, eager men and quite capable. One I brought up from St. Louis where he had worked with me and had seen how we had used management by objectives and knowledge of results. Please refer to chapter 6 in my book, MBO: Blue Collar to Top Executives, for a description of how that program was installed. This man was a great help in helping get the same type of program installed in the stockyards plant. Owing to the short time I was there, the stockyard program was not setup as well and in as much depth as the St. Louis program.

329

The problem was that four levels of management lay between me and the blue collar worker. Obviously, when you have three management levels below you, It takes time to get this programs down to their lowest level. Incidentally, I have learned during the last 25 years how to reduce this time considerably. The older foremen and department staff did not formally greet the young additions to the team. I learned a valuable lesson. I had hired the lower-level management persons. What I should had done was have this new men screened by the men they were to report to, and allow them to pick the men who would be working for them. That would have assure their backing of the choices and a commitment to their success.

As every experienced line executive knows, there is a tendency to let the boss stew in his own juice if he (the subordinate) is not committed. I had let myself get caught in the stew.

Let me cite one example of the competence displayed by one of the young men. I made him totally responsible for spoilage. In management thinking this would be analogous to a one-man matrix organization. He established a plan and carried it out. Spoilage was reduced to acceptable levels within about six weeks. This action was taken only after the normal line channels had failed to achieve any acceptable improvements. I made a big mistake in one meeting when I criticized a maintainer "Dago A1" they called him in front of the whole group. I have sense learned "praise in public, criticize in private". It took a big time to repair my relationship with all.

Problem 11 - The Summer of 1970 / New product

In the early spring of 1970, I had become deeply involved as a consultant with Fred Rudge, an independent consultant in New York City. We had worked together in many different kinds of projects. We had worked closely in the Clearing Industrial District (See pages 37-51, 71-93 of is book, *Productivity Improvement, The key to increased production*). He began talking to me about working fulltime with him. I had received an offer from one of my former bosses to become corporate manager of industrial engineering for Central Can Co. The rumor mill buzzed that my next move with Continental was to become the liaison between manufacturing and marketing at the corporate level in New York

At age 30, I was flattered, but had started to become restless in my spirit. The stockyards plant had pulled out of a hole. It was running at maximum capacity. Production lines were running that had not been active in 10 years. New training programs were upgrading the needed technical help. Half of the relocation programs were still to go, as we launched a major training effort for more competent people. There was a severe shortage of electricians and we solved the problem. I felt I had done the job I had been brought there to do.

We decided to move to Tulsa Oklahoma in August 1970 to begin a career academia. I announced my intention of leave Continental in May. I had planned to join Fred Rudge for a month of work in July, and then get started in Tulsa in August. My boss at Continental Can urged me to stay during the summer to move organization through another set of problems. I didn't want to, but felt an obligation to do everything I could. It was a tough, hard summer, but we made it.

The chief problem that summer ended up being the Keep Cool can, promised for Andy Granatelli. I learned of the project while driving down the Dan Ryan Expressway one day in late February. Someone on the radio was announcing the product and promising consumers it would be on the shelf for the hot summer months around Memorial Day.

I remember thinking, "That's going to be some kind of project; I wonder who is going to get stuck making it?" I learned a few days later that I was the stuckee. The sales people had promised delivery on a can that hadn't even been through research and development, had no tooling and equipment with which to make it. A grueling period was ahead.

We finally made delivery in late July. It took almost all the resources of the 50th-biggest corporation in the country to pull it off. I spent the Fourth of July with 20 of the leading research, mathematical, and equipment specialists the company could muster. The mood of the meeting was hostile. We had all been thrown together at the last minute to solve some complex mechanical problems, and getting the equipment into production on a personal note we had scheduled a family vocation and planned to leave after work that friday. My wife Mari had our Station Wagon when I arrived home and announced we couldn't go. We finally solved the problem. It basically boiled down to new tooling in some equipment that was not made to house the tooling.

Slack in the cams and gears caused a buildup of centrifugal force in rotating parts of the production process. It was an interesting combination of the buildup of centrifugal force, a certain base weight of aluminium that had a particular grain that when all combined, would present a situation where there would be a leak.

It had taken a full six to eight weeks of around-the-clock work to nail down these variables. We had wasted the first four weeks using stopgap and nickel-and-dime procedures. We finally realized, after a month of all-out effort, that we were going in circles.

During this entire process, we had a tremendous amount of pressure from the corporate office. Granatelli was raising the roof because he was spending a fortune advertising a product that wasn't on the shelf. Marketing has a lot of clout and was causing a ruckus in head office. All head office cares about is results. Unfortunately, we were given the task to have those ends manufactured by Memorial Day. Again, that's just the way the game is played. I am sure that at higher levels of the company, my record is somewhat tarnished for not having met that deadline.

When I had submitted my resignation, I knew nothing of the upcoming project and the grueling summer ahead. Many times I thought through how different all would have been had I bailed out and been involved with Fred in some of the glory work in New York City. Instead of the glory, I was in the trenches in Chicago. How my wife Mari and the children survived, I know not.

Problem 12 - Marketing

The solution of the marketing problem was in productivity. Our grand scheme was to make the plant productive and profitable. We then used that as a lever to show the division office that we could competently handle new orders. Our strategy was to go after the Michigan fruit and berry business, specialty orders, and government business. We were converting capacity to pick up this new business. Top management went with us and started moving this business in. This necessitated acquisition of the latest technology available in can making. We had six brand-new production lines. Four of these were installed after I arrived. We were making this specialty products from our Chicago Stockyards plant.

We got the business because we proved we could produce, and the plant was only a mile from the Dan Ryan expressway. The Dan Ryan and the Calumet expressway provided a fast, easy four- to six- lane shot into Michigan and all of the profitable canneries. We continued making the ham cans and sending them into other parts of the country. The overhaul program, preventive maintenance, and lubrication programs had increased the capacity of the ham lines by a full 25 percent. The plant was running seven days a week on the ham lines when I came, and was still running that way when I left. The demand for ham cans in that section of the country was insatiable. We could sell everything we could make. With a 25 percent increase in productivity, all the gains were gravy. Since it was a profitable item, it obviously added tremendously to the profitability of the plant and generated handsome increases in standard line hours.

The third-floor press had brought in the new cheese can and had taken it through research stages. This provided another new product. Our marketing plan paid off. We got new profitable business which generated new opportunities and new capacities.

Problem 13 - Accounting

I found many mistakes during my stay there which plant, on how labor, spoilage, and materials were charged. I would say the statements were 90 percent accurate, but I always suspected problems. One thing I never could get to the bottom of was a $ 10,000 loss in litho materials. During the previous year we had used a certain dollar for coatings in the seam of the end. The next year we had used 10,000 more dollars. The price hadn't changed, and to the best of my knowledge, our equipment settings hadn't changed. It is highly unlikely that this product could be stolen and resold. I never felt the accounting people did the right kind of a job to try to track down the answer. Perhaps the supplier over billed us.

The old equipment, to my knowledge, had been almost fully depreciated. It was obviously combined to make an asset base with the new equipment that was brought in. I don't have information on the profitability of the plant. My management bonus the last year 17 percent of my annual salary, which is an indication that we were having a pretty profitable year.

Problem 14 - Ethical Problems

I saw a lot of ethical problems. It seemed to me that every political and social group was shaking down every organization in the district for pledges to support all kinds of things from parades to annual parties. A threat always seemed to underlie failure to contribute to any of these projects. We seemed to dole the cash out, no questions asked, whenever requested. The rail crews had interesting ways of shaking down different parts of the organization. If a proper cache of whiskey and other embellishments was not conveniently left, needed rail switchings wouldn't take place. The situation once became so bad we couldn't get rail cars moved for any reason.

We protested to the railroad management, which had very little power over the "mistakes" made at the lowest levels. One of my foreman who had worked in the plant for years said "Let me take care of this". Reluctantly I said "Ok". Rail pickup and deliveries were never a problem again. I never asked what he did.

There was the ever-present evidence of the Chicago underworld. I was not new to this since I saw how it worked a few years earlier at Plant 5 on the other side of Chicago. A daily and nightly fence of stolen materials was going on throughout the whole south side of Chicago. The syndicate character's took orders and delivered contraband almost at will in the locker rooms, parking lots, and other areas.

One day as I was coming to work and listening to the radio, the announcer told about a Shaeffer pen truck that had been hijacked with all the pens stolen. When I got to work at 6:45 a.m., the union steward walked up and handed me a package of about 50 $3 Shaeffer pens. He asked me if I wanted a bargain for $1.

I heard stories of custom delivery of stolen automobiles down to the color, engine size, and accessories. The bookies and numbers men were active all over the place. I could not and did not do anything about this situation. All I did was refuse to purchase all the bargains that were constantly available. I tried to set an example that even though these items were highly tempting, it wasn't really right to become involved. I can't say that example rubbed off on anyone

I was offered a wad of bills as "thanks" and a " consulting fee" from a company trying to persuade us to go to its product. We had been deeply involved in testing three major competitors for more than a three months. Ironically, we had just about decided to take its product anyway. I didn't accept the money, but suggested that it might have a good effect on the people if they put on a grand feed for the troops. It would help them be in a good mood to be sure that their new product was successful.

I will never forget leading that army of blue-collar mechanics into the second-floor ballroom of one of the South side's posher spots. I had let them reserve the entire second floor because I didn't want that mob exposed to the public, both for our protection and the protection of the public. I don't even want to discuss the outcome of the party. Let's just say the wine flowed and the food was enjoyed by all. It reminded me of what it must have been like when the Vikings conquered a new country, and hungrily ravaged everything in sight after a year at sea.

Of course, the whole episode had a marked effect on morale. The troops generally conceded that I had been the one to make sure the grand party took place. In that social climate, anytime your "beat the system," to use current parlance, that was status. I didn't feel it was wrong for the company to stage the big party. Naturally, it would have been wrong if I had stuffed the money in my pocket.

Problem 15 - Integrating the Workforce

I was assigned to a three-man committee in the Chicago area to set up a program for bringing hard-core unemployed blacks into the job market. To shorten the story, we had psychologists identify 40 incorrigibles for us, hired a university to train them to eat in a cafeteria, read bus schedules, and become trained in how to work for manufacturing. Some 80 percent of those hired didn't make it, but 20 percent did.

I will never forget one fellow who worked for me; ugly, dirty, filthy, foul-mouthed, and contemptible he was when he reported for work. He cried when I left, and made my rounds thanking each person. He had truly become a changed young man. He and I butted heads on a regular and steady basis. It was because of this, I'm, sure, that he learned to trust me and made a man of himself. I am proud, as I look back, to have had a positive effect on one person's life. I ran into him seven years later when I had dropped in to see friends, and he was still progressing very well and was pleased to see me.

CONCLUSION

At the risk of immodesty, the day I left, all production lines shut down at approximately 2:30 pm and a great crowd gathered outside my office. The troops presented me with a TV set and made some speeches. I was touched. All the women and at least a third of the men was openly crying as I walked out that door with a heavy heart.

As I walked to my car in the parking lot I couldn't look back. I too was shocked with emotion. I can remember walking across the parking lot, hardly believing that I was leaving what seemed to have been an empire that we had built. When we packed up and headed for Oklahoma, I left with a cheerful heart and a happy, expectant attitude. I didn't know what to expect, had never taught a college course, and most certainly had a lot to learn.

As the years went by I always come back and visited the plant. Sadly the new environmental laws on air pollution made it economically unfeasible to operate the plant a few years later. The cost to comply was just too expensive. It was cheaper for Continental Can to move the business to other Continental plants.

Now the operation was 25 percent of plant capacity. As I walked through the plant on a chilly day the mountains seemed cold and lifeless. Many sections of the plant had little lighting.

My memory recalled these cold quiet isles at one time were bustling with activity.......... As I look back I can see business has its cycles.

I'm grateful for the experience. As the 67 Colts who won the Super Bowl I felt like we won our big game....

If you were my replacement, what would you do?

T. D. WILLIAMSON, INC.
ONE COMPANY'S EXPERIENCE WITH
STRATEGIC PLANNING

by

R. Henry Migliore
Professor of Strategic Planning
and Management
Northeastern State University/
University Center at Tulsa

and

Richard B. Williamson
President & Chief Executive Officer

OUTLINE

ABSTRACT

T. D. Williamson, Inc., faced a problem in 1985 on how to plan, manage, and control the company in the wake of a rapidly changing environment. The strategic planning process helped TDW make those changes. TDW went from a functional to a regional organizational concept. T. D. Williamson, Inc., is a stronger, more profitable company today.

BACKGROUND

T. D. Williamson, Inc., faced a crossroads in the evolution of the company in 1985. In order to understand the situation at that point in time, it is important to understand the company: its founder, how it has evolved, as well as its planning, management, and control system.

T. D. Williamson, Inc., is a family-owned business based in Tulsa, Oklahoma. It has evolved into a team of over 600 individuals operating six engineering and manufacturing sites, 17 Service Centers, and 19 field sales management centers located in 12 countries. The sales representative and distribution program involves over 65 firms.

The purpose, mission, and reason for being evolved from the dreams and vision of its founders.

The T. D. Williamson, Inc., purpose statement today is . . .

To provide products and services for the monitoring, operation, and maintenance of essential piping systems.

To sustain profitable growth sufficient to meet the needs of the stakeholders in the business (i.e., providers, employees, community, customers, and shareholders).

Growth to be achieved primarily by expending our activities in related businesses.

To maintain a position of leadership and integrity in business as perceived by our customers, employees, and the community.

STAGES OF EVOLUTION
1920–1975

How do small companies evolve into larger ones? Why do some succeed and some fail? We know from an academic standpoint that every company that survives goes through three stages.

Stage I is where the founder/family start the business. They have a unique idea, product, or service. T. D. Williamson, Sr., started the business with Edna M. Williamson, his wife, in 1920. The company at that time had as its primary mission to offer General Electric's motor and related power equipment to the rapidly expanding oil industry.

We know the expected failure rate of small businesses in the first year is 90 percent; 80 percent over five years. T. D. Williamson, Inc., has passed both of those tests.

In Stage I, the culture for the business is established. As we develop the thought process to the point of strategic change, it is important to note the role that the culture of T. D. Williamson, Inc., plays in the kinds of decisions that have to be made when the company set about to making tough, strategic choices.

In Stage II, as successful businesses grow out of the garage and become bigger, functional organizational structure begins to emerge. There will be a point where Marketing, Production, Finance/Accounting, and Human Resources are the major functional areas. There is a need for more planning, as well as for the development of leadership. TDW entered Stage II circa 1948 during a period when the oil and gas industry was expanding dramatically in the U.S. to meet demand for gasoline and other energy products. TDW further refined the Stage II development circa 1958 and continued for over 20 years, as product lines were added and international markets expanded. It remained a basically functional organization.

Stage III evolves as the company gets bigger. It becomes more sophisticated, it usually becomes incorporated, does formal planning, and establishes a Board of Directors. More defined accountability and rewards for managerial performance is required in order to direct and motivate key personnel. The organization begins the process of mergers and acquisitions, as well as forms joint ventures, franchises, and other alliances.

During this stage, changes in organizational structure take place. The managerial team must consider how to strategically manage the plan and the culture of the organization, and how to manage culture.

APPROACHING THE DIFFICULT PERIOD
1982–1984

During the period from 1982 to 1984, a set of conditions dictated the need for a specific strategy change.

In 1985, T. D. Williamson, Inc., needed to adapt to a marketplace. What happened to create this opportunity in 1985? Following the conclusion of World War II, the U.S. energy industry embarked upon a major program of expansion—designed to fuel the return to consumer products manufacture and the "love affair" that Americans were having with the passenger car. New pipelines were being laid and older ones were expanded and modified to meet the seemingly unlimited requirements of the consumer. For these pipelines to stay on stream, it became necessary to develop tools that permitted branch connections to be made to existing pipeline systems. TDW built upon older "tapping" concepts and a new generation of tapping machines emerged.

In addition, lines needed to be relocated (for example—to make way for new interstate highway right-of-ways) and repaired, as pipelines became damaged or continued to age due to corrosion and other forces. A way to isolate sections of pipe, while still allowing flow to be maintained for downstream customers, was needed. For this, TDW created a plugging system called the stopple. With that, yet another industry, tapping and plugging, was born.

Unlike its predecessor product lines, tapping and plugging required a more intensive involvement in the processes of machining, welding, and forming of steel. The friendly acquisition of a local manufacturing business ushered TDW into a new stage of its evolution—with new (manufacturing) processes to manage and different technical and management skills to be employed. The served industry was still the transmission pipelines, though the scope was becoming more global. A manufacturing center was established in Canada and another in the U.K., with a sales network beginning to expand into Europe, the Middle East, Asia, and South America.

The management teams were beginning to focus overseas, as well. Though essentially "clones" of the home office—they, nevertheless, served to remind "corporate" that all customers did not think the same as the U.S. pipeline industry. For example, the stage of technical and operational development of the domestic European pipeline industry, as well as the collaborative relationship of the operating companies with host governments, tended to color their behavior—whether the pipeline company was nationalized or a "production-sharing" subsidiary of one of the original "7-sister" international oil companies.

To respond to this, TDW's home office, as well as the local operating center, had to become more internationally minded. The unique tools and technology developed for use in the niche markets of North America could not be easily exported to local TDW operating centers abroad, much less licensed to third parties. Over time, however, a network of semi-independent overseas operating divisions began to emerge.

TDW management practices evolved as well. Individuals who had participated in the technical development of tools and consumable products in the North American market were now being called upon to be overseas managers—often with little or no formal training in the field. This placed everyone in a relationship of trust and mutual interdependence as no one individual or group had the skills or resources to carry out its business plan in isolation to the others. Though this synergy allowed for conservation of resources at a time when high market and operational development cysts, as well as cyclical markets, would have swamped a stand-alone business, it also led to a symbiosis of roles that ultimately led to a slowing-down of new development as a sense of conservatism and "group think" began to emerge.

Until 1960, TDW's approach toward tapping and plugging was focused on the higher-pressure oil, gas, and products transmission pipelines. In the preceding decade, local gas distribution companies had begun to expand and upgrade their natural gas delivery systems. This was accomplished using many of the new technologies utilized in the expansion of the transmission pipeline industry—only operating at substantially lower pressures. A general conversion from cast iron to steel pipes took place, and with that, the raising of gas pressures from less than one atmosphere to 60 to 90 psi. This provided TDW the opportunity to scale-down its tapping and plugging technology to create a new line of intervention equipment suited for the different operational needs of the gas companies. However, TDW was not the first into that market—and so began a long struggle to find our way into a marketplace that, though strong in its commitment to quality and safety, proved to be slow to change and adopt new ways of operations.

Within a decade, markets were developed in North America, Western Europe, and Australia—the then mature energy-consuming markets of the world. Not until the advent of LNG (Liquefied Natural Gas), and the prospect of transporting large amounts of natural gas economically and safely far from the producing areas to industrialized markets, had the gas distribution industry begun to expand in many of the newly industrialized nations. When it did so, it then repeated a cycle of supplanting wood, coal, fuel oil, and LPG as the core industrial, commercial, and residential fuels.

During the 1970's, the technology for producing polyethylene pipe, valves, and fittings improved dramatically—creating a demand for "different" products (now made of polyethylene) to serve TDW. This business involves the use of intelligent pigs: devices that are transported through the pipeline propelled by the pressure of the fluid in the line. The purpose of the tool is to collect data on a variety of pipeline features, and then download this data into larger computers for analysis and reporting. The types of information sought are anomalies which address the safety and environmental integrity of the pipeline—buckles, dents, corrosion, and cracks.

TDW's entry into this market began in the late 1960's with tools to inspect buckles and dents—the KALIPER, as we call it, because it uses a number of fingers extended against the interior pipe wall to sense any changes in contour. TDW established itself as the premier provider of this service globally.

However, the need for corrosion surveys has grown more steadily over the last two decades. In 1980, TDW began a program of research to develop a new generation of tools for inspecting gas pipelines for corrosion. To give you an indication as to how long the developmental cycle can be for some of these products, that tool began its field tests in 1991—over 10 years after embarking on the research.

When TDW's markets began to shrink in the early 1980's—along with the overall decline of the energy industry globally—TDW had to address this directly, though not promptly.

In 1983, the company had its first-ever layoff. In keeping with the philosophy of concern for our employees and their families, the event took place perhaps 18 months later than it might have in other companies. Steps were taken to assure a proper evaluation of each individual's performance and ability/willingness to improve. Some terminations occurred as a result of this process. Then, an early retirement program was initiated. Finally, the layoffs were made. A similar downsizing took place in 1985 as the global energy markets continued to contract—with only a modest sense of bottoming out, and no indication of a return of growth.

REORGANIZATION
1985

It was at this time that TDW decided to rethink its entire organization. TDW formally moved into Stage III in 1985. Not only structure and staffing were to be included, but the way the organization interacted with the firm's strategic direction. To do so, TDW selected a major U.S. consulting firm to lead the senior management of the company through an organizational assessment. That process included:

1. *Business Assessment*
   The first step was to see who TDW was in a global market/industry perspective. The market position was examined from two standpoints:

   - The size and relative competitive strength of TDW in each of its core businesses globally and regionally, as well as
   - The degree to which each regional market tended to differentiate itself in terms of product features, local sales, distribution, sourcing, and servicing requirements.

2. *Regional Assessments*
   The consequence of this was the understanding that TDW had become operationally different in three major regions of the world:

   - Western Hemisphere
   - Europe/Africa/Middle East
   - Far East/Asia Pacific

In the *Western Hemisphere Region,* markets were large but mature and slow growing. Although our market position was strong in almost all business areas, there was little opportunity to grow through existing product line modification and extension. Therefore, the challenge was to:

- HOLD and PROTECT the core businesses.
- Seek to expand our business position in the three target industries through selective ACQUISITION & PARTNERSHIP.

In *Europe/Africa/Middle East,* the markets were still growing as the industrial infrastructure, particularly in the oil- and gas-producing markets, was expanding to create new capacity (much in excess of current demand). The technological preferences of the industrialized countries tended to drive a reinvestment in existing infrastructure throughout Western Europe. Though not fully recognized at the time, Central and Eastern Europe and, to a lesser extent, the USSR, were also beginning their program of reindustrialization. All these factors tended to place the region into a GROWTH & DEVELOPMENT Mode.

Given the substantial size of the served markets in the region, we decided to support the continued development of regional technology and manufacturing operating centers to serve these local markets.

Finally, the *Far East/Asia Pacific Region,* though anchored by the industrial centers of Australia and Japan, was experiencing significant development of the energy production infrastructure in the energy-producing states—primarily in Southeast Asia—and industrial development in the NIC's (Korea, Taiwan, Hong Kong, and Singapore, in particular) and, to a lesser extent, India and China. The TDW view was that these subregional markets would grow, but very selectively, as each, in some way, was constrained by capital, the state of development of the existing infrastructure, the level of industrial and technological development of its supporting industries, and the economic and political policies of each nation.

3. *Regionalization*
On the basis of this, the decision was made to form semi-autonomous business divisions organized around the three regional groupings. The strong functional departments of a centralized corporate system were dismantled in favor of smaller teams (still functionally based) positioned closer to key end markets.

4. *Organizational Climate*
TDW also sensed that the company had gotten itself into the posture of "we're okay, the problem is somewhere else" by a combination of attitudes and organizational practices that, though acceptable and in

some cases praiseworthy, together created an environment of internally-driven, functionally-focused organizational groups. Integration of effort, a sense of the customer, and the bottom line rarely existed anywhere except at the top, if at all.

Therefore, a climate study was undertaken using the consulting company and to confirm what had been recognized in earlier culture studies of TDW. The consulting study surveyed the attitudes and expectations of TDW's middle managers and compared them with that of other corporate populations. Though TDW was performing well in some areas, TDW failed to meet the test in: **Decision Making; **Integration; **Performance Orientation; **Vitality; **Incentive Plan; **Management Style.

The culture changes at T. D. Williamson, Inc., were measured over a 12-year period of time with a culture index[1]. It was important in the company to sense the culture of the organization, to create a measure, and then how that measure helped to direct efforts to change the culture over a period of years. The Culture Index (CI)/Management System Balance Sheet (MSBS) was given to T. D. Williamson, Inc.'s upper and middle managers from 1978 to 1988. Until 1984, scores were generally high. The low 1984 score was one of many indications that adverse change was taking place at T. D. Williamson, Inc.

Table I shows the CI/MSBS scores for 1979, 1981, and 1984. Note the decline from 6.35 to 4.78 to the 1984 score of 2.01.

Table I
T. D. Williamson, Inc.
Culture Index/Management Sysem Balance Sheet

ASSETS	1979	1981	1984
Goals	+0.79	+.82	.55
Planning	+0.97	+.88	.58
Planning Effectiveness	+0.52	+.26	(.03)
Morale	+0.75	+.32	(.13)
Performance Appraisal	+0.54	+.49	.23
Performance Reward System	+0.36	+.17	.47
Supervision Balance	+1.01	+.79	.32
Communication	+0.66	+.62	.16
Job Satisfaction	+0.75	+.43	2.29
TOTAL ASSETS	+6.35	+4.78	(.28)
LIABILITIES	-0-	-0-	-0-
Total Assets Over Liabilities	+6.35	+4.78	2.01

Concerns regarding planning effectiveness, morale, job satisfaction, supervision, and communication led the across-the-board perception by managers that the TDW planning, management, and control system was not effective. The managers, validated by the CI/MSBS, didn't feel the management system was working.

5. *Strategic Management*
   In order to transfer the sense of strategic direction from a centralized corporate functional team to regionalized groups, TDW embarked on a two-phase program:

   - To create a hierarchy of strategic planning and direction setting that involved key managers from the shop floor to the Board Room, and
   - To develop managers and professional staff to carry out their new roles in the restructured planning networks.

   a. *Planning Stages*
      Most firms go through stages of growth and development as they learn to plan. In general, TDW management sees these to be: **Day-to-Day Management; **Budgeting and Operational Planning; **Long-Range Planning; **Strategic Planning; **Strategic Management.

   b. *Planning Hierarchy*
      One of our objectives in restructuring the planning hierarchy was to define the role of each level in the organization as it relates to strategic planning and direction setting, as well as its accountability for carrying out essential tasks.

      For TDW, planning roles broke into the following levels:

      - Enterprise Statement
      - Strategic Direction
      - Corporate Strategy
      - Business Strategy
      - Functional Strategy

      The scope of planning for each level tends to emphasize the relative importance of those factors that are most essential to managers working at that level of the organization. Some of those factors would be:

      - Access to and need to manage detail.
      - Awareness of and interest in supporting related functional activities.
      - Degree to which the business/work environment is defined by the organization or by the marketplace.
      - The necessity for accepting risk in order to meet assigned objectives.

c. *Recasting of the Plan*

Finally, the plan had to be recast so that each organizational group would see what it is managing—somewhat in isolation to the others and to the company as a whole. For a medium-sized business with traditional operational information systems, the task to deal with interregional transactions and trading practices was substantial.

d. *Training*

TDW believed it was necessary to re-orient its managers to their new responsibilities and to give them a broader perspective of the business each was expected to manage. A team of educators from several universities was formed to develop a course on Strategic Management. This was offered to 40 of our middle and upper managers most affected by the organization change.

In order for the company to be successful in this reorganization, two things needed to happen:

- TDW needed to be more effective in addressing current markets with existing and enhanced products and services, and
- TDW needed to develop/acquire other (new) products and services targeted to its key industries capable of broadening TDW's market position and enhancing its prospect for future growth and profitability.

To meet the objectives of the expanding marketplace, growth of the company, and general complexity, TDW changed its organizational structure. It changed from a functional to a geographic/service structure. The Finance function remained at the corporate level in 1991. Table II shows this organizational change. Note the matrix concept was not used in 1991 but was added as a refinement in 1992.

TDW's first acquisition attempt was in North America. It came in two parts. The first was in-situ heat treating: a technical service targeted to the refining and hydrocarbon processing industry. Another part of the business was an internal pipeline crawler designed to X-ray the girth welds joining the ends of sections of pipe. Though each was new to TDW and offered entry into new sectors of the industries we served, we underestimated the degree of difference in operational and technical support required. And, given that no market exists without some competition, we were somewhat surprised by the aggressiveness of pricing and service responses we encountered. But, the crowning blow as the need to continue to make capital infusions at a time when we could not see an acceptable payout of the business in the future. So as we all have learned at one time or another in our careers, some acquisitions and mergers (like some marriages) are

Table II
Organizational Change at TDW

1984

1991

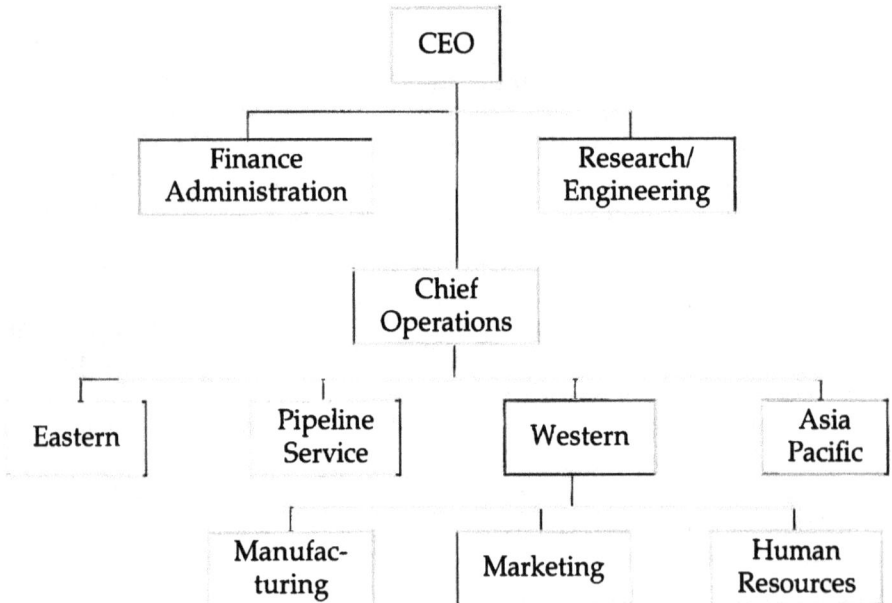

made in heaven, and some are not! When that occurs, exit is typically slow and painful.

TDW learned from the experiences. It was to do a more extensive job in examining the served markets—to better understand the dynamics of what makes them perform as they do. Also, it was to assess what sectors were more attractive for both existing providers as well as new entrants. During this time, we had opportunities to acquire a position in a number of businesses. Though each was studied to some appropriate degree, in general we backed away when we sensed we lacked the understanding of the end market. In other cases, it was when the competitive structure of that market appeared to be too aggressive—requiring the acquired entity to perform optimally (when often the reason for its being available was one or more performance deficiencies). Most of TDW's acquisitions have been small, focusing on product lines that address similar markets though occasionally incorporating modified selling and servicing channels. Manufacturing and technical support processes have typically not been stretched. As a result, the performance of these acquisitions has been acceptable, but not remarkable.

One strategic acquisition was made in 1988, that of FLAWSONIC. This is the intelligent pig designed to examine corrosion in liquid pipelines. At the time of its acquisition, it represented substantial risk to us inasmuch as it was for TDW new technology targeted to a related but not identical market. Also, the tool was still in a prototype stage of development. After two years of further development following acquisition, the tool was released to the market.

TDW immediately encountered the need to further enhance the underlying technology of the tool as well as the consistency of field performance. This raising of the ante forced TDW to pull the entire *Pipeline Surveys* business out of the three operating regions in 1989 and to create a new global business division. This allowed TDW to centralize technical development and to be more focused in how we addressed new markets with a product whose capabilities were and still are evolving.

It has also served to remind TDW of problems associated with the trend toward independence of the regional divisions (which has left us somewhat smaller and less capable of responding to global opportunities and threats). TDW has also come to recognize the value of joining with other firms in order to address markets too small, too remote, or too difficult for our own operating base to be effective. Typically, these have been in some of the developing markets, ones in which capital, technology, and market access are significant barriers. TDW has been willing to share the benefits in market development in order to attain a goal that would otherwise have been too risky or long term. In organizational change, one looks for behavioral signs that signal a fundamental change of attitude. This is one of them.

As a private, closely held business, TDW lacks the same strategic options as larger, publicly-capitalized firms. To move into that arena—either by a public offering, by acquiring, or by being acquired by a public company—has been considered. TDW management recognizes that we see our mission to serve end markets over the long-term with products that, by the nature of their technical development and acceptance cycle, create long periods of investment. A financially-driven investor environment that requires strong quarterly earnings would not allow such a business to survive—much less thrive. Among the many strategic options presented to senior managers, directors, and shareholders, this is one of the most critical. the board and shareholders of TDW have attempted to find a balance between consistently achieving acceptable short-term performance and appropriately investing in markets and technologies that will provide a future for the company when the current businesses mature and go into decline. As a consequence, the program for acquisition is still underway. Markets here and abroad are still being studied for acceptable entry points and "strategic alliances" are being developed to balance that which we can better achieve internally.

The net effect of TDW's efforts since 1985 has been to further diversify the company, its products, markets, and the operations that support them. Just as the Pipeline Surveys Division was created in 1989 as a global entity to deal with strategic technical development issues, other TDW businesses are being reformed within the context of regional management. In 1989 in Europe, TDW began a program to re-orient two sister plants to be more specialized around specific product lines—though the business management functions are still integrated as a part of regional management processes.

GO FORWARD
1992

In 1992, TDW began the process of creating three new product divisions from the shared functional operations of the past. Here, as in Europe, the intent is to create smaller business teams capable of integrating the essential operating functions (sales, engineering, and manufacturing) into groups capable of making the appropriate day-to-day decisions with a minimum of general management intervention. The development of products, markets, and business practices will remain the province of the more broadly skilled regional and corporate functional departments.

CASE STUDY
Nailing Down a Future for a Small
Wood-Products Business
By R. Henry Migliore and Ronald C. Ringness

Liberty Industries was founded in 1964 by its current President and Chairman of the Board, Charles E. Trebilcock. It began as a small industrial wholesale lumber firm located in northeastern Ohio, specializing in wood packaging products. The original plan called for a regionalized concentration of sales in a four- to five-state area. Liberty experienced moderate growth during its first nine years, when it functioned as a three-person organization. In 1973, the firm decided to increase field sales by developing an inside support department. A marketing manager was hired, as well as several product specialists. As a result, sales increased more than 13 times from 1972 through 1979. (See Exhibit I.)

Still a small company today, Liberty's rapid success was built on a low-cost base that generated excess available cash and fostered confidence among employees. When the recession of 1980-1982 began, the firm was still oeprating the same way it had in the rapid growth years of the mid-Seventies. But as excess cash was reduced, cash flow became tight and Liberty began to reconsider its aggressive plans for funding new product development and diversification.

NEED FOR PLANNING

During the early 1980s, management expanded its line from wood products to packaging systems and other consumable packaging items, and it also increased its sales force. This strategy was based on the assumption that the recession would be short-lived and that rapid growth would return. However, the firm also faced a conflict in management philosophies, along with a continuing need to establish tighter financial controls. Liberty's management felt there was no defined "path of progression," and they were unable to agree about long-term planning for their diversified product line. While the firm was still successful, its profitability had begun to diminish. This led Liberty's top management to seek outside help from a management consultant.

Liberty had fallen into the predictable pattern of difficulties many firms encounter when moving from a Stage I founder/manager level to a Stage II functional organization. This requires that the means of planning, managing, and controlling the organization shift as the company grows. To the credit of Liberty's management, they had recognized where they were and

349

had begun the process of change.

One of Liberty's problems was that the industrial product sector of the lumber industry had reached maturity, and projections indicated further reductions in the profit margins of Liberty's base product. The company needed to develop a strategic plan that would:

- Develop new direction in long-range marketing.
- Devise a selection process for new product lines.
- Mesh the conflicting management and planning philosophies.
- Establish operating controls throughout the organization.

A Strategic Planning/Management Committee was formed to assess past successes and failures and to sort the firm's future possibilities into a long-term strategic plan. This group was composed of the founder/ president, the strategic planner, the executive vice president of marketing, the vice president of product management, the regional sales manager, the senior buyer for the purchasing and customer service department, and a top regional product specialist. All had been employed by Liberty for a minimum of nine years. Each had been a part of the rapid growth of the 1970s and had experienced the frustrations and concerns of the early 1980s.

STRATEGIC LONG-RANGE PLANNING/ MANAGEMENT BY OBJECTIVES

Strategic long-range planning/management by objectives (SLRP/MBO) is a management philosophy based on identifying purpose, objectives, and desired results: establishing a realistic program for obtaining these results: and evaluating performance in achieving them. The addition of a preplanning, objective-setting process makes MBO a realistic system, capable of creating a significant change in attitudes as well as in productivity.

This philosophy involves nine steps:

1. Defining an organization's purpose and reason for being.
2. Monitoring the environment in which the organization operates.
3. Making a realistic assessment of its strengths and weaknesses.
4. Making assumptions about unpredictable future events.
5. Prescribing written, specific, and measurable objectives in the principal areas contributing to the organization's purpose. This requires:
   - Negotiating and bargaining at every level from senior management and staff positions down to the blue-collar level.
   - Writing a performance contract embracing the agreed-on objectives.
6. Developing strategies on how to use available resources to meet objectives.
7. Making long- and short-range plans to meet objectives.

8. Constantly appraising performance to determine if it's keeping pace with objectives and is consistent with the defined purpose. This requires:

   - A willingness to change or modify objectives, strategies, and plans when conditions change.
   - Evaluating progress at every stage so that needed changes can be made smoothly.
   - Making sure that rewards are thoughtfully considered and appropriate to the task; recognizing the strengths and weaknesses of the extrinsic and intrinsic rewards.

9. Re-evaluating purpose, environment, strengths, weaknesses, and assumptions before setting objectives for the next performance year.

This approach is based on involving people in the planning process and the commitment to keeping the plan updated and in writing. The nine steps of the strategic planning process impel management to consider the basic issues facing the business. Each step requires people at various organizational levels to discuss, study, and negotiate. This, in turn, fosters a planning mentality. When the nine steps are complete, you've created a product — a strategic plan. Although managing a business in accordance with a strategic plan is a learned art, the longer you do it, the better you get at it.

At Liberty, four subcommittees were established and headed by a member of the Strategic Planning/Management Committee. Subcommittees were set up to develop a statement of purpose; to conduct an analysis; to evaluate Liberty's strengths and weaknesses; and to investigate old and new assumptions. These four committees were made up of nearly everyone who worked for Liberty, and thus established a corporate family forum.

The process began in May 1985, and the initial reports were completed and ready for review by the Strategic Planning/Management Committee in August. Since the planning process involved everyone in varying degrees, all employees had the chance to contribute to the final plan. We carefully followed the old axiom: "The same people who execute the plan should also make the plan."

EXHIBIT 2 — How the Process Interacts*

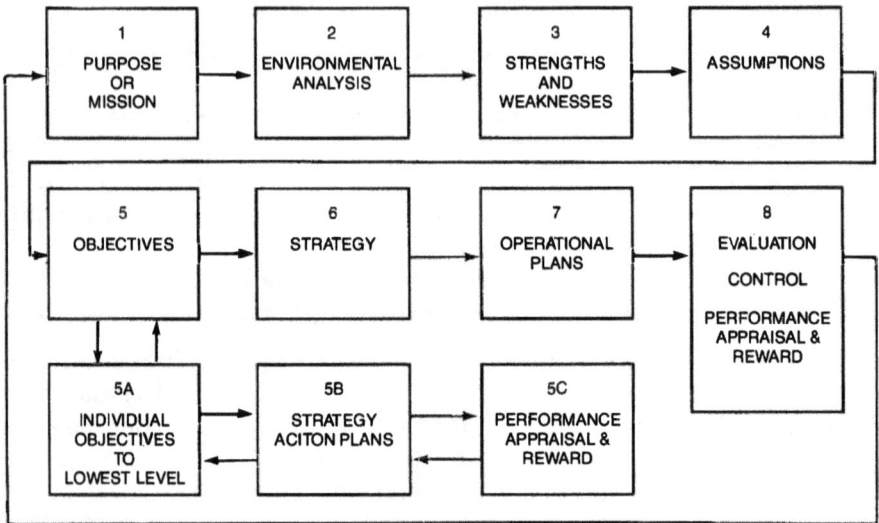

1 PURPOSE OR MISSION	2 ENVIRONMENTAL ANALYSIS	3 STRENGTHS AND WEAKNESSES	4 ASSUMPTIONS

5 OBJECTIVES	6 STRATEGY	7 OPERATIONAL PLANS	8 EVALUATION CONTROL PERFORMANCE APPRAISAL & REWARD

5A INDIVIDUAL OBJECTIVES TO LOWEST LEVEL	5B STRATEGY ACITON PLANS	5C PERFORMANCE APPRAISAL & REWARD

*Adapted from *An MBO Approach to Long-Range Planning* and *Long-Range Strategic Planning*

KEY EXCERPTS

The Committee's reports were highlighted with the following selections:

Purpose: Liberty is in the business of marketing industrial packaging products and services worldwide in order to realize a profit for the benefit of stockholders, employees, customers, and suppliers . . . Any industry that transports and/or warehouses its products is a potential recipient of Liberty Industries' services.

Environmental Analysis: Consumers of packaging materials are stressing cost reduction and control via spec revision and automation . . . Backward horizontal integration into supply network features joint ventures and acquisitions . . . New purchasing environment stresses long-term contracts, price protection guarantees, computer ordering, nonpartiality, and extended terms of payment . . . Annual growth for wood pallets is expected to be at 3-5 percent through 1990 (growing to a $3 billion industry) . . . Plastic packaging is expected to grow at a rate of 4-5 percent through 1990 and then increase substantially . . . Competing firms are forced to increase profits via market share rather than profit margins . . . Foreign competition is a major factor for U.S. firms to recognize within the developing global economy . . .

New regional sales territories are being encouraged in all industries by population shift trends.

Strengths: Liberty has nationwide market potential (regional sales offices in Virginia, Georgia, Ohio, Illinois, Texas, and California) . . . Its lumber products have historically been sold through wholesale channels . . . with a strong reputation of providing quality and service . . . Wood products generate reliable base of profit dollars . . . Liberty has a strong regional teams concept (two outside salesmen to one inside customer service representative . . . ability to expand supply base to meet sales requirements . . . commitment to success of all ventures . . . product and market knowledge . . . genuine concern for employees' well-being . . . stress on professionalism and creativity . . . competent inside staff working within excellent environment . . . new engineering and manufacturing capabilities generated through joint venture with established German packaging/machinery firm . . . strong personal contacts through top management associations capable of providing potential opportunities.

Weaknesses: Low profit margins of wood products . . . the cost of inventory in the new venture with packaging systems ($250,000 +) . . . need for strict budgetary controls in recessionary periods . . . lack of market research to determine viability of current and proposed products . . . sales staff too small, prohibiting maximum coverage . . . lack of in-house design and engineering capabilities . . . conflict of conservative versus aggressive management styles . . . lack of consistent sales and middle management . . . weak information transfer between corporate office and regional offices.

Assumptions: Potential reindustrialization of U.S. manufacturers coupled with a further transition into an information and service-based economy will establish the U.S. as part of the global economy . . . There will be more joint ventures between both domestic and foreign companies . . . The GNP will remain stable with 3-5 percent growth through 1988 . . . There may be an extended period of time with no recession . . . High technology (robotics, artificial intelligence, computer and telephone marriage), will replace current business methods . . . Liberty's cash flow will become more difficult to manage due to shorter accounts payable and longer accounts receivable periods . . . Rapid growth will require additional funds to manage accounts payable and accounts receivable . . . There will be a continued move toward alternate methods of product packaging and shipment . . . All products will require greater engineering/technical input to remain competitive . . . All packaging/material handling products will become more standardized resulting in a continued narrowing of profit margins . . . A distributor network is necessary for national marketing of low- and middle-range priced packaging equipment . . . Diversified manufacturers of packaging systems will decrease in number during the next five years.

These excerpts from the four committees' reports are a small part of the overall investigation done on the industry and the internal workings of the company. From these reports, the Strategic Planning/Management Committee developed priorities, sales objectives, strategy and controls to be implemented — and finally, an operating plan.

EXHIBIT 3

POTENTIAL
(Potential Market; Growth Oriented; Profitability)

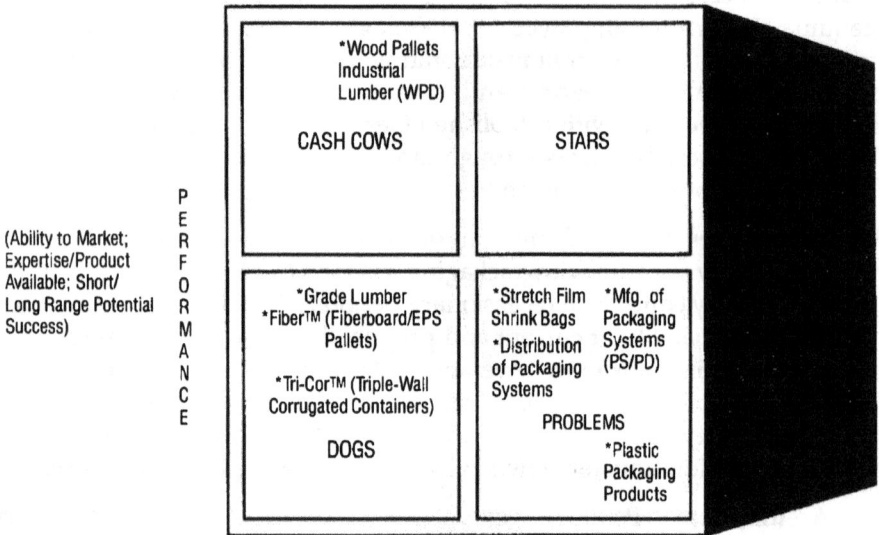

	CASH COWS	STARS
	*Wood Pallets Industrial Lumber (WPD)	

PERFORMANCE

(Ability to Market; Expertise/Product Available; Short/Long Range Potential Success)

DOGS	PROBLEMS
*Grade Lumber *Fiber™ (Fiberboard/EPS Pallets) *Tri-Cor™ (Triple-Wall Corrugated Containers)	*Stretch Film Shrink Bags *Distribution of Packaging Systems *Mfg. of Packaging Systems (PS/PD) *Plastic Packaging Products

IMPLEMENTING THE PLAN

The Strategic Planning/Management Committee met once a month, with the consultant attending quarterly. The rest of the group was to do the basic research, and compile the data. Individual concerns or confusion as to direction could be addressed not only to the group but to the consultant, if necessary, on a confidential basis.

Certain priorities evolved from the original committee reports. Each current product line as well as potential new products were evaluated using the classic matrix chart in Exhibit 3 to determine which product should be nurtured to create the profitable base Liberty needed to secure its future growth.

The Wood Products Division, Liberty's "Cash Cow," was a successful, nationally distributed line, but it was profitable only when just the direct expense of operating that division was charged to the division. However, the Packaging Systems/Design Division (PS/DD) had the potential for far greater profit percentages in its ability to expand into more sophisticated products and a worldwide market. The problem was, the cost of operating this venture was extremely high and there were greater risks involved. Expanding this division also meant increasing Liberty's involvement in engineering and manufacturing.

To finance the PS/DD, Liberty would have to milk its Wood Products Division cash cow. This was a key strategic decision that would alter the future of Liberty Industries. The problems associated with the PS/DD were potentially great, but the long-term rewards could be well worth the risk. The obvious planning objective would be to find solutions to the problems associated with the PS/DD and move it into the "star" category.

The firm had to accept the fact that shrinking profit margins within the maturing lumber industry meant that an aggressive growth plan had to be focused on new product development and diversification. They also decided that since there was a shortage of excess cash, and they were unwilling to create large debt in areas where Liberty lacked expertise, they would have to continue investigating available joint ventures and exclusive national marketing agreements. Finally, they reviewed the talents and commitment of key personnel to the potential future growth of the company.

As a result, sales objectives and net income levels were documented for the entire corporation to consider, along with a list of goals to be accomplished if certain income levels were met. Among these were:

- Computerizing the facilities to improve information flow and communication.
- Updating regional sales automobile fleet.
- Hiring PS/DD manufacturing/engineering coordinator.
- Expanding regional sales coverage by one specialist immediately; adding an additional representative during the next 6-12 months.
- Increasing home office clerical staff to maintain the flow of information more effectively, and to provide greater support to the outside staff.
- Publishing an organizational chart projecting the current expansion and diversification plan. Immediately promoting one individual to a middle-management positon.
- Moving ahead on diversifying the Packaging Systems/Design Division and other packaging products through continued negotiations and contractual ventures with other firms.

Commitment to these programs and the company's willingness to maintain an openness to new opportunities was unanimously approved by the Strategic Planning/Management Committee and supported by top management. Deviation from the plan would be subject to committee discussion and review. The consequences of change in products, trends, and organizational needs was to be analyzed regularly.

Along with a five year projection of sales objectives, priorities were established with built-in strategy and controls.

EXHIBIT 4
PROJECTED SALES (5-Year Plan)

Actual 1985	-$13,330,000	
1986 (original projection)	-$15,250,000	-$17,750,000 (actual)
1987	-$18,500,000	
1988	-$20,000,000	
1989	-$22,500,000	
1990	-$25,000,000	

EXHIBIT 5
MAJOR STRATEGIES IN THE 5-YEAR PLAN

- Expand to 12 sales regions to lower cost per regional base as well as to increase sales.
- Complete product/market research of plastic packaging products and begin marketing/manufacturing program.
- Expand PS/DD product line, marketing program, and promote internationally.
- Develop formal employee and management training program(s).
- Increase contribution(s) to Profit Sharing Retirement Trust to help secure employee's future.

EXHIBIT 6
Comparison of Actual to Target Figures

Corporate	Fiscal 1986 Target	Fiscal 1986 Actual	Variance
Sales			
Gross Dollar Profit			
Gross Profit Percentage			
Total Operating Expense %			
Average Collection Period			
Net Profit			

To facilitate implementation of major strategies in the five-year plan, and to measure their effectiveness, certain warning signals were singled out to alert management to review operations in detail. For example, the red flags went up in Packaging Systems/Design Division if:

- The joint venture with a West German partner was in serious jeopardy.
- A design engineer resigned.

- The gross profit on sales fell below a specified level for three consecutive months.
- They lost three major distributors.
- They faced a lawsuit on machinery products.

Although such simple, common-sense warning signals are easily installed at the planning stage, very few corporations take this important precaution.

ACTION/CURRENT STATUS

Along with its strategic plans, Liberty also needed to develop financial personnel, and support plans to handle current needs as well as to prepare for long-term growth. Objectives were instituted at both corporate and division levels to measure sales, gross profit on sales, and net profit objectives. These were to be monitored on a regular basis to compare actual results to target figures. Exhibit #6 demonstrates the simplicity of comparing actual numbers to target figures to measure how implementation is going at corporate and/or divisional levels.

Overall corporate performance was evaluated in December 1986 in a group review session. All results were on target to meet year-end objectives. Recognizing the need to expand the marketing coverage without exhausting available funds, a series of objectives, strategies, and actions were set up for each operating plan. For example:

Objective:

- Increase regional sales and profits of expanding into a minimum of two new territories by 1988.

Strategy:

- Add one new territory per year over the next five fiscal years to establish a total of 12 by 1990. Accelerate program if profits allow.
- Based on market potential, new territories will be identified and developed with one person covering both the purchasing and sales position until self-sufficiency is reached with a yearly profit of $150,000.

Action:

- Convert part-time purchasing/sales representative into a full-timer in Eastern region by January 1, 1987. Hire new buyer to provide inside support for Eastern Region and Mid-Atlantic Region by October 1, 1986.
- Hire Product Specialist for new Western Region by September 1987, or when net profit for the fiscal year reaches $250,000.
- Hire Product Specialist for new Midwestern Region by September

357

1988 or as soon as net profit in fiscal 1988 reaches $250,000.

The Strategic Planning/Management Committee tackled Liberty's greatest need by establishing several financial controls. Again, operating plans were designed to prepare Liberty for both the short and long term:

Objective:

- Operate within corporate budget established by top management team (President, Executive Vice President, and Vice President of Product Management).

Strategy:

- Prepare both a corporate and divisional budgeting forecast for each fiscal year.
- Prepare a monthly accrual fund to allow for severe seasonal fluctuations.
- At fiscal year end, review key expenses to determine realistic values for the upcoming fiscal year.

Action:

- Top management team to establish a budget and to review it on a monthly basis upon receipt of detailed financials from accountants.
- Founder/President to set up with accountants a monthly accrual fund to help defray seasonal fluctuations in profit/expense ratio.
- Assign expense control responsibility to specific individuals/areas wherever applicable.
- Assign PS/DD budgetary control to middle management by January 1, 1987.

Objective:

- Ease cash flow problems to eliminate the need to draw from Liberty's credit line.

Strategy:

- Reduce PS/DD inventories and prepaid stock items.
- Reduce accounts receivable by eliminating low-profit accounts and by reducing payment terms in Wood Products Division.
- Extend accounts payable terms with suppliers where feasible.

Action:

- Reduce PS/DD inventories by a minimum of 50 percent by January 1, 1987.
- Establish minimum/maximum levels of prepaid stock items by October 1, 1986.

- Establish minimum profit levels for new accounts. Set time allowances for raising profit percentages to acceptable levels on current accounts. Written report on status of accounts to be submitted to Executive Vice President by September 1, 1986.
- Investigate ways to reduce accounts receivable terms by August 1, 1986.
- Payment terms to suppliers to be reviewed and summarized by purchasing/customer service department by August 1, 1986.

What the Strategic Planning/Management Committee accomplished by developing these strategic plans was not only financial management, but the implementation of employee participation in developing strategic controls in Liberty's business activities. Everyone became involved. Reports were regularly submitted on a designated schedule, and follow-up meetings were held to review the information and make new assignments to continue current projects or to begin new ones.

A quarterly review process was set up. At the end of each financial quarter, the top management team meets to review progress on key corporate objectives. Each functional unit and/or division reports it progress as well. Many organizations develop plans and then never review them. Yet it's in the review process that accountability really takes hold, and that's the key to performance.

FUTURE PLANNING AT LIBERTY

Liberty's overall strategic plan will be refined and become more sharply focused in the years ahead. The 1987 reviews will further establish accountability and controls. More important will be the growth of the management group both as a team and as individuals. When changes are needed in response to the unexpected, or because of changing trends and cycles, the management team will have a structure and a process to use in making new decisions.

In 1988, Liberty's incentive plan will be reviewed and the version that most realistically rewards performance will be implemented for the future. Also, a "letter of commitment" concept, in which each employee will develop an individual plan and commit to it, will be reviewed and developed in late 1987 and 1988.

The planning "ABCs" Liberty followed were:

- There's a systematic, logical way to develop a long-range plan.
- Everyone can be and should be involved in the planning process.
- Commitment and self-control are the keys to the success of strategic planning/management by objectives.
- Every organization and each decentralized entity within that organi-

zation should develop an individual strategic plan in harmony with the corporation's overall plan.

- Goals must be negotiated whenever possible.
- Both extrinsic and intrinsic rewards must be attainable for the individual and/or group involved.
- Be prepared to spend time and effort keeping the program viable, especially in the first six months.
- Performance reviews must be conducted at regularly scheduled intervals. Be prepared to expose your management team to new ideas and new ways of approaching managerial problems.
- A person within the organization should be assigned to work with the consultant so that he or she can take over as the in-house expert during the consultant's absence.
- The system for setting, reviewing, and updating planning objectives should keep paperwork to a minimum.
- The decision to implement this management philosophy should not be made in haste.
- If you stop using management by objectives within the strategic planning process after everyone has begun, expect a big drop in morale.

In the stragetic planning and management process, Liberty is in its infancy. Yet, the company's future looks better than at any other point in its history. Expansion is taking place in regional sales coverage; a National Accounts Program has been introduced with a new manager in charge; negotiations are under way for exciting new products; the Packaging Systems/Design Division is rapidly establishing a quality name in the national marketplace; and determined work is being done to improve the profitability of the overall base product line to ensure the well-being and future of Liberty's corporate family.

LIBERTY/NUTRO PARTNERSHIP
Classic Example of Successful Organization

Three years ago Liberty Industries, said to be the nation's largest supplier of wooden pallets and other various packaged products, and Nutro Machinery Corporation, one of the largest packaging machinery and finishing equipment manufacturers in Europe, joined together in a venture to create Liberty/Nutro. This partnership is a classic example of two successful organizations marrying one another to form a solid, diversified marketing/ manufacturing company.

By having two manufacturing facilities, one located in Strongsville, Ohio (Cleveland), and the other in Youngstown, Ohio, it provided Liberty/ Nutro with great flexibility in production capacity, design creativity, and the plant space to expand into "turn-key" packaging systems. The bulk of the engineering/manufacturing management group is located in the Strongsville facility. Corporate headquarters and marketing management are located in Girard, Ohio.

While Liberty/Nutro is proud of the integration of German technology and ingenuity, all systems are manufactured in the United States. However, Nutro's Nurnberg, West Germany, facility is capable of manufacturing Liberty/Nutro's systems to meet the demands of European customers or U.S. accounts that include foreign installations.

Beginning with the popular Liberty/Nutro Series 500S Semi-Automatic Economy Wrapper, this organization has progressed up and beyond the new, uniquely designed Series 3000 Overhead Automatic. This system was a show-stopper at WestPack '87 and many consider it technologically superior to any stretch machine manufactured anywhere in the world. Its creative powered automatic film cutting and film gripping device is manufactured in such a way that this system is flexible enough to handle basically any type and size of conveyor system. In addition, there are other variations of the Series 3000, including a special agricultural industry unit. Liberty/Nutro regularly builds custom-designed systems throughout their stretch machine series.

When questioning part of the executive management and ownership of Liberty/Nutro (Ron Ringness and Jochen Grocke), they state that their long-term objective is to be considered the most quality-oriented, design flexible, and service dedicated company within their respective industry. They take pride in nurturing key, long-term employees and encourage an atmosphere of product development and friendly distributor/customer relations. They respect quality competition and feel that the future need for packaging systems in the United States has tremendous potential.

Their optimism and commitment to the future are spearheaded by a select group of quality distributor organizations which carry the Liberty/Nutro product line; balanced by an aggressive National Accounts Program; and supported by a strong distribution management team. A "partner" concept seems to exist between Liberty/Nutro and their western distributors as they prepare to tell the story of Liberty/Nutro packaging systems.

Strategic Planning: Define Mission, Objectives — Get Long-Term Results

William A. Sutton, Ed.D.
R. Henry Migliore, Ph.D.

The following is the first installment of a two-part article on "Strategic Long-Range Planning and the YMCA." In this issue, the authors discuss the first four steps of strategic long-range planning: defining the mission, monitoring the environment, assessing strengths and weaknesses and making assumptions. Part 2, appearing in the January issue, will cover goals and objectives, strategies, operational plans and performance appraisal.

Our definition of strategic planning and management (SLRP&M) is a philosophy of management based upon identifying purpose, objectives and desired results; establishing a realistic program for obtaining these results and evaluating the performance. The written plan then becomes the central theme of the direction and control of the YMCA programming. The nine steps in the process are:

1. Defining the purpose and reason for being of the YMCA in terms of membership/programmatic emphasis.
2. Monitoring the environment in which the YMCA and its programs function.
3. Realistically assessing the strengths and weaknesses of the YMCA and its programming.
4. Making assumptions about unpredictable future events that could impact the YMCA and its programs.
5. Prescribing written, specific and measurable objectives in the principal result areas that contribute to the organizational purpose. This requires:
   - Negotiating and bargaining at every level from top management positions to staff.
   - Recognizing a performance contract that embraces the agreed-upon objectives.
6. Developing strategies for allocation of resources to meet objectives.
7. Designing long-range and short-range plans to meet objectives.
8. Constantly appraising performance to determine if it is keeping pace with the attainment of objectives and if it is consistent with the defined purpose. This requires:
   - Willingness to change or modify objectives, strategies and plans when conditions change.
   - Evaluating progress at every stage so that needed changes can be

effected smoothly.
- Making sure that rewards are thoughtfully considered and are appropriate for accomplishment. Recognizing the strengths and weaknesses of the extrinsic and intrinsic reward system.
9. Reevaluating purpose, environment, strengths, weaknesses and assumptions before setting objectives for the next performance period. (See Figure 1.)

Figure 1

Strategic Long-Range Planning Process

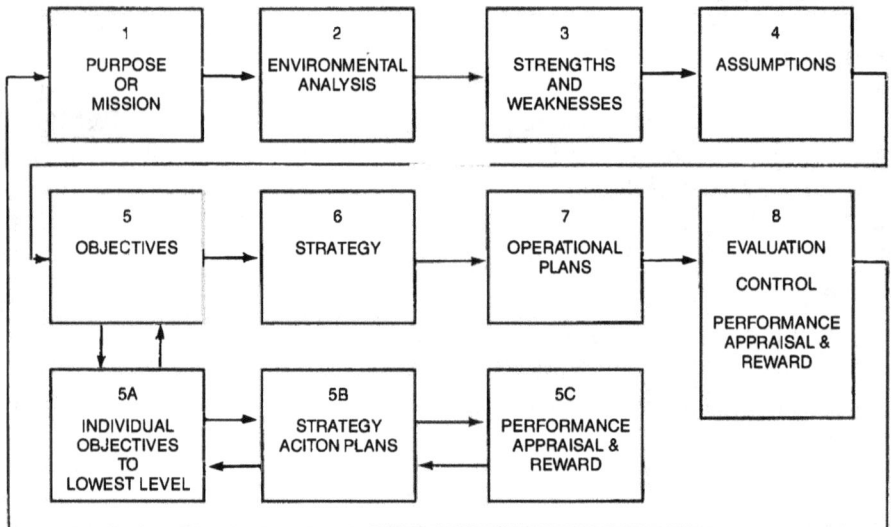

1 PURPOSE OR MISSION	2 ENVIRONMENTAL ANALYSIS	3 STRENGTHS AND WEAKNESSES	4 ASSUMPTIONS
5 OBJECTIVES	6 STRATEGY	7 OPERATIONAL PLANS	8 EVALUATION CONTROL PERFORMANCE APPRAISAL & REWARD
5A INDIVIDUAL OBJECTIVES TO LOWEST LEVEL	5B STRATEGY ACITON PLANS	5C PERFORMANCE APPRAISAL & REWARD	

The nine steps of the strategic planning process as illustrated in Figure 1 are important because they force the organization to consider certain questions. Each step requires the people at various organizational levels to discuss, study and negotiate; and the process as a whole fosters a planning mentality. When the nine steps are complete, you have a product: a strategic plan. Managing in accordance with a strategic plan is a learned art. The longer you use the tool, the better you are able to manage. Equally important is the process of involving people in the development and implementation of the plan.

In the YMCA and similar recreational or social service agencies, the SLRP&M concept has been successful in improving management practices. There are nine areas in which each YMCA director and board president needs to concern himself. The following sections examine each of these areas in greater detail and focus on their applicability to YMCA programming and management.

Defining the Purpose or Mission

A mission can be defined as a broad statement of the kind of organization that those directing it want it to be (Luck & Ferrell, 1985). A statement of purpose or mission should look towards the future but also relate to historical factors such as tradition and the present status quo. It should contain the dream and vision of what the organization wants to be (Migliore, 1983, 1987 & 1988). The statement of purpose for the YMCA of the USA is:

> *The Young Men's Christian Association we regard as being in its essential genius a world-wide fellowship united by a common loyalty to Jesus Christ for the purpose of developing Christian personality and building a Christian society.*

Relating metro or local Y mission statements to the YMCA of the USA position is essential. The statement of purpose for the YMCA of Greater Tulsa is an excellent example of how a statement of purpose at a lower organizational level can encompass the general principles mandated by the organizational hierarchy and at the same time state its own framework for adhering to this general purpose. The Tulsa statement of purpose is:

> *The Young Men's Christian Association of Greater Tulsa is a premier human service organization dedicated to meeting community needs for furthering the spiritual, mental, physical, and social growth of its constituents by developing and expanding value-intensive programs of health enhancement, youth leadership, family development, and international understanding through the use of appropriate facilities, trained volunteers and professional leadership.*

YMCAs and their programs relate to a variety of publics that must be addressed in day-to-day activities. Such groups include students (of all ages), single parents, traditional and extended family units, senior citizens, infants and preschoolers, business groups, civic clubs, teens, single adults and special interest groups relating to the social well being of the immediate service area, and political or charitable entities who may attempt to influence direction by controlling possible funding sources.

It would be highly impractical and perhaps impossible to develop a purpose statement that would satisfy the interests and concerns of all of these groups. The mission or purpose statement then, must be directed to those groups who have "core" concerns and relationships rather than those groups whose concerns and interests relate to the peripheral operations and benefits associated with the YMCA administration and subsequent programming.

In YMCA programming at all levels, certain implied purposes exist as well as concerns for participant growth and development. For example, it may be implied that certain programs within the YMCA "service umbrella" are expected to generate a profit, while other programs which fill a social service mission (Youth & Government; counseling services etc.) are expected to break even or operate within a given fiscal framework.

Monitoring the Environment

According to Drucker (1954) "decisions that are really important are strategic . . . they involve finding out what the situation is . . ." The YMCA director must constantly gauge the environment in which his program is located. This assessment should include factors that may affect the program's ability to fulfill its mission and purposes. In many cases this involves constructing a market analysis of the current marketplace (Smith and Cavusgil, 1984; Sutton, 1987). The growing impact of noneconomic factors, the acceleration of economic and social change caused by new technologies, the intensification of governmental influence upon the economy, the emergence of new political and social powers, and the changes in demographic structure as well as in educational standards are clear signs of the fact that growing markets cannot be considered in isolation (Reinhardt, 1984). When deciding on courses of action, commitments of time, or the use of resources, certain internal and external environmental factors from a variety of sources will impact the YMCA decision maker (Olson, Hirsch, Brietenbach and Saunders, 1987). The following list contains factors that merit attention and regular monitoring by the YMCA administration:

- Federal, state, and local legislation.
- Leadership and direction of leadership in local community.
- Economic and business indicators (local, regional and national).
- Political interpretations and implications of tax deductible and nondeductible expenses.
- Availability of corporate sponsorship.
- Competition from other organizations or enterprises (local and national).
- Media influences and exposure.
- Trends in financial contributions.
- Lifestyle changes: divorce rate, single parent family growth, increased life expectancy, double income families, unemployment rates.

The purpose of providing this list is to illustrate that a YMCA director's key responsibility in this process is to manage change. The only effective way to manage change is to constantly monitor our environment (Migliore, 1983, 1987 & 1988). By identifying and monitoring possible areas of change, the administrator is ready to take advantage of positive developments or to minimize the effects of negative factors. For example, if a YMCA director is able to monitor financial factors that affect overall income such as program enrollment and contributions, he might be better able to implement cost containment practices that minimize the impact of a shortfall in revenue rather than drop programs to achieve the same result.

An environmental analysis may also include survey data from the institution's various publics. This data may include enrollment records and patterns for YMCA sport or fitness programs, program/sport preferences, sustaining membership support, membership renewals, business community support, general community support and perceptions regarding program image and standing. This type of survey data can be inexpensively collected and analyzed, and provides important information regarding the relationship between the YMCA programs and the environment in which they function. An interesting area for examination might be the number of organizations and private enterprises offering fitness programming and how it compares with that offered by the YMCA in terms of facilities, cost, enrollment and personnel.

Strength and Weakness Assessment

After identifying the purpose and considering the environment, the YMCA director needs to assess the strengths and weaknesses of his program. A strengths/weaknesses analysis focuses on internal factors that might influence product success. Simply stated, strengths are attibutes to be emphasized . . . while weaknesses are problem areas to be resolved or at least controlled (Sutton, 1987). Some of the areas normally examined include human resources, financial resources, facilities, program enrollments, equipment, and geographic factors relating to location, proximity, and the demographics and psychographics of the local population.

The YMCA director must first identify those strengths which can be emphasized and utilized in the strategic planning process. In some cases this strength might be represented by new facilities or renovation, such as a swimming pool or Nautilus facility. Other strengths more commonly emphasized might be the skills or qualifications of staff or the quality and uniqueness of the program itself. For example, when the Stillwater Family YMCA introduced its comprehensive year-round child care program in 1979, several features became areas of strength for the program. The KinderKare program, featuring half-day programming and transportation for kindergarten students, was not available anywhere else. The staff became an area of strength due to an emphasis on hiring certified teachers possessing degrees in education or related fields. Finally, the facilities of the Y became an advantage to the child care program by offering swimming and gymnastics lessons as a standard part of the program curriculum. In all three cases the strengths were aspects of the program not available to the consumer through another enterprise, and the same could be true for most YMCAs offering child care programming if they make full use of the facilities at their disposal.

The following are several strengths listed by the Greater Tulsa YMCA in their Long-Range Planning Task Force Report:

- Possesses both facilities and expertise for health enhancement and wellness programs.
- Has the most attractive fee structure in Tulsa.
- Enjoys cooperation with public and private organizations in the community.

Identifying weaknesses is a painfull process. Objectivity must be maintained, which in some cases might necessitate using a consultant or outside party to candidly pinpoint the limitations. Realistic objectives cannot be set without a realistic appraisal of strengths and weaknesses (Migliore, 1988). For example, having a full station Nautilus facility as the only weight training apparatus might not be a weakness in some YMCAs, but in Ys catering to college students and a younger population, the lack of "free" weights and barbells might be perceived as a significant weakness. The following are several weaknesses identified by the Greater Tulsa YMCA during their strategic planning process:

- Lacks an adequate endowment program.
- Lacks a comprehensive public relations/marketing program for effectively informing the community of its YMCA programs and services.
- Programs are not currently attracting the adolescent age group.

Making Assumptions

This step involves analyzing the future and the current state of affairs. While futurists believe that the future cannot be forecast, they believe that decision makers should consciously assess the uncertainties, then develop and work toward a vision of the future (Taylor, 1984).

Major assumptions need to be made about those areas over which the YMCA director has little or absolutely no control (i.e., the external environment). This process can be initiated by extending some of the considerations examined in the environmental analysis.

The importance of assumption-making in developing long-range plans for YMCA programming is better understood by considering the given constraints in a YMCA program. For example, it can be assumed that the sustaining membership contribution program at the Woodville YMCA will be constant and that the levels of charitable giving will be the same or slightly higher than the previous year. This assumption enables the YMCA director to set objectives and to plan programs and offerings that are dependent upon income from the sustaining membership and charitable giving campaigns.

Other examples of making assumptions as they relate to YMCA program administration are:

- Revenues and sponsorship of programs by the business community will at least be equal to last year's revenues.
- Congressional legislation regarding changing the tax deductible nature of gifts and tax exempt status of the YMCA will not be implemented (although in some cases state or local legislation may be the more important issue).

The following assumptions come from the Greater Tulsa Long-Range Plan:

- Programs designed for personal health and social development will continue to be a high priority.
- Tulsa area economy will continue a slow improvement.
- Percent of subsidy from the United Way will continue to decrease.

Assumptions regarding corporate sponsorship and support of YMCA programs are becoming more and more critical. Dependence upon revenue that may fluctuate greatly or in some cases disappear over time has forced the YMCA director to constantly search for ways to stabilize, if not increase total income Dependence upon United Way funding or contributions could prevent a YMCA from fulfilling its mission through its operation and programming. By acknowledging this, the Greater Tulsa YMCA is forced to concentrate on developing alternative sources of income to augment those losses.

This step enables the administrator to identify important factors that are likely to remain constant. If there is a change that affects any one of these assumptions drastically, a reevaluation of the plan and appropriate revisions would be necessary.

Strategic Planning Sets Goals and Strategies For Running Smoothly

William A. Sutton, Ed.D.
R. Henry Migliore, Ph.D.

The following article is the second installment of a two-part article on strategic long-range planning for the YMCA. Part one, printed in the December issue, covered the first four steps of strategic long-range planning: defining the mission, monitoring the environment, assessing strengths and weaknesses and making assumptions. This month's article concludes with the coverage of goals and objectives, strategies, operational plans and performance appraisal.

Objectives and Goals

In any organization, goals and objectives must be geared to gain results (Edgington & Williams, 1978). In the term "management by objectives," management is the key — the use of objectives to help manage for results. Specifying objectives can only begin after the purpose of the organization has been defined, the environment has been analyzed, the strengths and weaknesses have been assessed, and the relevant assumptions have been made (Migliore, 1983, 1987 & 1988).

Objectives must be clear, concise, written, measurable statements outlining what is to be accomplished within a certain period of time. According to Drucker (1974), "objectives are not fate; they are direction. They are not commands; they are commitment. They do not determine the future; they are means to mobilize the resources and energies of the business for the making of the future."

Migliore (1983, 1987 & 1988) defines six types of objectives: routine, problem solving, team, innovative, personal and budget performance.

Routine objectives relate to activities, jobs, or work assignments that *occur regularly and predictably.* An example is conducting inventories and space and facility examinations relating to program management and functions to be used the day of the program or function.

Problem-solving objectives identify existing problem areas and state a deadline for solution. For example, a YMCA director might have the following objective: "Implement a computerized membership and program enrollment system prior to the initiation of advertising and enrollment for fall programming which begins August 1, 1989."

Team objectives are those that need to be accomplished with another member of the organizational team. For example, compiling a YMCA brochure may require the program director, aquatics director and fitness director to provide information to the executive director. Each of these individuals possesses a content knowledge apart from the others but the entire project is subject to their functioning independently and as a team to produce the necessary document.

Innovative objectives look to the future, suggest a completion date, and usually improve an existing situation. For example, a YMCA director might set as an objective of this type: "Devise a new methodology for performance evaluation for all fitness program participants by July 1, 1989."

Personal objectives relate directly to the individual, and consist of whatever that individual wishes to achieve during the year or other designated measure of time. An example might be in the area of personal growth and development: "Plan to attend the Aquatic Instructor Institute and become certified prior to December 31, 1989."

Objectives for budget performance are quantitative, measurable, and usually set on a yearly time frame consistent with the organizational fiscal year. A YMCA fundraising budget objective might be stated as follows: "The Child Care Programming Committee will solicit two vans for use by the child care program for the 1989-90 fiscal year by January 1, 1989."

Objectives should also be determined on the basis of internal and external strategy (Thompson & Strickland, 1984). Internal strategic objectives are concerned with desired organizational performance, such as membership retention, staff retention and training, sustaining membership goals and program enrollment. External strategic objectives relate to the reputation of the organization in the environment in which it competes and operates. Examples are publicity for learn-to-swim programs and the various social service programs conducted by the YMCA that do not generate direct income but do generate a favorable perception of the Y and its mission.

Once formulated, goals and objectives are stated in various types of plans and directives such as master plans, budgets, blueprints, schecules and committee structures. These objectives are subject to negotiation and clarification by all parties involved before they are accepted and become part of the strategic planning process. They are not to be dictated or determined without input from all concerned parties.

Once objectives have been negotiated and agreed upon by all concerned parties they become a performance contract. This performance contract is a personal commitment by a particular department or section to accomplish the objectives, as well as a commitment from the organization to provide the necessary resources and support to help the department or section to achieve these objectives.

The Greater YMCA of Tulsa has divided its objectives into the following categories: membership, program and participation, management and human resources, short-term tasks and finance. The key to this step is identifying relevant objectives that have a significant impact upon the operation of the YMCA.

Strategies

Luck and Ferrell (1985) define strategy as: "a scheme or principal idea through which an objective would be achieved." Strategies are, in sports-related terminology, "game plans." They are the "thinking" stage of the long-range plan, considering resources, thrusts, priorities and principles of accomplishing objectives (Broyles & Hay, 1979). For example, if one specified goal is to increase participation and enrollment in a particular YMCA program, there are several strategies that could be employed to achieve this particular objective:

- Offer the program or class at various times during the day so that everyone interested could participate if they choose.
- Offer a "free trial" of the program for one class meeting, or offer demonstrations prior to the beginning of the first class.
- Offer a discount to groups of three or more enrollees, or offer a program or cash rebate to an enrolled participant if that participant recruits and signs up other participants for the class or program.
- Offer a program or membership discount for non-members who are enrolled in the program but are not Y members.

Each of these strategies is capable of increasing program enrollment, but all are significantly different and according to Longest (1978), there is a relationship between the strategy used and the perceived environment. The most appropriate strategy for this particular example will be based upon the resources, administrative style, type of personnel available and other organizational factors. Various strategies relating to the stage of the product in the product life cycle will be developed. Such strategies may include price, promotion, place, personnel, pecuinary and market-related (Broyles & Hay 1979). Strategy is also intricately related to timing. Using a particular strategy to position your product a certain way might be successful at another time but not now.

The strategy phase receives more attention in each subsequent year of the strategic planning process because the mission, objectives etc. have already been stated and accepted. However, strategy changes as the internal and external environments dictate.

The administrator must keep in mind that the people who comprise the organization are the major limitation to successful implementation of strategies. On the other hand, these people are also the vehicle through which the strategy will be successful. In other words, involving these people in the strategy selection and verifying that the strategy is understood will encourage its acceptance and its eventual success.

Operational Plans: Long-Range and Short-Range

The operational plan, whether it involves long-range or short-range methodology, is the action or doing stage. This facet of the plan involves accomplishing, implementing, gathering, funding advertising and installing. Generally, a long-range plan requires a five-year operating plan for every phase of the business. In a YMCA program such a plan would include sub-plans for membership growth, general programming (youth or adult), fitness activities, aquatics, child care, charitable gift solicitation, capital and sustaining campaigns, marketing and promotion, public information and relations, fiscal management and data collection, analysis and utilization, and facility maintenance and management. Although this plan is a five-year plan, changes in the environment and other factors might bring about modifications from time to time. Each sub-unit must align itself with the mission, goals and objectives designated by the organization, and must make the proper contribution to insure organizational success.

A membership unit (personnel-staff and board/committee members) in a YMCA program might have as part of its five-year plan:

- Increase family membership enrollment by 33%.
- Increase individual membership enrollment by 50%.
- Implement discounted membership policies for the following groups: senior citizens; single parents; and college students (based on the academic calendar).

To make objectives and strategy really work for you, each objective should be organized according to the following format. Insure that everyone, including the program participants, have had input into the objectives, particularly those objectives relating to program offerings and capital issues. After the objectives have been agreed upon, various strategies can be developed to attain these objectives, and a system of control and follow-up can be developed in the operational plan area.

Performance Appraisal

This stage involves an overall appraisal of the performance of the YMCA and its personnel in terms of the accomplishment of goals and objectives. Several quetions should be asked by the YMCA director at this stage: What are the effects of accomplishing or not accomplishing the objectives? Could the objectives be accomplished in a more efficient or economical manner?

Have circumstances changed that necessitate changing objectives?

There are two other questions that also need to be answered at this stage. Will this appraisal be conducted annually or at regularly scheduled intervals throughout the year? Will there be a reward or other motivational factor associated with the performance appraisal?

All of these questions need answers at different stages of the strategic planning process. Frequency of the appraisal process and the reward system need to be determined in the initial stages of the strategic planning process. The remainder of the questions can be answered on an annual basis (summative) or during the process (formative) of the strategic planning process, depending upon organizational size and structure.

In terms of YMCA administration, the reward system (which in mainstream business can include performance bonuses, sales incentives, etc.) is quite limited, but should be included in hopes of greater productivity and in the interest of achieving organizational goals and objectives. A reward system in YMCA situation might be comprised of travel and training opportunities instead of direct compensation. These rewards could take the form of travel and expenses for the staff member (and family) to attend training sessions, conferences, or the annual meeting. Incentives might also be developed between local Ys, metros and the National Y to provide discounts and incentives for use of YMCA properties such as YMCA of the Rockies or similar facilities. Compensation and time off away from the job to attend classes to further one's career and professional capacity may also be seen as an incentive.

In a negotiated goals and objectives system of strategic planning and management, it might not be unrealistic in the near future to negotiate compensation increases directly relating to unit productivity and performance. Various financial increments could be agreed upon and granted if the staff member achieves those agreed-upon objectives. A bonus system could also be implemented and utilized if acceptable to all parties.

A third form of reward that may be effective in motivating performance in YMCA units is the allocation of future resources based upon departmental or unit performance. Those units or departments that achieve their objectives and maintain a high rate of productivity are given resources (budgetary, personnel, equipment etc.) as a reward for performance, while those areas low in productivity and achievement of goals and objectives are given a lower priority and in some cases not funded. Recognition is another area that could be used as a reward in YMCA program administration. Titles, offices and furnishings, privileges, changes in responsibilities and public acknowledgement can all be effective forms of recognition.

The key to this stage of the strategic planning process is communication.

Communication must occur prior to the initiation of the process, during the process, and during the performance evaluation. The administrator and co-workers should meet at regular intervals to determine what results should be achieved and what will constitute acceptable performance (Jensen, 1988). Effectiveness of the entire strategic planning process is dependent not only upon understanding and acceptance but upon the communication process involved. This communication process must be interactive and not merely directive. It must contain a medium for feedback from parties at all levels of this process.

For example, the membership director must have a means of informing the executive director and board of the status of sales and also how program offerings are being translated into sales and demand. Similarly the executive director needs to know from the membership director why the successful program enrollments are not being translated into demand or membership sales. This communication and feedback must occur throughout the year as well as in the planning sessions prior to and following that specific year. Perhaps the membership goals were unrealistic or a public relations gaffe or accident at the Y or scandal has affected sales, necessitating a revised goal in that particular area. Communication and feedback provide the organization with opportunities to remove obstacles to successful achievement of objectives during the process.

Feedback and formal appraisal should have two stages: an oral interactive stage and a written stage. The oral interview stage should take place first. This stage provides an opportunity for face-to-face interaction and interpretation of the factors that have contributed to or detracted from performance. The written stage should be a formalization of the discussion and evaluation of the oral meeting. Many times a second oral meeting can be arranged if the written stage does not seem to correctly summarize the initial oral evaluation.

Everything learned and discovered during the evaluation and appraisal process should be analyzed carefully, and the recommendations arising from this analysis should be formulated into alternatives and suggestions for affected areas of the strategic planning process. After careful analysis, these alternatives should be converted into actions and objectives and implemented into the strategic planning process in hopes of improving performance.

YMCA directors and presidents must take the framework presented here and develop their own SLRP&M plan consistent with their organizational size and mission. Once the plan has been developed and is in place, the management team must diligently monitor and adjust the initial plan to ensure its acceptance and success.

Bibliography

Broyles, F. & Hay, R. *Administration of Athletic Programs: A Managerial Approach.* Englewood Cliffs, N.J.: Prentice-Hall, 1979.

Drucker, P. F. *The Practice of Management.* New York: Harper & Row, 1954.

Drucker, P. F. *Management Tasks, Responsibilities, Practices.* New York: Harper & Row, 1974.

Edginton, C. R. & Williams, J. *Productive Management of Leisure Service Organizations.* New York: Macmillan, 1978.

Jensen, C. R. *Administrative Management of Physical Education and Athletic Programs.* Philadelphia: Lea & Febiger, 1988.

Keidel, R. *Game Plans.* New York: E. P. Dutton, 1985.

Longest, B. B. Jr. "An explanation of the relationship between the environment facing community hospitals and their strategies." Working paper No. 17, presented to the Academy of Management. San Francisco, August, 1978.

Luck, D. J. & Ferrell, O. C. *Marketing Strategy and Plans.* Englewood Cliffs, N.J.: Prentice-Hall, 1985.

Migliore, R. H. *An MBO Approach to Long Range Planning.* Englewood Cliffs, N.J.: Prentice-Hall, 1983.

Migliore, R. *Strategic Long Range Planning.* Jenks, Oklahoma: RHM & Associates, 1987.

_____ *Strategic Planning for Church Growth.* Tulsa: Harrison House, 1988.

Olson, Jr., Hirsch, E., Brietenbach, O., & Saunders K. (1987). *Administration of High School and Collegiate Athletic Programs.* Philadelphia: Saunders.

Pfeiffer, Ray *Long Range Planning Task Force Report.* Unpublished report, Tulsa, OK, 1983.

Reinhardt, W. A. "An Early Warning System for Strategic Planning." *Long Range Planning,* October 1984, p. 17, pp. 25-34.

Smith, L. R. & Cavusgil, S. T. "Marketing Planning for Colleges and Universities." *Long Range Planning,* December 1984, p. 17, pp. 104-117.

Sutton, W. A. "Developing an Initial Marketing Plan for Intercollegiate Athletic Programs." *Journal of Sport Management.* July 1987, p. 1, pp. 146-158.

Taylor, B. "Strategic Planning — Which Style Do You Need?" *Long Range Planning.* June, 1984, p. 17, pp. 51-62.

Thompson, A. & Strickland, A. *Strategic Management: Concepts and Cases.* Plano, Texas. Business Publications, Inc., 1984.

Readings Section

Improving Worker Productivity Through Communicating Knowledge of Work Results

R. Henry Migliore

The behavioral science technique of informing workers of the results of the past work performance, or knowledge-of-results," is analogous to the function of "feedback" in cybernetics: it supplies the work group with information on their performance level in order to signal the need of corrective action if behavior deviates from standard. It is the mechanism through which management can encourage the transition from random behavior to performance. Knowledge of work-results can be the catalyst for enabling the worker to attain his personal goals and to satisfy his higher level needs by becoming aware of his performance level against that of his co-workers and by meeting or surpassing standards of job performance.

In an attempt to evaluate the effectiveness of employing the "knowledge-of-results" technique in a unionized industrial setting, the author conducted two experimental studies using knowledge-of-results as a technique for improving employee productivity in a unionized production department of a mass-production manufacturing plant. The plant is located in the Midwest. The work layout and methods are highly standardized according to the best available technology. There is adequate capital and equipment to run an efficient operation. Management realized that the greatest additional gains to be made would have to come through the cooperation and morale of the work force. Within this environment, the technique of knowledge-of-results was evaluated.

The first study was made in the Press Department on the third shift during the two-year period from January 1, 1964 through December 31, 1965. The second study was made in the Press and Assembly Departments on all three shifts during the period from January 1, 1966 through December 31, 1966. After a control period in both studies, knowledge-of-results was introduced. The studies measure and evaluate the performance levels before and after knowledge-of-results was introduced. Study I utilizes five methods for presenting knowledge-of-work results in comparison to one method use in Study II.

Study I

The study is divided into three stages: control, preliminary, and full-scale implementation. During the control stage, when a planned knowledge-of-results program was not being utilized, existing relative performance levels of the skilled workers were studied. During the preliminary stage, knowledge-of-results was introduced into the work environment, and the best means for supplying knowledge-of-results to the work group were perfected. The full-scale implementation stage covers the period when the more sophisiticated and complete methods of supplying knowledge-of-results were used.

The study was conducted on the third shift, that is, the last shift in an around-the-clock operation (11:30 p.m. to 6:30 a.m.). The third shift has about 60 of approximately 200 employees in the department. The department mass-produces parts that are later assembled in another department or by the customer. The employees are organized in groups around the physical layout of the production lines. Two operations are completed on the raw material before it is brought to the Press Department. All of the material is altered at operation A. It is then transferred by trucks to operation B for fabrication. Approximately 50% of the parts are finished in the Press Department after operation B and are taken away by trucks to be assembled later by the customer or in the Assembly Department. The other 50% of the parts leave operation B and are transferred by trucks to operation C where they receive further fabrication and are taken to the Assembly Department or shipped to the customer.

Knowledge-of-results was introduced through a specially designed system of communications. In order to facilitate communications, the following techniques and practices were introduced:

- A separate monthly meeting was held with employees in each labor grade; for example, all members of the highest labor grade, 14, would attend a meeting separate from those held for individuals in the lowest labor grade, 4.

- A communications center, consisting of a group of bulletin boards for the posting of important information for the employees, was established.

- Personal contact by the supervisor with each employee was stressed. Informal conversations, usually on the production floor, were to place emphasis on progress toward attaining individual and group performance goals.

- Various employee activities were organized. A bowling league, golf league, and softball team were organized in an effort to improve morale, communications, working relationships and to give the satisfaction of participating with fellow employees in social activities.

Through the use of these communication channels, knowledge-of-results was presented to individuals and the work group in the following manner. (1) The department efficiency was charted every day on a large line graph (approximately three feet by four feet) which was attached to the bulletin board. (2) A form was posted on the bulletin board daily to inform the members of the workforce about the actual production and efficiency compared to the standard for each production line, and the names of the individuals working on each production line. (3) Informal contact by the supervisor with individuals in the skilled labor classification (labor group 14) periodically emphasized individual and group performance statisics. 4) Formal meetings were held with the trainees in skilled labor grade 14. These men completed a 4000 hour training program. They had previously completed formal classroom training and were now taking part in on-the-job training. These meetings emphasized their performance level. 5) Performance statistics were always discussed in the monthly meetings with the various labor grades. Shift and department performance levels were compared with goals set for the next period.

STATISTICS FOR STUDY I:
Control, Preliminary and Full Scale Implementation Stages
Third Shift Press Department Average Daily Productivity

Skilled Employees and Crews	Control Stage	Preliminary Stage	Full Scale Implementation
A	105	107	110
B	108	109	109
C	76	92	105
D**	—	80	105
E	71	78	98
F	86	83	96
G	75	76	94
H	80	89	92
I	80	80	91
J**	—	105	87
K**	73	73	86

Table I presents the performance of the line crews on the third shift for all three stages. It is calculated by taking the average daily output index, based on 100 as equal to standard, for the skilled labor grade 14 workers and their line crews. **Trainee in skilled labor grade.

SUMMARY

1. Mean	83.5	88.4	97.0
2. Median	80.0	83.0	96.0
3. Range	37.0	36.0	23.0
4. Std. Deviation	4.07	3.93	2.67

Through these specially designed communication channels, knowledge-of-results was presented to individuals and work groups. The hypothesis that knowledge-of-results will increase productivity was tested within this environment and was dependent on the following assumptions: 1) Changes in the supervisors assigned to the shift had no effect on the performance of the shift; 2) Factors other than the experimental variables had, at most, random effects on worker productivity; (these factors include variables such as union-management relationships, disciplinary actions, and levels and hours of employment[1]); 3) the "Hawthorne Effect" had no effect on the outcome of the study since the work group was not aware that a study was being made[2]; 4) The general changes in communication techniques and recreation programs for the workers did not have an independent effect on worker productivity.

It must be recognized at this point that the third shift of the Press Department could not be segregated into a separate entity. Control over the study would have been stronger if the work group could have functioned in a closed environment. The study, was, however, conducted as part of a normal manufacturing operation. Conversely this could be a strong point when considering the factors that could affect the study. A more realistic environment does avoid the problems introduced by the artificiality of the laboratory experiment in studies of human behavior.

Control Stage

The control stage for the study covered the period from January 1, 1964 through April 30, 1964. Knowledge-of-results as a mechanism for encouraging increased productivity was not yet introduced during this period, rather a method of ranking the relative performance levels of the skilled labor grade and their crews within the plant was perfected.

---

[1]There is some evidence available to support this assumption. After the work group had reached a certain stage in the productive and motivational process, outside factors, though important, did not seem to detour their efforts to maintain efficiency. There were two occasions in which dramatic changes in outside factors occurred. The entire third shift of the plant became emotionally involved in a situation in January, 1965 concerned with the changing of working hours. Shortly after that, in March, the national union declared a strike in which the local union participated. Manufacturing efficiency during this period remained constant around 90 percent. It was 6 percent higher than the previous three-month period. It is noted that the rate of improvement in performance remained relatively constant during the entire study, including the period between January and March, 1965. This further emphasizes the fact that outside factors had little effect, if any, on the outcome of the study.

[2]The "Hawthorne Effect" is referred to when the results of an experiment or study are positive because the group knew they were being experimented upon. The term originated with the Hawthorne Studies.

Although the entire crew is important, the skilled labor grade 14 workers do the actual maintenance, minor repair and play the biggest role in the line's productivity. Each labor crew consisted of from two to five people depending on equipment utilization. The crews were generally made up of the same members with the skilled labor grade member as the head of the crew. However, vacations, lay-offs, absenteeism, sabbatical leaves, sick leaves, and shift changes introduced some variation in crew composition.

Criteria for their ranking was based on production line performance figures during the control period. The performance figures used were: 1) production line percent efficiency measuring total parts produced against standard, 2) product quality based on quality control standards, 3) excess spoilage over standard, and 4) a qualitative judgment made by the foreman of expected line performance.

When completed, the ranking gave management a composite picture of the performance level of the skilled workers and their crews. The primary use of this information was to help identify individual performance problems and serve as a measuring tool to help them improve.

During the control stage, the third shift Press Department efficiency index mean was 83.5, the median 10.0, with a range of 37.0 and a standard deviation of 4.07. (See table 1)

Preliminary Stage

During the preliminary stage (the period July 1, 1964 through February 28, 1965), the techniques for introducing knowledge-of-results were perfected. The results of this stage were measured between October 1, 1964 and February 28, 1965. The new monthly meetings with each labor group were geared to the further opening of communication channels. Quality, efficiency, safety, and business trends were the chief topics of discussion. Occasionally members of the staff and other line departments presented their comments to the groups.

After the meetings became a routine part of the operation, a portion of each meeting was reserved for discussing problems. The meetings proved very beneficial. New ideas were brought out, misunderstandings clarified, better work techniques were introduced and an atmosphere for the free exchange of ideas was fostered. At each meeting, the group was given feedback on their performance level during the preceding period. Goals and how to achieve them were regularly discussed.

When the communications center was established, it provided another avenue for communicating with the work group. A portion of one bulletin board was used by the department general foreman. All supervisors in the press department used another board to post important information: a weekly newsletter, informative newspaper articles, magazine and journal articles, safety posters and letters written to the employees by upper management. And one of the most important uses of the communications center was to serve as a means of presenting daily performance figures: the posting of third shift performance levels on the bulletin board went through crude stages to arrive at the finished form. The first method of presenting knowledge-of-results was on a board with the heading, "Here's what the 3rd shift did yesterday." The shift's daily efficiency was posted on it. The next form showed the performance by production line.

As time went on the form became more sophisticated and included more information such as production line, line crew, actual production in units and efficiency based on standard. After a short period of time the members of the workforce became interested in the form and usually stopped at the bulletin board to check it before reporting to their work stations. To test the reaction and get a better idea of how this form was accepted, mistakes were purposely made in production counts, wrong names, etc. Workers were paying very close attention to it. In every case the error was noticed immediately and pointed out to the supervisors.

From the results of the performance ranking made during the control stage, management has a good idea of who the individuals with performance problems were. These individuals were then given a high degree of attention by the supervisor. Their performance trends were continually emphasized. This was always done informally and as a part of a conversation on the production floor. It was found during the preliminary stage that formal meetings in the office for this purpose were unsuccessful. This kind of meeting seemed to put the individual on the defensive, and did not prove to be constructive. After the poor performers started to make progress, this part of the program was expanded to include all members of the skilled classification.

Those members of the skilled classification that were taking part in on-the-job training were handled differently. They were rated and counseled periodically in the foreman's office. The progress of their training and the previous month's efficiency were discussed. Each trainee was assigned to work in different areas to facilitate his training. In each of these meetings, a goal was set for the next period's performance level, a joint figure arrived at by both the trainee and the supervisor.

The monthly meetings with each separate labor grade provided an opportunity for the supervisor to reinforce the members of the group as the production goals were being met and the shift efficiency steadily grew higher.

The results of the preliminary stage were determined from performance figures for October 1, 1964 through February 28, 1965. The first few months of this stage were not used in the calculation because the full effects of knowledge-of-results had not set in. The efficiency index mean rose from 83.5 during the control period, to 88.4 in the preliminary period. The median performance level rose from 80.0 to 83.0 The range improved slightly from 37.0 to 36.0 in the respective periods. The standard deviation reflects the changes by improving from 4.07 during the control period to 3.93 during the preliminary period.

Full Scale Implementation Stage

The last stage of the study is called full scale implementation because it was during this period that a fairly sophisiticated approach was developed for encouraging production through the mechanism of knowledge-of-results. This stage lasted from March 1, 1965 to December 30, 1965. The performance during this period is measured from August 1, 1965 through December 30, 1965. Again the later months of the period were used to better measure the full effects of knowledge-of-results during that period.

It appeared that individuals became more aware of the importance of their performance contribution to that of the group. Members of various line crews tried to break existing production records. When exceptional production records were set, the supervisors bought coffee for the workers involved. During April, 1965 the third shift ran over 100 per cent on a regular work day for the first time. The supervisors bought the entire shift a cup of coffee as a reward for meeting the goal. In the next nine months of the study the third shift production efficiency was over 100 per cent forty-one more times.

Top production runs were underlined with a marking pen on the daily sheet that was posted with performance information. This practice became the topic of humorous bragging among the workers. Many members of the skilled labor classification became so interested in their efficiency averages that they started requesting their totals every week. A few kept their own records. The trend toward higher efficiency made its greatest gains during this period; the mean efficiency index rose to a peak of 97.0 in comparison with the 83.5 and 88.4 efficiency index means attained during the two previous periods. Gains were also made in the other areas: median up to 96.0 range down to 23.0 and the standard deviation reflected these improvements by going down to 2.67 in comparison to the 4.07 and 3.93 during the previous two periods.

Results: Study I

Analyzing the individual and group performance levels during the two-year study supports the hypothesis that knowledge-of-results is a factor in increasing employee productivity. Significant improvements were made in productivity after the introduction of knowledge-of-results. All quantitative measures improved:

1. Performance index mean rose from 83.5 to 97.0.
2. Performance index median rose from 80.0 to 96.0.
3. Performance index range reduced from 37.0 and 23.0.
4. Performance index standard deviation reduced from 4.07 to 2.67.
5. Graphical interpretation shows steady performance increase.

It must also be noted that two of the three trainees and all of the experienced workers in the skilled labor grade improved their performance. It can therefore be postulated that knowledge-of-results will have a favorable effect on the performance of both experienced and inexperienced workers in an industrial work situation. Being aware of their performance let employees know how they were doing and provided a means for reinforcing constructive, production-oriented behavior. This contributed to better morale through stimulating the satisfaction of higher level human needs. The outside activities such as bowling, golf, and softball also contributed to better morale. Subjective impressions through observation by the researcher and other supervisors all agreed that morale seemed to have increased during the experimental time period. Many statements offered by members of the work group further substantiated this observation.

Study II

The second study made in the same metal fabrication plant covers a one-year period from January 1, 1966 through December 31, 1966. Two departments were used, the Press and Assembly Departments. Knowledge-of-results was introduced in the two departments after a control period to measure any changes in productivity. The scope of the second study is wider than that of the first because more workers and supervisors are involved in two complete departments. (The first study was made on one shift in one department). There are approximately 18 supervisors and 400 workers involved in the second study. But although wider in scope, Study II was not as deep as Study I since only one means of presenting knowledge-of-results was used. (Study I used five methods).

Knowledge-of-results was given the workers in Study II by posting on the bulletin board a revised copy of the daily production report. The primary use of the production report had been to supply management information. After it was altered it could be used for supplying the workforce knowledge-of-results. This was an efficient method of presenting the information because it was part of the normal duties already being done by the department clerks.

Press Department

Approximately 50 per cent of the Press Department employees were already exposed to knowledge-of-results through Study I and the activities of a few other supervisors. The form used for posting on the bulletin board was changed for Study II. It was changed in order to facilitate efforts already being made by the department clerk, thereby relieving the supervisor of the task. The revised form carried the same information as the one used in Study I, but was changed to include performance figures for all three shifts.

During the control period for this portion of the study, from January 1, 1966 through June 30, 1966, approximately 50 percent of the department employees were receiving knowledge-of-results. The mean efficiency index during this period was 91.6 Knowledge-of-results was introduced to the complete department the first week of July, 1966. The effect, if any, of complete knowledge-of-results is negligible. Performance did go up slightly in September and October after the control period. The mean efficiency after knowledge-of-results was 91.6, exactly the same as the control period.

CONTROL PERIOD
RELATIVE PERFORMANCE RANKING
OF THE SKILLED LABOR GRADE

The ranking of the performance levels of the skilled labor grade and their crews was made by totaling their performance statistics during the control period expressing these statistics in the form of an index.

The performance statistics were expressed in two factors; Efficiency Factor and Quality Factor. These factors were arrived at through the use of the formulas:

1. Quality Factor = $\dfrac{H + 4S}{P}$

with
   H = number of parts held for rework
   S = number of parts scrapped
   P = number of parts produced in thousands

2. Efficiency Factor $= \dfrac{A - E}{N}$

with

A = daily production line per cent efficiency measuring total parts produced against standard. $A = P/Q \times 100$; where $P =$ parts produced, $Q =$ standard.

E = daily production line per cent efficiency expected by the immediate supervisor.

N = number of days during the control period.

To arrive at the final index the Quality Factor and the Efficiency Factor were combined using the following formula:

3. Final Index $= \dfrac{QF + EF}{2}$

with

QF = quality factor
EF = efficiency factor

When the final index figure was calculated for each member of the skilled labor grade and his crew it was ranked with the other indexes. This gave management a clearer picture of the relative performance levels and was a basis for taking positive corrective action.

Assembly Department

The second portion of Study II was made in the Assembly Department where ten production lines bring the subassemblies together to make the finished product. The production lines are continuous, automatically moving from one piece of equipment to another. Eight supervisors and approximately 200 workers on all three shifts run the department. When the fabrication processes are complete the finished product flows to the Shipping Department to be packed and sent to the customer.

The Assembly portion of Study II is broken down into three stages: 1) the control stage ran from January 1, 1966 through April 30, 1966 with no formal knowledge-of-results presented to the group; 2) the preliminary stage, from May 1, 1966 through July 31, 1966, was the period when simple feedback in the form of the production report was posted daily; and 3) the full scale stage, from August 1, 1966 through December 31, 1966, is the period in which complete knowledge-of-results was posted through the revised production report. The information on this report included the amount of actual production, efficiency, spoilage, the number of quality incidents, and the key members of the line crew. All of this information was broken down by each production line.

Also included was the department efficiency and efficiency of each shift. The report was posted daily on the department bulletin board.

During the control stage the efficiency index mean was 84.0. After the introduction of knowledge-of-results in the preliminary stage the efficiency index mean went up to 87.5. The more complete knowledge-of-results was introduced in the full scale stage. The efficiency index mean improved to 88.6. The results of the Assembly portion of Study II show a slight improvement when knowledge-of-results was introduced to the work group. Average performance improved from 84.0 to 88.6.

Results: Study II

Although the study did not provide evidence of a high degree of improvement in performance, the results were in the hypothesized direction. While productivity increased to a small degree or was at least maintained in both portions of Study II, these results are not conclusive enough to substantiate the hypothesis that knowledge-of-results will increase productivity. The significant difference in the results of the two studies indicates that the daily form posted on the bulletin board is important, but it must be backed up with other methods of presenting knowledge-of-results to be most effective.

The greatest gains in productivity for production workers in the first part of this century can be associated with the application of the principles of scientific management to rank-and-file job design. Productivity gains through task specialization and work simplification techniques seem to have reached the point of diminishing returns. We may have reached a stage in industrial management where the greatest gains in productivity are now to be realized through the cooperative efforts of a motivated work force.

The key to controlling the attitudes, moral and resultant productivity of the work force is through an understanding and use of the behavioral sciences. Human motivation, according to many behavioral scientists, is based on man's basic and higher level needs. In order to motivate the industrial worker, the working environment must have characteristics that will reinforce and help satisfy his needs. The worker will contribute his best efforts to productivity in a working environment that offers him opportunities and stimuli for the fulfillment of his needs.

Management can use the mechanism of knowledge-of-results as a means through which the worker can receive reinforcement for productive, cooperative behavior. By receiving reinforcement for this behavior and better satisfying his higher level needs the worker is likely to continue this type of behavior. This is of utmost importance in industry because the workers do play a large part in the ultimate success of the firm.

R. Henry Migliore is the Manager of the Press Department of Continental Can Company. He received his degree in production management from Oklahoma State University and a Master's degree in commerce from the St. Louis University. He has done consulting work with Fred Rudge and Associates in Princeton, New Jersey.

Note—Update 2000 the philosopy, methods and strategy used at Continental Can Company in late 1960's has been used many times over. Everything mentioned in this article has been used, revised and updated. Increased productivity, better quality, lower spoilage cost and higher moral have become the NORM. Cardone Industries, Cross Manufacturing, T.D. Williamson Inc, Applied Automation, Colowyo Coal to name a few have enjoyed the benefits of "Knowledge of Results."

SUPPLY CHAIN MANAGEMENT PURCHASING / INVENTORY / MATERIALS

ABSTRACT

This is an approach to the development of the Supply Chain Management Strategic Plan. It emphasizes coordination with the purchasing, production and marketing plans. It introduces the concept of strategic thinking for supply chain integration. Each participant will develop a plan for his or her responsible area.

Purchasing and Materials Management plays an increasingly important role in the performance of a firm with many facets to consider. This is evident from the pursuit of the best value when selecting suppliers, establishing quality standards, to negotiating payment terms that best affect a firm's cash flow. A 1996 study reported 82.78 percent of 242 Southeastern firms reporting, Purchasing and Materials Management, had some level of involvement in Corporate Strategic Planning (Ferguson, 1996). Since this particular function can be such an intricate factor, long-range functional planning can create a competitive advantage for the firm who masters it.

A recent reader survey conducted by the National Association of Purchasing Management (NAPM) indicated one of the developing trends in the industry was the growing importance of Supply Chain Strategic Planning. (Savoie, 1998)

The Strategic Planning/Management Model

Just as important as knowing where you want to go is having a way to get there. The Strategic Planning/MBO model as presented in Strategic Planning and Management (Migliore, 1994) provides such a road map, whether for the overall organization or operational. It is necessary that the overall strategic plan of the company be established before attempting to develop a plan for a specific functional area. The reasoning for this is the functional plan should directly support the larger plan. Ideally and in many companies, Purchasing and Material Management will have an active role in the creation of the overall plan. (See Figure 1.)

Step 1: Developing the Purpose or Mission

"Supply Chain Management doesn't work if you don't have the right people involved, with the right strategic vision to look at the supply chain from a total process perspective." (Isikoff, 1998)

The purpose or mission statement of a Supply Chain Management Plan defines and describes the role played by the department. It states the department's *reason for being,* that is, the service provided to the organization by the department. This statement, though conceptually simple, provides the basis for the plan as well as a reference for decision making. An example of such a statement is presented in Example 1.

Example 1: Ferro Union Purchasing Purpose Statement

Purchasing Material for processing and distribution from suppliers at proven quality and service records at price levels, which will ensure competitive placement in our market. This particular statement ensures price will not be the only criteria assessed, but also quality and service records will be combined to focus on the overall value rather than merely price.

See Appendix A for more purpose statements.

Step 2: Environmental Analysis

The environmental analysis helps set the stage for subsequent steps. Fortunately purchasing is positioned well to perform environmental analysis. "Due to purchasing's external interaction, the function occupies a unique position for monitoring the external environment on a macro and a micro level. Purchasing can monitor the company's external environment for competitive advantages/disadvantages by providing input on forecasted supply market changes, which may result in supply advantages or disadvantages. On the micro level, purchasing provides input on specific suppliers, materials, and potential supply problems." (Ferguson, 1996)

Some items to consider are:

1. Economic Trends - There are those who believe the economy is headed for a downturn after more than eight consecutive years of expansion (Kiplinger, 1998).

2. Emerging Technologies - New products and services, internally and externally, can improve, supplement, or speed obsolescence of current inventories or commitments. New Technologies may also affect the distribution channels. With new technology provided through the computer, electronic data interchanges have become common. More recently, purchasing over the Internet has fostered

a great deal of attention, especially with the pursuit of purchasing standards (Cronin, 1997).

3. Mark IV Automotive watches not only the commodities they use, but also the commodities their suppliers use. This attention has allowed them to identify periods when a supplier price reduction was appropriate and has been used as a negotiation tool to acquire lower prices.

4. Government/Regulatory Trends - The regulatory environment plays a very large role in many organizations. This is especially true for government contractors and subcontractors. For example, strengthened or weakened affirmative action supplier requirements may further restrict or allow a greater degree of freedom in selecting suppliers.

5. Labor Agreements - Purchasing professionals must keep current on labor agreements affecting their suppliers and other external companies like transportation.

6. Expected quality levels - When searching for new suppliers for current or new product, it is wise to choose suppliers with documented business quality plans which have been regularly adhered to ensuring long term dependable performance. There are many suppliers in today's market with ISO certification, which proves their own level and commitment to continuous improvement.

7. Business Cycles - Traditional business cycle theory of expansion, peak, contraction, and recession should be incorporated in the environmental analysis as economic indicators apply to your specific business.

Cross Manufacturing, Overland Park, Kansas uses cycle forecasting to predict economic trends. Over the past 15 years the cycle forecasting model has been very accurate.

Step 3: Strengths and Weaknesses

A compilation of internal strengths and weaknesses allows the firm to strengthen its competence and address potentially self-inflicted barriers. This examination should look not only within the Supply Chain Management group but also at the other functional groups within the firm whose performances could affect the outcome of the functional plan. Functional areas of responsibility must create a supportive plan for the entire company's strategic plan. In some cases, the Supply Chain Management Group may be unable to address a particular weakness. In such cases, a collaborative effort between functions is necessary.

Step 4: Assumption

Unfortunately, the most thorough of environmental and internal analysis of the past and current situations cannot predict the future. Therefore, it is necessary to make certain assumptions about things outside the firm's control that could have a significant effect on the outcome of your plan. For this particular step, your plan should identify several factors over which you have no control. This will allow you to incorporate this later in the strategy and operational planning stages. For example, if a commodity type material experiences wide price fluctuations during a time period, your plan should allow for a marketing adjustment (example: sell less/more of this family of parts, or increase/decrease sales price thereby changing the product mix necessary to sustain profits or capitalize on positive fluctuations.)

Examples of assumptions made in the Mark IV plan:

1. *The prices for linerboard have reached their bottom, so price increases of 4-6 percent are expected in 1999.*

2. *Sales growth for auto filters belts and hoses will continue at a 6 percent per year pace.*

3. *Petroleum related products would continue to have soft prices throughout 1999 due to low oil prices.*

Examples of assumptions made in the ASEC plan:

1. *Foreign exchange rates are assumed at certain levels for the development of standard cost internationally.*

2. *Assume legislation requiring catalytic after treatment of vehicle exhaust will remain in place and strengthen over time requiring technological advancements.*

3. *In purchasing, it must be assumed the forecasts provided by marketing environmental analysis are correct. The favorable PPV (Purchase Price Variance) is based on controlled savings per unit but variations in demand volumes will affect total PPV for all material.*

Step 5: Objectives

In establishing objectives for Supply Chain Management, we begin at the highest level of the strategic planning process. Here we first develop specific, measurable goals necessary to support the overall objectives of the firm, which are identified in the corporate strategic plan.

Examples of key supply chain areas are:

1. Delivery performance of suppliers as well as to customers.

2. Inventory levels and turns of not only your raw materials, Work in Process (WIP), Finished Goods (F.G.), but also that of your suppliers and customers. It is not enough for our firm to use JIT manufacturing techniques but our suppliers must also. We can extend this process through the entire supply chain through demand management techniques with our customers.

3. Obtain favorable PPV through negotiation, supplier partnerships, component commodity tracking, technological advance releases from suppliers, and information share of MRP forecast and inventory levels.

4. Establish excellent inventory accuracy through cycle counting programs and controlled issues and receipts to the system.

5. Education and development of supply chain personnel. Staff developing a life and career plan and negotiating the career plan with their bosses to ensure continued growth of the department.

6. Establish and maintain ISO 9000 and/or QS 9000 compliance. See appendix B for specific objectives for a number of companies.

Step 6: Strategy

In developing the strategies to meet objectives, we enter the thinking stage of the Purchasing and Materials Management Strategic Plan. This involves the development of programs and/or policies aimed at building the framework for the operational plans. Many firms have developed Preferred Supplier programs as part of their purchasing strategy to provide incentives to the supplier through certain guarantees earned when performance reaches a certain level. These programs benefit the firm by enticing the supplier to improve performance. The supplier also benefits from the customer for increased

Purchasing and supplier partnerships or joint study teams working to improve shared processes have gained popularity as a strategy. These arrangements have allowed the purchaser and supplier to deal at a positive level, acting in collusion rather than in confrontation. Another benefit is the improved communications and understanding that can be accomplished as perceptions are shared and unknown barriers are exposed and eliminated. (Murphee, 1992).

An example of a strategy in motion is the trend of many companies moving toward Internet based commerce. American Express set a strategy of channeling the multitude of office supply purchases through their financial service.

Examples of Strategies used by ASEC MFG.:

1. Track key commodities of suppliers' products, which influence your pricing.

2. Develop preferred supplier program including quality audits based on ISO-9000 standards, price reductions, and on-line deliveries and reject rates.

3. Increase frequency of delivery of items to reduce inventory.

4. Demand management of customer's inventory turns.

5. Share MRP forecast to support inventory level.

6. Measure and graph PPV working toward a goal.

7. Measure and graph cycle counting results toward goal.

8. Take classes and certify as a CPIM and CPM.

Step 7: Operational Plans

Developing the operational plans requires entering the trenches to examine the fundamental activities necessary to implement the strategies. This particular activity reaches deeply into the SCM function. Within the department, it is critical that the strategies become integral to the way the department functions and are pursued individually and jointly to gain synergy. To ensure this occurs it is imperative to involve the members of the department in the development of the operational plan.

An Example of an operational plan in action is the use of purchasing cards. American Express set a strategy of channeling the multitude of office supply purchases through their financial service. The strategy evolved into the offering to companies to help them cut cost by offering an

Step 8: Evaluation, Control, Performance Appraisals and Reward

The step of evaluation involves the presentation of functional plans to the firm's management team. The presentations of every function plan, not only Purchasing and Materials Management, but also Marketing, Operations, Human Resources, etc., launches the discussion and debate about how the plans fit one another. The outcome of this discussion and debate should be a modified plan that conforms and connects with the other plans and supports the firm's overall strategic direction.

Control and performance appraisal fit with the old adage: "What gets measured, gets done." It is clear, to reach a destination one should employ the proper tools of navigation to determine position, direction, and speed. These tools for the purpose of strategic planning and management are the metrics a firm would refer to when determining whether objectives are being met. What should be measured are those things the firm can act upon or things outside the firm's control that may explain certain situations. Put another way, a firm should measure and display information that detects changes that may hurt or help the firm. How often a firm measures these should depend on the availability of the information and the benefit of the measurement in relation to the cost, and the potential exposure to the firm as a result of a change.

Caution must be taken establishing supply chain objectives to ensure they are not driven in a vacuum. For example, the purchasing department in a Midwest manufacturing company changed suppliers of lubricants. They were able to cut the total lubricant costs by over 50 percent. In the short term, the purchasing department met cost reduction objectives and the firm's profit position improved in that year.

Over the next few years; however, the company began to experience progressively worse equipment wear and breakdown problems. The effect was poor manufacturing efficiency and customer deliveries became a significant problem. Management was slow to react to the problem. Every measurable area indicated there was a problem: breakdown, repair costs, etc. After the cause of the problem was finally determined, the company returned to the higher grade, more costly lubricant. A combination of improved preventative maintenance, check maintenance and running maintenance along with the superior lubrication dramatically improved the plant operation. This example illustrates the issue that arises when a metric is examined in isolation rather than in conjunction with others to produce a more robust examination of benefit-cost analysis.

Another adage proclaims, "what gets rewarded, gets done well." This statement demonstrates the simple philosophy that people perform best when their contribution is recognized and rewarded. Many different options exist when trying to determine the best method of reward but the selected option should provide incentives for current and future performance.

One should not only limit this to within the organization. For example, a division of Mark IV Automotive hosted a Supplier Recognition Day in order to honor their top suppliers in the areas of quality and customer satisfaction.

REVIEW

The plan is reviewed quarterly. Cross Manufacturing, Overland Park, Kansas, has used this planning process for years. Progress on the overall plan is reviewed by Cross President, John Cross. Each functional area presents their plan and gives a status report on progress toward meeting each of the objectives.

All members of the management team have the opportunity to ask questions and give their input. This interaction gives the opportunity for teamwork among all the functional areas. When adjustments are needed for Cross Manufacturing, all areas, including material control, have the opportunity to adjust their plans. The key is a coordinated effort.

CONCLUSION

The authors have a combined 70 years experience in manufacturing, operations, engineering, and supply chain management. We believe this area needs to be a key part to the firm strategy. This article encourages the vendor to think strategically and maximize the contribution of the supply chain professional to the support of firm mission and objective.

SUPPLY CHAIN MANAGEMENT PURCHASING / INVENTORY / MATERIALS / LOGISTICS

PURPOSE / MISSION / REASON FOR BEING

Who are your "customers"?

Why are you needed?

What service do you provide?

Write out your purpose statement.

ENVIRONMENTAL FACTORS

What is going on external to your company in the Supply Chain Management area?

What are the latest technological advances utilized by your competition?

ASSUMPTIONS (Things over which you have no control.)

1.)

2.)

3.)

STRENGTHS AND WEAKNESSES

YOUR DEPARTMENT STRENGTHS

1.)

2.)

3.)

YOUR DEPARTMENT WEAKNESSES

1.)

2.)

3.)

ASSUMPTIONS (Things over which you have no control.)

1.)

2.)

3.)

KEY RESULT / OBJECTIVES / TARGETS

AREA   OBJECTIVES

	Last Year	This Year	Next Year	Five Years
1.)				
2.)				
3.)				
4.)				
5.)				

STRATEGY
Game Plan to achieve objectives.

1.)

2.)

3.)

4.)

5.)

OPERATIONAL PLANS

MAJOR PROBLEM FACING YOUR DEPARTMENT

ANALYSIS

ALTERNATIVES TO SOLVING THE MAJOR PROBLEM

1.)

2.)

3.)

RECOMMENDATION

CROSS MANUFACTURING, INC.
THREE-YEAR OPERATING PLAN
MATERIAL CONTROL DEPARTMENT

OBJECTIVES	FY 1993	FY 1994	FY 1994	FY 1994	FY 1994	FY 1994	FY 1994
Objectives #1-Material Cost	Last Year Reference	Current Year 1st Quarter	Current Year 2nd Quarter	Current Year 3rd Quarter	Current Year 4th Quarter	Total Year	3rd Year
Obtain % material cost as a % of net sales for the cylinder line							
Target	41%	44.9%	43.5%	43.4%	43.2%	43.8%	41.0%
Actual	43.1%	42.5%	40.3%	42.1%	44.8%	42.6%	–
Variance	2.1%U	2.4%F	3.2%F	1.3%F	1.6%U	1.2%F	–

OBJECTIVES	FY 1993	FY 1994	FY 1994	FY 1994	FY 1994	FY 1994	FY 1995
Objectives #6-PPVl Cost	Last Year Reference	Current Year 1st Quarter	Current Year 2nd Quarter	Current Year 3rd Quarter	Current Year 4th Quarter	Total Year	3rd Year
Achieve 0% variance on Lewis PPV each quarter							
Target	0.0%	0.0%	0.0%	0.0%	0.0%	0.0%	0.0%
Actual	2.2%U	.14%U	1.4%U	1.8%U	2.0%U	1.4%U	–
Variance	2.2%U	.14%U	1.4%U	1.8%U	2.0%U	1.4%U	–

APPENDIX B
MORE SPECIFIC
SAMPLE OBJECTIVES
FROM THE MARK IV PLAN

MARK IV AUTOMOTIVE
YEAR 2000 PURCHASING OBJECTIVES

MATERIAL PRICING

Potentials to reduce material cost 5%

Achieve $5,000,000 Reduction for Year 2000

How-Negotiations

Consolidation of supply base

Standardization of materials

WORKING CAPITAL IMPROVEMENTS

Terms

Extend payable terms by 5%

Reduce raw material inventory by 10%

Work with logistics, and supply management, on the following

Improved lead-times and supplier delivery performance

Inventory consignment programs

Elimination of remaining MOQ's

Pull systems

Work with technical teams to standardize product/materials.

Maintain 100% either ISO 9000 or QS 9000 certification of suppliers,

SAMPLE OBJECTIVES FROM CARDONE PLAN

CARDONE

OBJECTIVE PLAN	1998 PLAN	1997 ACTUAL	% CHANGE
A. R/M Back Order (to mfg)	0	4	100%
B. R/M Back Order (X-number)	25	31	20%
C. R/M Inventory Turns	5.5	5	10%
D. R/M Parts Shipments Reject	10	36	72%
E. Net Savings	$2.0 mil	$2.5 mil	20%
F. Total RM Vendor Base	325	376	14%
G. VPI	95%	88%	8%
H. VCAR Performance	15 days	N/A	N/A
I. Payable Days outstanding	40	35.5	13%

HOW BIG: A PLAN OR ACCIDENT

Abstract

The question of how big the firm should be is analyzed. We discuss four considerations. First is the general pattern of firm growth. Second is availability of the correct amounts and types of resources-both tangible and intangible. The third, to grow the business, what is the most efficient use of resources? To be considered is the direction and potential growth of the industry, current firm market share, and where the firm is operating on the Long Run Average Cost Curve. And fourth is the vision, ability, desire of management and the management team to create value for the organization. The authors reject the notion that the decision for growth and size is not because of ego and arrogance.

The authors conclude that the organization should plan toward an optimum size based on total revenue. Size must be profitable as measured by a rate of return. The plan has a specified horizon. Each year and when conditions warrant, the strategic plan is updated and revised.

WHAT SIZE IS BEST?

How should the firm grow and expand? The central question is whether to chase the market or control growth. Another question has to do with size of the firm in the long run. Or maybe it's time to retrench? When you chase the market you are reacting to opportunity. This was the strategy of General Patton in World War II: "Take as much ground every day as you can." Good strategy until the Army ran out of gas and supplies. Aggressive growth must have support. For the firm, it's "expand your market as fast as possible." The notion is "big is better." Many believe the opportunity is there and you better not pass it by or perhaps it is gone forever. However, a support base must be developed to support the growth.

Should the company grow and expand? While the answer to that question may seem obvious, it is not as clear as it might seem. While we suggest that the company should grow, growth does not always mean expansion. In addition to getting larger, growth may mean getting smaller, better or simply changing into something different. To make the choice as to how to grow and how much, it is necessary to understand why firms should grow in the first place. Consider the fall of the Roman empire. After 12 centuries, what happened? At one time Rome ruled the world. Most scholars agree on two overriding reasons for Rome's fall. One is decay from within. The second, and what is important here, is Rome over-expanded and didn't adopt its management system. The empire got too big. They tried to continue to manage with the centralized government and management system. The Romans couldn't manage and control the very empire they built.

Why should firms grow?

To answer the question-why should firms grow-we must understand how organizations grow as systems. We start with the presumption that any organization is a system. We know that all systems by nature may self-destruct in a process theorists call entropy. Entropy is the tendency for an organized system to become disorganized-essentially to fall apart. We can explain the tendency toward falling apart by borrowing liberally from Newton's laws and applying them to business firms.

First Law of organizations-An organization at rest tends to stay at rest

We know that organizations don't like to change, that inactivity breeds inactivity and finally complacency. This complacency takes the form of the organizational "couch potato," the firm that has a routine from which it does not want to detour. However, in the rapidly changing world of today's business environment, complacency can spell trouble as we see from the second law.

Second Law of Organizations-Organizations at rest tend to decay (or at least get in trouble)

There is an old business saying that goes something like "if you snooze, you lose!" While there is much to recommend stability, the business world is not a particularly stable place. As a result, complacency means that firms fall behind technology, product innovation, market changes, customer tastes, etc. In fast-moving industries, change occurs at ever increasing rates. The complacent firm falls behind even more rapidly. For example, in the late 1980's both IBM and Compaq seemed to rest on their laurels and didn't maintain their technological edge. As a result, both firms lost market leadership and market share. In fact, they came perilously close to being forced out of the personal computer business.

Even in slow-moving industries, complacency breeds trouble. Even for the fortunate firm that has little effective competition, if skills aren't used they will decay. Prior to the 1981 breakup, AT&T hadn't worried about competition. When the firm was split into the long distance firm and the "baby bells," James Olsen and the AT&T management had to revive long moribund competitive skills. It was a Herculean effort to transform the firm back into a competitive organization after decades of the status quo as a monopoly. However, the slide into complacency is not the only problem as we see in the third law.

Third Law of Organizations-Organizations in trouble tend to get worse!

In his research on bankruptcy, Don Hambrick of Columbia University coined the term "flailing about" to describe the death throes of an organization. When firms decline, panic often sets in so managers start doing anything they can-as long as they are doing something. Hambrick suggests they flail about looking for a solution. As managers get increasingly desperate, they also get increasingly poor at making choices, creating a spiral of decline. American Motors may be a good example of this death spiral. When it became increasingly clear that American Motors could not compete with the "Big 3" or the foreign firms like Toyota and Nissan, they rapidly brought out several new models, tried a wide variety of sales and dealer promotions, sold assets, closed plants and tried to strike deals. In the end, Chrysler got a bargain on the venerable Jeep nameplate and virtually everything else that American Motors had left was worthless.

How does the firm combat the forces of the three laws?

Beating the inevitable decline described above simply requires planned growth. In our terms, growth means ongoing development of the organization and its capacity. However, growth, as we indicated previously does not always mean expansion. Growth can mean getting better. As we mentioned above, AT&T went through a wrenching change in 1981 and again in 1996. In 1981 the firm had to transform itself into a competitive power after decades of complacent monopoly status. In 1996 the firm had to rid itself of an unsuccessful acquisition NCR (National Cash Register) plus get its businesses back to a size that will allow them to change as conditions dictate-something that has rewarded Lucent's shareholders quite handsomely.

Growth may mean a different direction. The Mother's March of Dimes started out to fight Polio. In 1957 the organization helped Drs. Salk and Sabin defeat polio for good.

Instead of accepting victory and disbanding, the organization took stock of itself, realized the potential good this effective group could do and took on a new challenge. The new focus, birth defects, sadly is one that the organization will have reason to battle forever.

Describing specifically how firms get better or different is beyond the scope of this article. What we can discuss is growth in size. To most people, firms growing means they are getting bigger. We see countless examples of firms expanding from their own success (e.g. Microsoft), from buying up other firms (Disney's acquisition of Capital Cities/ABC) or from merging with equals (Packard Bell's merger with Zenith and NEC's personal computer businesses.)

However, not all size decisions mean the firm is getting bigger. The downsizing rage of the 1990s indicates that many firms have begun to believe that growth can be achieved by getting smaller. Sometimes the leaner size can be very effective. As an example, when the federal government consolidated the Northeastern railroads in Conrail, the combined organization had in excess of 100,000 employees and was losing (collectively) hundreds of millions of dollars. When the U.S. government sold the new Conrail to the public in 1988, the revitalized firm had approximately 36,000 employees and profits in excess of $200 million. While not all downsizings are as successful as Conrail, the direction of growth does not have to be up.

The central question for managers is one of how big the firm should be for the long run. . . . The argument for controlled growth is to be conservatively aggressive. Controlled growth requires more analysis. It is proactive not reactive. In this scenario the opportunity is minimized for costly mistakes.

Peter Drucker, noted business consultant and author, (973: 638-649) believes a firm has an optimum size in every industry. Good theory, but how does the firm determine size?

An interesting case in point is Johns-Mansville, which wanted to always maintain 20 percent of market share. (Doer, 1977:10) W. Richard Goodwin took over the company in 1970 and aggressively expanded the market share, growth and earnings were a company record in 1976. Goodwin was removed from office because he assumed the need for growth. His assumption was wrong. The Board of Directors wanted to maintain a conservative company.

Another way is to determine the firm's market share in the total market. What are the strategies of your competitor? Are you expanding your share of an expanding market or are you taking customers from your competition?

FIGURE 1

Market Share

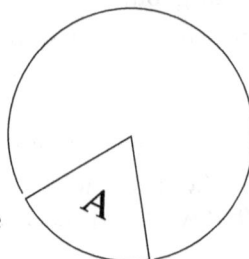

A-Your Market Share

In order for organizations to respond to the call for growth, each area of the business must have resources. As such, we need to understand the role that resources play. Webster's defines a resource as "something that lies ready for use or can be drawn upon for aid." Traditionally, economists have classified organizational resources into three general categories-land, labor and capital. However, as we will discuss below, several intangible resources are also essential for firm survival and growth.

Resource Characteristics

In the previous sections it was argued that the firm needs the right types and amounts of resources in order to grow. In this section we add the idea that to support that growth the firm needs to identify resources that have the right characteristics as well. Several contemporary management researchers including Jay Barney at Ohio State University and Margaret Peteraf at the University of Minnesota have developed what they call the "Resource Based View" of the modern organization. In this view, the organization succeeds or fails competitively on the basis of the characteristics of the resources it possesses, for example, the degree to which there are substitutes available for the resource, the extent to which the resource can be used in multiple ways, etc. Dependent on these resource characteristics, the firm is able to develop and maintain advantage in the competitive marketplace. This article is concerned with the growth of some type that must be part of the firm's strategic plan, growth that must be supported by resources with the correct characteristics. If the firm wishes to grow larger, possessing resources for which competitors cannot find substitutes will make that easier by making the firm distinctive. If the firm is trying to grow by going in a different direction, then resources that may be used a wide variety of ways will give the firm the flexibility it needs to change. When the firm wishes to grow by getting smaller, then resources which cannot be imitated by competitors will give the new, smaller firm more "bang for the buck" (efficiency) so as to help it keep up with larger competitors.

While having resources is necessary for growth, just having resources is not sufficient. Firms can be in the midst of plenty only to die. An example comes from a software firm that was founded, grew, and died in the early 80s. The company, called Dakota Software, developed inexpensive programming language compilers that would run on personal computers. Each compiler package cost about $50. While they were not as complete as the compilers that ran on mammoth mainframes, they were perfectly sufficient for most individual programmers. As such, Dakota was able sell millions of copies of their software. The problem was that the huge influx of orders overwhelmed the firm. They did not have sufficient cash flow (resources) to even buy the disks necessary to distribute the software or to print the manuals for their products. In the midst of massive orders for their products, the firm went out of business.

The lesson we learn from Dakota software is that not only does growth require resources per se but requires that the firm have the right amount and types of resources as well. A key part of managing growth is figuring out what resources are needed, in what amounts and when those elements are needed. There are a variety of tools available to managers to help with tangible resource planning so we won't belabor the point here. Inventory and production management tools such as Materials Requirements Planning (MRP), Just-in-Time inventory systems and other production planning tools can help managers determine how much of what resources are needed.

While tangible resources are critical, we suggest that there are several intangible resources organizations also must have in order to grow. We discuss three, key intangible resources-specifically information, time, and legitimacy.

The phrase "information age" is often used to describe the world today. While the ability to produce things is still valuable, the currency of the late 20th century is information. The role of information is seen most vividly in the growth of "network" organizations. Network organizations are firms that themselves may not produce much (or anything) but rather contract for needed elements of production and distribution. These virtual organizations parlay information about the capabilities of others into business success. Two well-known examples of network organizations are Nike and Dell Computer. While both organizations have some production capacity, much of what they sell is produced by others under contract. These firms manage information about their suppliers as much as they manage their own plants. Both firms have used this information-intensive approach to achieve massive growth.

Even to more traditional organizations, information has become more and more valuable. With innovation occurring in both technology and finance at increasingly faster rates, the firm that cannot process these changes will be left behind. Further, the advent of powerful database management tools gives firms vastly improved ability to process information concerning their customers and target markets. The increased precision that these new tools provide may make the difference between success and bankruptcy. The above examples are but a few reasons why, in order to grow, firms have to manage information as a resource. As the firm decides how much it wishes to grow, it can decide how much information it needs to manage that growth.

The second intangible resource critical to firm growth is time. As we discussed above, as we enter the 21st century, the pace of change is increasing. If firms wish to grow, they must put "time on their side." A vivid example of how time can defeat a growth strategy came in the early 1980s during the beginnings of the takeover battles that were to epitomize that era. When Conoco became a takeover target, several firms were in the thick of the battle. One of the combatants, Texaco, however, came under the anti-trust scrutiny of the U.S. government costing the firm precious time. While many analysts of the era suggested that Texaco's bid was a better deal for Conoco shareholders, Texaco ran out of time while being stalled by the Justice Department's inquiry, resulting in the victory to DuPont. Texaco's growth plans were stopped because of time as a critical resource. The management of growth requires sufficient time in which to allow that growth to occur in a planned way.

The last intangible resource that is critical to organizational growth is legitimacy. There are two types of legitimacy-market legitimacy and social legitimacy. Society confers market legitimacy when it determines that there are no (few) questions that can be raised about the firm's products or services and confers social legitimacy when there are no concerns about a firm's behavior as a member of society. You cannot go down to the corner store and buy legitimacy (although many firms have tried). It has to be earned and regularly maintained. Interesting examples of firms facing market and social legitimacy concerns are Sony and Betamax for market legitimacy plus McNeil Labs (Johnson and Johnson) and Tylenol for social legitimacy. In the Sony Betamax case, it was widely acknowledged that the "Beta" format was argued to be technically superior to the VHS format for home videotape recorders. However, consumers selected (legitimized) VHS as the format of choice. As the movie studios put fewer and fewer titles out in Beta format, Sony was not allowed to grow with the brand to the point where they eventually had to pull the product altogether.

In the case of Johnson and Johnson's McNeil Labs and Tylenol, social legitimacy helped the brand grow. After the second series of poisonings using tainted Tylenol, Johnson and Johnson's McNeil Labs pulled Tylenol capsules off the market saying that the firm could not guarantee the safety of the product. The firm took a charge in excess of $250 million causing Johnson and Johnson's first quarterly loss in decades. However, within a year, society's reaction to the firm's response was to increase Tylenol's market share by seven (7) percent. Consumers saw the firm's forthright response to the crisis as deserving of even more social legitimacy and hence were more willing to buy the product.

In each of the above examples, we see how intangible resources helped or impeded growth. Unfortunately, there are no software tools to help managers determine how much in the way of these intangible resources are necessary for growth. Rather, each manager must rely on his or her knowledge, background and training to make that decision. Here are some guidelines to help managers decide how much of each tangible resource is necessary-depending on how much the firm wishes to grow.

The key to management of intangible resources is the recognition of their importance. Again, intangibles are just as critical to success as the tangible elements in the firm-in some cases more so. Managers must not only recognize this fact themselves but also communicate the importance of intangibles to every member of the team.

Secondly, managers must realize that the acquisition and maintenance of intangible resources has a cost just like those of tangible resources. Some of those costs are fairly obvious, e.g. gathering, storing and processing information has clear costs for equipment and staff. With the goal of legitimacy, the costs may not be as clear. In any case, it is essential that managers understand what these intangible resources cost and manage these costs just like any other resource.

Further, as with all costs in firms, there is a point where more is not better, regardless of the resource. The cost of acquiring or maintaining any intangible resource may outweigh its benefit. While it is likely that one can only crudely estimate the cost and benefits of intangible resources, it is essential that these estimates are made. As the costs of acquiring and maintaining intangibles are often buried in overhead, the firm can run up huge charges rapidly unless a close watch is kept. These charges will deprive the firm of needed cash resources in the service of elusive intangibles. As we saw in the Dakota Software example above, even in the midst of plenty the firm can starve to death.

Finally, in the management of intangibles, managers must learn to tolerate ambiguity. With cash or inventory, it is pretty clear when the firm has a sufficient amount of the resource. This is much less likely with intangibles. How much information is enough? How legitimate do you need to be given the size you wish to have the firm achieve? These are questions for which there is likely not a good answer.

Even if there is a good answer, it is likely that the answer will change rapidly. Tolerating and managing the ambiguity inherent in the use of intangible resources are capabilities that managers must develop in order to be successful. As managers decide how much to grow, they will have to decide how much of what type of both tangible and intangible resources are necessary for that growth. It is through the efficient management of these resources that the firm will be able to operate at its ideal point-the bottom of the long-run average cost curve.

After making this determination, consideration must be made on the effects growth strategy has on production, plant capacity, quality, finance, transportation, engineering, human resources, etc. Every area of the business must respond if the firm chooses to grow.

The closer the firm operates at the bottom of the long-run average curve, the better its opportunity to use pricing at a competitive strategy. The optimum position at the bottom of the curve gives the firm optimum flexibility in whatever growth trajectory it chooses. Notice how Wal-Mart uses low prices because of controlled costs as a competitive advantage.

FIGURE 2

Long Run Average Cost Curve

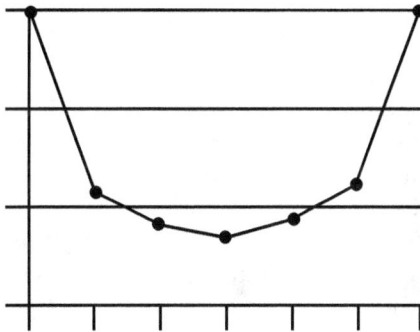

Drucker (Drucker, et al. 1973, 638) emphasizes the need to manage increased complexity. As the firm grows, its universe becomes increasingly complex. Even if all other factors fall in place, does management have the ability to manage the new proposed growth? Can a Piper Cub pilot fly a 747? Can the management team grow in philosophy, planning, communication and delegation? Even Henry Ford at Ford Motor Company and IBM's Thomas J. Watson had problems.

Resources and Growth

In deciding how and how much to grow, managers must examine not only the amount and type of resources they need to support that growth but what characteristics the resources must possess. By making these decisions ahead of time as part of a strategic planning process, managers are in a much better position to be able to identify and obtain the specific resources they need to support the type of growth the firm seeks.

Another way to view long-term success of the firms is with the formula:

$$X = f(a,b,c,d,e,\ldots?)$$

The "X" represents the dependent variable, long-term success. In the formula, X is function of the various combinations of independent variable, a,b,c,d,e, on to infinity. The discussion could be expanded to independent variables; political climate, national monetary policy, national security, organizational culture, technology, etc. For example, in the best case scenario, long-term success (X) for Wal-Mart could be a function of market share and quality which, according to the PIMS (Buzzell, 1988) model, are the two most important variables. Other independent Wal-Mart variables: expanding market, weak competitor (K-Mart), successful management taking over the for the late Sam Walton, with favorable U.S. economic conditions, low interest rates, etc.

CONCLUSION

The recommendation for planned growth is a thoughtful, creative approach to strategic planning. The strategic plan is developed by taking all factors into consideration. This process forces the size decision. The options could be to double in size, have modest growth, or as we have seen in the past decades-downsize. The emphasis here is proactive planning. Too often, for example, downsizing is done in small increments. It is like cutting the dog's tail one segment at a time. Every cut is painful. A better approach is proactive retrenching and then an aggressive scaled-back attack plan.

Too often a company chasing the market with uncontrolled growth ends up with disillusioned leaders, harassed management, confusion, declining quality, and poor customer service. It can be likened to an army outrunning its fuel and food. The excitement of the rapid advance is sobering as the firm (and the army) become vulnerable to attack mired in their self-imposed quicksand.

We believe the long-term size based on revenue should be established. Short-term targets are developed to control and coordinate the growth.

As conditions change, the plan can be altered. The size decision, once made, is not cast in stone. A little farfetched, perhaps, but who is to say that Wal-Mart might not buy out K-Mart? The current Wal-Mart plan calls for optimistic growth over the next five years. Wal-Mart seems to be going for a 200-billion-dollar objective in the next five years. The last twelve months' revenue has been around $150 million. K-Mart's last twelve months have been about $35 billion. With the industry average profit margin of 2.9%, Wal-Mart is doing exceptionally well at 3.3%. All Wal-Mart financial figures are better than K-Mart's. K-Mart's profit margin has been 1.0%. A K-Mart takeover, however, could be too tempting. The question is: Would the larger entity with a purported current size of $185 billion perform to meet stockholders' expectations?

A worst-case scenario would feature many of the medium-size firms in Mexico. Let's say half of the products/services of a Mexican company are exported into a foreign market, and they are operating an efficient, cost-conscious manufacturing operation at or near the bottom of the long-run average cost curve with a reasonable market share. These are certainly two important variables. Realistically the peso is at an all-time low exchange rate and the political climate is uncertain. Problems with inflation are quite likely given Mexico's instability. As such, planning for growth in such an uncertain environment would certainly require a much different planning scenario. It is very likely that in this climate modest growth is best.

REFERENCES

Business Week, Doe, John "Management Principles", Oct. 31, 1977, p. 10-15.

- Management, Drucker, Peter (Harper and Row) 1973, p. 638-649.
- Drucker chapter 53 addresses the issue of being the right size. Chapter 55 is on the issue of being the wrong size and chapter 60 is on managing growth.

The PIMS Principles, Buzzell, Robert D. and Gale, Bradley, T. (New York: The Free Press, 1988) p. 15.

Scott, W.R., & Meyer, J.W. (1983). The organization of societal sectors. In J. Meyer & W.R. Scott (Eds.), *Organizational Environments: Ritual and Rationality*, 129154, Beverly Hills, CA: Sage Publications.

How Big: A Plan or Accident; growth strategy for the small and medium size enterprise." Article adapted from a presentation at ICSB 1999 Conference June 19-23, Naples, Italy

415

GLOBAL EXPANSION STRATEGY

EXAMPLES

PURPOSE:

Molex:

To be leaders in the interconnection industry in terms of growth of revenue and and profitability. This will be accomplished by being the preferred suppliers for our customers in our core competitive markets.

Hershey:

To enhance shareholder value as a focused, snack food company in North America and selected international markets and to be a leader in every aspect of business.

SCI

SCI is committed to total customer satisfaction by providing the highest quality of products and services in the industry. SCI achieves this by understanding customer needs and by consistently meeting and exceeding customers expectations.

Biomedicine

Is an international company dedicated to making high specialty medical products, especially catheters.

McDonald's

McDonald's vision is to be the world's best quick service restaurant experience. Being   the best means consistently satisfying customers better than anyone else through   outstanding quality, service, cleanliness and value. Develops, operates, franchises and   services a worldwide system of restaurants which prepare, assemble, package and sell value~priced foods.

Ben & Jerry's

Ben and Jerry's is an international company dedicated to the making of all natural ice cream and related products such as: super premium ice cream, ice cream novelties, low-fat ice cream, low-fat and non-fat frozen yogurt, and sorbet using Vermont dairy products. Ben and Jelly's are based on profitable growth by increasing value for their shareholders and employees. Ben and Jelly's is a company that recognizes the role they play in society by initiating ways to improve the quality of life for community, local, national and international.

ENVIRONMENTAL ANALYSIS

Molex

- Primary SIC: 3577
- SIC codes: 7373,3572
- Molex has 10% Net Profit compared with 7% in the industry.
- Top competitor is AMP with 10% of the interconnect industry in terms of revenue.
- S& P states that over and above 18 million people per month will be new users at the internet through out 2000.

Hershey

SIC CODE 2060

Chocolate market is expected to growth by 2 to 3% over the next year.

Hershey has 41.5% of the market.

SCI:

The high amount of local competitors

McDonald's

Environmental Analysis: SIC Code 7sl`f F6 T4 p. IIy

Global tourism last year totaled over 593 million tourist arrivals, generating $413 billion in tourism receipts.

World tourism spending grew at double the rate of the above mentioned

Biomedics:

SIC: 3841

In 1999 300 people out of 1 million suffered with renal failure

STRENGTHS

Molex

- Last year Molex grew 3 times more than the industry average.
- Molex is the second place in terms of revenue in the interconnect industry with 6.3% of the total market estimated in $27.1 billion
- Molex paid more profit per share than the rest of the industry in 1998

SCI

Good procurement

Surface Mount Technology

High quality

SCI testing service.

Biomedics

High quality products

High efficiency in Marketing

High technological products

The company has been in business for over 90 years - was originally started by the Williams brothers. The company is diversified - Energy and Communications, as well as regulated and deregulated entities. Actively pursuing acquisition opportunities to enhance shareholder return. Attempting to expand international operations - will own or will partner with existing firm to be in more than 25 countries worldwide. Will improve the credit ratings of both the energy business and communication business by offering an IPO on the communication sector.

WEAKNESSES

Molex

- Industry is cost driven but Molex is not cost oriented
- Slow time to market on new product
- Molex is very careful when taking risk in acquisitions or expansions, this makes us slow.

Hershey

Big competition

Price is very fluctuant

High freight costs

SCI

High turn over

Few prepared people

Not enough facilities to host new products in Mexico.

Bioedics

High competition

Less financial buying power than the competitors

Lack of experience in exporting and globalization

High costs in training.

A portion of the business is highly regulated-returns are limited

Highly leveraged company-the company has a large amount of debt

The facilities for the communications are unfinished and are still being built - incurring plenty of expenses at the present time.

Fluctuating energy commodity prices.

Will need to significantly develop their international business in order to be a player. in the Global Market.

GENERAL STRATEGY
GAP

GENERAL STRATEGY:

Currently, there are 1,862 Gap, Banana Republic and Old Navy stores in the United States and 321 in other countries. Open 200 stores in the United States in the year 2000~ open 80 stores overseas. Expand Gap, GapKids and Baby Gap, along with Banana Republic and Old Navy. Expand Old Navy/Launch restaurants reminiscent of WWI Naval mess halls, in an Old Navy Flagship, in current U. S. Markets.

GENERAL GLOBAL STRATEGY:

Ben and Jerry's not only in the United States, but also in Europe, Asia and recently open one franchise in Peru, Canada, Israel and a joint venture in Russia. Ben and Jelly's also sell their products in super markets and special stores. In order to expand globally they are planning on opening more franchises and company owned outlets in selected new foreign countries. At this moment Ben and Jelly's have over 170 franchise ice cream scoop shops and partnerships in the United States. They have four stores in The Netherlands, four in Canada, three in France, eight in Israel, one in Lebanon, one in Peru and one in the United Kingdom.

CISCO

Global Strategy:

Cisco's products encompass the broadest range of networking solutions available from any single supplier. These solutions include routers, LAN and WAN switches, dial and other access solutions, Web site management tools, Internet appliances, and network management software. The thread that ties these products together is the Cisco IOS software platform, which delivers Internet services and enables networked applications. Cisco's offerings also include indusb)T-leading customer services for network design, implementation, maintenance and support.

MC DONALD'S

1. Develop our people at every level of the organization, beginning in our restaurants.

2. Foster innovation in our menu, facilities, marketing, operations and technology.

3. Expand our global mindset by sharing best practices and leveraging our

best people resources around the world.

4. Long term, reinvent the category in which we compete and develop other business and growth opportunities.

5. Continue the successful implementation of changes underway in McDonald's USA.

6. Increase the number of franchisees in high- growth areas.

7. Boost salaries, add bonuses, and increase hourly wages and compensation packages.

8. Due to the shortage of highly skilled workers it is important to add more training programs to upgrade the level of skills for all employees.

HERSHEY

To expand it's revenue by 5% in the next 5 years by entering the markets of Singapore, Brazil and Venezuela.

CORE STRATEGY

GAP

SUMMARY OF EXPANSION (CORE) STRATEGY:

United States: (200) Add more in the Midwestern states and Southwestern U. S. Singapore: (3) Population is growing, low labor costs and GNP is growing, diverse group of citizens;

Mexico: (12) Labor is cheaper, low tariffs taxes on items, close to U. S. border;

Brazil: (8) Free-spirited community~ low stress/less formal clothing style;

Japan: (12) 39 stores already successful~ use past strategies;

England: (12) Culture difference is low; Well-developed country with high GNP; similar clothing preferences;

Australia: (15) Banana Republic line of clothing focuses on the "outback"; low culture difference, speak virtually same language; low law and tariff bamers;

Canada: (13) Currently have 130 stores; positive quarterly revenues;

China: (12) Joint ventures with clothing companies~ spread into other provinces/cities. Argentina: (5) Wealthiest country ~ middle class is highest population;

BEN & JERRY

South America, especially in three countries: Peru, Chile and Argentina. There is some competition in the ice cream industry, because people in Peru as well as in Chile and Argentina are used to eating fruit ice creams, that is why we are going to have to introduce new and different flavors.I would like to open three more stores in Lima, Peru, two stores in Chile and one store in Argentina. The stores will be opened in cities where the climate is warm and nice and invites people to have ice creams. These three countries are characterized eating ice cream as a day to day labor.

CISCO

Telecommunication Carriers

Intemet Service Providers

Cable Companies

Wireless Service Communication providers

Small/Medium Business

Companies in need of a network as well as an Internet connection

MOLEX

The markets that Molex will explore with this new service, are the same markets that Molex is already attending (Automotive, Data, Telecom, etc.) The manufacturing sites will be established in different areas of the world to cope with our costumer expectations in terms of communication, deliveries, and service.

WAL-MART

Wal-Mart has done an exceptional job in developing and implementing a Global and Core International Strategy. The last five years of the 20th century recorded very profitable international growth. In the 21st century already their British and German expansion has bee aggressive.

CONTEMPORARY MARKETING

INTRODUCTION

What goes around comes around. Here we are in the new millennium. Has anything really changed in marketing?

The new trend for the marketing manager in the millennium has to be customer focused. This new trend has been called "IBM CO" or customer oriented selling. Xerox Canada calls it "solution selling," and Xerox USA calls it "buyer-centered selling." The "new' concept calls for going to the customer and finding out about their future plans, problems, and products.

The key is to find out how your organization can help the customer solve problems, gain market share, and be more profitable. LISTEN TO YOUR CUSTOMER. Listen, listen, listen... said the late Frank "Pat" Murphy, Sr., the founder and CEO of the F.W. Murphy Company. (1) Listen and find out what the customer's problem is. The customer doesn't want you to sell them something, but help them solve their problem. With this information your organization can take a creative and innovative look at the customer and their needs. By putting together a multi-level, multi-disciplined task force your company can see what specific products, services, and solutions they can come up with. The "solution" might mean a capital investment or could require a complete change in the company's time-honored policy and procedure.

MARKETING PLAN

The marketing plan is coordinated with the finance, production, and human resource plan to implement the overall corporate strategy. The product must always be better than the sales pitch. The product isn't sold until it's paid for. A good marketing/production plan can only sell a product or service once. The marketing plan has a focus on meeting customer needs. It keeps existing customers and develops new ones. Over the past few years, marketing strategy has been compared to warfare. This creates a view of the competitor, their strategy, and how your strategy combats theirs.

The purpose of the promotion plan is to support the marketing plan. The promotion plan is aimed at the specific customer outlined in the overall plan. The message in the promotion plan appeals to the perceived and real needs of the customer. The promotion plan is the mix of image, logo, television, radio, direct sales, direct mail, telemarketing, newspaper, magazine, and referrals to get the message to the target market.

The sales management plan coordinates the work of direct sales people, wholesalers, marketing representatives, etc. The ultimate success of the organization is the coordination of all segments of the overall plan, top to bottom.

The organization must empower, train, encourage, and reward its people. When it's all said and done, PEOPLE get the job done.

A strategy must be developed to take advantage of goodwill and minimize customer complaints. Research indicates that a good product/service/experience will likely cause the customer to repeat it seven times. Poor service or a bad product can be repeated 47 times. These issues must be addressed in the marketing plan.

CUSTOMER SATISFACTION

Satisfied customers translate into business success. A customer is the most important asset a company possesses. The customer is the source from which all cash flow is generated. You always want to keep the customers you have and gain new customers who would be loyal to you.

(2), "if you cannot demonstrate the link between increased customer satisfaction and improved financial results, you're not measuring customer satisfaction correctly." Satisfied customers should exhibit at least one of three measurable characteristics: loyalty (retention rates), increased business (share of market), and insusceptibility to your rivals' blandishments (price tolerance).

Companies think of capturing a customer as a singular event. Providing quality service includes recapturing the existing customer each time you are in contact with them. When you do this successfully and repeatedly, the customer becomes comfortable and satisfied with the relationship, thus reducing their chances of leaving. Customer comfort means that the customer's needs have been met. Customers do business with organizations that they rate highly in: services, products, support and costs. If the customer's comfort level is strong in all four categories, the overall value will be highly rated.

According to Dawn Lacobucci, of the Financial Times (5), managers are seeking to enhance customer service, to offer customers added value and gain the competitive edge. Managers should consider the implications of the basic characteristics of customer services; such as the differences in services, and the fact that they are simultaneously produced and consumed and that they are intangible.

Measuring Customer Cost

Frederick Reichheld of Bain & Co. says that, "long-term customers tend to buy more, pay more, and create fewer bad debts. Reichheld stated that by raising customer retention rates by five percentage points, a company can increase the value of an average customer by 25% to 100%."

Based on the work by Reichheld and the University of Michigan's Class Foretell, here is a summary of how to calculate what a customer is worth. First, decide on a meaningful period of time over which to do the calculations. This will vary depending on you planning cycles and your business. Secondly, calculate the profit (net cash flow) customers produce each year. Track several samples; and find out how much business the customers gave to you each year and how much it cost you to serve them. It's better to, segment them by age, income, sales channel, and so on.

For year one, subtract the cost of acquiring the customers. Costs will include things such as, advertising, commissions, and back office costs of setting up a new account. Be sure to get specific numbers. For example: profit per customer in year one, year two and so on, and not averages for all customers or all years. Lastly, you chart the customer life expectancy, using the samples to find out how much your customer base erodes each year.

Once you know the profit per customer per year and the retention figures, it is simple to calculate the net present value. This information can assist businesses in finding out how much to spend to attract new customers. 'Repeat business is the ultimate measure of customer satisfaction and almost certainly merits bigger investments that you make." According to Reichheld, "for advertising agencies a 5% increase in retention rates translates into a 95% increase in customer NPV and for credit card companies a 75% increase in customer NPV."

Measuring Customer Satisfaction

Thomas Stewart states that (2), "Customers define a business and the meaning of economic activity. The final analysis of what matters is how well an economy satisfies its customers needs and wants." The University of Michigan's business school and the American Society for Quality Control, released the American Customer Satisfaction Index (ACSI), making it possible to keep track of customer satisfaction.

The ACSI monitors customer satisfaction in more than two dozen manufacturing and service industries and several public-sector functions, totaling about 40% of US gross domestic product (GDP). As a result, this makes the ACSI the first large-scale, methodical attempt to measure the quality of economic output. According to economist, Claes Fornell, a professor at the Michigan business school and designer of the index, "At the macro level, you should consider this an economic indicator, like indicators of price and productivity."

Using ACSI, industries, especially domestic automobile makers, have made significant gains in customer satisfaction. The overall degree of customer satisfaction among U.S. companies has decreased, most noticeably in the computer industry. According to ACSI, the reasons could be attributed to the failure to respond to customers' increasing expectations, and insufficiently stringent ways of tracking customer's attitudes.

The ACSI is too new to judge its ability to contribute to forecasts of the economy as a whole, but it appears to be able to foretell corporate performance. A study by David Larcker of the Wharton School, using data from the National Quality Research Center, showed those companies that ranked highest in the first year's ACSI, significantly outpaced lower-ranked companies in the stock market.

The ACSI results suggest at least three wrong turns businesses may have made in their drive to improve customer satisfaction.

1. Customer service is a cost to be incurred, rather than an investment.
2. There is a rising awareness of customer expectations
3. ACSI cannot yet define customer satisfaction to financial results.

According to Ray Schneider of Perspective magazine, (3) your customers are sitting on a wealth of information that can help you improve your business opportunities with them. Conducting a customer survey can bring in this valuable information, by removing the guesswork out of the way you do business, so that you can do more of it. A customer survey specifically does the following:

1. Establishes a baseline of measurement for improving customer satisfaction.
2. Helps focus improvement efforts.
3. Increases customer perception that you're listening.
4. Increases ability to be customer focused.
5. Increases ability to stay quality focused.
6. Improves market position.

And if properly crafted, analyzed and utilized, money spent will eventually become money earned. According to Schneider (3), in conducting a customer survey, hold the following in mind:

1. Keep customer surveys short so customers are more willing to participate.

2. Open-ended essay questions take time and should be kept to a minimum.

3. Customer surveys can be administered by phone or mail.

4. Response rates for customer surveys are typically far lower than employee surveys, between 5-25%.

5. To increase response rate, a letter of introduction, personalized or

   not, serves as your essential communication device.

6. Confidentiality is less of an issue in customer surveys, some customers may prefer to let the company know their comments.

7. Incentives can increase response rate in customer surveys.

8. Demographic information adds value.

9. Demonstrating respect for your customers helps them to think of you similarly.

The managers of the Clarkson Company of Sparks, Nevada also agree that conducting surveys provides many advantages. According to the managers, having an outside firm conduct the surveys offered substantial benefits both internally and externally to the firm. Respondents felt freer to share information more candidly with a third party. The Clarkson Company used The Voice of the Customer surveys developed by Colleen "Coco" Crum (4), to find out how their customers felt about their services and products in relation to their competitor performance.

The methodology Crum employs, enables companies to determine their competitive strengths and weaknesses as well as customer expectations for customer service, product design and quality, product costs, and other performance attributes

New tools for Customer Service

Database software is the choice of many organizations for tracking customer service. Database software can follow the buying behavior of customers and help companies' meet specific product or service marketing needs. A well-managed customer database is especially helpful for small companies competing with large ones.

Terry Boyle, vice president of Game-Set-Match, a tennis services firm in Englewood, Colorado, attributes getting his customers to return with the use of the computerized database his company uses. He says "the company has increased its revenues at an average annual rate of 45 percent over the past four years by focusing on existing customers for repeat sales and by providing personalized service." The use of the computerized database has made Game-Set-Match's marketing campaigns more effective and cost efficient

The database used at Game-Set-Match tracks the buying behavior of every person who takes lessons from the firm, plays in one of the leagues it organizes, or makes a purchase in its small retail shop. A total of more than 10,000 people in 4,800 families. "The use and marketing of our database has kept us ahead of the competition," says Boyle. "We can target search our customer base. If there's a program we need to promote, such as a league, we can look up who was in that league last year and put a notice out to that particular group" (6)

According to Claudio Marcus, vice president of marketing with Target-Smart! Inc., a marketing software company in Denver; "generating repeat business costs less than attracting new customers and a lot less than winning back dissatisfied customers." So, it's important for growth oriented small firms such as Game-Set-Match to concentrate on giving buyers reasons to return.

Donna Fluss, a research director at Gartner Group, a technology consulting company based in Stanford, Conn., says, "the more you know about your customers, the more effective you'll be at increasing their value to your organization." Fluss says "that every contact that a company has with its customers is an opportunity to impress them with your service." Customer databases help companies achieve these goals by providing employees with quick, convenient, access to relevant information before they call customers. Such information includes previous purchase, questions asked, and problems incurred.

This form of relationship marketing is sometimes called, "one-to-one" marketing and is a strategy that large firms have been using for more than a decade to increase customer retention. Now small businesses can hold their own with their big business competitors by using point-of-sale, database, contact management, call center, and customer-service and support software.

Technology can also help the company automate the way it serves customers and responds to problems. Automated processes, such as fax-on-demand and automated call-distribution (ACD) systems can be very effective ways to serve customers.

Fax-on-demand systems allow customers to dial in and request that specified information is faxed to them. While ACD systems, allow customers to call in and choose among a number of service options, either by touching a number on their telephone keypad or by using voice commands.

The system routes each call to recorded information or to a person who can help the caller.

In addition to these systems, many companies provide service on Internet sites. The Internet enables even small companies to provide around the clock customer service. Customers may find Web-based service frustrating and impersonal if it isn't implemented correctly. To be successful, customer service Web sites must provide easily accessible, up-to-date information as well as a mechanism for resolving service problems quickly and completely.

Companies can use the Internet to complement their telephone service offerings using CustomerSoft's ESP Li@ison. The product works in concert with the company's Expert Support Program customer-support software, a database of problem solutions that a firm's telephone support personnel can use to help customers. Many companies are also using "Instant Messenger" to help with customer questions while online.

Internet Message Center (IMC) is an electronic mail based support solution, which makes it easier for companies to automate and manage customer inquiries from a Web site or via direct e-mail. Internet Message Center creates a queue of incoming messages that shows the time they were sent and there related topics. The message can then be forwarded to staff members. IMC also provides a mechanism for monitoring message volume and response time. It works with leading e-mail programs, including Qualcomm Eudora, Microsoft Outlook, and Netscape Messenger.

Even online customers want to communicate with a person sometimes, by using iServe. Companies can offer live interactive support on their Web sites. Customers who visit a firm's Web site and type in questions and receive answers immediately from a customer support representative. Support personnel can also display on the customer's screen Web pages containing detailed information and send helpful software files to the customer's PC.

Technology can also give employees the knowledge they need to serve customers better. Building a knowledge base has allowed Paradigm4 to establish a reputation for fast and expert service after just three years in business. The Fairfield, N.Y. firm installs wireless telephone networks for corporations and government agencies, such as police departments. One of Paradigm4's selling points is its customer support desk, which responds to problems 24 hours a day, seven days a week. To increase the effectiveness of its help-desk workers, Paradigm4 installed knowledge management software called, Top of Mind from Molloy Group Inc., a software developer in Parsippany, N.J.

Lastly, always make sure that employees are trained to help customers. Not only do they need to know to use the company's customer's service databases, but also need to have the personal skills to provide the attention that customers demand (6).

CONCLUSION

Contemporary marketing is simple, basic, and based on common-sense fundamentals. Contemporary marketing means you get to know your customer. Contemporary marketing means shut up and listen. Contemporary marketing means organize your efforts to help your customer succeed. Contemporary marketing means to be honest have character and integrity. Integrity in what you do, in what you say, and in how you conduct business. Your product must be better than your sales pitch.

Work Cited

Crum Coco, "Listening to The Voice of The Customer," *Voice of The Customer*, Jan. 1996, p.1-3.

Coleman-Lochnel Lauren, "New-Jersey Shoppers Find Customer Service Is Getting Worse," *Knight Ridder/Tribune Business News*, Nov. 21, 1998, p. 1-3.

Job Applicant Data From Hreasy Points to Lax Attitudes on Customer Service," *PR Newswire*,

Nov. 4, 1998, p.1-2.

Iacobucci Dawn, "Golden Rules For Customer Service: Mastering Marketing Supplement," *The Financial Times*, Oct. 26, 1998, p.2.

McCollum Tim, "Tools For Targeting Customer Service," *Nations Business*, Nov. 1, 1998, p. 1.

S.C. Columbia The State, "Improved Customer Service Can Lessen Anxiety," *Knight Ridder/ Tribune Business News*, Nov. 2, 1998, p.1.

Schneider Ray, "The External Customer Survey," *Perspective*, 1997, p.1-3.

Stewart Thomas A., "Managing," *Fortune*, Dec. 11,1995, p.180.

http://web7.searchbank.com/infotrac/session/300/307/27972956w3/6 2!xrn_17

http://web7.searchbank.com/infotrac/session/300/307/27972956w3/3 5!xrn_6 http://web7.searchbank.com/infotrac/session/300/307 /27972956w3/38!xrn_7

http://web7.searchbank.com/infotrac/session/300/307/27972956w3/2 0!xrn_1

http://web7.searchbank.com/infotrac/session/300/307/27972956w3/4
3!xrn_13

Reference

1. "F. W. Murphy's manufacturers' Overseas Operations" speech given to the Engineers Society of Tulsa meeting, Sept. 19, 1994.

2. Thomas A. Stewart, "Managing," Fortune, Dec. 11, 1995, 181.

3. Ray Schneider, "The External Customer Survey ," Perspective, 1997, 1-3.

4. Coco Crum, "Listening to The Voice of The Customer," Voice of The Customer, Jan. 1996, 1-3.

5. Dawn Iacobucci, "Golden Rules For Customer Service: Mastering Marketing Supplement," The Financial Times, Oct. 26, 1998, 2.

6. Tim McCollum, "Tools For Targeting Customer Service." Nations Business, Nov. 1, 1998, 1.

"EMPLOYEE HEALTH: A COMPETITIVE ADVANTAGE"

EXECUTIVE OVERVIEW

This article discusses the importance of employee health and the effect health has on the total organization. The author believes a positive climate for good health is essential to create a competitive advantage for the organization. Organizations are pressured for both survival and performance in the world's competitive environment. The author urges organizations to develop a total health strategy (THS). The hypothesis is that organizations with a positive health climate will have a competitive advantage over those that continue to do business as usual.

A NEW STRATEGY EMPHASIS

A well thought out Total Health Strategy (THS) can contribute to a positive work culture. The culture, climate, and environment create the opportunity for the organization to perform. Organizational performance can be measured in profit, nonprofit, government, religious, and social organizations. In a for-profit business we measure profit, market share, return, or investments. Nonprofit organizations have measures of performance such as number and quality of clients served. All organizations define strategy for viable existence. This article suggests a new emphasis on total health planning, management, and strategy implementation.

TOTAL HEALTH STRATEGY

The Profit Impact of Market Strategy (PIMS) model (1) defines the two most important individual independent variables for success in profit-making organizations as market share and quality. The dependent variable is normal profit, indicated in the formula as an x. Normal profit is a function of an infinite number of dependent variables. These dependent variables are a, b, c on to infinity in the formula.

$$x = f\ (a,\ b,\ c,\ d,\ \ldots\ \text{infinity})$$

In the two previously discussed formula variables, market share and quality are designated as independent variables a and b. This paper suggests and introduces another independent variable as Total Health Strategy (THS).

WHAT IS A TOTAL HEALTH STRATEGY?

A total health strategy is a comprehensive audit and measure of total organization health. This strategy includes an audit of employee health with the potential for an annual physical of all employees in the organization. Specific health objectives are set for the total organization. Sub-units in the organization have support health objectives. It is suggested that each employee has or develops a life/career health plan (2). Such a plan includes health, exercise, and nutrition objectives and strategies. These factors are all part of the THS for the organization. Allen C. Elliott (3) made a good point when he stated, "What good is it to become wealthy, successful or famous when you cannot enjoy life, because of depression or if you die early because of poor health? Good health must be a high priority in your life."

Competitive advantage is those organizational strengths, uniqueness, and differentiation of products and/or services that give that organization an edge over its competition in the market place. The central point of this paper, aside from the moral obligation of an organization to encourage a healthier workplace, is that the group functions better with improved performance from an alert, healthy, invigorated workforce. A healthy workforce is also more likely to deliver higher profits, higher market share, and quality products and/or service. A healthy work force will miss fewer days at work, have a lower injury rate, and lower turnover. An organization with healthy workers outperforms the organization without a THS. This creates competitive advantage (4).

WHY IS HEALTH IMPORTANT?

Fewer people in the U.S. are physically active today than 20 years ago. A report by the Federal Centers for Disease Control and Prevention points out that physical inactivity plagues all areas of the United States (5). In the mid to late 1970's, the jogging craze, inspired largely by Cooper Aerobics Center founder and well-known author Dr. Kenneth H. Cooper, was at its pinnacle. The formerly fit baby boomers that have slowed down or dropped out may need to be reminded of the overwhelming scientific evidence of the benefit of a regular exercise program. Exercise helps control weight and stress, increases HDL (the good type) cholesterol, protects against high blood pressure and, in some cases, even treats hypertension effectively.

There also is a need to break cigarette-smoking habits. Tobacco causes 420,000 deaths annually. Tobacco is the primary nongenetic contributor to death in the United States. Surprisingly, an estimated 50 million people still smoke.

More than 25 percent of all Americans are considered overweight. Because excess weight is associated with high blood pressure, stroke, heart disease, and certain cancers, overweight employees are a greater risk to themselves and their organization. It has been shown that 85 percent of recipients of a health-risk appraisal make significant lifestyle changes: 67 percent begin eating healthier, 48 percent start or increase their exercise, 33 percent begin losing weight, 19 percent reduce or quit alcohol consumption, and 12 percent reduce or quit using other tobacco products (6).

About 75 percent of health-care costs can be linked directly to unhealthy lifestyles-an encouraging statistic for individuals and corporate managers who work in organizations with a THS. Company executives can begin simply by setting a good example. They also can provide wellness and lifestyle retreats for key executives and employee fitness facilities.

EFFECT ON ORGANIZATION PERFORMANCE

The Washington Business Group on Health and numerous other sources report that employee fitness programs achieve long-term savings of $3.00 to $6.00 for every dollar spent. Other experts believe the savings are greater (7). William M. Mercher, Inc., a benefit-consulting firm, found that one group saved $5.50 for each dollar invested (8).

Kim E. Anderson's new book *Promoting Employee Health: A Guide to Workplace Wellness* (9) provides information to implement a worksite wellness program. The book provides cost benefit, program structure, and advice on how to evaluate and/or improve existing programs.

Research in the health field documents positive results. Employees are healthier, more productive, and report higher morale, while employers are documenting savings of 3 percent to 8 percent of their total health and medical expenses. Typically, 30 percent to 32 percent of claims are linked to preventable health conditions. Studies conducted by the Association for Worksite Health Promotion and Wellness Councils of America reveal that corporate wellness programs increase productivity, morale, and loyalty and reduce health care costs, use of health care benefits, workers' compensation and disability management costs, injuries, and absenteeism (10). San Bernardino County, California, reported a 20 percent decrease in lost-time expenses from sick leaves. They instituted a wellness program (11). Carpenter Technology Corporation has used on-site clinics for five years to serve 2,200 of the 5,900 employees and dependents. The company estimates it saved more than $108,000 in 1997 (12).

If you are a manager, what is your responsibility for employee health? Do health issues have an economic impact on your organization? The obvious answer is "yes." (As managers and organization professionals, here are buzzwords that continue to surface: "strategy" and "competitive advantage.") The focus on profits, market share, and customer service occupies the thoughts of professional managers. Health issues must go beyond the notion of "it's the right thing to do." Human resources, training, employee retention, work culture, building and maintaining an empowered, motivated performing work force are on everyone's mind. Should an organization have key measurable health objectives and strategies? Ask any athletic coach and the answer is "yes." As a businessperson, why wouldn't your answer also be a BIG "yes?"

THS is not only the organization's responsibility to full-time employees, but extends to part-time employees. Labor shortages around the world have created the need for temporary workers and increased immigration.

The Cooper Clinic in Dallas, Texas developed a program called LifeLinks (13). LifeLinks is committed to providing all Cooper Aerobics Center employees with an integrated program promoting total well-being and employee unity. LifeLinks monetarily rewards employees who participate. It improves employee health and fitness, and maintains a high level of productivity through a positive atmosphere. LifeLinks provides a wide variety of programs to meet the needs of all employees. It has been reported that incentives doubled the participation rate. The reward system does not always work. Hershey Foods has maintained a fitness center on corporate grounds since 1979. Participation is not required. Employee feedback indicated they were not pleased with the incentive program. Hershey management dropped the incentive program (14). Hershey should consider a health bonus plan for its organization?

And don't forget nutrition! Along with an active lifestyle, much attention must be paid to diet. As a general rule, Cooper nutritionists suggest a range of 1,300 to 1,500 calories a day for women and 1,600 to 2,000 for men. What we eat has a lot to do with who we are, how we feel, our energy level etc., and, yes, how we look.

At the Cooper Aerobics Center, employees eat at a healthy food bar, where tasty, low-fat recipes are available that help promote health-conscious eating. Recipes from the food bar come from Cooper's nutrition staff and two books *The Guilt-Free Comfort Food Cookbook* (15) and *What's Cooking at the Cooper Clinic?* (16). At Texaco and Conoco in Houston and Exxon in Dallas, employees have the same option, a special healthy cafeteria food bar.

This article suggests that the positive effect of a wellness program go beyond better health and the contribution to the profitability of the organization. Healthy employees feel better about themselves. There is a new vigor in the organization. Dr. Aunna Herbst found in her experience "that employees participating in these programs have better attitudes and behavior, are more loyal, more enthusiastic and highly motivated." (17) This author agrees with Dr. Herbst. A management culture that promotes all aspects of a well-rounded person is more likely to succeed.

CONCLUSION

A comprehensive, organization health strategy, a THS, pays off in the long run for organizations. Employee health and physical fitness are vital. The ethically responsible organization must provide the right priority and emphasis on health for workers whose well being, vigor, and energy are critical to the company's success. Alert, healthy employees create a competitive advantage for the organization, lower the costs of medical insurance, and minimize time off for sick days. "There's no question that people who are fit are more productive; they enjoy their work more and accomplish more." (18)

ENDNOTES

1. Buzzell, Robert D., Bradley T. Gale. *The PIMS Principles*. (New York: The Free Press, 1987), pp. 7, 8

2. Migliore, R. Henry. *Personal Planning*. (Jenks: Managed for Success, 1994).

3. Elliott, Allen C. *A Daily Dose of the American Dream*. p. 121, 1997.

4. Porter, Michael E. Competitive Advantage: Creating and Sustaining Superior Performance. (New York: Free Press, 1985) and "How Competitive Forces Shape Strategy." *Harvard Business Review*. March/April 1979.

5. *Morbidity and Morality Weekly Report*, Dec. 23, 1998. http://www.cdc.gov/epo/mmwr/mmwr.html.

6. "The Checkup, Part II." *Fortune*. October 26, 1998. P. 329.

7. "The Global Aging Crisis." *Denver Post*. February 7, 1999. P 1.

8. Sullivan, Bernard J. "New Wellness Programs Can Produce Big Savings." *Baltimore Business Journal*. Oct. 17, 199. 15 N 22, p. 26, 1998.

9. Anderson, Kim E. *Promoting Employee Health: A Guide to Workplace Wellness*. 2nd ed. (Des Plaines, IL; ASSE, 1999).

10. Geonie, Paula. "Wellness Programs Can Help Your Company Run the Race." *L. I. Business News*. April 20, 1998, N 16, p. 31.

11. Szalai, George. "Plan Brings County Savings: Programs for Wellness, Productivity, and Expanded in California." *Business Insurance.* July 13, 1998. 13.

12. Shinkman, Ron. "Healthy Workplaces: Employees Look to On-site Clinics to Control Costs." *Modern HealthCare.* April 20, 1998, v. 28, N 16, p. 64.

13. Interview by author at Cooper Clinic, December 31, 1999.

14. Ziegler, Jan. "The Worker's Health: Whose Business is it?" *Business and Health.* December 1997, v. 15, N 12, p. 26 (4).

15. Kostas, Georgia. *The Guilt-Free Comfort Food Cookbook.* Nashville: Thomas Nelson, 1996

16. Kostas, Georgia. *What's Cooking at Cooper Clinic?* Dallas: Cooper Clinic, 1992.

17. Ingram, Morrow "The Healthy Workplace" Oklahoma Business Monthly, Feb. 2000 pp 18-20

18. Christopher Neck and Kenneth Cooper. *The fit executive; Exercise and diet guideline for enhancing performance.* Academy of Management Executive 2000 Vol. 14 No. 2

Appendix A

What will this Seminar do for the Company?

1. "Gives top management the chance to help develop the path of travel during the next five years."

2. "Gives us a soapbox to voice our true feelings."

3. "Gives us a chance to formulate and consolidate ideas and mature."

4. "Gives us a format to follow."

5. "Helps organize and clarify communication from the top down."

6. "Involves all employees in a way that can be managed."

7. "Gives us faith internally in helping our financial status."

8. "We will now have a better defined objective to market."

9. "Develop a real business atmosphere and teamwork in an already healthy management team."

10. "Help those of us who are leaders to field problems before they occur in a positive way that effects the overall plan."

11. "It places into effect controls on past temptations to yield to whims and impetuousness."

12. "Provides a basis for decision making."

13. "Provides measurable goals and the attendant reward that comes with accomplishment."

14. "Creates a forum for all levels of management to have a steering influence on company direction."

15. "Helps us deal more with contingent circumstances and less with panic."

16. "Helps all employees to define a reason to rally."

17. "Employees will be more ready to fully participate and make commitments."

18. "Enables us to work as a team in becoming financially successful."

19. "Helps everyone realize that reaching our goals is going to take hard

work and teamwork, but will be worth the effort."

20. "Gives the team direction, makes for more labor and cost-effective measures, and sets the stage for more productivity."

What will this Seminar do for me as an individual?

1. "Will help me develop methods in management decision making."

2. "Will help me plan objectives."

3. "Will help me produce finished plans for management responsibilities."

4. "Will enable me to set a definite direction and go for it."

5. "Will let me know that I am an important part of the team and that the team feels the same way."

6. "Will give me the tools, support, and encouragement to contribute to and reach team goals."

7. "Will give me a sense that communication is improving."

8. "Will make me more efficient, more goal oriented."

9. "This strategic planning can be used in full or in part in all of life's challenges and opportunities."

10. "Will depersonalize difficult management decisions."

11. "Will develop measurable targets so that subordinates can be more easily evaluated."

12. "This plan will steer me away from frustration and discouragement."

13. "Will give me more ability to use my gifts and strengthen my weaker point."

14. "Will get me organized in a way that will create results."

15. "Will give me more job satisfaction, and will make me a more active part of the whole."

16. "Will make me more efficient and help my growth."

17. "Will force me to become the most effective manager possible."

18. "The seminar will give me a very powerful and directional place to start."

19. "With this plan, my potential can be tremendous."

20. "Will boost my morale and give me a clearer, overall picture to achieve my desired goals."

About The Author

R. Henry Migliore

Dr. Migliore is presently Professor of Strategic Planning and Management at Northeastern State University/ Oklahoma State University*Tulsa; Dr. Migliore teaches at the graduate and undergraduate levels. He was formerly Professor of Management and former Dean of the ORU School of Business from 1975 until 1987. He was a visiting professor at the University of Calgary, fall 1991, and a visiting professor at ITESM Campus Guadalajara, Guadalajara, Jalisco, Mexico, spring 1995 and Singapore in 1997.

He is former manager of the press manufacturing operations of Continental Can Company's Stockyard Plant. Prior to that he was responsible for the industrial engineering function at Continental's Indiana plant. In this capacity, Dr. Migliore was responsible for coordinating the Long-Range planning process. In addition, he has had various consulting experiences with Fred Rudge & Associates in New York and has served large and small businesses, associations, and nonprofit organizations in various capacities. He has made presentations to a wide variety of clubs, groups, and professional associations. Dr. Migliore has been selected to be on the faculty for the International Conferences on Management by Objectives and the Strategic Planning Institute Seminar Series. He is also a frequent contributor to the Academy of Management, including a paper at the 50th anniversary national conference. He served for 12 years on the Board of Directors of T. D. Williamson, Inc., and was previously on the Boards of the International MBO Institute and Brush Creek Ranch, American Red Cross/Tulsa Chapter, and is chairman of a scholarship fund for Eastern State College. In 1984 he was elected into the Eastern State College Athletic Hall of Fame. Dr. Migliore has been a guest lecturer on a number of college campuses. He has lectured for the Texas A & M, Pepperdine ITESM, Guadalajara, and University of Calgary Executive Development programs. He serves on Chamber/Civic Committees and served on the Administrative Board at The First United Methodist Church, Tulsa, Oklahoma. He was selected Who's Who on a list of 31 top echelon writers and consultants in America.

To date previous articles on management and business subjects have appeared in *AIIE Journal, Construction News, Management World, Management of Personnel Quarterly, Journal of Long-Range Planning, Dental Economics, Health Care Management Review, MBO Journal, Business and Society Review, Parks and Recreation Journal, The Journal of Business Strategy, Daily Blessing, Ozark Mountaineer, On Line, Real Estate Today, Communication Briefings, Journal of Sports Management, Alberta Business Review, The Planning Review, Hospital Topics, Journal of East-West Business, Journal of Ministry Management, IIE Solutions,* and two Mexican journals. His books, *MBO: Blue Collar to Top Executive, An MBO Approach to Long-Range Planning, A Strategic Plan for Your Life, Strategic Long-Range Planning, Strategic Planning for Church and Ministry Growth, Common Sense Management; A Biblical Perspective, Personal Action Planning: How To Know What You Want And Get It,* and *Tales of Uncle Henry,* describe personal theories and experiences. He contributed to the book, *Readings in Interpersonal and Organizational Communication and International Handbook on MBO.* The book *The Management of Production: A Productivity Approach* is coauthored. Other books include *Strategic Planning and Management, Strategic Life Planning,* and *Common Sense Management.* The manuscript *People Productivity and Profits* has been completed. He is co-authoring a series of books with Haworth Press. Released so far are *Church and Ministry Growth* (1995), *Planning for Nonprofit Management* (1995), *Strategic Planning and Health Care* (1996), *Strategic Planning for Private Universities* (1997), and *Strategy Planning for Collegiate Athletics* (spring 2000). *Strategy Planning for Higher Education and Planning for City Government* will be completed in the year 2000. *Strategic Long-Range Planning for the New Millennium* is being updated for release in late 2000. His books have been translated into Russian, Chinese, Korean, Spanish, German, and Japanese. A Spanish version of *Strategic Planning* is coauthored with Gonzalo Rivero, and will be published late 2000. He has also produced "Personal Financial Success," an ORU video training kit offered on nationwide television, and video/audio tapes to go with his books. Dr. Migliore has developed three complete videotaped correspondence courses.

In November 1985, the daily "Managing for Success" cable television program was inaugurated and was on the air until March 1986. It was on Tulsa Cable. The series began again on Tulsa Cable in September 1986. He writes occasional columns for the *Tulsa World, Tahlequah Pictorial Press, Collinsville News, Jenks Journal,* and *Muskogee County Times.* A complete video series with four summary units and 36 support units covering planning, management, and common sense management supports other material.

November 1998 R. Migliore was inducted into the Eastern Oklahoma State Hall of Fame. This followed his induction in 1988 into the Eastern Athletic Hall of Fame.

Dr. Migliore has been a small business consultant for the Oklahoma Small Business Development Center for 13 years. Dr. Migliore holds degrees from Eastern Oklahoma State, Oklahoma State University, St. Louis University, and completed his doctorate at the University of Arkansas. He belongs to the Academy of Management, Planning Executives Institute and is a senior member of the American Institute of Industrial Engineers.

Other Books by
Dr. R. Henry Migliore

COMMON SENSE MANAGEMENT

ISBN: 0-87683-633-3

PERSONAL ACTION PLANNING

ISBN: 0-87683-637-6

THE MANAGEMENT OF PRODUCTION:
A PRODUCTIVITY APPROACH

ISBN: 0-87683-631-7

STRATEGIC PLANNING FOR UNIVERSITY ATHLETICS

ISBN: 0-7890-089-10

CHURCH AND MINISTRY STRATEGIC PLANNING

ISBN: 5-56024-346-5 Hard cover

ISBN: 5-56024-347-3 Soft cover

STRATEGIC PLANNING IN NONPROFIT ORGANIZATIONS

ISBN: 1-56024-919-3 Hard cover

ISBN: 5-56024-920 Soft cover

STRATEGIC PLANNING FOR PRIVATE HIGHER EDUCATION

ISBN: 0-7890-0098-9 Hard cover

ISBN: 0-7890-0191-8 Soft cover

APPLYING PLANNING PRINCIPLES TO THE MANAGING OF HEALTH CARE ORGANIZATIONS

ISBN: 0-7890-0060-1

STRATEGIC LONG RANGE PLANNING; A PLANNING AND MANAGEMENT SOURCE FOR LATIN AMERICAN BUSINESS

**Here's what the
professional managers are saying:**

I know Dr. Migliore to be a highly skilled academician with an impressive list of credentials. I believe his greatest strength is his ability to clearly and easily communicate facts, ideas, and methodologies to both traditional and non-traditional students and professional managers.

Hughes, Jack B. ReVelle, Leader, Continuous Improvement

I have known Henry Migliore for nearly ten years. He was instrumental in the start-up of our Colowyo mine in northwestern Colorado, and his writings, particularly, Strategic Long-Range Planning and A Strategic Plan for Your Life: A Biblical Perspective demonstrate his keen understanding of strategic business concepts and their application.

W. R. Grace & Co., J. Peter Grace, Former Chairman

"Strategic Long-Range Planning" has proven to be critical in the success of my Industrial Engineering Division. Dr. Henry Migliore took my entire Industrial Engineering staff through the planning process. His common-sense principles and manufacturing experience helped my engineers be more successful in their area.

Cardone Industries, Mark Spuler, Executive Vice President

Dr. R. Henry Migliore has worked with our Government Marketing Division of Canon, U.S.A., Inc. in developing a format and completing a five-year business plan. Specifically, Dr. Migliore helped us refine our marketing plan. His approach helped us analyze our market niche, competition, products and services. We feel we are in a better position to meet the needs of our customers. Henry's assistance has placed us on a track that will enable our company to objectively approach our market and include our profit objectives.

CANON U.S.A., INC, Jerry Robinson, Former Director of Field Sales

In the twelve years since I graduated from Oklahoma State University, I've heard a plethora of speakers and Dr. Migliore consistently places at the top. Equal to his charm as a speaker, is his thorough knowledge of the many facets of strategic management and tactical implementation.

ROX Corp, Darren Keller, Manager of Operations

Williams has worked with Dr. Migliore and his students to lend assistance and bring an important minority owned business out of bankruptcy. We believe this company has now turned the corner and will have a bright future.

Williams Communications Corp., David L. Willis, Project Manager

It is unique to find an individual who has been capable of providing publications that are of interest to all of these audiences. Moreover, his publications spans the areas of policy, strategy, management, and marketing. His ability to teach within colleges and universities at all professional levels-undergraduate, general masters, Executive MBA, and management development-is special. He has a nice ability to adjust his presentations to the needs and interest of these various target markets.

Texas A & M University, Dr. Don Hellriegel, Lowry Mays College, Graduate School of Business,

Several years ago, Henry had the opportunity to assist Colowyo in its strategic planning process. At that time, Colowyo was a new start-up company owned by W. R. Grace. The relatively new management at Colowyo was having trouble working together. They were not a cohesive team going toward the same goal. Henry came in as a Strategic Planning consultant for Colowyo and over a period of time, taught management the process and skills necessary to work together as a team. While he taught strategic planning processes and skills to management, the real, lasting benefit of his time at Colowyo was the training Henry provided the management team at Colowyo. Through written assignments, role-playing, and his strong encouragement of open communications, walls were broken down and a strategic planning process was put in place the helped Colowyo become the most successful start-up operation in the history of W. R. Grace.

Kennecott Energy, Colowyo Coal Company L.P., Mark A. Hulstine, Chief Consultant

Professor R. Henry Migliore and I first met in the mid-1980's as we teamed up in the development of a five-year strategic business plan. Professor Migliore served as a consultant to our $100MM per year high technology manufacturing business. Professor Migliore's writings are on target with what business should be about in today's economic environment. His leadership and strategic plan assisted our company in enhancing its growth and development opportunities. He is both practical and far-sighted.

Phillips 66 Company, Warren H. Alfred, Director of Human Resources

In his unified approach to management Henry blends the current state-of-the-art and science of management thinking and communicates it in a professional, tough-minded, common sense manner.

Southwestern Bell, David Johnsen, Ph.D, Director Marketing Research

R. Henry Migliore has worked with our top management team developing a long-range strategic plan. Dr. Migliore has been a major contributor to our improved efficiency and enhanced understanding of the need of strategic planning and implementation.

Crown Auto World, Henry Primeaux, Former President

Henry Migliore led a seminar for employees on various levels reporting to me. The people attending the seminar were impressed with the way Henry Migliore reduced extremely complex processes to more simple, understandable and workable methods. As I reviewed the seminar, it was amazing how much material we covered and learned in such a short period of time.

Oxy Petroleum, Charles E. Creekmore,
Former Operations Services Manager

Henry is a quality professor because his involvement in consulting with businesses helps him to stay on the cutting edge of the problems and challenges facing businesses today. He knows how to teach effective solution process to his students and professional managers. He is an effective consultant because of his vast experience and knowledge.

Mazzio's, Craig E. Bothwell, President & CEO

Our firm retained the service of Dr. Henry Migliore. His seminar series in Mexico was professionally presented and, with a few exceptions, was viewed as very successful. Dr. Migliore assisted our top management team in the development of a strategic plan. The session assisted in re-thinking all aspects of our business. We feel we have a better grasp of how to be more successful in the future.

Plus Consultants, Jose Luis Acevedo, General Director

Over the years, I have witnessed Dr. Migliore's work with several different types of groups: executives within my own unit; adult students; and industry professionals. Regardless of his audience, he has a unique way of mesmerizing with his stories, getting a laugh with his anecdotes, and all the while making several key points about leadership. Most recently, Dr. Migliore has been instrumental in assisting the College of Human Environmental Sciences in its strategic planning for the next several years. He helped our executive group not only see the best way to plan for an uncertain future, but guided them through exercises designed to make them a better team.

Oklahoma State University/Tulsa, Dana Schuler,
Manager, Extension Programs

The seminar was informative and stimulating and provided a basis for improving our long range planning. Many of the ideas presented were incorporated and are still being used today.

Colowyo Coal Company, R. D. Usilton, Vice-President, Finance

"Dr. R. Henry Migliore has been a consultant for Cross Manufacturing, Inc. for 21 years. He has been instrumental in our planning and strategy process. We have used all his materials and books. We have a sophisticated ongoing planning and review process in place. Dr. Migliore continues to provide leadership to the top management Cross team

Cross Manufacturing, Inc. John H. Cross, President & CEO

Three years ago, Dr. Migliore took our entire top management team on an off site planning retreat. That experience has been a major turning point for the continued success of our company. We used his updated book, Strategic Planning for the New Millennium, as a guide for management development. All areas of our business have developed support functional plans to insure the success of the overall Aftermarket plan.

AfterMarket, Steve Pittenrigh, President & CEO

Dr. Migliore served on our board of directors and as a consultant for two decades. He was instrumental in helping us develop the TDW planning and management system. We used his Corporate Culture Index to monitor the culture of our company. Dr. Migliore was valuable in training and assisting all levels of our employees. He participated with me as part of our First Presbyterian-Tulsa Strategic Planning Committee. We used his expertise, books, and workbooks while guiding us through the planning process. My observation has been that the concepts are valuable in all types of organizations.

*T. D. Williamson, Inc., Richard B. Williamson, President & CEO*Dr. Migliore has been a volunteer consultant for 17 local non-profit groups, including Salvation Army, Goodwill Industries, YMCA, and American Red Cross. The past few years he has concentrated on working with minority and other small businesses. It is my pleasure to give the highest recommendations to Dr. Migliore.

Metropolitan Tulsa Chamber of Commerce, Clyde C. Cole, Former President

In utilizing Dr. Migliore's concepts at staff planning retreats and annual job reviews, we have found these sessions to be more meaningful, directive and productive. His practical, common-sense approach to work and life management allows me to recommend his work for its contribution to both professional and personal progress.

Cooper Clinic, Georgia Kostas, M.H.P., R.D., L.D., Nutrition Director, Cooper Clinic

Informal and formal feedback from seminar participants confirmed my impression that Dr. Migliore is a master at moving things along at a fast and interesting pace. All the seminars he did with the University of Calgary have been well received. His books and materials have been of great value to our seminar participants.

University of Calgary, Brad Jackson, Director Management Seminars

Dr. Migliore's academic interests are evidenced by his new book on Strategic Planning and Management for the New Millennium. He worked closely with a colleague assisting management cultures in different countries. He introduced the corporate culture index in his latest book.

University of Calgary, Mansour Javidan, Chairman Policy and Environment

Dr. Migliore possesses the unique ability to apply business concepts in real world situations to achieve successful results. His new book outlines workable theory and concepts.

Howco Metals Inc., Richard R. Rocha, Materials Manager

Dr. Migliore came to us highly recommended both for his academic achievements as well as his total experience base. His introduction to KTUL was very timely as we were positioned to review and update our five-year strategic plan.

Prior to entering a weekend retreat, Dr. Migliore challenged the members of the leadership Team with guidelines to insure their preparation would be thought provoking. The guidance he provided enabled the team to better understand their role in strategic planning and review. Through the use of his writings, knowledge, and instruction, our team quickly learned the process necessary for such planning. He was supportive as he guided the leadership team on their weekend journey into the future. His abilities to facilitate kept them focused on the task at hand as they developed KTUL's strategic plan.

Oklahoma's Channel 8, KTUL-Tulsa, Dan Bates,
Former President and General Mgr.

I have reviewed many of Dr. Migliore's published works but have also contracted for his services in the field of strategic planning. I have found Henry to be an extremely intelligent individual with an excellent ability to communicate at any level.

Hampton-Tilley Associates, Inc., Don A. Hampton, President

**Here's what
religious leaders are saying:**

Through your assistance, we will capitalize on the potential God has given us.

B. J. Daughtery, Victory Christian Center

Dr. Migliore was able to quickly teach the elements in the MBO approach. He gained the confidence of our top management team and helped us in developing long-range objectives.

B. Erickson, "Back-to-the-Bible" Broadcast

I can quickly and openly attest that the high-quality work performed by Dean Migliore in our recent Tulsa YMCA project exceeds all other experiences.

R. A. Pfeiffer, YMCA of Tulsa

Migliore played a crucial role in the development of an administrative plan for the growing ministries of the Christian Legal Society.

L. R. Buzzard, Christian Legal Society

All of my top executives . . . jobs have become more meaningful as a result of being filled with great management purposes and clear objectives.

M. Cerullo, World Evangelism

www.ingramcontent.com/pod-product-compliance
Lightning Source LLC
Chambersburg PA
CBHW031626210326
41599CB00021B/3316